THE KING MONTEZUMA TRILOGY

Keith H. Adkins

Copyright © 2025 by Keith H. Adkins

All rights reserved.

No part of this book may be reproduced, or stored in a retrieval system, or transmitted in any form or by any means, electronic, mechanical, photocopying, recording, or otherwise, without express written permission of the publisher.

This is a work of historical fiction.
Names, places, and events are used fictitiously.

ISBN 979-8-9895776-7-5
Made in the United States of America
ChrisJen Publications
www.keithhadkins.com
Cover design by: ebooklaunch.com

Contents

A MESOAMERICAN TIMELINE v
INTRODUCTION TO THE TRILOGY vii

THE FORMING OF THE EMPIRE
A King Montezuma Story – Book 1

PREFACE: Heading for the Jungle...... 2
ACT I: Becoming God's People.. 8
ACT II: Liberation. 50
ACT III: Settling into the Promised Land 87
ACT IV: The Demand for Leadership 124

THE SECRET OF THE EMPIRE
A King Montezuma Story – Book 2

PREFACE: A Border Crossing 169
ACT I: Before the Exile 176
ACT II: The Fall of the Empires 216
ACT III: During the Exile 259
ACT IV: After the Exile....... 299

THE VALUE OF THE EMPIRE
A King Montezuma Story – Book 3

PREFACE: An Aztec Synagogue..........................338
ACT I: Poetry in Tucson 346
ACT II: Wisdom in Tubac 393
ACT III: Stories in Phoenix 417
ACT IV: Liturgies in Flagstaff............................461

ACKNOWLEDGMENTS 508
BOOKS BY THIS AUTHOR 509

A MESOAMERICAN TIMELINE

The Formative Period (1500 BCE–CE 300)

The Olmec Civilization flourished from 1200–400 BCE, centered near modern-day Veracruz, and reaching as far south as present-day Nicaragua. They also had an extensive trade network, as Guatemalan jade artifacts have been found in Olmec sites.

The Maya Civilization flourished from 1000 BCE-CE 1521 They developed a writing system, produced beautiful art and created a calendar system. The ruins of their pyramids can be found all over the Yucatan Peninsula, including Chichen Itza and Tulum.

The Zapotec Civilization flourished from 500 BCE–CE 1000, centered near modern-day Oaxaca. They established trade links with the Olmecs, and had a sophisticated knowledge of engineering. They had a highly organized governance system, and developed the predecessor to the Maya and Aztec calendars.

The Classic Period (CE 300 – 950)

The Teotihuacan Civilization flourished from CE 1-650 and was one of the largest cities in the world. Monuments found there, with hieroglyphic texts, describe its divine origins, in a societal transformation from shamans to kings.

The Tajin civilization flourished from CE 550-1100. Located near Veracruz, this was a ceremonial center renowned for outstanding artistic developments in intricate mosaic stone facades and colorful fresco painting.

The Postclassic Period (CE 950 – 1521)

The Mixtec Civilization flourished from CE 900-1521. Their craftspeople used exotic materials of gold, silver, and copper from Central and South America, while turquoise from the American southwest was exchanged for the plumage of Scarlet Macaws.

The Aztec Civilization flourished from CE 1200-1521. Spanish conquistadors, led by Hernan Cortés, overthrew the Aztec Empire and captured Tenochtitlan. The Aztec or Mexica people gave their name to the nation of Mexico, while their city of Tenochtitlan became what we know as Mexico City.

INTRODUCTION TO THE TRILOGY

Casting the Bible into fiction is what this volume is about. It tells the stories from the three parts of the Old Testament, known as the Law, the Prophets, and the Writings. Beginning in Guatemala and ending in what is now Mexico City, our stories take place during Mesoamerican times, centered on the battle with Cortes in the 1500s. The other volume, *The Jim Caldwell Trilogy*, reimagines the New Testament set as a battle with the Russians in the 1880s. Together, they offer a fresh experience with the Holy Bible.

This trilogy begins with *The Forming of the Empire: A King Montezuma Story – Book 1*. The stories are told by Geraldo, a Mexican guide, leading Jameson and his father to points along the way where the stories took place. It features the patriarchs Aapo, Hugo, Tobillo, and Eloy, as they slowly become God's people. Liberation is next up, as Abund leads his people out of bondage, into the wilderness and receive the commandments on top of Cerro Raxon. Geovanni then takes them into the Promised Land, but they wanted leadership. Luis proved unworthy, so the people chose Montezuma to be their king. After his death, the Empire divides. The Northern Empire is conquered by the cartel, then the Southern Empire falls at the hand of Cortés and his Conquistadors.

The next book is *The Secret of the Empire: A King Montezuma Story – Book 2*. This time, the stories are shared in context by the father, to his wife Sol, and their son Jameson. It is a flashback to see more detail of what went wrong. It runs through the pleading of the gloom and doom prophets, and covers life for the Aztec people before, during, and after the Exile. Here you will experience the pain of the fall of the Empire and subsequent deportation of the Mexicans to Spain. There we will hear the stories anew, like the Valley of Dry Bones, where the Mexicans receive a vision of hope. Finally, more prophets talk about problems encountered in rebuilding Tenochtitlan after their return to Mexico.

In *The Value of the Empire: A King Montezuma Story – Book 3*, the father continues to be the storyteller. He and Jameson first head to the Poetry Center in Tucson, to discuss the book of Psalms with students at the University of Arizona. Then they head for Wisdom's Café near Tubac, to enliven Proverbs and the book of Job through discussions with patrons. A third trip goes to The Nature Conservancy in Phoenix, to disuss storytelling with the staff, to see if we can learn from Ezra, Nehemiah, Chronicles, and Daniel. Finally, Sol again joins her husband and son, this time for a trip to the Flagstaff Aztec Synagogue. A docent named Atzi shows them copies of the Megillot, and she talks about them, one at a time: Lamentations, Ecclesiastes, Solomon, Esther, and Ruth.

These two volumes, also available as six separate books, become a fresh, new way to experience the Bible. Together they tell what I call *The God Story: An Empire and A Diamond*. It is my hope that it will bring the Bible alive at a time when the world is deeply divided, and spirituality is desperately needed. It is my prayer that The Old Testament, properly known as the Hebrew Sciptures, and The New Testament, what I call The Christian Sequel, will symbolize unity as God's Story.

The King Montezuma Trilogy

THE FORMING OF THE EMPIRE
A King Montezuma Story – Book 1

The King Montezuma Trilogy

PREFACE
Heading for the Jungle

As we came in for a landing in Mexico City, a fierce wind shear pushed us forty-five degrees off center. It was strange seeing the runway straight ahead, and several passengers screamed as the pilot fought to gain control. We ended up touching down at about a twenty-three-degree angle, but as the tires gripped the tarmac, the plane lurched back into position. I thought this must be a sign that we were in for a memorable journey, and we were.

My son and I deplaned, as we had to change planes for our final flight to Belize City. The Mexico City airport is a sprawling piece of property, serving as testimony to being Latin America's busiest. We hustled to our next gate, which was already boarding by the time we arrived. Finding our seats, we smiled at each other, and Jameson thanked me again for his eighteenth birthday gift.

My family lives in Phoenix, Arizona, where my wife and I are dedicated members at Main Street Caldwellian Church. Jim Caldwell started the faith in Phoenix in 1881, so it was fun to visit nearby places that had become holy sites. My son grew up hearing the stories of Jim Caldwell from Sunday sermons, but it was especially powerful to stand in places like Prescott where Jim delivered what became known as the Teachings on the Hill. We even visited where Pablo had his Road to Tucson experience. We were blessed that it didn't take long for the stories to be written down and published, and we cherish our copy of The Caldwellian Scriptures.

Our faith is very important to us, and it was great

The King Montezuma Trilogy

explaining our son's name to him when he was old enough to understand. We named him Jameson, after Jim Caldwell, not after the Irish Whiskey. We always hoped he would grow up as a believer in the one God, and he did. He came to understand that Jim Caldwell became the son of God after the resurrection, and Jim's Spirit can live within us to give us guidance on how to live the Caldwellian life. Our dreams for Jameson became reality, and now I was fulfilling my desire for a pilgrimage to the holy sites of Jim Caldwell's heritage. It was a win-win, because Jameson's birthday gift was doubling as my dream come true. It also served well that Jameson was thinking of going into the ministry.

It was a much shorter flight to Belize City, and thankfully uneventful. We rented a car for a very long, one-way trip back to Mexico City, to be accompanied by a guide whom we would meet in Guatemala. The plan was to stop at ancient ruins along the way, to see the places and hear the stories from the beginnings of the Aztec people in the Peten jungles of Guatemala, to several pyramids along the way, ending in Mexico City.

The first thing Jameson noticed was that so many women had the same round face as his mother. I laughed and said, "Mom's of Mayan descent."

Jameson furrowed his eyebrows and said, "I thought the Mayans had disappeared!"

"Many people think that," I responded, "but there are about 8 million descendants of the Mayans living today."

Being a teenager, Jameson whipped out his trusty iPhone and googled it. "Wow!" he exclaimed, "Mom has relatives." We laughed again and were on our way. "I'm hungry," Jameson announced. It had been a long trip so far, so we stopped at a

The King Montezuma Trilogy

roadside stand and got some tacos. The attendant was happy to take American dollars, so I asked in broken Spanish how much it would cost for six tacos.

The man said, "Three for a dollar," holding up three fingers. In a bit of a shock at the low price, I handed him a five-dollar bill and motioned for him to keep the change. After humbly refusing, he finally kept the money with a smile and thanked me. We devoured a delicious dinner, then got back on the road. I was anxious to get going because we had a four-hour drive ahead of us. Fortunately, we had reservations at the Jungle Lodge Hotel in the midst of the Peten jungle at the Tikal National Park.

We arrived at 10 p.m. and were greeted with a delightful glass of fresh papaya juice. After some more gracious hospitality, we checked into our little jungle bungalow. It was hot and humid but served its purpose. We weren't there for luxury, we were there to learn about ancient history at old ruins, to bring the heritage of Jim Caldwell alive, and to have a father-son adventure. Exhausted, we opened the mosquito netting around each of the twin beds, climbed in and quickly drifted off to sleep.

The morning greeted us with the very loud sounds of howler monkeys. Looking through the netting I saw Jameson smiling, and asked what was going on?

Jameson laughed and said, "We're not in Arizona anymore!"

The shower was outside. It was still relatively private, and somewhat enclosed, but just seemed unusual to go outside to clean up. The jungle was all around, so the only ones watching were some birds and a few monkeys. The resplendent quetzal is the national bird, and one just sat on a tree branch a few feet away. His iridescent green plumage was offset by a red breast,

The King Montezuma Trilogy

black innerwings, and a white undertail. After Jameson got ready, we headed next door for breakfast, then off to meet our guide Geraldo.

It was another hot, sunny, and muggy day, but we were finally ready to truly begin our adventure. This was the place where it all started. Where God called the Aztecs to leave Aztlan and go to a land of promise. There they built Tenochtitlan, the capital of the Aztec Empire, and their ruins are still being unearthed in the middle of what is now Mexico City. The Aztec religion continues to serve the people well, and it was humbling to begin the process of seeing the sights and sounds of the places that ultimately led to Jim Caldwell, a descendent of King Montezuma.

I was like a kid in a candy store, as we walked over to the ancient ruins of Tikal. The crowds were already there, and so was Geraldo. He was looking for a father-son duo, and we were told our guide was a short, stocky Mexican man with a sense of humor. He walked up to us and said, "Dr. Livingstone, I presume," in very good English, with a strong Spanish accent.

Jameson was confused, but I caught the reference. I laughed and smiled and said, "You must be Geraldo." He returned a big smile and a powerful handshake, then we marveled for a moment about the momentous trip ahead. I introduced him to my son and shared my gratitude for his willingness to lead this unique experience. He really was ideal because he grew up with the Aztec religion and recently became a Caldwellian.

We sat on a step at the base of the Tikal Temple and Geraldo began sharing about the Aztec Bible we now have. He said that Jim Caldwell often quoted from it, but the main thing was that it recorded the stories of the Aztec people over a long

The King Montezuma Trilogy

period of time. They first tell the stories of how the Aztecs became God's people, and then tell the stories of how they gained God's promised land of Mexico. He stopped at that and flashed a big smile, then continued with his tour guide voice, "Tikal National Park is now a UNESCO World Heritage Center. The word Tikal means waterhole, because this ancient site in the jungle was dependent on water for life. This city in the Peten jungles of Guatemala started around 600 BCE and lasted until about CE 909. It grew to over 50 square miles and around 50,000 people. It had a sophisticated water management system, and lots of cultures living together."

"Obviously, this place came to an end, since its lying in ruins, but do you know why?" asked Jameson.

"Ah," he sighed. "The secret of the empire. Nobody knows for sure why it fell apart, nor any of the other Aztec Empires, but that's getting ahead of ourselves. First, we need to be looking at the forming of the empire, and it all began right here in this jungle."

"So this is the mythical Aztlan?" asked Jameson.

"That's what I think," responded Geraldo. "Some have even called it Ur of the Chaldeans, but the point is that God called the Aztecs to leave their homeland and go to a land of promise. You know, Mexico, right?" he asked with that same glowing grin. We agreed, then he continued. "They would know when they finally got there, when they saw an eagle perched on a cactus, eating a snake. When they saw this exact sign, at the end of a long journey, over many centuries, they founded Tenochtitlan. That place is now Mexico City, the capital of Mexico, and a city of over 9 million people."

"I'm excited!" stated Jameson, and I agreed. This was going to be a great experience traveling to several pyramids

The King Montezuma Trilogy

throughout Mexico, seeing the context of where the stories of the Aztec Scriptures took place. It already felt like Geraldo was going to be a great guide, helping us understand how that holy book came to be, and this is where our story begins.

The King Montezuma Trilogy

ACT I
Becoming God's People

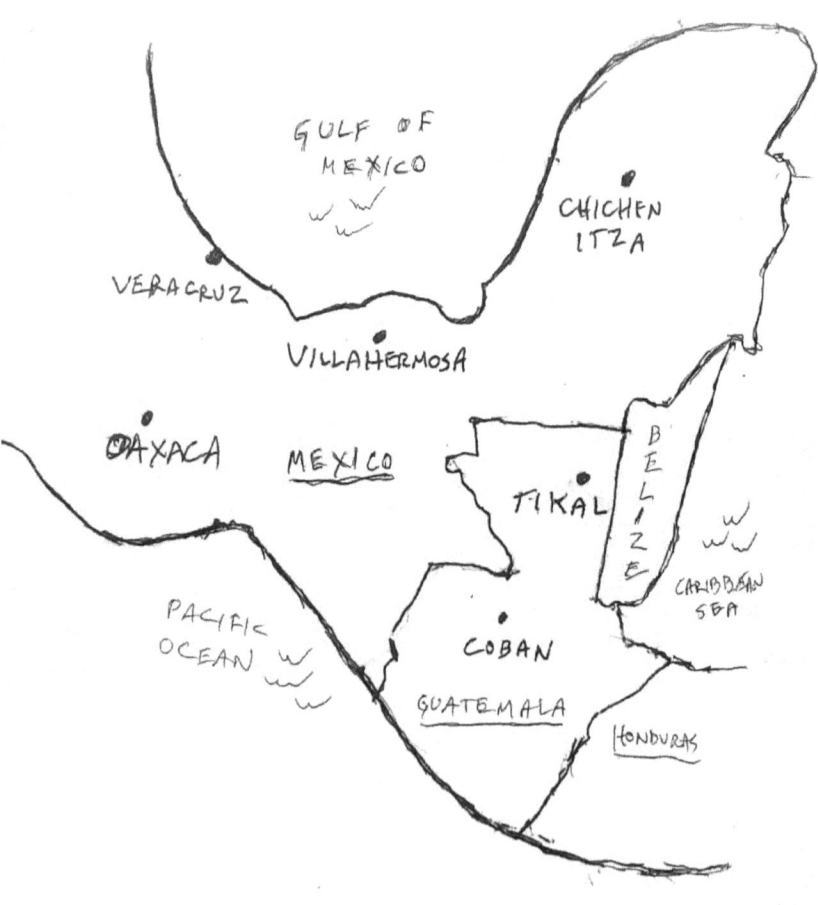

The King Montezuma Trilogy

SCENE ONE
Aapo and Hugo

Geraldo loved to share the stories. He was a well-trained tour guide in Mexico, but had never taken on a job quite this extensive. Jameson and I continued sitting at the base of the Tikal Temple as he began with, "Please get comfortable." We shifted to a shadier spot, and leaned back against the next set of steps. Jameson complained that sitting on rocks wasn't exactly a comfortable thing, and Geraldo took the cue like it was delivered by the straight man in a comedy duo. "Ah, yes, but life was comfortable in Aztlan."

"Good one," proclaimed Jameson, as he squirmed in his seat trying to find an Aztlan feel.

Geraldo said, "Aztlan means 'place of herons,' and it's where the mythical origin of the Aztec people took place. As legend is told, someone cut down a forbidden tree in this garden of beauty."

"Where's the garden?" inquired Jameson, as he looked around at the jungle encroaching on this small window into the past.

"That's what I want you to see," explained Geraldo. "You need to use your imagination." After a short pause, he continued, "So when the forbidden tree was removed, God was offended. He wanted the Aztecs to leave, but nobody had ever heard of God. They had plenty of gods, like Quetzalcoatl, Huitzilopochti, Tezcatlipoca, and Tlaloc, but certainly not a nameless god, who simply became known as God. So how do you think God convinced the Aztecs to leave?"

After we shrugged our shoulders, Geraldo said, "God didn't,

The King Montezuma Trilogy

because God's call was to an individual. His name was Aapo, the Guatemalan name that means 'father of many.' Then God said to Aapo, 'I want you to leave your country and go to the land that I will show you.' To say the least, Aapo was disturbed by this unusual request, so he asked, 'Who are you?' God said, 'I am the one and only God. I will make of you a great empire, and I will bless you, and make your name great, so that you will be a blessing. I will bless those who bless you, and the one who curses you I will curse; and in you all the families of the earth shall be blessed.'"

"Wait a minute," Jameson said. "So God curses people?"

"That's what you heard?" questioned Geraldo, trying to hide a bit of annoyance. "Let's try this a bit differently. God was choosing Aapo among all the Aztecs because God found him to be a righteous person. Aapo still wasn't too sure about this very strange experience, but he liked being called righteous. After all, he was outside cutting down a tree, as his father had told him to do, when this God thing happened. Then again he worried that God might have thought he was the one who cut down the forbidden tree. Aapo finally realized he couldn't talk about this to anybody, since nothing like this had ever happened. So he decided to follow this call on his heart, mind, and soul by the one God, because he felt a strong urge within to do so. He gathered up a few things, left his home without saying goodbye to anyone, and took his wife with him. Her name was Beatrice, the Guatemalan name that means 'voyager through life.'"

"I'm still not ready to move past that curses thing," Jameson said. "So God will curse those who curse you?"

"Now you're sounding like Aapo," I said, with a tinge of frustration. "Let's get back to the storyline."

The King Montezuma Trilogy

"Okay," said Geraldo, "but first we have to drive to Oaxaca, where Aapo got a taste of the Promised Land of Mexico."

"How far is that?" asked Jameson with a concerned look on his face.

Geraldo said, "A little over eight hundred miles, one border crossing, and more than nineteen hours. We'll do it in two days, with a hotel stop in Villahermosa."

Jameson settled into the back seat with headphones, while I got in on the passenger side, and Geraldo drove. It was an uneventful trip, passing beautiful scenery, while Jameson wiled away the time on his phone. Arriving at our hotel, Geraldo proudly announced that "Villahermosa means beautiful village."

"What are those stone heads about?" inquired Jameson, as we passed by the entrance to the Parque Museo La Venta.

"Those are very ancient artifacts from the Olmec Civilization. They date back to the time of Aapo. Who knows? Maybe he even saw the one you're looking at."

Jameson thought that was pretty cool. Then we had some dinner and settled in for the night. The second day was similar to the first, and we arrived at our hotel in Oaxaca at dusk. This time we went out for dinner and were delighted to find a vibrant and colorful city. It's known for its mole, a thick and complex sauce served with meat. I looked forward to ordering it. Jameson stayed with a nice, safe taco, and was glad because when he tried my mole, his face shriveled up. "Eww, its chocolate sauce on turkey! Thanksgiving just got ruined."

The next morning we headed out to the Monte Alban pyramid. It was dramatically larger than Tikal, so we surveyed the surroundings for a while, then sat attentively on the steps of Monte Alban. It was a pleasantly warm and sunny day as Geraldo asked, "Do you know where the largest pyramid in the

The King Montezuma Trilogy

world is?"

I quickly volunteered "Egypt," and Geraldo said, "No. It is the Great Pyramid of Cholula, just north of us in the outskirts of the city of Puebla." You could tell Geraldo was beaming with pride as he explained, "It is the largest pyramid by volume in the world. It is more than four football fields wide. It's not as tall as the ones in Giza, but it is still the biggest. Oh, sorry for that commercial. Here, of course, is the wonderful Monte Alban pyramid. It comes from the Zapotec civilization, and it's where God said to Aapo, 'To your offspring I will give this land. Raise your eyes now, and look from the place where you are, northward and southward and eastward and westward; for all the land that you see I will give you and to your offspring forever.'"

Jameson and I looked around and agreed it was an impressive site, overlooking the city of Oaxaca. Geraldo returned to his tour guide voice. "Just like Tikal, these magnificent ruins are also on the list of UNESCO World Heritage sites. The ancient Zapotec civilization considered Monte Alban a sacred site that doubled as a fortification against invading forces. The impressive structure sits high on a plateau above the valley, and it is where our story continues. Soon after arriving in Oaxaca, there were kings who were waging war over trade routes through their empires. Aapo ended up being at the right place at the right time, and rescued the son of King Melchizedek, and when it was found out, the king met Aapo in the Valley of Oaxaca. And King Melchizedek brought out bread and wine; he was a shaman of God Most High. He blessed him and said,

'Blessed be Aapo by God Most High,

The King Montezuma Trilogy

maker of heaven and earth;
and blessed be God Most High,
who has delivered my son into your hand!'"

"I guess I like the blessing stuff," Jameson said with a wry smile. "By the way, doesn't the name Melchizedek mean righteousness?"

"Yes," I responded, "and interestingly, he was from the city of peace."

"And the King gave Aapo bread and wine," continued Geraldo. "Doesn't that remind you of Jim Caldwell at the last supper he shared with his Hole in the Rock Gang?"

"Intriguing, isn't it?" I confirmed. "That's one reason I love the Aztec Scriptures. The texts are very real, and challenging, and exciting."

Geraldo agreed, then said, "After these things the word of God came to Aapo in a vision. 'You shall have as many descendants as there are stars in the sky, because I have promised that your people will be my people. And I have brought you from Ur of the Chaldeans to give you this land. But know this: your offspring shall be aliens in a land that is not theirs, and shall be slaves there, and they shall be oppressed for four hundred years. Then they will come back here in the fourth generation.' Aapo was less than impressed, but then God made a verbal covenant with Aapo, saying, 'To your descendants I give this land, from the great river in the north, to the body of water in the west, and from the sea in the east, to Guatemala in the south.'"

"So that made everything okay?" asked a puzzled Jameson.

"Of course not," said Geraldo, "but the promises were in

The King Montezuma Trilogy

place for the Aztecs to become God's people living on God's Promised Land. To make the covenant with God binding, Aapo needed to respond to it, to guarantee its validity. Then God said, 'This is my covenant, which you shall keep, between me and you and your offspring after you: Every male among you shall be circumcised.'"

Jameson glanced down for a moment and said, "Thanks a lot, dad. I know what that's all about." Then said, "Hey Geraldo, isn't that a bit prejudiced? Why not some sort of covenant that includes women?"

"God did it for their health," explained Geraldo. "Then God said, 'So my covenant shall be in your flesh as an everlasting covenant. As for Beatrice your wife...'"

"Now we're getting somewhere," interrupted Jameson. "What happened to her?"

"God blessed her," said Geraldo.

"Wow. Are you kidding?" asked Jameson with frustration.

"Not at all. Then God said, 'I will give you a son by her, and kings shall come from her.' Do you want to know what happened next?" We nodded, so Geraldo continued. "Aapo fell on his face and laughed, and muttered under his breath, 'I'm an old man and Beatrice is past the child bearing years.' God replied, 'Beatrice will bear a son, and you shall name him Hugo (the Guatemalan name that means "the intelligent one"). I will establish my covenant with him as an everlasting covenant for his offspring after him. And Beatrice will give birth next year.'"

"All of this happened in this area?" Jameson asked inquisitively.

Geraldo confirmed, then said, "God appeared to Aapo at the door to his home in the heat of the day, and when Aapo went to the door, he saw three men standing there. He didn't

The King Montezuma Trilogy

know they were angels. Aapo invited them in to stay for lunch and when they agreed, he asked Beatrice to prepare some of her renowned carne asada. After they ate, one of the men asked, 'Where is your wife, Beatrice?' Aapo replied, 'She's outside in the kitchen.' Then one of the other men said, 'When I return, your wife shall have a son.' Now Beatrice was listening, and since she was beyond child-bearing years, she laughed. It then became apparent that this was a divine visit, as the angels asked Aapo, 'Is anything too difficult for God?'"

Geraldo said, "Let's go up the pyramid for the next part of the story." Jameson jumped up and happily ran to the top. When I breathlessly got there, Geraldo continued. "Then the three men took Aapo to the top of the Monte Alban pyramid in Oaxaca, and pointed north and a little bit east. At that moment the angels disappeared, and God's voice said, 'Just over the Sierra Juarez Mountains is the village of Veracruz. The Olmecs live among its rivers and coastal plain, and their sin is very great. I shall wipe them off the face of the earth.'"

Jameson was properly horrified, and asked, "Would God kill the good as well as the bad?"

"Listen to how the story went down," suggested Geraldo. "Aapo said, 'Suppose there are fifty righteous Olmecs who live there. Will you not spare them? Will you not do the just and right thing?' And God said, 'If I find fifty righteous Olmecs in Veracruz, I will forgive the whole place for their sake.' Then Aapo asked, 'What if you find forty-five righteous people there?' and God answered, 'For the sake of forty-five, I will not do it.' Aapo then negotiated, 'How about forty?' God answered, 'For the sake of forty, I will not do it.' So Aapo requested, 'Please don't get angry, but what about for the sake of thirty?' God said, 'If I find thirty, I will spare them all.' Then Aapo asked, 'What

The King Montezuma Trilogy

about twenty?' When God agreed, Aapo had one last request. 'Suppose ten are found there.' God said, 'I chose you for your righteousness, and you are proving to be a good choice, so, yes. For the sake of ten I will not destroy it.' As soon as Aapo realized he was standing alone on top of the pyramid, and the voice was no longer being heard, he returned home."

Jameson started to head down the pyramid, but Geraldo said, "There's more to the story." When Jameson was seated, the story continued. "Aapo's nephew Francisco, the Guatemalan name that means 'the free one,' lived in Veracruz. That evening, two of the three men who had visited Aapo, came to Veracruz. Francisco was at the entrance to the village, and invited them to his house for the night, so they went with him and had dinner. Men of the city surrounded Francisco's house and demanded to see his visitors. He went out and asked the evil people to leave them alone, because they weren't practicing proper hospitality. But they were enraged about strangers in their midst, and tried to break down his door. The men inside grabbed Francisco, pulled him inside, shut the door, and caused the men outside to become blind. Then the two men asked Francisco if he had any relatives in the village, because they were about to destroy the place. None of his friends nor family believed Francisco, so when morning dawned, they told him to take his wife and two daughters and leave town. Once outside the village, the two men said to the family of four, 'Flee for your life and do not look back. Flee to the hills, or else you will be consumed, for God is preparing to rain fire on the village and wipe it off the face of the earth.' As they departed, Francisco's wife couldn't bear the thought of losing her life back in the village, so when she did, she turned into a cactus."

"Gotta' admit," said Jameson, "I don't much care for that

The King Montezuma Trilogy

story."

"It's sad," I agreed, "but don't forget what Jim Crawford had to say about it: 'Remember Francisco's wife. Those who try to make their life secure will lose it, but those who lose their life will keep it.'"

"Okay dad, but what does that mean?" Jameson asked.

"It's part of your destiny, son," I said. "If you go into ministry, you will lose the life you had. In fact, anyone who follows the Caldwellian lifestyle will lose the old life, like Pablo did on his Road to Tucson experience, and find the new life of following the Spirit of Jim."

Jameson suggested, "It sounds like a tough decision. Why would anyone do it?"

"Few take that road," I solemnly shared, "because the journey through this life is more attractive doing what we want rather than what God wants."

Geraldo agreed with a nod and announced it was time to travel to the next pyramid for more stories. It was a twenty hour drive to Chichen Itza, so we would do an overnight once again in Villahermosa. Jameson settled into the backseat and got out his cell phone while I broke out my laptop. Geraldo liked to talk, but he kindly gave us some quiet time. The next day brought us close to Chichen Itza, and we stayed in the quaint little village of Piste, about twenty-five miles northwest of the ruins.

In the morning it was Geraldo who was excited. As soon as we parked, he hurried us to a nice viewing spot and went into his guide voice. "This is one of the most visited archaeological sites in Mexico today," he said with a sense of pride. "Chichen Itza was named a UNESCO World Heritage Site in 1988 and, in 2007 it was named as one of the New Seven Wonders of the World." Some oohs and aahs were heard by tourists who were

The King Montezuma Trilogy

listening in. "The name Chichen Itza is Mayan meaning 'at the mouth of the well of the Itza.' The Itza were an ethnic group of Mayans in the northern part of the Yucatan peninsula. The main pyramid of Chichen Itza is El Castillo, also known as the Temple of Kukulkan. Around it lies a myriad of structures that were built for this city that, at its height, is believed to have had as many as 50,000 people. The well in the name refers to a number of underground rivers that served as that indispensable gift of water. It became an important commercial center, trading in gold and other treasures. This is why it became a dangerous place for those who were not from there, and it is where Aapo and Beatrice settled after Monte Alban." People started moving on when they realized the guide was moving into a religious discussion.

"To protect his wife in a dangerous and foreign land, Aapo told people that Beatrice was his sister. When King Canek of Chichen Itza heard about Aapo's sister, he sent for her. But God came to Canek in a dream by night, and said to him, 'you are about to die because of the woman whom you have taken; for she is a married woman.' Now Canek felt panic in his dream and asked, 'Who are you?' God said, 'I am the one who destroyed Veracruz.' Canek had just heard about that event, so he was even further frightened. He had not approached Beatrice, so he asked the mysterious voice in his dream, 'Will you now destroy an innocent person? After all, he said she was his sister. I have done nothing without integrity and everything with innocence.' Then God said to him in the dream, 'Yes, I know that you did this in the integrity of your heart; furthermore it was I who kept you from sinning by not letting you touch her. Now then, return the man's wife, for he is a prophet, and he will pray for you and you shall live. But if you do not return her, know that you surely will die, you and all that are yours.'"

"Still not liking this God of the Aztec Scriptures," said Jameson, but I put a hand on his shoulder and suggested that we were here to listen to the stories where they originated. Geraldo continued, "So Canek got up in the morning, and called all his servants and told them all these things; and the men were very much afraid. Then the king called Aapo and said to him, 'What have you done to us? Have I sinned against you, that you have brought such great guilt on me and my kingdom? You have done things to me that ought not to be done. What were you thinking of, that you did this thing?' Aapo said, 'I did it because I thought there is no reverence of God in this place, and they will kill me because of my wife.'"

Geraldo had a bit of a concerned look on his face and asked us, "Do you think there was no reverence in this place before Aapo brought the Aztec faith?"

Honestly, we were a bit stunned at his question. We looked at each and Jameson shrugged his shoulders. I thought for a moment, then carefully parsed my words, "This feels like a spiritual place…and I suppose there are many ways to God."

Geraldo liked my answer and continued with the story. "Aapo then said she is indeed my sister, the daughter of my father but not the daughter of my mother, and she became my wife. And when God caused me to wander from my father's house in Guatemala, I said to her, 'this is the kindness you must do me: at every place to which we come, say of me, he is my brother.' Then Canek took some donkeys and horses and gave them to Aapo, and returned Beatrice to him. Canek said, 'My land is before you; settle where it pleases you.' Then he said to Beatrice, 'I have given your brother a thousand pieces of gold; it is your exoneration before all who are with you. You are

The King Montezuma Trilogy

completely vindicated.' Then Aapo prayed to God, and God healed Canek and his wife so they were able to have children. For God had closed all the wombs of the house of Canek because of Beatrice, Aapo's wife."

"Seems like things were going pretty good for Aapo," declared Jameson.

"Yes," Geraldo agreed, "and now the impossible was getting ready to happen. As promised by God, Beatrice, in her old age, bore Aapo a son. Aapo named him Hugo, as God had previously instructed, then obediently had his son circumcised. Now Beatrice said, 'God has brought laughter for me; everyone who hears will laugh with me. Who would ever have said to Aapo that Beatrice would nurse a child, yet I have born a son in my old age.' At that time Canek said to Aapo, 'God is with you in all that you do; now therefore swear to me here by God that you will not deal falsely with me or with my offspring or with my posterity. But as I have dealt loyally with you, you will deal with me and with the land where you have resided as an outsider.' And Aapo said, 'I swear it.'"

We all took a break, then Geraldo led us to the site of a well to continue the story. "One day, when Aapo complained to Canek about a well of water that Canek's servants had seized, Canek said, 'I do not know who has done this; you did not tell me, and I have not heard of it until today.' So Aapo took two of his donkeys and gave them to Canek, and the two men made a covenant. And Canek said to Aapo, 'What is the meaning of the two donkeys that you have set apart?' Aapo said, 'These two donkeys you shall accept from my hand, in order that you may be a witness for me that I dug this well.' Therefore that place was called Beersheba, because both of them swore an oath. Afterwards, Canek left and Aapo planted a jacaranda tree

The King Montezuma Trilogy

to commemorate the event as a religious experience. And Aapo resided there as an outsider for many days.'"

"I remember what's next," said Jameson, "the sacrifice of Hugo."

"Well, not exactly," Geraldo said. "God definitely commanded Aapo to sacrifice Hugo, but the story has come to be known as either 'The Testing of Aapo' or 'The Binding of Hugo,' based on what you want to focus on."

Jameson asked, "So why would human sacrifice even be considered? And why would that be considered spiritual?"

Geraldo explained, "Human sacrifice was commonly practiced among the Mayans, and some say that the story of Aapo and Hugo was where human sacrifice ended. Now let's get back to the story." After we gave an approving smile, he said, "God then tested Aapo. While he was still at Chichen Itza, God said 'Take your son, your only son Hugo, whom you love, and go to the pyramid near Oaxaca, and offer him there as a burnt offering.'"

Jameson immediately interrupted, "We don't have to drive back there now, do we?"

"Of course not," said Geraldo. "You already know what that area is like." He then went on, "After a terrible and sleepless night, Aapo got up. It was before dawn, and he found himself stumbling around in a dazed confusion. As he struggled to saddle a horse, Beatrice heard him and asked what was going on. He responded in a gruff voice, 'Don't ask! And don't wait up for us either.' He then cut some wood for the burnt offering, gathered Hugo, and set out for Monte Alban. When Aapo saw the pyramid in the distance, he tied up his horse and asked Hugo to carry the firewood and a knife. 'What are we doing?' asked Hugo. 'We are going to the top of the pyramid to worship,

The King Montezuma Trilogy

and make a burnt offering to God,' Aapo replied. So the two of them ascended the great pyramid. Hugo said to his father, 'The fire and the wood are here, but where is the animal for a burnt offering?' Aapo had visible tears in his eyes as he said, 'God himself will provide the animal for the burnt offering, my son.' There they built an altar and piled the wood for the burnt offering. Aapo said, 'It is time to worship. I know it seems strange, but I need to bind you for the ceremony.' After binding Hugo, he laid him on the altar, on top of the wood, and took the knife to slaughter his son. Then God called to him from heaven and said, 'Do not lay your hand on the boy or do anything to him; for now I know that you revere me, since you have not withheld your son, your only son, from me.'

"And Aapo looked around and saw a young deer near the base of the pyramid, caught in a thicket by its horns. Aapo took the deer to the top of Monte Alban, unbound his son, and offered up the deer as a burnt offering. So Aapo called that place 'God will provide.' God called to him a second time and said, 'by myself I have sworn that, because you have done this, and have not withheld your son, your only son, I will indeed bless you, and I will make your offspring as numerous as the stars of heaven and as the sand that is on the seashore. By your offspring shall all the nations of the earth gain blessing for themselves, because you have obeyed my voice.' So Aapo and Hugo came down from the pyramid and returned to their home."

"I'll bet Hugo's mom had a lot of questions when they got back," laughed Jameson. "And think about Hugo! What happened between him and his dad on their three day journey to the pyramid, and three days back? Did Hugo hear God's voice at the pyramid, or just his dad? Wasn't he curious about being tied up and laid on top of the wood? Did he see the knife?

The King Montezuma Trilogy

Did he have concern when he saw tears in his Dad's eyes? Did he ask about the unusual worship ceremony?"

"Very good, Jameson," Geraldo said. "It's an important insight to realize that both the Aztec Scriptures and the Caldwellian Scriptures open a very brief window into their times. This story from the Aztec Scriptures is one of the most troubling of all the stories. While it is indeed a supreme act of obedience, it is a terrible example of genuine worship, and even worse it puts God's morality in jeopardy. Does it mean that God is above all human moral codes to use divine wisdom? Or does it mean cultural norms have vastly changed? After all, human sacrifice indeed was practiced all over the Mayan and Aztec world."

They had plenty to think about, so they took another break and got some refreshments from a street food vendor. It was a warm afternoon with bright sun as they sat at a bench and enjoyed some authentic, no frills Mexican food. Geraldo really loved being a tour guide, so pretty soon he got them back to the story.

"Beatrice lived a long and prosperous life, and died in the land of Chichen Itza. Aapo mourned and wept for her, then said, 'I am a stranger residing among you; give me property for a burial place.' The people of the Yucatan Peninsula answered him, 'You are a mighty prince among us. Bury your dead in the choicest of our burial places; none of us will withhold from you any burial ground.' Aapo bowed to them and said, 'If you are willing that I should bury my dead anywhere I want, I would like the cave at the end of this field.'"

The three of them walked to the end of the field, and Geraldo said, "When King Canek of Chichen Itza heard of the request he said, 'You may have the cave at the end of the field.' So the cave passed to Aapo as a possession. After this, Aapo

The King Montezuma Trilogy

buried Beatrice in the cave in the land of the Mayans. Now Aapo was old, and God had blessed him in all things. Aapo said to his servant, 'Put your hand under my thigh and I will make you swear, by the God of heaven and earth that you will not get a wife for my son from among the local Mayans. Instead, go back to my homeland in Guatemala and get an Aztec wife for my son Hugo.' The servant said, 'Perhaps the woman may not be willing to follow me to this land. Shouldn't I take Hugo with me?'

"Aapo explained, 'God took me from my father's house and from the land of my birth, and spoke to me, and swore that he would give my offspring this land. Here, not there. So don't worry. God will send an angel with you, to help you take a wife for my son from there. If the woman is not willing to follow you, then you will be free from this oath.' So the servant put his hand under the thigh of Aapo and swore to him concerning this matter, then traveled to Tikal, Aapo's homeland, in the Peten jungles of northern Guatemala."

Jameson was quick to confirm, "And we don't have to drive back there either, right?"

"That's right," Geraldo said. "When he arrived, he stopped at the well outside the city, because it was toward evening, when women were coming to draw water. He prayed, 'God of my master Aapo, please grant me success today and show steadfast love to my master. I am standing here by the spring of water, and the daughters of the townspeople are here. Let the girl to whom I speak be the one whom you have appointed for your servant Hugo.' Before he had finished praying, Alejandra showed up with her water jar on her shoulder. The girl was very attractive to look upon. Then the servant said, 'Please let me sip a little water from your jar.'

"Alejandra never spoke to men at the well, so she was

The King Montezuma Trilogy

surprised when he talked to her. She reluctantly decided to give him a drink, so he was encouraged, and asked if there was room in her father's house to spend the night. Now she understood why she wasn't supposed to speak to men at the well, but something strange happened. It was almost like she was outside of her body looking at the man, and then she said 'yes,' so the servant bowed his head and worshiped God.

"Then Alejandra ran and told her mother's household about these things. Her brother ran to the well to find out what this man's intentions were, and he could have sworn he saw an angel standing by the servant. They talked for a while and the servant came across as genuine. When he found it was all true, he invited the servant to their house. Once inside, the traveler said, 'I am Aapo's servant. God has greatly blessed him, and he has become wealthy. And his wife Beatrice bore him a son. My master made me swear, saying, 'You shall not take a wife for my son from the daughters of Chichen Itza, in whose land I live, but you shall go to my father's house, to my kindred, and get a wife for my son.' He then told them about his prayer to God for help in finding the right woman. Then he said, 'If you will deal loyally and truly with my master, tell me; and if not, tell me, so that I may be on my way.'

"Alejandra's father said, 'I believe this is all true. Take her and go, and let her be the wife of your master's son, as God has spoken.' In the morning, Alejandra's brother and mother decided she should remain at least ten days, and then could go. The servant asked them not to delay, so they asked her what she wanted. Alejandra said it was her desire to go, so her brother blessed her,

'May you, our sister, have offspring

The King Montezuma Trilogy

as numerous as the stars;
and may they gain possession
of the gates of their foes.'

Then Alejandra rose up, mounted a horse, and followed the servant back to Chichen Itza.

"Now Hugo went out in the evening to walk in the field, and looking up he saw horses coming. And Alejandra looked up, and when she saw Hugo, she slipped down from her horse. She asked, 'Who is the man over there, walking in the field to meet us?' When the servant said it was his master, she took her veil and covered herself. And the servant told Hugo all the things that had happened on his journey to Aapo's homeland. Then Hugo took her into the home where his mother had lived. They got married, and he loved her very much, which comforted him after his mother's death. Aapo died in a good old age, an old man full of years, and was gathered to his people. Hugo buried him in the cave with his wife Beatrice. After the death of Aapo, God continued the blessings to Hugo, from generation to generation.

"Okay, it's been a good day of storytelling. Let's head back to our hotel and have some dinner. Tomorrow we'll pick the story back up with Hugo. Just remember that the stories we are experiencing from Genesis are about the four patriarchs of the Aztec Scriptures. We heard a lot about Aapo and Hugo, and next we will hear about Tobillo and Eloy."

The King Montezuma Trilogy

SCENE TWO
Tobillo and Eloy

We had a good night's sleep, and I found it rewarding to hear Jameson say he was enjoying the trip. After breakfast, we met Geraldo, who was his normal enthusiastic self, as we headed back to the ruins. He shared a lot of details about the area, like it is one of the most visited sites in Mexico, then he parked and took us to the north end of the expanse. We walked on a raised pathway for about a football field in length and came to the Sacred Cenote. It's a water-filled sinkhole about 200 feet in diameter and surrounded by sheer cliffs. He asked us to find a comfortable place to sit in the shade and listen to the next biblical story.

"Hugo was forty years old when he married Alejandra. They struggled to have a child, so Hugo prayed to God for a child. He told God that it would be difficult to pass the blessings on if he didn't have progeny. God knew that, and soon enough she conceived. Twins were in her womb, and they struggled within her, and she said, 'If it is to be this way, why do I live?' God surprised her with a response:

'Two nations are in your womb,
    and two peoples born of you shall be divided;
the one shall be stronger than the other,
    the elder shall serve the younger.'

Alejandra didn't care very much for this word from God. How could she become excited about having twins if they were going to fight all of the time?

The King Montezuma Trilogy

"When her time finally came to give birth, the first came out red, and she and Hugo named their eldest son Rojo. The second child came out gripping Rojo's heel. Sure enough, the fighting that started in the womb continued as soon as they were born. They thought for quite a while about a name for the younger child. Since he grabbed at his brother's heel, they decided to name him Tobillo, which means ankle. When the boys grew up, Rojo was a skillful hunter, while Tobillo liked to sit around the house and help his mom cook. A problem quickly developed because Hugo loved meat, and since the eldest was a successful hunter, Hugo loved Rojo more than Tobillo. Alejandra loved having the companionship of her son in the kitchen, so she loved Tobillo the most."

"Kinda glad," mentioned Jameson, "I was an only child."

"Not me," said Geraldo. "I am the youngest of eight children, but back to the story. Once when Tobillo was cooking a stew in the kitchen, Rojo came in from the field and was famished. Rojo said to Tobillo, 'Let me eat some of that stew!' Even though Tobillo was the younger of the two, he loved throwing it in Rojo's face about God's proclamation, 'The elder shall serve the younger.' Tobillo said, 'Let me get this straight. You need what I have, so you should give me something I need.' Rojo questioned, 'What's your point? I'm starving!' to which Tobillo requested, 'First sell me your birthright.'

"Rojo didn't really care about anything Tobillo ever said, so he replied, 'How could I care less?' Rojo then said, 'Swear to me first.' So he swore to him and sold his birthright to Tobillo, and Rojo despised his birthright and his brother.

Now there was a famine in the land, and Hugo thought about going to his ancestral home. God appeared to Hugo and said, 'Do not go down to Guatemala. Continue to reside in this

The King Montezuma Trilogy

land, and I will be with you, and will bless you. For to you and to your descendants I will give all these lands, and I will fulfill the oath that I swore to your father Aapo. I will make your offspring as numerous as the stars of heaven, and will give to your offspring all these lands. And all the nations of the earth shall gain blessing for themselves through your offspring.' So Hugo remained in the Yucatan peninsula."

"Do you think he swam in this cenote?" asked Jameson.

"Definitely not," said Geraldo. "Before human sacrifice ended with the binding of Isaac, this waterhole was used for depositing valuables and human bodies to appease the rain god Chaac. That's why it is called sacred, but there are several other cenotes in the area used for drinking water and swimming."

"What happened next in the story?" I asked, gently moving them away from majoring in the minors.

Geraldo happily continued with "God blessed Hugo, and he became rich. Then Hugo prospered more and more and became very wealthy. He had a great house and the local Mayans envied him. And King Canek said to Hugo, 'Go away from us; you have become too powerful for us.' So Hugo departed from there and settled near the Monte Alban pyramid."

"Been there, done that," retorted Jameson.

"Very good," announced Geraldo, "so now just return there in your imagination." We paused and closed our eyes. We had seen a lot of places already, so needed to conjure for a moment the memory of that particular pyramid, then he continued. "But when Hugo's servants found a well of spring water in their new location, the Zapotec people quarreled with them, saying, 'The water is ours.' When they didn't quarrel about another well, Hugo said, 'Now God has made room for us, and we shall be

The King Montezuma Trilogy

fruitful in the land.'"

"Those guys moved around as much as we did, Dad," said Jameson with a smirk on his face.

I responded that, "change of scenery is good. It keeps things fresh."

"Let's see how things were refreshed in this story," suggested Geraldo. "When Hugo was old and his eyes were dim so that he could not see, he called his elder son Rojo and said to him, 'My son, I'm old. Hunt some game for me so I can enjoy it before I die, then I will give you my blessings,' and Rojo went and did as his father instructed. Now Alejandra was listening, so she went to her son Tobillo and said, 'Obey my word as I command you. Prepare your father's favorite dish and give it to him, so that he may bless you before he dies. Then Alejandra took Rojo's favorite garments, and put them on Tobillo. After Alejandra perfected her son's dish, she handed it to her favorite son and said, 'Take this to your father, but do not talk.'

"Hugo smelled the fragrant dish as Alejandra and Tobillo entered the room, and said, 'How is it that you have found it so quickly my son?' Alejandra answered, 'Please, Hugo, just enjoy the meal you requested. Rojo has fallen ill from rushing so hard in this task and he can barely talk.' Hugo dipped a tortilla into the caldo, and was so pleased that he blessed his son, the wrong son, right then and there. A smile crossed Hugo's face when he smelled Rojo's garments, and he said,

> "Ah, the smell of my son
>   is like the smell of a field that God has
>   blessed.
> May God give you of the dew of heaven,

The King Montezuma Trilogy

    and of the fatness of the earth,
    and plenty of grain and wine.
Let peoples serve you,
    and nations bow down to you.
Be lord over your brothers,
    and may your mother's sons bow down to you.
Cursed be everyone who curses you,
    and blessed be everyone who blesses you!"

"Wow!" said Jameson. "A story of deception. I would never have guessed the Aztec Scriptures would have such unethical behavior."

"As I said before, my son, the stories pull no punches. They deal with the good, bad, and ugly, just like the church today."

Geraldo was getting used to being interrupted. It wasn't a normal tour, so he was fine with the change in style. "As soon as Hugo had finished blessing Tobillo, Rojo returned from his hunting. Hugo quickly realized he had blessed the wrong son, but the deed was done. Rojo begged to be blessed anyway, so Hugo gave him a hunting blessing, since the political blessing was already given. Rojo was so infuriated, that he pledged to kill his brother as soon as his father died. With the encouragement of his mother, Tobillo decided to leave, so his father blessed him, and sent him to the ancestral home in Guatemala to find a wife. Tobillo left Monte Alban and headed for Tikal."

"Should we think about Tikal now?" asked Jameson.

"Not yet," said Geraldo. "First, we have a few more things to hear. On the first night of his journey, he laid his head on a stone, and went fast to sleep. And he dreamt that there was a stairway to heaven with angels walking up it and down it. Then

The King Montezuma Trilogy

God confirmed that the promises made to his father and grandfather would continue to Tobillo. And that God would take care of him on his trip away from the Promised Land. Waking up in a great mood, Tobillo made a vow, saying, 'If God will be with me, and will keep me in this way that I go, then the one God shall be my God.'"

"Wait a minute," said Jameson. "I know about if/then stories, as in 'if you do this, then I'll do that.' So you mean to tell me that Tobillo received an unconditional covenant from God and placed a condition of his own on it?"

"Kind of like," I said, "when people experience the unconditional love of God and do nothing about it." Jameson and I sat and pondered that one for a while. Then Geraldo went on.

"As Tobillo neared Tikal, he came upon a well, capped with a heavy stone that normally took several men to move. When Tobillo saw a beautiful woman approaching, he was filled with excitement and moved the stone by himself. After impressing her they talked, and Tobillo discovered she was his uncle's daughter. The woman immediately ran and told her father, who ran back to greet him. After a quick embrace, Tobillo was brought back to his uncle's home. His uncle was so thrilled that he said, 'Surely you are my bone and my flesh!' And he invited him to stay.

"Tobillo was so enamored with the woman, that he offered to work seven years for her hand in marriage. The years passed quickly and he told his uncle, 'my time is completed, I'm ready to marry your daughter.' So his uncle threw a wedding feast, veiled his ugly daughter, and gave the wrong daughter away. Tobillo got so drunk at the party, that evening came, and he didn't even notice the deception…until the morning.

The King Montezuma Trilogy

"He was enraged, went to his uncle and demanded an explanation. His uncle said, 'It is tradition here to give away the first born before the younger daughter. But if you give me another seven years of work, I will give you my younger daughter.' Tobillo agreed to the deal and in the meantime had a fruitful seven years with both daughters, and ended up with eleven sons and one daughter."

"Wait, what?" asked Jameson. "That doesn't seem right."

I simply explained, "Different time, different customs."

Geraldo continued, "Tobillo also became exceedingly rich and said to his uncle, 'Send me away that I may go to my own home and country.' As Tobillo gathered his family and flocks, his nephews said, 'Tobillo has taken all that was our father's; he has gained all of his wealth from what belonged to our father.' Then God said to Tobillo, 'Return to the land of your birth.' So Tobillo set his family on horses and headed for Chichen Itza.

"His uncle was a cruel man, so he decided to pursue Tobillo. When he caught up with Tobillo he said, 'What have you done? You have deceived me, and carried away my daughters like captives of the sword. Why did you flee secretly and deceive me and not tell me? I would have sent you away with a party. It is in my power to do you harm, but God told me not to.' Tobillo responded, 'I thought you would try to take your daughters by force.' Then his uncle searched where Tobillo was at and found nothing that had been his. So Tobillo became angry and said, 'What is my offense? What is my sin, that you have hotly pursued me? Now that you have searched my belongings, set them before your sons, so that they may decide between us two.'

"Then his uncle said, 'The daughters are my daughters, the children are my children, the flocks are my flocks, and all that

The King Montezuma Trilogy

you see is mine. Come now, let us make a covenant, you and I; and let it be a witness between you and me.' He literally drew a line in the sand and said, 'I will no longer cross into your land and you will no longer cross into my land.' He then offered a threat that he'd better not mistreat his daughters because God has witnessed this covenant. Early in the morning, Tobillo's uncle got up, and kissed his grandchildren and his daughters and blessed them. Then he departed and returned home."

"Don't think I care too much for that uncle," said Jameson.

"Of course, not," I agreed. "The problem is that you're going to find people like that throughout your life. To keep from getting too bothered by them, you have to come to grips with the fact that life is unfair."

"Could I argue with God about that when I get to heaven?" asked Jameson.

"Sure," I said. "Just don't be in a hurry to get there."

Geraldo was patient as usual, then said, "As Tobillo continued his journey back home, he sent messengers ahead of him to meet with his brother Rojo. He wanted them to tell his brother that he had lived with their uncle until now, and he was returning with wealth and seeking peace. They returned to Tobillo and said, 'Your brother is coming to meet you, but he's bringing an army worth of men with him.' So Tobillo prayed to God, 'I am not worthy, but please deliver me from my brother.' Not really trusting God, Tobillo sent gifts ahead of himself to be given to Rojo.

"That night Tobillo sent his wife and children back across the line that he and his uncle had drawn in the sand. It was the boundary between Guatemala and the Promised Land. That way they could be returned to his uncle if he dies. When Jacob was left alone, a man showed up at his campsite. Tobillo was wary of strangers, especially considering his brother may be sending messengers ahead of him, so he welcomed him in a cautious manner.

"May I help you?" questioned Tobillo. The mysterious man said nothing, and for a moment, Tobillo thought he saw wings behind the man's back. All of a sudden he remembered the story about his grandfather meeting three men who later turned out to be God, but this strange man seemed to be anything but God. Then it happened. The shadowy figure approached Tobillo and knocked him down. 'What kind of greeting is that?' complained Tobillo, but the man remained silent. 'Have you come to kill me?' Tobillo begged for an answer, but none came. Then the sinister visitor knocked him down again. 'Sir. I believe you have forgotten your manners!' No matter how hard he tried, he couldn't engage the enigmatic man in conversation.

"Then the perplexing man put Tobillo in a head lock. At that point he definitely saw a wing and asked, 'Are you an angel?' Frustratingly, there was still no answer, but the quiet man let go, stepped back, then lurched toward him and went into full wrestling mode. Now Tobillo was strong as an ox, so he flipped him over and pinned him. 'That'll teach you a lesson!' laughed Tobillo, just before he found himself flipped over and pinned.

"This went on all night, with Tobillo offering all kinds of wrestling holds that never seemed to work. They both grew weary, and at daybreak the perplexing guest decided to end the match. Before Tobillo knew what happened, the man did a spin kick that landed on his hip. 'Ouch!' yelled Tobillo angrily. 'You dislocated my hip!' Tobillo then lurched forward from his good hip and pinned the man, who finally spoke: 'Let me go, for the day is breaking.' Tobillo asked, 'Why? Because you failed to break my hip?' But Tobillo knew this was a messenger from God

The King Montezuma Trilogy

in some fashion, so he said, 'I will not let you go, unless you bless me.'

"The angel asked, 'What is your name?' and Tobillo thought it a strange question for a messenger from God, but answered him anyway. Then the messenger said, 'You shall no longer be called Tobillo, but Mexica, for you have mixed it up with God and prevailed.' And then he blessed him and vanished. When Tobillo/Mexica looked up he saw his brother Rojo coming, along with that army worth of men. He quickly rose and paid deference to his brother as he approached, but the strangest thing happened. Rojo embraced him and they stood there and wept. Rojo asked, 'Where is your family?' to which he responded by calling to them just over the boundary line. As they arrived, Rojo was pleased to see that his brother had accumulated a great many family members and much wealth. Then he said, 'Let us return home.' God said to Mexica, 'Don't return to Chichen Itza, but go settle at Tulum.'"

"Aha!" announced Jameson. "I smell a trip coming, because we haven't been to Tulum."

"That's right, son," I said. "It's only about a two-hour drive, so would you mind driving?" Jameson nearly knocked me down grabbing the keys and running to the car. I moved to the backseat so Geraldo could navigate, we made it without incident, and Geraldo returned to his tour guide voice.

"The Tulum area was first inhabited more than 10,000 years ago, and it is believed to be the last great settlement built by the Maya. It was the only port city they built, and was a major trade center for land and sea. The ancient city was built like a fortress during the Formative Period, to protect the luxury items the Maya traded in. By the time Tobillo/Mexica arrived, it was a vibrant and colorful city.

The King Montezuma Trilogy

"When Mexica was getting close to Tulum, he said to his family and servants, 'Put away the foreign gods that are among you, and purify yourselves, and change your clothes; then come, let us go to Tulum.' God said to him, 'I am God: be fruitful and multiply. The land that I gave to Aapo and Hugo I will give to you, and I will give the land to your offspring after you.' As they arrived in Tulum, Alejandra began labor pains. It was a very difficult childbirth, and the family was able to secure a midwife for assistance. Alejandra knew she would not survive the birth, so she hurriedly announced that the name she wanted for the child was Amadis, which means 'love of God.'"

"So," stated Jameson, "now Mexica had twelve sons?"

I said, "Yes," then mentioned that the sons would become the names of the twelve tribes of Mexico, which got its name from Mexica.

"Then what happened?" asked Jameson, and I replied, "Alejandra died and was buried. Then Hugo, her father-in-law, died and Rojo and Mexica buried him."

"Not wanting to be around the place his wife was buried," explained Geraldo, "Mexica settled back in Oaxaca. Now the name of the eleventh son of Mexica was Eloy, which means 'chosen.' When Eloy turned seventeen, he was watching the flock with his brothers, and he complained to his father about their work. Now here's the real problem: Mexica loved Eloy more than any of his other children. Maybe because he was a son of his old age, but it doesn't matter, what matters is the favoritism. In fact, his father loved Eloy so much, he made him a beautiful sarape of many colors. But when his brothers saw that their father loved him more than them, they hated him.

"To make things worse, Eloy had a symbolic dream about his brothers bowing down to him. Dreams are fine, but it wasn't

The King Montezuma Trilogy

in Eloy's best interest to tell it to his brothers. So, strangely, he did, because youthful exuberance often outstrips intelligence. As to be expected, they hated him even more. Then he had another dream, and not learning lessons from his experience, he again told it to them. Now the brothers were combining their hatred with jealousy, a lethal combination.

"One day, Eloy was spending the day lazing around, while his brothers tended their father's flocks. Mexica found his young son and admonished him, saying, 'Go help your brothers.' As he was getting close to where they were, they saw him coming. That's when all of their venom reached a peak and they decided to kill him. They said, 'Here comes this dreamer. Let's kill him and throw him into one of the pits. Then we'll tell dad that a jaguar ate him.' But one of the brothers disagreed, saying, 'Let's not kill him, but throw him into the pit.' So when Eloy arrived, they stripped him of his colorful sarape, and threw him into the barren, waterless pit.

"Then a caravan of Olmec traders came into view carrying Guatemalan jade. The brothers quickly discussed the situation and decided to offer Eloy to them. They pulled him out of the pit and sold him for one jade trinket, then the Olmecs took Eloy with them to Coban in central Guatemala. The brothers returned home and told their father that Eloy had been killed and eaten by a jaguar. Then Mexica was grief-stricken, and would not leave his home for many months.

"Meanwhile, the Olmecs sold Eloy in Guatemala to Adelmo, one of the king's officials. Now Adelmo could see that Eloy was a good man, so he put him in charge of all that he had. Eloy was also a good-looking man, and after a while, Adelmo's wife yearned for him. Day after day she tried to seduce him, and finally she grabbed his kilt and it fell off as he ran outside. She

The King Montezuma Trilogy

yelled, 'This man tried to have his way with me!' When Adelmo got home, she told her side of the story and he became enraged. He then had Eloy put in prison.

"Some time later, two of the king's servants offended the king of Guatemala, and were sent to the same prison as Eloy. One night, both servants had a dream, and Eloy saw their fallen countenance. When he asked what the problem was, they both said they had confusing dreams. When Eloy told them that 'nothing is impossible for God,' they told him their dreams. Giving God the credit, Eloy interpreted their dreams, and they came true.

"Two years later, the king had a dream that terrified him. Finding nobody to interpret the dream, he put out a call for anyone who could understand it. Still finding no one, word came to him about Eloy, and the king sent for him. Upon arriving, the king asked if he could be of help, and he answered, 'It is not I, but God who will help.' So the king told him the dream, and Eloy said, 'It is about seven years of plenty, followed by seven years of famine. You should select a man to be in charge of Guatemala, who will store up produce of the land during the years of plenty. Then you will survive through the famine.'

"The king decided to put Eloy over Guatemala as second-in-command. And Eloy went throughout the land during the seven years of plenty, and had the people store up food. When the seven years of famine arrived, just as Eloy said, the Guatemala did just fine. All of the surrounding countries were in terrible trouble, so people from all over came to Guatemala, and Eloy sold grain and became famous. That's when things got strange, because Mexica decided to send his sons to Guatemala to buy grain.

"When they got there, they stood in an enormous line, and

The King Montezuma Trilogy

had no idea it was there brother who was so famous. When it was their turn to purchase food, they bowed their heads to the ground in deference to Eloy's authority, and Eloy recognized them. 'Where have you come from?' asked Eloy. His brothers responded, 'From the land of Oaxaca, where the great Monte Alban pyramid lies.' Eloy inquired, 'Are you spies?' They said, 'No, my lord. We have only come here to buy food.' Eloy frightened them when he said, 'No, you have come here as spies!' Then they said, 'We are your servants.'

"Eloy continued his interrogation with, 'Do you have any other brothers?' They said, 'Yes, my lord. Our youngest brother stayed home with our father and another one died.' After quickly composing himself about them saying that he was dead, Eloy said, 'Here is how I shall test you spies, to see if there is truth in you. One of you shall go and get your brother to bring here while the rest of you remain in prison.' Three days later Eloy returned to the prison and said, 'If you are honest men, you may leave only one brother here, while the rest of you carry grain back to your household. If you return with your youngest brother, you all shall live.'

"They agreed to this contract, and when Eloy left they said, 'We are surely paying the penalty for what we did to our brother. Remember the fear he had in his eyes when we threw him in that pit?' Another brother said, 'I told you not to harm him, but you wouldn't listen to me!' Eloy returned after a quick break to shed some tears over what had been done to him, then took one of the brothers and said, 'This one shall stay.' Eloy then ordered their bags to be filled with grain and to give them provisions for their journey.

"When they came to their father in Oaxaca, they told him all that happened. They then opened their bags of grain and found

The King Montezuma Trilogy

that their money was returned to them. Their father was not interested in the money because he did not want to send his youngest son back with them. Then one of the brothers said, 'You may kill my two sons if I do not bring our brother back.' Their father said, 'My son shall not go back with you,' so they unhappily remained. The problem was that the famine around Oaxaca worsened, so their father told them to return to Guatemala and get more food. One of the brothers reminded his father that the man in charge in Guatemala warned them that they would not be get any produce unless they brought their other brother. Out of exasperation, Mexica said, 'Take your brother, and be on your way,' then they took their youngest brother and headed off to Guatemala. Eloy was overjoyed when he discovered his brothers had returned with Mateo (which means gift of God), so he sent word to have them brought to his house for dinner."

"I'll bet that scared them!" announced Jameson, with his eyes wide open.

I agreed by saying, "Of course it did. They were being invited to the home of nobility, when they had no ability."

"Please, Dad," begged Jameson. "Your jokes leave something to be desired. Let's get back to the story."

"Indeed, they were afraid. They concocted all sorts of reasons why they were being invited, and none of them were good. When they arrived, they stood warily on the porch, and didn't even have to knock before the steward came out to greet them. The brothers immediately launched into sharing some of their fears, when the steward said, 'You have no reason to be afraid.'

"Yah," said Jameson, "I heard that line in a scary movie." I frowned, then the story continued.

The King Montezuma Trilogy

"The brothers were brought to an inner courtyard where, to their surprise, the brother who had been held captive until their return, was brought to them. They ecstatically embraced, shed some tears of joy, and shared their recent stories. When Eloy came home that evening, the brothers bowed before him. He asked, 'Is your father well? Is he still alive?' They said, 'He is still alive,' then bowed again before him. Eloy looked at his brothers, saw their youngest brother, and asked if it was him. Before they could answer, Eloy abruptly left. They looked at one another in confusion, but Eloy had gone out of the room because he was overcome with emotion. After composing himself, Eloy returned and said, 'Serve the meal.'

"The brothers were brought into the dining room and seated by order of birth. This shocked the brothers, but they didn't dare ask how this Guatemalan noble knew such information. In a continuing surprise, their youngest brother was brought five times as much food as the rest of them. Fear began to creep through them, but they smiled and ate and drank and made merry as they could.

"After dinner, Eloy privately instructed his steward to fill the men's sacks with food for their return journey, but add his precious jade cup at the top of one of the sacks. When morning came, the men were allowed to leave, and again they were in disbelief. As they rode away, they kept looking back, as none of this made any sense. Sure enough, they soon saw a large group of Eloy's servants chasing after them. When they overtook the brothers, the steward asked, 'Why have you stolen my master's green goblet?'

"One of the brother's assured him that nothing of the sort happened, but the servants searched the bags anyway. Terror filled their eyes when the item was produced, then the steward

The King Montezuma Trilogy

pointed at Mateo and said, 'Since it was in his bag, he shall return to become a slave.' After angrily asking Mateo why he stole it, they returned to the city to see what they could do to get their brother out of trouble."

"But he didn't do it!" complained Jameson, to which I said, "Remember what I said about life being unfair."

"When they returned to Eloy's home, one of the brothers asked, 'How can we clear ourselves?' Eloy said, 'The one who was in possession of the chalice shall be my slave. As for the rest of you, go in peace to your father.' Another brother said, 'Please let me speak.' Before Eloy could say anything, he continued, 'We cannot very well return to our father without our youngest brother. He has already lost one son. Surely he has been torn to pieces because nobody has seen him again, and if we return without our youngest brother our father will surely die. So now, I beg you, take me in place of Mateo.'

"They were all amazed when Eloy broke down and cried right there in front of them. Then he said something that shocked them to their soul: 'I am Eloy.' The brothers stepped back and fell to the ground, but Eloy said, 'Come closer.' They slowly got on their feet and hesitantly approached him. He said, 'I am your brother Eloy, whom you sold to jade traders headed to Guatemala. Now do not fear, because God has taken your terrible deed and turned it into good.' They stared at him, and while in their joy they were disbelieving. One of them finally asked, 'How can any good come from what we did to you?'

"Eloy explained, 'It is I who interpreted the king's dreams, which in turn saved us from famine. So it is not you who sent me here, but God. Now hurry back to our father and tell him that God has put Eloy in charge of Guatemala. Then tell him to come back with you and do not delay, because there are five more

The King Montezuma Trilogy

years of famine to endure. He will be safe here. And tell him how greatly I am honored in Guatemala.'

"The brothers talked for a long time, during which the King heard that Eloy's brothers had come. The King called for Eloy to come to his house, so he asked his brothers to remain until he got back. The King said, 'Tell your brothers that when they return, I will give them the best of the land. Give no thought to your possessions, for Guatemala's best is yours.' Eloy returned and told his brothers the good news. He then gave them provisions for their journey back to Oaxaca, and when they got there, they screamed, 'Eloy is alive!' Their father nearly fainted, so they carefully washed his face with cool water and said, 'He is even ruler over all of Guatemala.' This was too much for Mexica to take in, so he said that he didn't believe them. Several brothers spoke up at the same time and said, 'We didn't believe it either.' Then one of them said, 'He did things that defied logic.'

"Mexica then said, 'I'm listening.' The oldest brother said, 'He invited us to dinner. That scared us because we didn't know that the man who was second-in-command in all of Guatemala was also our brother. When we got to his house, he seated us in order of our birth.' Mexica said, 'Okay, that is strange.' The oldest continued, 'Then he showered Mateo with gifts, and allowed us to come back here.' Mexica asked, 'So why do you think he was Eloy?'

The oldest brother said, 'His steward brought several servants and stopped us as we traveled. They searched our bags and found a precious jade cup in Mateo's bag.' Mexica frowned, but the brother continued, 'he didn't do it. When we got back, Mateo was going to be made a slave, so I offered to take his place.' Mexica had a look of shock on his face, while another brother said with a laugh, 'You think you were

The King Montezuma Trilogy

surprised!' Then they all said, 'This great leader of Guatemala broke down right in front of us and cried.' Mexica suggested, 'Surely he was no great leader.' Then another brother said, 'He was greater than that.' Then the man said, 'I am Eloy.' We got up close to him and he said, 'I am your brother whom you sold...' All of the brothers quickly interrupted, and one brother finished his sentence, 'your heart to.'

"Mexica said, 'That doesn't sound like the way you treated Eloy, but it sounds like what Eloy would have done.' Then the oldest brother asked his father to step outside and showed him a great wealth sent from the King. As Mexica stood their stunned, they finished the stories, ending with the fact that the King was offering him a great place to live while the rest of the world suffered from famine. This revived Mexica's spirit and he said, 'Enough! My son Eloy is alive. I must go and see him before I die.'

"When Mexica set out on his journey, he stopped at Chichen Itza for a short visit in the land of his ancestors. There he had a vision in the night and God told him, 'Do not be afraid to go down to Guatemala, for I will make of you a great nation there, and I will be with you.' Then they came to Guatemala, and Mexica sent one of his sons ahead to Eloy. He was so excited that he mounted his horse and rode out to meet his father. They embraced for a long time, then Mexica said to Eloy, 'I can die now, having seen for myself that you are still alive.'

"When the King found out that all of Eloy's family had arrived, he sent word that the best part of the land was in the northern part of their country, and that he was going to be true to his word. They were beyond joyful, then Eloy brought Mexica to meet the King, and Mexica blessed him. After the King left, Eloy took all of his family to the best part of the land, and

The King Montezuma Trilogy

granted it to them, as the King had instructed. So Mexica settled in the land of Guatemala with his family, and they were fruitful and multiplied.

"One day Mexica called his family together and said, 'I do not have long to live, and I have one request.' Matteo asked, 'What is it father?' Mexica said, 'Do not bury me here when I die. I wish to have my body returned to Chichen Itza, so I can be buried by my wife.' Eloy said, 'I will do as you request.' Not many days later, Eloy was told that his father was ill. When he got to his father's house, Mexica summoned his strength and sat up in bed. Mexica said to Eloy, 'God told me in a dream, while I was in Chichen Itza, on my way here, that the blessings passed down from God to Aapo and to Hugo, then to me, will continue to you.' When Mexica saw Eloy's sons, he said, 'Whose are these?' Eloy proudly announced, 'These are my sons, whom God has given me here.' Mexica embraced the boys, then blessed them, saying,

> 'The God before whom my ancestors
>   Aapo and Hugo walked,
> the God who has been my guide
>   all my life to this day,
> the angel who has redeemed me from
>   all harm, bless these boys;
> and in them let my name be
>   perpetuated, and the name of
>   my ancestors Aapo and
>   Hugo;
> and let them grow into a multitude on
>   the earth.'

The King Montezuma Trilogy

"Then Mexica called all of his sons, and said: 'Gather around, that I may tell you what will happen to you in days to come.'"

"Wait, dad," requested Jameson. "Isn't this where Mexica drones on about blessings for all twelve of his children?"

I said, "Yes." Then he begged to move the story along, so Geraldo agreed.

"Then Mexica said, 'Do not forget to bury me with my wife,' and he breathed his last. After a lengthy period of mourning, Eloy asked the King for permission to bury his father at Chichen Itza, and the King said, 'Go, bury your father, as he wished.' Eloy and his brothers then fulfilled their father's request, and afterwards they returned to Guatemala.

"One day the brothers were talking, and it occurred to them that Eloy could still hold a grudge against them. Now that their father was gone and Eloy was famous, they might finally incur his wrath. So they concocted a plan. They went to Eloy and said, 'Before dad died, he asked us to beg you to forgive us of anything we may have done to you.'

"Eloy smiled and said, 'I don't believe you.' Before his brothers could say anything, he continued. 'But don't worry, am I in the place of God? Even though you intended evil, God turned it into good.' The kindness in his voice calmed them, and they put that concern to rest. So Eloy stayed in Guatemala with all of his relatives. Many years later, Eloy called his brothers together and announced, 'I am about to die, but trust the promise from God that you will return to the land promised to Aapo, Hugo, and Mexica.' When he gave his last breath, they took his body to Chichen Itza and buried him with their mother and father."

Geraldo had a satisfied look on his face and said, "Well,

The King Montezuma Trilogy

men, that completes the book of Genesis. What has the experience been like?"

"My favorite story," said Jameson, "was about Tobillo getting renamed Mexica."

"Why?" inquired Geraldo.

Jameson said, "Well, first of all, wrestling with God is a pretty cool idea. But mainly because it reminds me of Jose Maria Perez being renamed Pablo after his road to Tucson experience. In a sense, I'm like Tobillo and Jose Maria Perez, because a new name shows a change of heart, and when I became a believer I became known as a Caldwellian."

My heart warmed hearing my son talk so graciously about his faith. I shared with them that "I just loved being in the Peten Jungle where the whole story of God having a relationship with people got started. Sitting at the Pyramid in Tikal and hearing those early stories brought them alive, because they became more than just words on paper in the Aztec Scriptures. Somehow the characters were no longer just literature. They took on a personality with flesh and blood because I could smell and see and hear the sites they were at."

Geraldo shared that it had all been very special to him, also. He thanked me for hiring him, then suggested we stop for the day before moving into the stories from the book of Exodus.

"I want to go swimming," announced Jameson.

"Great idea," agreed Geraldo, "and here in Tulum is a wonderful white sand beach with gentle turquoise waves. Let's check into our hotel and get ready for the beach."

After we arrived at the shore, we could look up a rocky cliff and see El Castillo, the largest of the ruins in Tulum. It wasn't long before I heard Jameson scream. He was running out of the water and a gentle giant of a manatee went swimming by. We

The King Montezuma Trilogy

all had a good laugh, and then enjoyed a wonderful dinner when we got back in town.

The King Montezuma Trilogy

ACT II
Liberation

The King Montezuma Trilogy

SCENE ONE
Abund

The skies were cloudless when we reached our destination, so we settled in under a tree and prepared for the next set of stories. Geraldo wiped a little sweat from his brow, due to the humidity, then began. "After all of Eloy's family died, the Aztecs in Guatemala were fruitful and multiplied and became exceedingly strong. A new king arose over Guatemala who did not know Eloy, and was threatened by their power that came from the sheer number of people. He decided to oppress them, but they responded by multiplying even more. Soon the Guatemalans dreaded the Aztecs.

"That's when the king made a terrible decision. He told the midwives, 'Kill all baby boys who are born, but baby girls can be left alone.' The midwives feared God, so they decided to let the baby boys live. When the king asked them why they were disobedient, they lied to him, so he commanded all Guatemalans to kill any newborn Aztec boys. One particular baby boy was rescued from death by having him hidden when he was born. When the mother could not hide him anymore, she made him a little ark and floated him out on a river.

"The daughter of the king happened to walk by and saw the baby in the ark. She found he was an Aztec child, but decided to keep him. When the child grew up, she named him Abund (which means 'living in abundance') because he would be living a much better life than if he were raised as an Aztec."

Jameson had been squirming a bit through this story, and finally asked, "Isn't killing wrong?" I replied that it sounded like God's people were going to be needing some commandments.

The King Montezuma Trilogy

Geraldo nodded, then continued. "One day, after Abund had grown up and learned about his identity, he saw a Guatemalan beating an Aztec. He was so enraged that he killed the Guatemalan. The next day, Abund discovered that people knew of the killing. He feared the king would want to kill him, so he fled to Copan in western Honduras. There he met a shaman who had a daughter, and they soon married. After a long time, the king of Guatemala died and the Aztecs prayed for relief.

"One day, Abund came to Cerro Montecristo, the mountain of God. About half way up the mountain, he saw a mahogany tree that was on fire. Out of concern, he went toward it to see if he could save other trees nearby. To his surprise, when he got there, it wasn't on fire at all. Then the most amazing thing happened. God called to him and said, 'Abund, come no closer! Remove your sandals, for the place on which you are standing is holy ground.'

"Then the LORD said, 'I have heard the cry of my people in Guatemala, and I have come down to liberate them. So come, I will send you to the king of Guatemala to bring my people, the Aztecs, out of that land.' But Abund didn't feel up to the task, so God said, 'I will be with you.' Abund felt a little better, then asked, 'If they want to know your name, what shall I say?' At that point, God disclosed a very private part of divine identity. He said, 'Names are important, so to show how much I care, I shall tell you that my name is "I LET BE WHAT I LET BE." This is my name forever.'

Jameson interrupted with, "I love that! I guess if God lets people be, then I maybe I should, too."

"Yes," said Geraldo, "except God didn't let the Guatemalans be!" I suggested that when things are wrong, it must be the time to not let people be, same as God. After we

The King Montezuma Trilogy

thought about that for a moment, Geraldo continued. "Abund asked God, 'What happens if they don't believe me?' and another one of those uncomfortable silences happened. A bit frustrated, he complained again that he just wasn't up to the task. Then the LORD said, 'Don't you know it is I who gives speech to mortals?' But Abund begged, 'Please send someone else.' Then the anger of the LORD was kindled against Abund and God just said, 'Go and do as I say.'

"God was feeling benevolent after that, so he sent Abund's brother to meet him at Cerro Montecristo. There they talked about how God told Abund that everyone who wanted to kill him was dead, so they were to return without fear. Back in Guatemala, Abund gathered all the elders of the Aztecs and told them that God had seen their misery. They immediately bowed down and worshiped.

"At that point, Abund and his brother went to the king of Guatemala and said, 'The God of the Aztecs says, "Libertas a mi gente," which means 'free my people,' or 'let my people go.' The king laughed and said, 'I do not know your God, and I will not let the Aztecs go. I need them to assist with building my pyramids.' He then instructed the taskmasters to let heavier work be laid upon them. God then told Abund to tell the Aztecs, 'I will free you from the burdens of the Guatemalans and deliver you from slavery. I will take you as my people, and I will be your God. Then I will bring you into the land that I swore to give to Aapo, Hugo, and Mexica. I will give it to you for a possession. I am the LORD.' So Moses told this to the Aztecs, but they would not listen.

"Abund then returned to the king and said, 'Let God's people go,' but his heart was hardened and he still refused. Abund said, 'Because of God's great power, and because you

The King Montezuma Trilogy

have not listened, I will strike the water of Lake Atitlan and it shall dry up. Then you will have no water to drink.' The king laughed, so Abund struck the water and it dried up, but the king arrogantly turned his back on them and returned to his palace.

"A week later, the LORD said to Abund, 'Go to the king and tell him to let my people go. If he does not, I will send a plague of typhoid fever.' The king ignored him, so Abund said, 'Because of God's great power I now call on this disease to come upon the land.' When that happened, the king said, 'Tell your God to take away the disease from me and my people, and I will let them go.' Abund said, 'So that you may know that there is no one like the LORD our God, the fever shall go away.' When it did, the king again hardened his heart.

"Then the LORD said to Abund, 'Now I shall bring Chikungunya on the land,' and it came upon every human and animal."

"What is that?" asked a concerned Jameson. "And could I get it?"

Geraldo laughed and said, "We are in Mexico, and you are with a Mexican, so surely you are safe." Jameson wasn't impressed, then asked what it is. Geraldo explained "it is a virus that is spread by mosquitos."

Jameson asked, "So there are no mosquitos in Mexico?"

I said, "Of course there are. And in the United States, too, but I think we're getting away from the story."

Jameson seemed a bit disgruntled, then Geraldo said, "The story doesn't get any better, because the king had little concern for his people. The LORD then said to Abund, 'Go back to the king and tell him I say, "Let my people go. If you do not, I will send dengue fever tomorrow." The king didn't, so the LORD did. Again the king relented, and he agreed to let the Aztecs worship

The King Montezuma Trilogy

away from the Guatemalans, so as not to be offensive, but told them to not go far. When they were gone, so was the disease, but the king still had a hardened heart.

"Once again, the LORD told Abund to return to the king and say to him, 'The LORD says, let my people go. If you do not, I will strike down your cattle, hogs, sheep, horses, and chickens with swine fever. This will be done tomorrow.' Sure enough, the king ignored Abund and their livestock became sick and died, yet the king would not let the people go. Then the LORD brought malaria to the people, but the king would not change his mind. Next the LORD told Abund to tell the king, 'The LORD says I have let you live, so you can see my power. Tomorrow I will bring flooding to the land, but my people will be safe.' The next day, torrents of rain fell on the land. The open fields became an inland sea and every tree was downed, yet the king remained with a hardened heart.

"Then the LORD said to Abund, 'Go to the king and tell him that I have done these things, so that you may know that I am the LORD.' So Abund went and said, 'How long will you refuse to humble yourself before God? If you refuse again, God will send Chagas disease, and this time it was Abund who turned and left. The king's court advised him to let the people go before all of Guatemala was destroyed, so Abund was brought back. The king said that only the men could go worship the LORD, and Abund humbly turned down the offer, so he was rudely dismissed.

"Then Chagas came upon the land, and doubly so for the king. This time the king summoned Abund and said, 'I have sinned against the LORD your God, and against you. Forgive my sin and remove this deadly pestilence from me. When he was healed, his heart hardened, and he would not let God's

The King Montezuma Trilogy

people go. Then the LORD said to Abund, 'There will be scorching heat across the land for three days, and it was so. The king summoned Abund and this time offered to let the children go, and again Abund said he would not compromise. Then the king said, 'Get away from me! If I ever see you again, you will die.' Abund responded, 'It is true, I will never see you again.'

"This time, when Abund left, he asked the LORD, 'What will it take to convince the king?' The LORD answered, 'One more plague, then he will let you all go. Tell the Aztec people that every firstborn Guatemalan will die.'"

"Okay," complained Jameson, "I have to interrupt. Is all of that misery and death necessary?"

I said, "No, but there are consequences when we don't follow the way of the LORD."

Jameson followed with another question. "How did the Guatemalans know when they saw an Aztec?"

"Great question!" announced Geraldo. "The Guatemalans were Mayan."

"Okay," said Jameson, "but I don't know the difference."

I said, "Sure you do. Remember that mom is of Mayan descent, and the Mayans have round faces."

Jameson nodded that it made sense. Geraldo was glad to have a little break, because he was struggling with the pain of the story. He took a deep breath and continued, "Abund told the Aztecs, the LORD said, 'about midnight I will go through the land, and every firstborn Guatemalan shall die. Then the Guatemalans will beg for you to leave. Every family needs to take a year-old llama that is faultless, and hang it by the neck until it dies. This will become your last supper in Guatemala, so be prepared to depart after you eat.'"

The King Montezuma Trilogy

"Hmm," said Jameson, "doesn't that remind you of Jim Caldwell?"

"Yes," I said, "but then again Jim Caldwell's heritage was Aztec."

Geraldo continued with, "What the LORD was saying was 'I will then strike down every firstborn Guatemalan, so put the blood of the llama from your meal on your door, and when I see the blood I will pass over that house. This day shall be a day of remembrance for you. You shall celebrate it as a festival to the LORD for the rest of time, and you shall call it the Festival of Pan Dulce. However, add a bitter flavor to the bread so it will be a bittersweet memory.' Then Abund called the Aztecs to him and said, 'It is time. Tonight the LORD will pass over your house, and your firstborn will live, if you have the blood of the llama on your door.'

"At midnight, it happened. The king arose, and all of Guatemala cried out in despair over their losses. The king then sent word to Abund to 'Leave my people alone. I want your people to go away.' So the Aztec people gathered up their meager belongings, and the ingredients they needed to make a bitter pan dulce.' The Aztecs, about one thousand in all, journeyed away from Coban in the interior of Guatemala, toward Cerro Raxon, a nearly 10,000 foot mountain that was easy to see. The first night they camped out, they baked pan dulce in memory of the bittersweet times enslaved in Guatemala. Sitting around the campfire, the eldest among them shared stories that had been passed on from generation to generation. The time the Aztecs lived in Guatemala was four hundred thirty years, so there were many stories shared that night.

"Then the LORD told Abund, 'All Aztecs shall celebrate the

The King Montezuma Trilogy

time their firstborn children were passed over and allowed to live,' and the Aztec people did just as the LORD commanded. Abund said to the campers in the wilderness, 'Remember this day on which you came out of Guatemala, out of the house of slavery, because the LORD brought you out from there by strength. When the LORD brings us into the Promised Land, we will celebrate for seven days, and on the seventh day there will be a festival to the LORD. Tell your children on that day that the purpose of the festival is to remind us what the LORD did for us when we were liberated from Guatemala.'

"When the king let the people go, God led them in a roundabout way through the wilderness toward Lake Izabal. The LORD went in front of them in a pillar of cloud by day, to lead them, and in a pillar of fire by night, to give them light. Neither the cloud by day nor the fire by night left its place in front of the people. When the king of Guatemala was told that the people had fled, he had a change of mind about letting them go. He had his army mount their horses to pursue them, and he led the way.

"As the king and his army drew near, the Aztecs looked back, and the Guatemalans were advancing on them. They complained to Abund asking, 'Why did you take us into the wilderness to die? Didn't we tell you to leave us alone and let us serve the Guatemalans? It would have been far better to serve the Guatemalans than to die in the wilderness.' But Abund said, 'Do not be afraid, stand firm, and see what the LORD will do for us.'

"Then the LORD said to Abund, 'Why do you cry out to me? Tell the Aztecs to go forward to Lake Izabal and go around it to the south.' Abund questioned this, because then they would be trapped by the Caribbean Sea. Again, numbing silence, but the

The King Montezuma Trilogy

pillar of cloud moved from in front of them and took its place behind them. Abund then called out to his people and said, 'See, the LORD is between us and the king's army,' and it was there all night.

"The next morning Abund led his people on around the Lake, and they were encouraged to see that it narrowed to a much smaller river that emptied the lake into the sea. At that point, Abund stretched out his hand over the water and the LORD drove the river back. The water was divided and the riverbed became dry ground. The Aztecs carefully stepped onto the riverbed and the river formed a wall of water on their right and on their left. In their joy they were disbelieving, then noticed the Guatemalan army coming after them.

"The one thousand strong community of Aztecs rushed to the other side and stepped out, as the Guatemalan army entered the riverbed on their horses. The LORD responded by having the water slowly seep back onto the dry ground, and turn the riverbed into mud. The horses were getting stuck so that they turned with difficulty. The Guatemalans were frightened and said, 'Let us flee from the Aztecs. Surely they are God's people.'

"Next they jumped off their horses and tried to escape on foot, but their own weight was too much so they continued to sink. Then the LORD said to Abund, 'Stretch out your hand over the river, so that the water may come back upon the Guatemalans and their horses.' So Abund obeyed and the waters slowly returned across the riverbed, drowning the entire army of the king. The LORD saved the Aztecs that day from the Guatemalans, and they truly felt like they were God's people. From that day on, the people feared the LORD and believed in the LORD and in his servant Abund."

The King Montezuma Trilogy

Geraldo said, "I have one more story to tell, and then we can take a break. It is actually a song by Abund, followed by a song by his sister, but they are recognized as some of the oldest and most important poems in the Aztec Scriptures."

"Why?" asked a curious Jameson.

"Because," explained Geraldo, "they share the earliest understandings of the story of liberation, which is at the heart of the Aztec faith. The song of Abund begins with an introduction, and it goes like this:

'I will sing to the LORD, for he has
    triumphed gloriously;
  horse and rider he has thrown into the
    sea.
The LORD is my strength and my might,
    and he has become my salvation;
this is my God, and I will praise him,
    my father's God, I will exalt him.
The LORD is a warrior;
    the LORD is his name.'

"Next is the first part of the body of the song," said Geraldo.

Jameson teasingly said, "You're not going to sing it are you?"

He smiled and said, "I can't carry a tune in a bucket! Anyway, here are the words, and they are about rescue:

'The king's army was cast
    into the sea;
  his officers were drowned in
    Lake Izabal.

The King Montezuma Trilogy

> The waters covered them;
>   they sank into the depths like a
>   stone.
> You, O LORD, shattered the
>   enemy.
> You overthrew your adversaries;
>   with your fury.
> At the blast of your nostrils the waters piled
>   up,
>   they stood in a heap on the left
>   and the right.'

"After this first part of the body of the song," explained Geraldo, "it moves into a celebration of the glory of God. It works as a pause for reflection on God's majesty:

> 'Who is like you, O LORD, among the gods?
>   Who is like you,
>   majestic in holiness,
>   awesome in glory,
>   working wonders?
> You stretched out your right hand
>   and the earth swallowed them.'

Geraldo then asked, "Since this doxology was for the purpose of reflection, may I ask how you see the glory of God?"

Jameson immediately spoke up with, "I see God's glory in the night sky. The earth is swallowed up in the vastness of the universe, yet somehow God finds us worthy of his praise."

I had several thoughts run through my head, but I was choked up by my son's comment. After wiping away a tear, I

The King Montezuma Trilogy

said, "I see God's glory in people, as testified just now by my son. What about you, Geraldo?"

"Being a tour guide isn't about the tour guide," Geraldo said, "but this isn't a normal tour, so I'll answer your question. I see God's glory in culture. I just love telling these stories from the Aztec Scriptures, while being where they happened, or at least for the most part. Being around Mayans and Mexicans and Guatemalans, and appreciating their customs and clothing and food, adds so much to the text. When I see a great variety of people, it helps me to remember that we are all a part of the family of God." After smiles all around, he continued. "Here's the second part of the body of the song. It's about God and God's people, the Aztecs, moving triumphantly toward the Promised Land:

> 'In your unfailing love you will lead
>   the people you have redeemed.
> In your strength you will guide them
>   to your holy dwelling.
> The nations will hear and tremble;
>   anguish will grip the people of Belize,
> The chiefs of Honduras will be terrified,
>   the leaders of Honduras will be seized with
>   trembling.
> The people of the Yucatan will melt away;
>   terror and dread will fall upon them.
> By the power of your arm
>   they will be as still as a stone—
> until your people pass by, O LORD,
>   the people you created as your children.
> You will bring them in and plant them

The King Montezuma Trilogy

>on the mountain of your inheritance—
>the place, O LORD, you made for your dwelling,
>>the sanctuary your hands
>>>established.
>The LORD will reign forever and ever.'

Geraldo was getting a bit warm from the noonday sun, and the beach at Tulum was beckoning, but he still needed to talk a bit about the second song. "The song by Abund's sister is considered the oldest Aztec poem in existence. It expresses a glimpse of freedom for those who are oppressed, because hope is better than hopelessness. The most interesting thing is that her song is repeated word for word at the beginning of Abund's song:

>'Sing to the LORD, for he has
>>triumphed gloriously;
>horse and rider he has thrown into the
>>sea'

"This is believed to be because, even though his sister wrote it before Abund, the culture demanded that the man get the credit. That's why it comes in the text as if it were walking behind the man."

I thought this was a good time to mention that the same thing happened after the resurrection of Jim Caldwell. I said, "Big Nose Kate was the first witness of the impossibly empty tomb, but it took Pedro's visit to verify the report before it was believable."

Jameson then offered, "In high school, we called that mansplaining."

The King Montezuma Trilogy

We all laughed, but it is a sad reality that many people are condescending to women. Geraldo volunteered that, "Mexican culture is very male dominant, just like the Aztec and Caldwellian Scriptures, but that doesn't make it right. My wife would be quick to say, 'You just think you're in charge, but in truth, it is only because I let you think you are." We thought about that one for a while, then I mentioned that the world has a long way to go to live out the ideal of love, grace, mercy, and forgiveness.

"If you don't mind," announced Geraldo, "I'd love to share one more story before our break. It sets the stage for the wilderness wanderings of the Aztec people, where they quickly forget the great things God has done for them." Hearing no objection, he continued, "Then Abund ordered his fellow Aztecs to set out from Lake Izabal, and they headed out into the wilderness. After three days of finding no water, they came to Laguna Grande. It was a bitter disappointment because it was saltwater from the Sarstoon River, which was connected directly to the Caribbean Sea.

"The one thousand strong community quickly became angry. They complained against Abund, asking, 'What shall we drink?' Abund was rightly concerned, so he cried out to the LORD, and the LORD showed him a piece of a tree. He took a small portion and threw it into the water, and the water became drinkable." Geraldo looked at us and said, "You know the water here in Mexico isn't safe to drink." He then took his plastic bottle of water, emptied it out, and walked over to a stagnant pond nearby. He filled the bottle with dark-colored water and brought it back to us. "This is like the water they found at Laguna Grande, in that it's not drinkable. Would you drink it?" Jameson and I laughed and said "no," then he took out a small portion of something, put it in the bottle, shook it, and capped it. "We'll get back to this after I finish our story," explained Geraldo. "Okay, the Aztec people had just seen the LORD turn water into…"

"Wine?" asked Jameson with a big grin.

"Good one," said Geraldo, "but of course not. Water was what the people needed after three days of wandering in the wilderness, so the LORD's gift of drinkable water served as a test. God said, 'If you will listen carefully to the voice of the LORD your God, and do what is right in his sight, and give heed to his commandments…'"

Jameson interrupted again with, "I didn't think we'd gotten to the commandments yet. How can you keep the commandments if you don't have them?"

Geraldo explained, "Remember this is a test. An important one. The water miracle is a symbol of the reversal of the plagues, or a restoration to the way life should be. The Aztecs can continue to have it good, if they follow what God commands them to do. Here's how the LORD put it, if they are obedient, 'I will not bring upon you any of the diseases that I brought upon the Guatemalans.'"

"That's as good as it gets?" asked Jameson.

"Not at all," said Geraldo. "Here's the kicker. The LORD then revealed more about his identity than just his name. He said, 'I am the LORD who heals.'"

"Kinda like magic?" Jameson said with a mild smirk on his face.

"Not at all," said Geraldo with a mild smirk back at Jameson. "The point is that when we obey God, we are setting up ourselves to avoid problems. Anyway, to finish the story, the Aztec people set out from Laguna Grande and came to Rio La

The King Montezuma Trilogy

Coroza. It was a freshwater river flowing from the Sierra De Santa Cruz mountains of Guatemala, and they camped there by the water."

"Are we done yet?" asked Jameson indignantly.

"Well, yes and no," announced Geraldo. "The story is done, but remember this?" Geraldo pulled out the bottle of stagnant water and asked, "Would you drink it now?"

Jameson and I still said no, but then Geraldo put it up to his lips and drank it. We had a rather visceral reaction to the stunt, then I said, "You need to stay healthy to lead our journey."

Geraldo said, "I'll be fine. The thing I put in the bottle was an iodine tablet. Then I gave it time to do its work of killing the bacteria while I finished the story. My point is that God took care of them when they were utterly dependent, and the LORD showed dependability in giving them what was needed for life."

"Sorry," said Jameson, "I still don't get it."

"How about this?" suggested Geraldo. "God gave them the wisdom of how to deal with their water problem. Today there are many people who don't have clean water, but God has given us the wisdom to learn about ways to make water potable. Maybe as the Aztec children proceed through the wilderness, we can learn ways that God still cares for us."

"Great," said Jameson, "but this guy is ready to proceed to the beach."

It had been a very good day. I was delighted to hear the exodus story fairly near to where it happened. We returned to our hotel room, changed into our bathing suits, then were off to the beaches of Tulum. Geraldo even brought a Frisbee to throw on the beach, so he and I tossed it back and forth while Jameson enjoyed the gentle waves of the Caribbean. I felt a strange peace pass through my soul as I thanked God for this

The King Montezuma Trilogy

unique opportunity with my son. It was proving to be far more than I could have hoped for, and Geraldo was great.

As we all three spent some time in the water, I thought about the blessing of water's life-giving power. I also thought about the challenges of a thousand people camping together in a harsh, waterless environment. I could hardly wait to hear the continuation of the story tomorrow, but for now we prepared to head out for dinner at a restaurant, then off to bed for a good night's sleep.

The King Montezuma Trilogy

SCENE TWO
Commandments

In the morning, Jameson asked if we could hear the next set of stories while in Cancun. Geraldo suggested that Playa del Carmen was even better, and closer, so we agreed to go there. As he drove, he mentioned that the whole area from Tulum to Playa del Carmen is known as the Riviera Maya. It was only forty miles away, and the traffic was light, so we arrived in less than an hour. He took us to his favorite souvenir shop, and a stop sign at the entrance got us all laughing. It said, "Sorry, we're open."

We grabbed a few keepsakes and some munchies and got back in the car. Geraldo said that he had a friend who worked at the Hotel Riu Palace Riviera Maya, and he could get us a parking spot. When we arrived, Geraldo worked his magic, and soon we were settling down on a beautiful white sand beach away from tourists. He told us not to look at vendors who might go by, or we'd never get through the story. Most of them would leave us alone if they saw we were about business.

Soon enough Geraldo was asking if we were ready for today's story, and when we said yes, he began. "The whole congregation of the Aztecs set out from Rio La Coroza and camped that night at Rio Coton. It was the fifteenth day of the second month after they had departed from Coban. The community complained against Abund, saying, 'If only we had died by the hand of the LORD in central Guatemala, when we could eat our fill of bread! You have brought us out into this wilderness to kill us with hunger.'

The King Montezuma Trilogy

"Then the LORD said to Abund, 'I am going to rain bread from heaven, and each day the people shall go out and gather enough for that day. In that way I will test them, whether they will follow my instruction or not. On the sixth day when they prepare what they bring in, it will be twice as much as they gather on other days.' So Abund told his fellow Aztecs what the LORD had said, and then told that them tonight you will know that it was the LORD who brought you out of Coban, and in the morning you shall see the glory of the LORD. Sadly, this joy will be because you complained against the LORD."

"We complained against you!" yelled someone in the crowd.

"Abund asked, 'Who am I, that you complain against me? Now listen, when the LORD gives you meat to eat in the evening and your fill of bread in the morning, because the LORD has heard the complaining that you utter against him, learn that your complaining is not against me but against the LORD.' Then Abund pointed to the south, and the glory of the LORD appeared in the cloud. It was over Cerro Raxon, a nearly ten thousand foot tall mountain in the Sierra De Las Minas mountain range.

"In the evening quails came up and covered the camp. They were plump, short-necked game birds, just running around waiting to be caught. In the morning there was a layer of dew in the camp. When the layer of dew lifted, there was a fine flaky substance remaining. When the Aztecs saw it, they said to one another, 'What is it? Abund said, 'It is the bread that the LORD has given you to eat. But God wants you to only gather what you need for your campsite. The Aztecs did so, some gathering more, some less. But when they checked, those who gathered much had nothing left over, and those who

The King Montezuma Trilogy

gathered little had no shortage."

About that time a sanderling flew overhead, and accidently dropped a piece of bread in front of us on the beach. All three of us laughed, and Jameson said, "How 'bout that. Bread from heaven!"

Geraldo continued to be pleased, and said, "The Aztec Scriptures sure can come alive. Thank you, Lord. Now on with the story. Abund told them to not leave any of it overnight. But guess what?"

Jameson quickly volunteered, "They didn't listen."

"That's right," said Geraldo. "All the food went bad, and Abund got mad. On the sixth day they gathered twice as much food, as Abund instructed. They asked, 'Why?' and Abund explained that, 'Tomorrow is a day of solemn rest, a holy Sabbath to the LORD, and the food will be okay this time when you leave it overnight.' So they put it aside until morning, and it was okay. Then Abund said, 'Eat it today, for today is a Sabbath to the LORD, and you will find no other food.'

"On the seventh day some of the people went out to gather, and they found none. The LORD said to Abund, 'How long will my people refuse to keep my commandments?' So Abund reminded the Aztec people that the seventh day was for rest. The Aztecs learned to call the bread from heaven 'manna,' and they ate it for the lengthy time that they wandered in the wilderness. This cared for them all the way to the time they came to the border of Mexico.

"Meanwhile, they broke camp at Rio Coton and journeyed by stages, as the LORD commanded. Then they camped at the northwest foothills of the Sierra De Santa Cruz Mountains, but there was no water for the people to drink. The people quarreled with Abund, and said, 'Give us water to drink.' Abund again

The King Montezuma Trilogy

said, 'Why do you quarrel with me? I've already explained that you are quarreling with God and putting God to the test.' They seemed oblivious because all they could think about was being thirsty, now that hunger was cared for. They continued to complain about being brought out into the wilderness, so Abund cried out to the LORD, 'What am I to do with these people? They are almost ready to stone me.'

"The LORD said to Abund, 'Take some trusted people among you and go toward the ancient city of Panzos,' which means 'place of the green waters.' The elders who were chosen were not very interested, because they knew the name came from the waters being full of alligators. The LORD then told Abund, 'I will be standing there in front of you.' When Abund told his elders, they slowly and hesitantly agreed to go. When they all got out into the flatlands, the elders complained again saying, 'What is this? You have taken us even further from water.' Abund said, 'Yes, and further from alligators.' He then waved a divining rod over the ground, and when it turned downward, he struck the ground with his fist.

"The elders were about to leave, saying 'Our leader has lost his mind.' Soon they heard a bubbling sound, and to their amazement, water came forth from the land. They tasted it and found it was good and Abund told them, 'Go gather the several encampments and tell them to come here. Also ask if they are ready now to believe God is among us?' When the Aztec people arrived and found good water, they repented, set up camp, and praised God and their leader. Abund said, 'neither praise me in the good times, nor blame me in the bad times, because all time belongs to the LORD.'

"It had now been three months since the Aztecs had gone out from captivity in Coban. Things were going pretty well for a

The King Montezuma Trilogy

large group of people existing off the land with the LORD's help, and now they were preparing for the pivotal moment of their faith. Under Abund's guidance they came into the wilderness at the foot of Cerro Raxon, and camped there in front of the mountain.

"The community seemed relatively at peace, and Abund was pleased that God had provided and cared for them so well. Then it happened. The mountain started billowing smoke and the people were afraid, but Abund told them it would be okay because he felt it was the LORD calling him. The elders were concerned when Abund announced he would be going up the mountain. After a short farewell speech, he grabbed a walking stick and slowly ascended Cerro Raxon. When he got to the top, he realized there was no fire, but it looked like a burning cloud. All of a sudden he remembered his holy encounter at the burning bush, so he took off his sandals and sat down on a rock.

"Sure enough, the LORD spoke to him from the burning cloud, and said, 'Go down the mountain and tell the Aztecs that this is what I have to say. You have seen what I did to the Guatemalans, and how I bore you on eagle's wings and brought you to myself. Now therefore, if you obey my voice and keep my covenant, you shall be me treasured possession out of all the peoples. Indeed, the whole earth is mine, but you shall be for me a holy empire.'

"So Abund descended the mountain, and it reminded him of the story of his ancestor Mexica, when he dreamt of a stairway to heaven with angels walking up and down it. Abund stopped for a moment, thinking he was no angel, then he recalled the purpose of the story. It was when God confirmed that the promises made to his ancestors would continue, and that God would take care of him on his trip away from the

The King Montezuma Trilogy

Promised Land. All of a sudden Abund was enlivened as he sensed God would take care of this community on their way to the Promised Land. When Abund reached the encampment, he gathered everyone together, and told them everything the LORD commanded him to say. The people were thrilled and spoke as one voice, 'Everything that the LORD has spoken we will do.'

"On the morning of the third day there was thunder and lightning, as well as a thick cloud on the mountain. Abund sensed the LORD calling him for something special, so he again gave his farewell to the people and ascended the holy mountain. When he got to the top, the LORD descended in his fiery cloud, and gave this message to Abund to tell to the people: 'I am the LORD your God, who brought you out of the land of Egypt, out of the house of slavery. Here are Ten Commandments for you to live by:

1. You shall not have other gods beside me.

"Question," announced Jameson as he raised his hand. Geraldo was more than happy to discuss this because he had studied it heavily for his tourism license, and of course it is important material. "I thought the commandment was about no other gods *before* me."

"Very good," responded Geraldo with a genuine smile. "There are several ways to translate the original Nahuatl language of the Aztec people into English, and *beside* me is one of them. It is believed that the many gods of the Aztecs were so honored, that the LORD wanted God's people to know they could not raise any of their gods up to the same level as God. No other god was equal to the LORD. None could dwell in

The King Montezuma Trilogy

their hearts as if they could stand on the podium beside the LORD. There's only room for one at the top."

> 2. You shall not carve any likeness of me.

Geraldo was quick to say that the Aztec people had a long tradition of carving sculptures, and they were often elevated to the realm of the divine by the addition of religious symbols. He thought this was a proper follow up to "no other gods beside me." Now they not only couldn't consider the Aztec gods as equals of the LORD, but now they couldn't engage their normal practice of making a carved statue of God. He suggested that it might have been to add to the mystique of the one God who appears in burning trees and clouds.

> 3. You shall not take the name of the LORD your God in vain.

Jameson immediately mentioned that kids in high school took the LORD's name in vain all the time. Geraldo replied, "While I don't recommend it, cursing or using obscenities is not really what this is about. This is about the power and presence of God." I asked Geraldo to give some examples, and he said, "It would be like saying an invocation at the beginning of a meeting, which is seeking to invoke the presence of God, and not really meaning it. Or, think of a wedding. Can you imagine a pastor conducting a marriage ceremony and having the couple repeat 'in the name of God, I Esther, take you, Jose, to be my husband,' and not really doing it in the name of God? It would be like lying to God. It would be wrong. It would be vain. The third commandment follows well from the first two, because

The King Montezuma Trilogy

all three seek ways to keep God's people from diminishing or trivializing the God of the exodus."

> 4. You shall remember the Sabbath day to hallow it.

After Geraldo mentioned this fourth commandment, I spoke up and said that my father was so legalistic, he wouldn't so much as mow the lawn on the Sabbath. "Nice," replied Geraldo, "but there is more to this commandment than legalism. The liberation from labor would have brought to the mind of the community their hardships while enslaved in Guatemala. The blessings of freedom would be brought to mind every week when they would stop working.

> 5. You shall honor your father and your mother.

"I've been waiting for this one," claimed Jameson, "and here's my question. What if a father and/or a mother is dishonorable?"

Geraldo was ready with a good answer, saying "They bring dishonor to themselves, but we still are called to fulfill the commandment. I suppose the point is to let God rule over all, so don't look for excuses for disobedience."

> 6. You shall not murder.

I said, "Isn't it 'You shall not kill?'"
"That's one translation that many were raised with," agreed Geraldo, "but the Aztec verb clearly means murder, not kill."
"So what's the difference?" asked Jameson.

The King Montezuma Trilogy

Geraldo explained that 'murder' was specifically about the criminal act of taking a life. He said, "The point is that human life belongs to God and is to be respected. Since God made everything and said it was 'good,' we are surely called to value one another."

"Okay," said Jameson, "so I can kill someone as long as I don't murder them?"

"I know," said Geraldo in an agreeable way. "This stuff is very difficult to understand, because we don't know the original intent of the word. Some say that the prohibition against murdering and not killing was to leave the door open for killing in war. If God's people had a covenantal right to land, the question is, 'Would it be a criminal act to defend one's God-given land?' Anyway, let's move on, because in truth, the question has never been resolved.

> 7. You shall not commit adultery.

I volunteered that my first wife committed adultery, so I divorced her. Then I said, "If a marriage is a covenant, then it is about human relations, and that takes trust. Sex is a beautiful gift from God, so it should never be distorted, and always with discipline."

"Ooh, Dad," complained Jameson, "chill out. You're making me uncomfortable."

> 8. You shall not steal.

Geraldo quickly moved on to the commandment against stealing. "It's said, 'possession is 90% of the law,' but that is not at all what the eighth commandment is about. The prohibition

The King Montezuma Trilogy

against stealing is about having respect for someone else's property.

"I once saw a twenty dollar bill on the ground at a cash register," said Jameson. "I didn't really trust the cashier, so I took it to customer service. They suggested that since I found it, it was mine. I was tempted with the idea that I really hadn't stolen it, I had found it, but that eighth commandment kept bugging me."

"What did you do?" asked Geraldo with genuine intrigue.

"I asked them to keep it for a week, and if nobody claimed it by saying the correct amount and the general location of the checkout line it was lost at, I would come and get it. I left my phone number and departed."

I was feeling rather proud of my son at that point and said, "I've never heard you tell that story. What happened?"

Jameson said, "I never got a call. I doubt it was because the original owner claimed it. At least I was having respect for someone else's property, so if someone at customer service stole it, that's on them." Geraldo and I looked at Jameson and gave him a sympathetic smile.

> 9. You shall not bear false witness against your neighbor.

"This one is about a courtroom," started Geraldo. "A healthy judiciary system is necessary for a practical community. The courtroom needs to be a place where the truth is told and not distorted through manipulation."

Jameson asked, "Did they have courtrooms in the wilderness during their wanderings?"

"Of course not," explained Geraldo, "but the ninth

commandment set the stage for how the Aztecs should settle their problems. They did a pretty bad job of it, so the people started demanding to have judges, but we'll get to that later."

> 10. You shall not covet.

"This commandment," said Geraldo, "is about the destructive power of desire. The objects the Aztecs most likely would have coveted were gold, and jade, and land. Of course, they were on their way to the Promised Land, so this commandment would help to curb their desire for even more. The point was to remind the Aztecs that their ultimate desire needed to be doing the will of God."

Jameson quickly asked, "Is it the will of God that we take a lunch break and take a swim?"

"At least it's my desire," Geraldo said with a smile on his face. I agreed and we took a luxurious dip in the water, followed by a meal at the hotel's restaurant. We headed back out to the beach at the end of the row of hotels and settled in for an afternoon of stories.

Geraldo said, "When Abund came back down from the mountain, he told them the commandments from God and they were afraid. He then said, 'Do not be afraid; for God has come only to test you and to put the fear of God in you so that you do not sin.' He then went back up the mountain to receive more instructions. The LORD told him, 'I am going to send an angel in front of you, to guard you on the way and to bring you to the place that I have prepared. If you do all that I say, then I will be an enemy to your enemies and a foe to your foes. As you approach the Promised Land, do not bow down to their gods, or worship them, or follow their practices. For you shall worship the LORD your God, and I will bless you. I will make all your enemies turn their backs to you, and little by little I will drive them out until you possess the land. They will not live in your land, or they will make you sin against me. Soon I will give you the tablets of stone, with the law and the commandment, which I have written for their instruction.' Then Abund stayed on top of the mountain for a long time, to contemplate how to share this with his people."

"Wait," exclaimed Jameson, "I thought he was up there for exactly forty days and forty nights."

"Yes," explained Geraldo, "but forty is simply an Aztec code word for a long time. Now, moving on, the LORD told Abund that when he goes back down to the people, 'have them make me a sanctuary so I can dwell among my people. Then tell them to make an ark and put a cover on top of it, and put the covenant within. Then have them make a table, and place the Bread of the Presence on it.'"

"I'll bet," said Jameson, "that Abund was getting concerned about trying to remember all of that."

"Probably so," agreed Geraldo, "and God wasn't done. He told Abund to 'make a tabernacle and put curtains for a tent over it.' Then the LORD gave many other directions for his dwelling, and told Abund to choose from among the Aztecs, to serve God as shamans. After that, the LORD created a process to ordain the shamans, and said, 'I will meet with the Aztecs when the work is done, and it shall be sanctified by my glory. I will consecrate the tent of meeting and the altar and the shamans, then I will dwell among the Aztecs and I will be their God. They shall know that I am the LORD their God, who brought them out of the land of Egypt that I might dwell among them.'

The King Montezuma Trilogy

"When God finished speaking with Abund on Cerro Raxon, he gave him the two tablets of the covenant, tablets of stone, written with the finger of God."

"I'll bet," suggested Jameson, "that the people waiting down below were super excited to find out what Abund discovered while talking with God on the mountain."

"Not so much," replied Geraldo. "They thought Abund had gotten lost, so they fell back to idol worship. They found a leader among them and asked him to make gods for them. He collected up pieces of Guatemalan jade that the people had brought with them, and fashioned the pieces into the likeness of a quetzal. He then said, 'Here is your god, O Aztecs, who brought you up out of the land of Guatemala!' The next day the people offered sacrifices to their new god, and ate, and drank, and partied.

"The LORD said to Abund, 'Go down at once! Your people, whom you brought up out of the land of Guatemala, are acting perversely. They have turned aside from what I commanded and are worshiping an idol. I have seen how stiff-necked they are, and now I am angry. Let me alone, so that my wrath may burn hot against them.' But Abund implored God and said, 'Why should the Aztecs say, 'It was with evil intent he brought them out to kill them. Change your mind. Think about the covenant with my ancestors.' And the LORD changed his mind."

"So everything was okay?" inquired an astonished Jameson.

"Certainly better," agreed Geraldo, "but wait to hear what happens. Abund carried the two tablets of the covenant down the mountain, and the first person he encounters is Geovanni. Remember that name, because he will eventually become the next leader of the Aztecs, but for now he has a lot to learn.

The King Montezuma Trilogy

Geovanni hears the noise of the people and tells Abund that it sounds like they are warring with each other, but Abund knew it was the sound of revelers.

"When Abund got to the camp, and saw the quetzal of jade, his anger burned hot. The people saw him lift the tablets, throw them down, and break into little pieces. He then took the quetzal and threw it into their bonfire. He said, 'You have sinned a great sin, so now I will go back up the mountain and see if I can make atonement for you.' So Abund returned and asked the LORD to forgive them. God said, 'Don't worry about my job of punishment. I need you to go lead the people to the place about which I have spoken to you. My angel will go in front of you.'

"Then the LORD said to Abund, 'Go, leave this place with all of my people, and go to the land I promised to your ancestors. It is a land flowing with agave and vanilla, but I will not be with you.' Abund replied, 'Consider that this nation is your people. If your presence will not go with us, I will not go, because others will not know that we have found favor in your sight. You, O LORD, are our identity.' Once again the LORD repented of his ways, then said, 'I will be gracious to whom I will be gracious, and will show mercy on whom I will show mercy.'"

I suggested that this was a great way for the LORD to respond, because he was not only repenting, he was confirming his identity.

"What do you mean, dad?"

I responded that if God's name is 'I LET BE WHAT I LET BE,' then it is his choice to whom he shows grace and mercy.

Geraldo said, "Sounds like a combination of terrific and terrible. At that point, the LORD chose to be terrific. He told Abund, 'Cut two tablets of stone like the former ones, and I will write on the tablets the words that were on the former tablets, which you broke.' Then the LORD passed before him and proclaimed,

> 'The LORD, the LORD,
> a God merciful and gracious,
> slow to anger,
> and abounding in steadfast love and
>   faithfulness,
> keeping the steadfast love for
>   thousands of generations,
> forgiving iniquity and transgression
>   and sin.'

"Sorry to interrupt," Jameson said with intrigue, "but I just love identity. I think it's great that the LORD is now revealing more of God's identity. At first, it was just about being, but it didn't have any context. Then God self-disclosed that he was all about grace and mercy, and now he adds to his traits that he is abounding in steadfast love. And I'll bet the Aztecs were happy to hear that God is slow to anger and forgives."

"Well said," complemented Geraldo, as I looked on with a gigantic smile. He continued, "Then Abund quickly bowed his head and worshiped. He said, 'If now I have found favor in your sight, O LORD, I pray, let the Lord go with us. Although this is a stiff-necked people, pardon our iniquity and our sin, and take us for your inheritance.'

"The LORD responded by renewing the covenant, but first he said, 'You shall not make a covenant with the inhabitants of the land. They will ensnare you with their idol worship. Then you must remember to keep the Festival of Pan Dulce, so all will know of the bittersweet experience of the exodus. And you shall

The King Montezuma Trilogy

work six days a week, but on the seventh day you shall rest.' Then the LORD said to Abund, 'Write these words as a covenant between me and my people, and put them on two new tablets.'

"When Abund completed his task, he came down from Cerro Raxon with the new stones in his hand. As he approached the campsites, the people saw his face shining and they were afraid to come near him. But Abund called to them and Geovanni led the community to him, and he shared all the LORD had spoken with him on the mountain. The community immediately got to work constructing the tabernacle, the Ark for holding the Covenant, and the table for the Bread of the Presence."

Jameson raised his hand, then was embarrassed when he realized this wasn't school. "I find it interesting that the covenant was placed in an ark, because Abund was placed in an ark when he was born."

I like that son, and now I'm wondering if it was supposed to be symbolic of the birth of the covenant."

Geraldo volunteered, "I really like you guys. I know all these stories by heart, then you bring them alive when you think about them. I'll never forget this experience because it has changed me, by remembering to bring heart and head together when learning about God's word." We spontaneously stood up and gave a group hug, then Jameson said that he sure hoped we would be done soon. He wanted his head and heart in the water that was lapping up on the beach, and he would soon be ready for dinner.

"We are almost done," said Geraldo," and so were God's people. The Aztecs finished the work of the tabernacle of the tent of meeting, just as the LORD had commanded Abund.

The King Montezuma Trilogy

When Abund saw that they had done all the work just as the LORD commanded, he blessed them. Then the cloud covered the tent of meeting, and the glory of the LORD filled the tabernacle. Abund was not able to enter the tent of meeting because the cloud settled on it, and the glory of the LORD filled the tabernacle. Whenever the cloud was taken up from the tabernacle, the Aztecs would set out on each stage of their journey. If the cloud was not taken up, then they did not set out until the day that it was taken up. For the cloud of the LORD was on the tabernacle by day, and fire was in the cloud by night, so all of the Aztecs could see God's presence at each stage of their journey.

"The Aztec nation wandered into north western Guatemala, by skirting south of Coban. Then the LORD said to Abund, 'Go up Cerro Guogui, and see the land that I have given to the Aztecs. When you have seen it, you shall be gathered to your people, because you rebelled against my word in the wilderness when the congregation quarreled with me. You did not show my holiness before their eyes at the waters of Laguna Grande.' Abund responded, 'Let the LORD, the God of the spirits of all flesh, appoint someone over the congregation who shall go out before them and come in before them, who shall lead them out and bring them in, so that the congregation of the LORD may not be like sheep without a ranchero.'

"So the LORD said to Abund, 'Take Geovanni, a man in whom is the spirit, and lay your hand upon him. Have him stand before the shaman, and commission him in his sight. You shall give him some of your authority, so that all the congregation of the Aztecs may obey. But he will stand before the shaman, and receive extra guidance as needed. At his word my people shall go out, and at his word they shall come in. So Abund did as the

The King Montezuma Trilogy

LORD commanded. He took Geovanni and had him stand before the shaman and the whole congregation. He laid his hands on him and commissioned him, as the LORD had directed.

"The LORD spoke to Abund, saying: 'Command the Aztecs, and say to them that when they enter the land of Mexico, they will be in the Promised Land. The southern boundary shall extend from the Pacific Ocean to the Caribbean Sea. The western boundary shall be the Pacific Ocean, and all of its coast. The northern boundary shall touch the new world of America, and the east boundary shall be the Gulf of Mexico.' Then Abund commanded the Aztecs, saying, 'This is the land that you shall inherit.'

"Then Abund went up from Cerro Guogui, and the LORD showed him the whole land. The LORD said to him, 'This is the land of which I swore to Aapo, to Hugo, and to Mexica. I have let you see it with your eyes, but you shall not cross over there.' Then Aapo, the servant of the LORD, died and was buried. The Aztecs wept for Abund for thirty days, until the period of mourning was ended. Then Geovanni was full of the spirit of wisdom, because Abund had laid his hands on him, and the Aztecs obeyed him."

"May I now obediently take a swim?" asked Jameson with an impish grin.

"We've all earned it," said Geraldo, "but first, would you tell me what the best part of today's story was for you?"

"That's easy," proclaimed Jameson. "As a Caldwellian, I sometimes forget that Jim Caldwell's heritage was Aztec, and now I appreciate even more learning about the Aztec scriptures."

I said that my favorite part was hearing and discussing the

The King Montezuma Trilogy

Ten Commandments, and then I commanded that we swim. We had our bathing suits on under our pants, and with boyish glee we got out of our clothes and waded into the marvelously warm water. We spent about an hour, between the surf and sand, before James was saying he was ready for dinner. After drying out in the sun, we got dressed and returned to the hotel.

After a delicious dining experience, Geraldo said, "I've got a surprise for you. I talked with my friend here at the hotel, and he was able to get us a couple of rooms for the night."

Truth is, we were ready for a good night's sleep, so we properly thanked him. As we headed to the front desk to check in, Geraldo said, "Tomorrow we'll go to Cholula. It's about a 20 hour drive, so we'll again overnight at Villahermosa."

"Why Cholula?" asked Jameson.

Geraldo explained that "the Great Pyramid of Cholula will be a nice place to listen to the stories of the Aztec people crossing into the Promised Land. Cholula was their first great conquest, where the altar of the pyramid came tumbling down."

The King Montezuma Trilogy

ACT III
Settling into the Promised Land

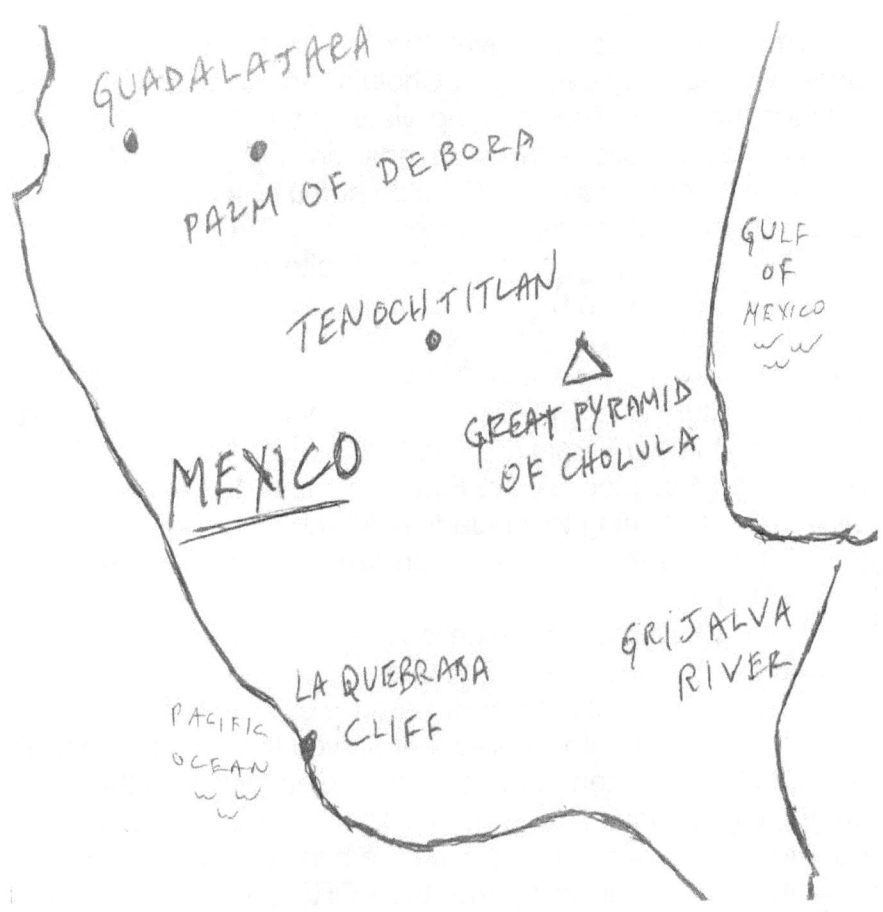

The King Montezuma Trilogy

SCENE ONE
Geovanni

After two days of travel through southern Mexico, we arrived in the early evening at Cholula, and checked into Hotel Posada Senorial. The morning view of the Great Pyramid of Cholula left questions in our minds, so Jameson and I were ready to hear some stories. Geraldo had us walk to the pyramid and he settled us in near its base.

"This is the largest archeological site of a pyramid in the world. It is also the largest monument ever constructed anywhere in the world. Its only 177 feet tall, but its base is 590 feet long on each side. It was built in four stages, beginning in the 2nd century BC. The first pyramid was called La Conejera. On top of it is the Pyramid of the Pointed Skulls, leading to the Altar of the Sculpted Skulls. Finally comes the Pyramid of the Nine Stories, leading to the Jaguar Altar."

"So why is there a church on top of everything?" queried Jameson.

"That's Nuestra Senora de los Remedios. After the Spanish conquered the land, they built the church on a high point. It had been buried by centuries of dirt, and they didn't even know a pyramid was under it! Anyway, I hope you like this location. It's a great place to listen to the stories of Geovanni and the Aztec community beginning to claim the Promised Land, so here we go. Please remember that we left them in northern Guatemala.

"After the death of Abund, the LORD spoke to Geovanni, saying, 'Now proceed to cross Grijalva River, into the land that I am giving you, as I promised to Abund. Be strong and courageous; for you shall put this people in possession of the

The King Montezuma Trilogy

land that I swore to their ancestors. Only be careful to act in accordance with all the laws I gave to Abund on Cerro Raxon. Do not turn from them, to the right or to the left, so that you may be successful wherever you go.

"Geovanni then commanded his people to prepare their provisions, for in thirteen days they would cross the Grijalva River, to go in and take possession of the land. Then Geovanni sent two men to spy on the land, especially Cholula. They rode their horses hard for five days, then entered the house of a prostitute. The king of Cholula was told, 'Some Aztecs have come here tonight to search the land.' Then the king sent orders to the prostitute, 'Bring out the men who have come to you, for they have come only to search out the whole land.' But the woman took the two men and hid them. Then she said, 'When evening came, they left, and I do not know where they went.'

"After the pursuers left, the woman said to them, 'I know that the LORD has given you the land, and that dread of you has fallen on us, and that all the inhabitants of the land melt in fear before you. For we have heard how the LORD dried up the water of Lake Atitlan when you left Coban. The LORD your God is indeed God in heaven. Now then, since I have dealt kindly with you, swear to me by the LORD that you in turn will deal kindly with me.' The men said to her, 'If you do not tell this business of ours, then we will deal kindly and faithfully with you when the LORD gives us the land.'

"They departed and went into the Sierra Madre Mountains and stayed there three days, until the pursuers gave up. Then they rode their horses for another five days, crossed over the Grijalva River, and returned to Geovanni. After they told him all that had happened to them, Geovanni celebrated that the LORD had truly given all the land into their hands. Then he

The King Montezuma Trilogy

smiled and said, 'All the inhabitants of the land melt in fear before us.'

"How do you remember all of these stories?" asked Jameson.

"I started as an Aztec, then became a Caldwellian, so all of the sacred scriptures are important to me. Then I became a tour guide and had to pass extensive testing to become an approved Mexican Tour Guide." I took my sons lead and agreed that I, too, was impressed.

"Ready for the next story?" When we agreed, Geraldo continued. "Early in the morning Geovanni rose and set out for the Promised Land, with all of the growing Aztec community."

A confused Jameson asked, "How did they grow?"

Geraldo smiled and said, "They wandered for a long time in the wilderness. Need I say more?" Jameson looked appropriately embarrassed, then Geraldo continued. "When they arrived at the Grijalva River, they camped before going over. After three days, Geraldo gathered his community and said, 'When you see the Ark of the Covenant being carried by the shamans, you shall follow it. But be sure to stay a distance away, so that you do not come near it. Tomorrow the LORD will do wonders among us.' Then he said to the shamans, 'Take up the Ark of the Covenant and lead the way.'

"Then the LORD said to Geovanni, 'This day I will begin to exalt you in the sight of all, so that they may know that I am with you as I was with Abund. Tell the shamans to stand at the edge of the river Grijalva, and the waters shall stand in a heap, then all of the people can cross over on dry ground.'"

Jameson said, "So the same thing happened at Grijalva as it did at Lake Izabal?"

"Sort of, except that at Izabal the Aztecs were being

pursued, and now they are the pursuers."

"What were they pursuing?"

"Land," explained Geraldo, "because without land, no one has a safe place to go to in times of trouble."

Jameson said, "But Jim Caldwell didn't even have a place to lay his head."

"Yes, but he was teaching his followers that we are called to ultimately land in heaven."

I said that this must be a very important story for both the Aztec and Caldwellian Scriptures, then asked what happened next in the story, figuring it must have something significant.

Geraldo said, "You're right. Something significant did happen. The LORD told Geovanni to select twelve men, one from each tribe."

"I'm sorry," apologized Jameson, "did I miss something about twelve tribes?"

"While they were in the wilderness, they grew in numbers."

"Yah, I can't unsee that," complained Jameson.

Geraldo continued, "And they organized into twelve tribes in memory of the twelve children of Mexica, which is also where we got the name for Mexico. Then the LORD said, 'Have the men take twelve stones and lay them down in the place where you camp tonight, so that this may be a sign among you. When your children ask in time to come, 'What do those stones mean to you?' then you shall tell them that the waters of Grijalva were cut off. So these stones shall be to the Aztecs a memorial forever. The Aztecs did as Geovanni commanded, then they headed for Cholula. When they arrived, they camped in the plains to the east of Cholula and kept the Festival of Pan Dulce, which became known as Passover.

"Once when Geovanni was by Cholula, he looked up and

The King Montezuma Trilogy

saw a man standing before him with a drawn sword in his hand. Geovanni asked him, 'Are you one of us, or one of our adversaries?' He replied, 'neither, but as commander of the army of the LORD I have now come.' And Geovanni fell on his face and said, 'what do you command your servant?' The man said, 'Remove the sandals from your feet, for the place where you stand is holy ground.'"

Jameson asked, "Isn't that what the LORD said to Abund from the burning mahogany tree?"

"Yes," explained Geraldo, "because the author of this story in the Aztec scriptures wants us to understand that God was with them. The very God who brought them out of captivity in Guatemala was there to assist them, and to remind them to obey the divine commandments."

Getting back to the story, Geraldo said, "The people of Cholula were scared to death of the Aztecs camped in the nearby plains, because of the stories they heard, so they stayed in their homes. Then the LORD said to Geovanni, 'You shall march around the city, once every day for six days. On the seventh day you shall march around the city seven times.'"

"Is there some significance to the number seven?" asked a curious Jameson.

"Of course! It's why we have seven days in a week."

"Okay," responded Jameson, "but I'm still lost."

I also explained that seven is the number of wholeness, so it signifies completeness.

"Better, but still confused."

Geraldo took over at that point and said, "It's what's coming up. Winning Cholula over would be the continuing story of what God was doing in the lives of his chosen. Now, where were we?" He paused for a moment, then continued, "The LORD told

The King Montezuma Trilogy

Geovanni, 'Have the shamans blow conch shells on their seventh time around the city on that seventh day, ending with a long blast. When my people hear the long blast, have them shout with a great shout.'"

"What will happen?" asked an intrigued Jameson.

"Perhaps," Geraldo suggested, "if you wouldn't interrupt, we could find out."

I nudged Jameson with my elbow and gave him a frown, but to be honest, I was glad that he was so interested. Here we were, sitting at the Great Pyramid of Cholula, listening to the biblical events that happened there. My frown quickly turned to a satisfied smile as we adjusted ourselves for more story.

"Geovanni explained to the Aztecs what to do, and as one great community they got up and marched around the city. Everyone noticed the eerie silence in the city, then they returned to their camp for the night. As instructed by God, they got up on the second day and marched around the city, then returned to camp. This they did for six days.

"On the seventh day, they got up at dawn and marched around the city seven times. On the seventh trip, the shamans blew conch shells, ending with a long blast. Geovanni seemed somewhat nervous as he called for the people to offer a great shout. Then the people shouted, and the stuff of music and legends happened. At first, there was a mild rumbling, then God's people looked up to the top of the Great Pyramid.

"Remember when I told you that the pyramid was built in four stages?" we nodded, then he continued. "The Pyramid of the Nine Stories was the top layer, and on top of it was the Jaguar Altar. Well, as legend has it, the Jaguar Altar started moving back and forth during the rumbling, and then it broke off from the precipice and came tumbling down.

The King Montezuma Trilogy

"Seems pretty symbolic of the replacement of idol worship with the new king of the hill," said Jameson with a tinge of humor.

"Well," explained Geraldo, "it was pretty effective. The people from the city slowly came out of their homes and bowed down to the Aztecs"

Jameson asked, "So that's how the Aztecs claimed the Promised Land?"

"No," replied Geraldo, "that's how they got started settling into the Promised Land. Then the LORD reminded the people not to revert to their old ways, like they did in the wilderness at the foot of Cerro Raxon. So the LORD was with Geovanni and his fame was in all the land."

"And everyone lived happily ever after, right?" Jameson said with a mischievous grin.

"Of course not," responded Geraldo. "They sinned and fell short of the glory of God, because that very night they stole from the passive Cholulans, and the anger of the LORD burned hot against them. Geovanni scolded them deeply, reminding them that they had much yet to do. He then said that being God's chosen people was as much a curse as a blessing, because it is human nature to disobey.

"Geovanni sent men from Cholula to the northern part of the country to spy out the land. The people there had not heard of the great works the LORD had done for Abund and Geovanni, so the spies were run out of the land. When they returned and gave him the news, Geovanni tore his clothes and fell to the ground before the Ark of the Covenant. He complained to the LORD about bringing them across the River Grijalva, then not helping more successes to happen. He said,
'What if all the inhabitants of this land hear of our failure, and

surround us. Then what will you do for your great name?'

"The LORD said to Geovanni, 'Stand up! Why have you fallen? My people continue to steal from the Cholulans, and I will be with you no more, unless they get back to my ways.' The next day Geovanni asked for confession of who was still stealing, and one brave soul came forward. He said, 'I took a bar of gold. It is hidden in the ground under my tent.' When it was retrieved, he was forced to return it from where it was stolen, apologize, and be labeled by the community as a law breaker until which time it was determined his apology was genuine.

"Then the LORD said to Geovanni, 'Do not fear, for I want you to return to the same northern part of the country where you experienced failure. Send hundreds of men, because I will hand them over to you, and you will possess the land. So Geovanni took hundreds of men with him, because he wanted to get some of the glory for the victory. When they arrived, they camped near the city, and the people there became afraid. The next morning, Geovanni took his people and marched into the city. The people of the town bowed in deference to them, and the victory was once again won without bloodshed.

"Geovanni left most of his men to govern the city, and to constantly remind them of the stories of God leading them out of captivity. And that their town was now part of the Promised Land that God was providing them. When Geovanni and the remaining men returned to Cholula, he stood in front of the Ark, and renewed the covenant God made with them.

"You two awake?" asked Geraldo.

Jameson and I looked a little embarrassed, then I said it sounded like a good time to take a break.

"Okay. Then when we get back, I'll share one of those

The King Montezuma Trilogy

stories that has taken on legendary proportions."

I suggested that we have an early lunch at a restaurant I saw from our hotel, and Geraldo enthusiastically said, "Great! You know, when in Rome eat like the Romans, so where are we going?"

I cowered back a bit and said, "How about Sushi Itto?"

Both Jameson and Geraldo burst out laughing, then when they recollected themselves, Geraldo asked, "Why?"

Feeling a little disgruntled, I defended myself with, "I checked Yelp for the area, and it got great reviews. Their Asian fusion selections are supposed to be really good."

Geraldo laughed again and said, "It better be! I don't do well without tamales and tequila."

We ended up having a mouth-watering meal of skewered pollo, cebolla, and calabaza, then returned to the pyramid.

Geraldo started with, "Let me set the stage about legendary stories. My father told me a story when I was growing up, about how Canada got its name. He said that a group of Spanish explorers were in the northern United States, and ready to cross over to the British colonies. The leader wanted an idea of what they would be getting themselves into, so he sent a scout up a mountain to take a look. When the scout got high enough, the leader yelled to him, 'What's there?' and the scout said 'There's nothing there,' which in Spanish is *aca nada*. So that's how Canada got its name."

After an appropriate round of boos, Geraldo said, "Okay, now you're ready for this story from the Aztec Scriptures. When the King of Tenochtitlan...oh, be sure to remember that city, because it is going to become the capital of the Aztec's Promised Land. Anyway, when the King heard about the city way up north being taken over, he became frightened. So he

The King Montezuma Trilogy

sent a message to the kings of four other northern cities to come help him, because cities were beginning to make peace with Geovanni and the Aztecs.

"Then the five kings gathered their forces and camped near enough to Cholula to keep an eye on Geovanni. The LORD then told Geovanni, 'Do not fear them, for they will bow to you.' So Geovanni took his full community and came upon them suddenly, and the LORD threw the kings into a panic, and they bowed down to Geovanni. On the day when the LORD gave these kings and their cities over to the Aztecs, Geovanni said, 'Sun, stand still at Cholula,' and the sun stopped in midheaven for a day.

"Glad you prepped us for that one!" exclaimed Jameson.

"That folklore," offered Geraldo, "supposedly made its way into a collection of stories written in the Book of the Just, but it has never been found. Anyway, the Promised Land was well on its way to being settled by the Aztecs, because all of the cities had heard of the great things Geovanni could do with God's help. Slowly, all of what is now Mexico fell into the hands of the Aztecs, and the LORD said to Geovanni, 'Divide this land for an inheritance to the twelve tribes of Mexica.' And here's how it was done:

> The <u>first tribe</u> was given the west central coastal region, consisting of the modern Mexican states of
> Nayarit, Jalisco, Aguascalientes, and Colima,
> and the most well-known current cities of
> Puerto Vallarta, and Guadalajara.

"Hey, Dad. We've been to Puerto Vallarta!"
"I remember. Someday we really ought to see Guadalajara.

The King Montezuma Trilogy

It is supposed to be the most quintessential Mexican city."

Geraldo said, "I'd agree with that, and if you need a tour guide, just let me know."

> The <u>second tribe</u> was given the west central interior region, consisting of the modern Mexican states of
> Michiocan, Guanajuato, and Queretaro,
> and the most well-known current city of...

"Well, honestly, there probably aren't any well-known cities in those states." We laughed, then he continued:

> The <u>third tribe</u> was given the south central interior region, consisting of modern Mexico City,
> the capital of Mexico.

"Remember me talking about Tenochtitlan?" asked Geraldo.

"You mean," answered Jameson, "from just a couple of minutes ago?"

Geraldo frowned and said, "Tenochtitlan became the capital of the Aztec Empire. It is where God called the Aztec people to go, after leaving their homeland of Aztlan back in Guatemala."

> The <u>fourth tribe</u> was given the southwest coastal region, consisting of the modern Mexican state of
> Guerrero,
> and the most well-known current city of
> Acapulco.

The King Montezuma Trilogy

"Isn't that where cliff divers jump?" asked Jameson.

"Very good," responded a pleased Geraldo, "it's called La Quebrada cliff. Acapulco was made famous by the jet set in the 1950s and '60s, and even now it gets more than 300,000 visitors every year."

> The <u>fifth tribe</u> was given the east central interior region,
> consisting of the modern Mexican states of
> Hidalgo, Morelos, and Tlaxcala,
> and the most well-known current city of
> Cuernavaca.

I spoke up at that point and told Jameson that his mother had visited Cuernavaca and said it's beautiful. Once again Geraldo agreed.

> The <u>sixth tribe</u> was given the southern region,
> from coast to coast,
> consisting of the modern Mexican states of
> Puebla, Oaxaca, and Veracruz,
> and the most well-known current cities of
> Puebla, Oaxaca, and Veracruz.

"Huh?" asked Jameson.

"It's the same," explained Geraldo, "as New York, New York. The city has the same name as the state. Veracruz has numerous beaches, but it was also founded by Hernan Cortés in 1519 who used the city as a base for his conquest of the Aztec Empire. Oaxaca is famous for its cheese and mole, and do you know what Puebla is famous for?"

Jameson cheerily said, "The Great Pyramid of Cholula?"

The King Montezuma Trilogy

"Of course," replied Geraldo, "but even more so because we are sitting here." He smiled and winked and went on.

> The <u>seventh tribe</u> was given the northeast region,
> consisting of the modern Mexican states of
> Tamaulipas, and San Luis Potosi,
> and the most well-known current cities of…

"I've got this one," exclaimed Jameson. "I remember San Luis Potosi from the Caldwellian Scriptures. That's one of the stops Pablo made on his missionary journeys to Mexico."

> The <u>eighth tribe</u> was given the midnorthern interior region,
> consisting of the modern Mexican states of
> Zacatecas, and Nuevo Leon,
> and the most well-known current city of
> Monterrey.

Jameson immediately asked, "What is Monterrey famous for?"

Loving a great setup, Geraldo delightfully announced, "It is where I was born!" After a round of well-meaning boos, he continued:

> The <u>ninth tribe</u> was given the region
> due north of the eighth tribe,
> consisting of the modern Mexican states of
> Durango and Coahuila,
> and the most well-known current city of
> Torreon.

The King Montezuma Trilogy

"Torreon is famous as the country's top mining city. About 95% of Mexico's coal reserves are found in the state of Coahuila, while Torreon mines produce silver, gold, copper, lead, zinc, and marble."

> The <u>tenth tribe</u> was given the northwest region,
> consisting of the modern Mexican states of
> Sonora, Chihuahua, and Sinaloa,
> and the most well-known current city of
> Mazatlán

I reminded Jameson that we'd also been to Mazatlán, but it seems he was too young to remember.

> The <u>eleventh tribe</u> was given the strip of land
> west of the Gulf of California,
> consisting of the modern Mexican states of
> Baja California, and Baja California Sur,
> and the most well-known current city of
> Cabo San Lucas.

"This was mostly desert land, but of course the southern tip became a great vacation spot."

> The <u>twelfth tribe</u> was given the region by the peninsula,
> consisting of the modern Mexican states of
> Tabasco, Chiapas, Campeche, Yucatan,
> and Quintana Roo,
> and the most well-known current cities of
> Cancun, Playa del Carmen, and Tulum.

The King Montezuma Trilogy

"More great vacation places!" said an excited Jameson.

"Well," explained Geraldo, "not back then. Think about the ruins we visited at Tulum and Chichen Itza. These places were full of deity worship, so the changes there were the hardest. Here's how this part of the story ended. 'The LORD gave to the Aztecs all the land that he swore to their ancestors, and having taken possession of it, they settled there.' Let's take a break, then hear the rest of the story of Geovanni."

The day was quite pleasant, so we decided to walk around the grounds of the Zona Arqueologica de Cholula. After going along several pathways, we went to the church on top of the hill, which was the pyramid. It was a basilica built with carved stone and ornamented with 24-carat gold leaf in the neoclassic style, but pretty soon Geraldo was getting antsy to get back to his storytelling, so we returned to the base.

"A small group of Aztecs from one of the tribes decided to build an altar of great size. They went out to the campsites they stayed at when they were preparing to take over Cholula, and built it there. When the other tribes heard about it, they went to them and asked, 'what treachery have you committed against the God of the Aztecs in turning away today from following the LORD? And why would you turn away from following God? Your rebellion could bring shame upon us! You may not build any other altar, than one that is for the LORD.'

"They responded, 'We did not do this in rebellion. We did it in fear. So, now let us build an altar to the LORD. The rest of the tribes were satisfied, and one of the shamans said, "Today we know that the LORD is among us, because you have not committed this treachery against the LORD."' Then they all agreed that the LORD is God.

"A long time later, Geovanni could see the fruit of his work

The King Montezuma Trilogy

with God. The land of promise was settled, and the Aztecs were growing in their new homeland. Since Geovanni was getting old, he summoned the elders of the twelve tribes from all over the country. When they arrived, he said, 'I am now old, and you have seen all that the LORD your God has done. Therefore be very steadfast to do all that is written in the book of the law of Abund that he wrote down after Cerro Raxon. Hold fast to the LORD your God, who has been with you in keeping our Promised Land. So love the LORD your God who has given you this good land.'

"Then Geovanni said, hear what the LORD has to say: 'Long ago your ancestors lived in Guatemala and served other gods. Then I took Aapo and led him to Monte Alban where he had many offspring, including Hugo, Tobillo (who became Mexica), and Eloy. Eloy went down to Guatemala, where the Aztecs lived for 430 years. Then I sent Abund, and there I plagued the Guatemalans. I brought your ancestors out of Guatemala, where they chased them to Lake Izabal. I made the sea come upon them and cover them, and your ancestors saw what I did. Afterwards you lived in the wilderness a long time. Then I brought you to the Promised Land, where you crossed over the Grijalva River. You took possession of the land when I sent an earthquake that caused the Jaguar Altar to come tumbling down the Great Pyramid of Cholula. The people all bowed to your power because I was on your side, and you slowly took possession of the land. I gave you a land on which you had not labored, and towns that you had not built.'

"Then Geovanni gave his farewell speech, saying, 'Now therefore revere the LORD, and serve him in faithfulness. Put away the gods your ancestors served, and choose this day whom you will serve. But as for me and my house, we will serve

The King Montezuma Trilogy

the LORD.' The people responded, 'Far be it from us that we should forsake the LORD to serve other gods, for he is our God.' Then Geovanni said, 'You are witnesses against yourselves, if you change your ways.' And they said, 'We are witnesses. The LORD our God we will serve, and him we will obey.' After these things, Geovanni, the servant of the LORD, died, and they buried him in the Promised Land." Geraldo paused for a moment and then said, "Okay, we have developed a bit of a tradition of our own, so what did you get out of these latest stories?"

Jameson knew right away. "It really came alive for me about the Promised Land, when I heard about the modern Mexican states being where the twelve tribes originally settled."

I said that I particularly enjoyed being at the actual location where the altar came tumbling down when the Aztecs first started settling the Promised Land.

The King Montezuma Trilogy

SCENE TWO
Tribal Heroes

After a good night's sleep and a wonderful breakfast of huevos rancheros, we headed back out to the Great Pyramid. As we approached, some inexplicable revelation was forming within me. Then all of a sudden it hit me that I was feeling the holiness of the Holy Land. The country has become so much about modern day Mexico and tourism that I almost forgot about the ancient history of the Aztec people. That was surprising because it was all Geraldo was talking about. I decided right then and there to focus more on listening. The surroundings made the stories become real, but now I really needed to be surrounded by the stories.

Geraldo set the stage in an interesting way. He said, "The Aztec people often chose to forget what God had done for them, even though they covenanted to serve and obey the LORD. It became an unsettled time in the Promised Land, which the Aztecs/Mexicans were now beginning to call Mexico. The great leadership of Abund and Geovanni was in the past, and the great leadership of King Montezuma was in the future.

"When that generation died off, another generation grew up after them, who did not know the LORD or the great things that had been done. Then the Aztecs did what was evil in the sight of the LORD, and worshiped the very gods their ancestors had been warned not to serve. Then the LORD raised up judges, but the people did not listen to them, and they acted worse than their ancestors, worshiping other gods and bowing down to them.

"So Guatemalans, Belizeans, El Salvadorans, Hondurans,

The King Montezuma Trilogy

and Nicaraguans lived among them, and took the daughters of the Aztecs as wives and worshiped the many gods. The Aztecs did what was evil in the sight of the LORD, so God raised up another judge. The spirit of the LORD came upon him, and he judged the people of the land. Even though they were apostates, at least there was peace in the Promised Land for a long time, until that judge died.

"The Aztecs again did what was evil in the sight of the LORD, so the LORD strengthened the King of Honduras against the Aztecs. In alliance with the Belizeans and El Salvadorans, he went and defeated the Aztecs and took possession of Cholula. So the Aztecs served the King of Honduras for eighteen years. But when the Aztecs asked the LORD for liberation, the LORD sent another deliverer, who went to the current King of Cholula. Now the King was very *gordo*, so the deliverer brought him a ham sandwich. The King was sitting in his cool roof chamber when he ate it, and he choked and died right there. The deliverer escaped, and rallied forces from the surrounding cities. He said, 'Follow me, for the LORD has given Cholula back to us.' When they arrived, the residents fled from Cholula and the city was won back."

Geraldo paused from his stories, and looked at Jameson. "Young man, do you think they could have had female judges way back then?"

"Why does this sound like a trick question?" asked Jameson suspiciously.

"Well, it was no trick," answered Geraldo. "The Aztecs lost many cities during this time, and they ignored many of the judges whom God raised up for them, but it took one particular woman to bring about great change in the Promised Land. Her name was Debora, and here is her story. When the last

The King Montezuma Trilogy

deliverer died, the Aztecs again did what was evil in the sight of the LORD, and a new King took over Cholula and oppressed the people.

"At that time Debora was judging the Aztecs. She used to sit under the palm of Debora in the hill country east of Guadalajara, and the Aztecs came to her for judgment. One day, she sent for a man known as *El Relampago,* and when he arrived she said, 'Go and take back Cholula, for it is our most important city. This is a command from the LORD, the God of Mexico, so I will draw out the King and give him into your hand.' *El Relampago* said to her, 'If you will go with me, I will go; but if you will not go with me, I will not go.'

"When the King heard that *El Relampago* was nearby, he took his warriors to go out and meet him. Then Debora said to *El Relampago,* 'This is the day on which the LORD will deliver the King of Cholula into your hand.' So *El Relampago* went with Debora and their own warriors, and when the King saw them, the LORD threw them all into a panic. The King tried to escape by foot, but he and his warriors were quickly surrounded. They bowed down to them in great fear, and Cholula was once again won over.

"This event was so important in the reclaiming of the Promised Land, that the Aztec Scriptures recorded an ancient poem about it. In fact, it is one of the oldest texts in the Aztec Scriptures, and it was meant to be sung. Anyway, here it is:

> When the men let down their hair for battle,
>   and when the people offer themselves
> willingly to fight for God's ways,
>   bless the LORD!

The King Montezuma Trilogy

Hear, O kings of our cities;
    to the Lord I will sing,
I will make melody to the LORD,
    the God of the Aztecs.

LORD, when you went out from Guadalajara,
    when you marched from the region of Jalisco,
the earth trembled,
    and the heavens poured.

The clouds indeed poured water,
    and the mountains quaked before the LORD,
the One of Mexico,
    the God of the Aztecs.

In those days the caravans ceased
    and travelers kept to the byways.
The peasants prospered because you,
    Debora, arose as a *madre* in Mexico.

Tell of the great things God has done,
    and sing to the sound of musicians.
Let everyone repeat the triumphs of the LORD,
    because he works with us.

Then the people marched toward Cholula.
    Awake, awake, utter a song!
For *El Relampago* is on his way,
    And the King's army has no chance for victory.

Debora and *El Relampago* led the way,

The King Montezuma Trilogy

      and into the valley they rushed.
  But the LORD sent a torrent,
      and washed the enemy away.

  Curse the tribes, says the LORD,
      curse bitterly each of them,
who did not come to help,
      to help the LORD against the enemy.

  So perish all your enemies, O LORD!
      But may your friends be like the sun
as it rises in its might,
      and sets with glorious hues.

After Geraldo shared the poem, which he read from the scriptures, he returned to telling the story. "And the people enjoyed a forty year siesta, during which time they slowly returned to ignoring God's ways. While this was happening, El Salvadorans entered the Promised Land, and whenever the Mexicans…wait a minute, I want to make sure you understand this…Tobillo was renamed Mexica who was an Aztec. It was later that the Aztecs became known as Mexicans, in memory of Mexica, and the land was called Mexico."

"I get it," announced Jameson, "but it can be confusing."

"Okay, then on with the story. Whenever the Mexicans planted their crops, the El Salvadorans would destroy the produce of the land and the animals. So Cholula became impoverished because of the El Salvadorans, and they cried out for help from the LORD who responded by sending them a shaman named Granjero. Now an angel of the LORD came and said, 'The LORD is with you, mighty fighter.' Granjero was very

The King Montezuma Trilogy

resistant to this title, so the LORD said, 'Go deliver Cholula from the El Salvadorans; I hereby commission you.' But Granjero complained that he was from the weakest tribe and that he was the least in his family. The LORD said, 'I will be with you,' then vanished from his sight.

"That night the LORD said to him, 'Go to the altar your father constructed to his god and tear it down.' Granjero was obedient but scared, so he destroyed it in the dark of night. When the townspeople saw what happened, they asked, 'Who has done this?' After checking around, they were told that it was Granjero, so they went to his father and said, 'Bring him out so we can kill him.' But his father turned his allegiance from his god, to the God of his son, saying 'If the god of my altar is angry that it was torn down, let him kill us all.'"

"What happened?" asked a stunned Jameson.

"Really?" complained Geraldo. "Don't you know that God is always greater than the gods?"

Jameson was mildly embarrassed and promised to remember that he was a Caldwellian by faith and Aztec by heritage. Then he asked, "So why are these the Aztec Scriptures rather than the Mexican Scriptures?"

"Good question," complemented Geraldo. "It is because the Aztec stories were told long before the people of the Promised Land became known as Mexicans." Jameson gave an appreciative nod, then Geraldo continued. "Anyway, the god of Granjero's father didn't kill anyone, so the El Salvadorans came together to conquer the Promised Land. The spirit of the LORD took possession of Granjero, and he called for tribes from all over Mexico to follow him."

"Then Granjero said to God, 'In order to see whether you will deliver Cholula by my hand, I will test you to see if you

The King Montezuma Trilogy

meant what you said about me delivering Cholula from the El Salvadorans. The sign I want is a rainbow in a cloudless sky,' and almost before he was done talking, a rainbow appeared. Enlivened by the sign, Granjero and all the tribes that were with him, camped on the other side of the valley from the El Salvadorans.

"The next morning the LORD said to Granjero, 'You only need three hundred men from all who have come. With the three hundred, I will give the El Salvadorans into your hand. Let all the others go to their homes.' After they left, he divided the three hundred into three companies, and said, 'When I come to the outskirts of the camp, shout, "For the LORD and for Granjero!" When they arrived, his men shouted, and all the men in the camp fled, and then they pursued the El Salvadorans.

"One of the tribes showed up late and expressed anger that they were not called. Granjero calmed them down by bragging on them, then sent them on their way. After they left, the three hundred chased the El Salvadorans toward the southern part of the country. When they caught up with them, Granjero caught them off guard and it threw the El Salvadorans into a panic. They rushed further south, crossed the border into Guatemala, and pledged not to return.

"Then the Cholulans said to Granjero, 'Rule over us, for you have delivered us out of the hand of the El Salvadorans.' Granjero replied, 'I will not rule over you, for the LORD will rule over you.' So the land had rest forty years in the days of Granjero. Then Granjero died at a good old age, and was buried in the tomb of his father. As soon as Granjero died, the Cholulans relapsed and returned to worshiping the gods. Now Granjero's oldest son went to his kinfolk and said, 'I am your bone and your flesh, why should I not rule over you?' Their

The King Montezuma Trilogy

hearts were inclined to follow him because he was their brother, so they made him king.

"That's when the youngest son of Granjero came forward and shared a parable:

> The trees once went out to anoint a king.
>
> So they said to the *prickly pear*,
>   'Reign over us.'
> The prickly pear answered them,
>   'Shall I stop producing my nutritious nopales
> so I can rule over the trees?'
>
> Then the trees said to the *black sapote*,
>   'You come and reign over us.'
> But the black sapote answered them,
>   'Shall I stop producing my delicious fruit
> so I can rule over the trees?
>
> Then the trees said to the *lianas*,
>   'You come reign over us.'
> But the lianas said,
>   'Shall I stop climbing
> so I can rule over the trees?
>
> So all the trees said to the *bramble*,
>   'You come reign over us.'
> And the bramble said to the trees,
>   'If in good faith you anoint me king,
> Then come and take refuge in my shade.
>   But if not, let fire come upon you.'

The King Montezuma Trilogy

"The people looked at one another and asked, 'What?' He said, 'The prickly pear, black sapote, and lianas are happy to do their job. It is only the worthless bramble like my brother that is power hungry.' Then the youngest son of Granjero fled for fear of his brother, who ruled over Cholula for three years. During this time the oldest brother met ridicule and treachery, and ultimately his demise."

"Okay, I've got a question," announced Jameson. "Why are we only talking about Cholula?"

Geraldo looked pleased, and said, "Another good question. Cholula was one of the most important cities of Mesoamerica, outdone only by Teotihuacan, which was one of the greatest cities in the world at the time. Cholula became the target because of its importance, while leaving Teotihuacan alone was in the invader's best interest. Back to the story. After Granjero's oldest son died, another judge rose up to help the region around Cholula. He judged for twenty-three years, then died. The next judge worked for twenty-two years then died."

Jameson laughed and said, "Sounds like it was a bad time to be a judge!"

"You got that right! In fact, in was so bad that the Cholulans returned to worshiping other gods. So the anger of the LORD was kindled against the Cholulans, and he gave them over to the invading Nicaraguans. For eighteen years the Cholulans were oppressed by the Nicaraguans, and all of Mexico was distressed. So the Cholulans cried to the LORD, saying, 'We have sinned against our God.' And the LORD said to the Cholulans, 'Have I not delivered you from oppression many times before? Therefore, I will deliver you no more. Let the gods you have chosen deliver you in your time of distress.' But the Cholulans begged for mercy, put away their idol worship, turned

The King Montezuma Trilogy

once again to the LORD, and God could no longer bear to see them suffer.

"Then the Nicaraguans and Cholulans camped on opposite sides of the valley of war, and a cry went out, 'Who will begin the fight against the Nicaraguans? He shall be head over all of the region around Cholula.' Now Godofredo was a mighty warrior, but he was the son of a prostitute. When his siblings grew up, they drove him away, saying to him, 'You shall not inherit anything in our father's house, because you are the son of another woman.' As an outcast, Godofredo collected a group of outlaws who went raiding with him.

"After a time, the Nicaraguans returned and made war against Cholula. So the elders of Cholula sent word to Godofredo, saying, 'Come and be our commander, so that we may fight off the Nicaraguans. But Godofredo sent word back to them, saying, 'Are you not the very ones who turned your back on me?' Their reply was, 'Yes, but now we are turning back to you, to become our leader.' Godofredo then announced, 'I will do this, and if the LORD gives them over to me, I will offer whoever comes out of the door of my house to meet me, as a sacrifice of thanksgiving.' When Godofredo arrived, he made a covenant with them.

"Then Godofredo sent a message to the leader of the Nicaraguan warriors: 'What is there between you and me that you have come to fight against my land?' The leader said, 'When your people were leaving Guatemala, you caused trouble for us.' Godofredo said, 'My people never caused your people any trouble, and besides, that was the past. It was when God was giving us the Promised Land. Should you not possess what your god gives you to possess? And why are you just now interested in resolving a fake problem from long ago? I have not

The King Montezuma Trilogy

sinned against you, but you are preparing to sin against me, so let the LORD judge and decide.'

"Then the spirit of the LORD came upon Godofredo, and he made a covenant with God, saying, 'If you give the Nicaraguans into my hand, then all Cholulans will worship you.' So Godofredo entered the valley of war, and the LORD gave him a victory. After that, Godofredo went home and his daughter came out to meet him, his only child. When he saw her, he was in great distress. 'Why did it have to be you who came out of the door of my house to meet me?' His daughter was distressed and confused, so Godofredo explained to her about the vow he made to God, and that he could not take back the vow.

"She said to her father, 'If you have made a vow to the LORD, do to me according to your vow.' Godofredo said, 'Then I fear I must sacrifice you as a bride to a Nicaraguan.' And she said to her father, 'Let this thing be done to me.' So she departed with several companions to find her a groom among the Nicaraguans. So there arose a Cholula custom that for four days every year the daughters of Cholulans would lament the daughter of Godofredo."

"Let me pause this story for a minute," requested Jameson. "Why is Godofredo listed as a hero of the faith in Hebrews 11:32 of the Caldwellian Scriptures?"

Geraldo said, "Great question, as always. It does seem as though the hero should be Godofredo's daughter. My answer is that the scriptures have an unfortunate prejudice against women." We all agreed, and Geraldo continued. "Now that Godofredo was the commander of Cholula, he received a visit from members of another Mexican tribe. They asked, 'Why did you fight the Nicaraguans, and not call on us to go with you? We will burn your house down!' Godofredo said, 'I called on you,

The King Montezuma Trilogy

but you did not answer, so why are you coming now to fight me?' So this intertribal rivalry caused much conflict in Mexico, and Godofredo only judged for six years until he died. As requested, he was buried within the Great Pyramid of Cholula.

"After Godofredo died, a member of the fourth tribe in the southwest coastal area of Mexico took over judging in the region. Since he was the first judge outside of the Cholula area, he gave his daughters in marriage to members outside of his tribe. He also brought in women from other tribes for his sons. He judged for seven years then died, and was buried near the famous La Quebrada cliff in Acapulco. The next judge lasted ten years before he died, and after him a judge served eight years and died.

"Okay. We're ready for the story of the fifteenth and final judge. Do either of you know who that was?"

After Jameson offered a blank stare, I said that it was Sebastian, then requested a short break. Geraldo decided to drive us over to the sister city of Puebla, and take a quick tour. I could see the proud gleam in his eyes as he slowly drove past the Catedral de Puebla with its twin bell towers. On our way back he mentioned that there where many wonderful museums and a great zocalo in the city. When we returned, we got into a comfortable spot near the Great Pyramid of Cholula, and Geraldo started the story of Sebastian.

"There was a man whose wife was barren, and an angel appeared and said, 'Although you are barren, having borne no children, you shall conceive and bear a son. He shall be consecrated to God from birth, and will some day deliver Mexico from the hand of the Panamanians.' She told her husband of her experience, and he was doubtful. The angel appeared again and told them to make a burnt offering to the LORD. When the

The King Montezuma Trilogy

flame went up, the angel ascended in the flame, and they believed their child would deliver the people of the Promised Land. She bore a son, and named him Sebastian. The boy grew and the LORD blessed him, and the spirit of the LORD began to stir within him.

"One day Sebastian saw a Panamanian woman, and wanted her for his wife. But his parents said, 'Is there not a woman among all our people that you must take a wife from the Panamanians?' But Sebastian said, 'No. I want her.' At that time the Panamanians had dominion over Mexico. So Sebastian went to talk with the woman he saw, and on the way he was attacked by a puma. The spirit of the LORD rushed on him, and he killed the puma with his bare hands. Finally, he arrived and talked with the woman, and she pleased him. After a while he returned again to marry her.

"Sebastian made a feast there as the young men were accustomed to do. When the people gathered, he said to them, 'Let me now put a riddle to you. If you can explain it to me within the seven days of the feast, I will give you a prize. But if you cannot explain it, then you will give me a prize.' So they said to him, 'Ask your riddle.' He asked them,

>'What is good in the ground,
>then great in the mouth,
>but terrible in the head?'

"For three days they could not explain the riddle. On the fourth day they said to Sebastian's wife, 'Find out the answer to the riddle or we'll burn your house down.' So she said to him, 'You must hate me, because you have a riddle that you have not explained to me.' She kept nagging him, so on the seventh day he told her, and she immediately went and told the people. Before the seventh day, the people answered the riddle

The King Montezuma Trilogy

correctly, and he was furious because he assumed she had shared the secret. In fact, he was so enraged that his father-in-law gave his daughter to another man."

"Interesting," said Jameson, "but what was the answer to the riddle?"

"Oh, sorry," apologized Geraldo. "The answer was tequila."

Jameson thought about it for a minute, then asked, "Hey, dad. Can I try some tequila?"

I quickly responded, "Sure, but don't tell your mother when we get home."

Geraldo seemed bewildered, and asked Jameson, "Have you not tried alcohol before?"

Jameson slightly blushed and said, "I think we need to get back to the story."

"The next day, Sebastian discovered the terrible thing that happened to him. His father-in-law said, 'I was sure you had rejected her, so I gave her to your best man from the wedding.' In more rage, he made torches and burned down the crops of the Panamanians, who asked, 'Who has done this?' Somebody who saw him do it said, 'It was Sebastian.' So the Panamanians killed his wife and father-in-law, and Sebastian swore to take revenge on them.

"So more Panamanians came up the Pacific coast from Panama to Acapulco and made a raid on the land. The men of Acapulco said, 'Why have you come up here against us?' They said, 'We have come up to bind Sebastian, to do to him as he did to us.' Then three thousand men of Acapulco went to the La Quebrada cliff where Sebastian was staying, and said to him, 'Do you not know that the Panamanians are rulers over us?' He replied, "It doesn't matter. As they did to me, so I have done to them.' They said to him, 'We have come to bind you and give

The King Montezuma Trilogy

you into the hands of the Panamanians.' Sebastian asked that they not attack him, and they agreed to only bind him. So they bound him with two new ropes, and brought him up from the cliff.

"When they all met, the spirit of the LORD rushed on him, and the ropes fell off. Then Sebastian found the jawbone of a donkey, and killed them all. This event became so famous that it became the words of a song:

'With the jawbone of a donkey,
heaps upon heaps,
with the jawbone of a donkey
I have slain a thousand men.'"

"Weird song if you ask me," offered Jameson. "And I'm not fond of glorifying killing."

"Fair enough," agreed Geraldo, "but remember these stories took place a long time ago. And they show the troubles the people experienced. Anyway, Sebastian judged in what is now the Mexican state of Guerrero for twenty years.

"Once Sebastian went to Oaxaca and slept with a prostitute. Being outside his tribal territory, the Oaxacans gathered at the city gate planning to kill him in the light of the morning. But Sebastian rose at midnight and got away in the dark of the night. After this he fell in love with a woman from the western edge of the Cuenca de Balsas Mountains, whose name was Dolores.

"The Panamanians came to her and said, 'Find out how Sebastian is able to bring harm to so many people, and we will make you rich.' So Dolores said to Sebastian, 'Please tell me how you are able to bring harm to so many people.' After lying to her a few times, she said, 'Surely you do not love me.' After nagging him day after day he grew weary, and told her his whole

The King Montezuma Trilogy

secret. 'You know the superstition of "el mal de ojo," which means evil eye?' She said, 'Of course. They are malevolent gazes that can bring harm to people.' Sebastian said, 'I am very good at it. If I were blindfolded, then my power would leave me.'

"So Dolores went to the Panamanians and said, "I have found the answer. Come to my home tonight and bring me the money.' When they arrived, she let him fall asleep, then invited them in. She carefully put a blindfold on him, and it woke him up. As Sebastian started to reach for the blindfold, the Panamanians gouged out his eyes, then imprisoned him. Now the Panamanians rejoiced, saying, 'Our god has given Sebastian into our hand.'

"In their merriment, they said, 'Call Sebastian, and let him entertain us.' So they retrieved Sebastian from his prison cell and humiliated him. Then he called to the LORD and said, 'Strengthen me only this once, so that with this one act of revenge I may pay back the Panamanians for my two eyes.' And Sebastian grasped the two middle pillars on which the house rested, and he leaned his weight against them. Then he said, 'Let me die with the Panamanians.' He strained with all his might and the house fell, and everyone died. Then his brothers and all his family came down and buried him. He had judged in Mexico twenty years."

Jameson said, "It sure seems like there isn't much interest in the Ark of the Covenant in these stories, and that confuses me."

"Funny you should mention that," said Geraldo, "because that's the direction this story is headed. There was a man from the hill country of Zacatecas who stole money from his mother, but he finally confessed and returned it. His mother said, 'May my son be blessed by the LORD!' then she used the money to

The King Montezuma Trilogy

make an idol. Now there was another man from the central tribe who decided to leave. He came upon the man from Zacatecas who invited him to stay, if he would be his priest. In those days there was no king in Mexico, and the priest decided that all the priests needed their own territory. So several priests went scouting the land on a mission from God. When they came to the peninsula, they found the ruins of Chichen Itza and Tulum, and decided this formerly godless land needed their presence. This is when the twelfth tribe took on its special identity. The land was the burial site of many of their ancestors, but it also had the ghosts of the many people sacrificed to idols.

"Then all the Mexicans came out, from all over the Promised Land, and assembled as one body at Guadalajara. The chiefs of all the tribes presented themselves, and questioned how some vile acts were occurring among the fifth tribe. They all agreed that the fifth tribe had become a disgrace and united against them, but the people of the fifth tribe fought back. After much loss of life, the Mexicans inquired of the LORD, 'Shall we again battle against our kinsfolk?' And the LORD said, 'Go up against them,' and they did, and they lost. So the Mexicans went to the Ark of the Covenant and inquired of the LORD, 'Shall we fight again?' The LORD answered, 'Yes, for tomorrow I will give them into your hand.'

"The Mexicans then thought through some strategy, and the fifth tribe did not realize that disaster was close upon them. The Mexicans lifted up their voices and said, 'O LORD, the God of Mexico, why has it come to pass that one tribe should be obliterated?' So the Mexicans had compassion for the remaining members of the fifth tribe, and they slowly began being fruitful and multiplying.

"Let's stop for a late lunch," said Geraldo, "then we'll come

The King Montezuma Trilogy

back for one more story. We also have one more trip to make before I tell the remaining stories."

"I want to try some enchiladas," requested Jameson.

I said that I like it all, so anywhere to eat was fine.

"So," teased Geraldo, "no Asian food this time?" We laughed and Geraldo drove us back to Puebla and took us to his favorite restaurant, Fonda de Santa Clara. "This is a typical Mexican restaurant, with colorful decorations, generous and flavorful portions, and friendly service." Jameson got his enchiladas and I tried some escamoles, an ancient food consumed in Mexico since the age of the Aztecs. I tried it and said it tasted kind of buttery and felt like cottage cheese in my mouth. Geraldo had a big grin on his face and said, "My friend, you just ate ant larvae." Jameson's eyes got real big, and I said I thought I was ordering a type of mole. After that, we drove around town a little more, then headed back to the pyramid.

"Remember back to the beginning of our journey," asked Geraldo, "when we were at the Tikal Temple?" We had to think a bit because we had been to many temples in many countries. When we finally nodded yes, he said, "There in Guatemala was Aztlan, the ancestral home of the Aztecs, which means people from Aztlan. It is also where God called Aapo to leave his homeland because someone cut down the forbidden tree. He was to go to a land of promise, and his progeny would know when they finally got there, when they saw an eagle perched on a cactus, eating a snake.

"For me, this is where it gets fun, because after many centuries, they finally saw this exact sign. As the legend goes, it was on an island, located in what was once known as Lake Texcoco. This is where they founded Tenochtitlan, which would become the capital of the Mexican Empire, which is now Mexico

The King Montezuma Trilogy

City."

"Great!" exclaimed Jameson, "so now we can go there?"

"Not yet. Remember that we need to talk about what we learned?"

"Okay," said Jameson, "but I have more of a question than a learning. How was this unique sign missed for so long?"

"It wasn't. It took this long before all three signs came together. Sometimes we have to wait for God's timing, rather than expect things to happen when we want them to."

The thing I liked best was that God rose up a woman to be a judge. I told them it vexed me that we struggle so much today to simply be God's people, humanity, living on God's Promised Land, the earth. What I learned is that the Aztec Scriptures testify as a microcosm of what the world and everything in it is called to be: holy.

The King Montezuma Trilogy

ACT IV
The Demand for Leadership

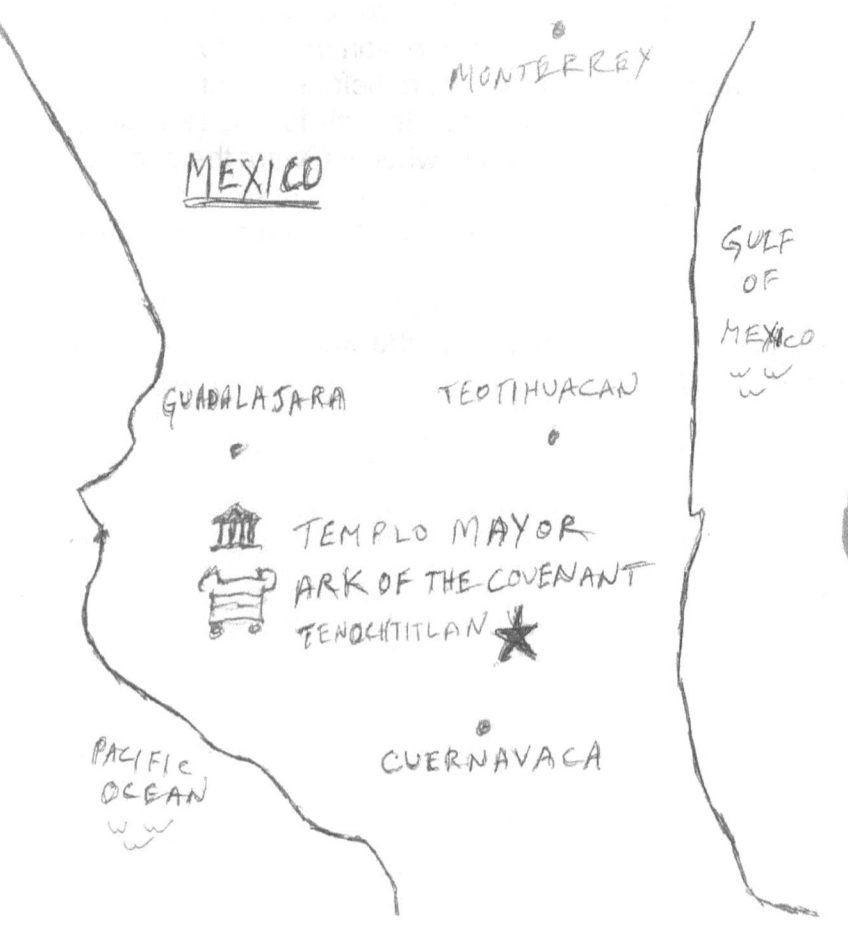

The King Montezuma Trilogy

SCENE ONE
The Forming of the Empire

    Since it was afternoon, we checked out of our hotel and headed for Mexico City. It was a bright and sunny day, and Geraldo talked as we entered the city. "I love this place. It has over twenty-two million people in the metropolitan area, and is always alive with music and events." We stopped at our hotel, checked in, and took a taxi to Templo Mayor. When we arrived, he said, "This is the historic center of the city, and it is where the Mexica people founded Tenochtitlan. What you are looking at are the excavated ruins, right here in the midst of Mexico City.
    "I wanted you to see this before it got dark, to give an idea of what the Mexican people built so long ago." Then with excitement in his eyes and the waving of hands, he described the area. "This is it. This is where God called his people. It took a long time to win over the Promised Land, and tomorrow we'll settle at the nearby zocalo to hear the rest of the stories. Is this making sense?" When we said, 'Yes,' he went into his guide voice. "Tenochtitlan eventually reached an area of more than five square miles, laid out symmetrically in four sectors.
    "Each area had its own services, like religious leaders and craftspeople, but the center of it all was the Templo Mayor. This became the holiest place in the Promised Land, which eventually gathered the political, military, and religious power together under one person. Who might that be?"
    "King Montezuma!" exclaimed a happy Jameson.
    "You bet," said a surprisingly exuberant Geraldo, "but we have much to do before we begin those stories. I hope this brief introduction was useful, but as for now it is starting to get dark,

The King Montezuma Trilogy

so we need to catch a taxi back to our hotel." We had a great dinner and discussion and Jameson and I were more than delighted with our journey so far. In the morning we taxied to the Plaza de la Constitucion. Geraldo said, 'This is commonly known as the zocalo, and it was the main ceremonial site for the Aztecs/Mexicans." There were no benches in this massive square, so we found a nice place to sit at the edge.

In an almost reverent way, Geraldo began, "They were finally God's people, Mexicans, living on their God-promised land, Mexico, but anarchy was about. It was time for God to act again, so God raised up another shaman. As Abund led the way to liberation and Geovanni led the way to the Promised Land, so Salvador led the way to the Empire.

"The change from tribal kinship to national kingship was very complex, but it began with the birth of Salvador. His mother was barren, and one day she made this vow: 'O LORD of hosts, if only you will look on the misery of your servant and give me a son, then I will dedicate him to your service.' After that, a priest told her, 'Go in peace. The God of Mexico will grant your petition.' In due time she conceived and bore a son, and named him Salvador. When he was old enough, his mother left him at the house of the LORD, then she prayed,

> 'My heart exults in the LORD,
>   there is no Holy One like you.
> The bows of the mighty will be broken,
>   but the feeble will be strong.
>
> The barren have borne children,
>   but the fruitful are forlorn.
> The LORD makes the poor and rich,

The King Montezuma Trilogy

> but those who are low he exalts.
>
> He raises up the poor from the dust,
>   and the needy from the ashes.
> To make them princes
>   and inherit seats of honor.'

"Now Salvador grew up in the presence of the LORD, and continued to grow both in stature and in favor with the LORD and with the people. He ministered to the LORD under the direction of the priest, but the word of the LORD was rare in those days, and visions were not widespread. One day Salvador was lying down in the temple where the Ark of the Covenant was. The LORD called to him, and Salvador said, 'Here I am!' He ran to the priest, but the priest said he did not call him. When the LORD called him a second and third time, the priest perceived that it was the LORD calling him.

"He told Salvador to respond to the next call saying, 'Speak, LORD, for your servant is listening.' When he did this, the LORD told him to let the priest know he would be punished because his sons were blaspheming God. When Salvador told him, he responded, 'It is the LORD. Let him do what seems good to him.' As Salvador grew up, the LORD was with him, and all Mexico knew he was a trustworthy shaman for the LORD.

"In those days the Colombians waged war against the Mexicans and won. When the elders returned they asked, 'Why has the LORD let the Colombians win against us?' so they sent for the Ark of the Covenant. When it arrived at their camp, word got out, and the Colombians were afraid because of the stories they had heard. But they decided to be men, fought again, and captured the Ark of the Covenant.

The King Montezuma Trilogy

"In very short order, things started going poorly for the Colombians, and they said, 'The ark of the God of Mexico must not remain with us. Send it away, and let it return to its own place, so that it may not destroy us.' So they put the ark of the LORD on a cart, and had it returned to Guadalajara.

"Then Salvador addressed the people of Mexico: 'Return to the LORD with all your heart. Put away the idols you worship. Direct your heart to the LORD, and serve him only, and he will deliver us from the hand of the Colombians.' So they obeyed, and Salvador acted as a shaman for them, and God worked as their helper. The Colombians made one last attack, God subdued them, and they left Mexico for good. Well, not all of them. A remnant took their boats north and settled in the state of Sinaloa.

"When Salvador became old, the elders of Mexico came to Salvador and said, 'You are old, and your sons do not follow in your ways. Appoint a king to govern us, like other nations.' Salvador turned to the LORD in prayer, and God said, 'They are not rejecting you, they are rejecting me, just like they did in Guatemala.' So Salvador told the elders, 'The LORD set our ancestors free in Guatemala, but if you demand a king, you will be giving up your freedom and choosing slavery to a king.' But the people refused to listen, so he said, 'We'll try it your way, but let's see how that works for you.'

"Now there was a man whose name was Luis, who was tall and handsome. The LORD revealed to Salvador that the next day he would see Luis and he was to anoint him to be the military ruler over Mexico. When Salvador saw Luis the next day, he said to him, 'You shall rule over Mexico.' He responded, 'I am from the least of the tribes of Mexico, and my family is the humblest in the tribe.' Then Salvador took a vial of oil and

The King Montezuma Trilogy

poured it on his head, saying, 'The LORD has anointed you the military ruler over Mexico. You shall save us from the hand of our enemies.' Then Salvador called the tribes of Mexico near and said, 'Do you see the one whom the LORD has chosen? There is no one like him among all the people.' And all the people shouted, 'Long live the king!'"

"And I'm praying for long life," complained Jameson, "because I won't last much longer if we don't stop for lunch!"

We all agreed, and fortunately the zocalo was packed with food carts, food trucks, and souvenir booths. Jameson acted like an old pro when he walked up to a food truck and said, 'I'd like a torta, some elote, and a bottle of Jarritos.' I proudly patted him on the back and ordered some ceviche de camaron, a plate of sopecitos surtidos, and a strawberry zocalo margarita.' Geraldo looked surprised and said, 'You must be hungry!' He then ordered a chicken tinga burrito, a plate of mole zocalo, and a bottle of cerveza. I asked if there were any problems with people getting sick, and Geraldo explained, 'The local police have an operation called "mala copa," where they close down any eatery that goes against regulations.'

When our orders came up, we went to a table reserved for customers, and the food was delicious. After a few minutes, Jameson pointed to a unique souvenir booth that was fairly close. A person would go up several steps and be helped onto a plastic donkey, then a photographer would take a picture of the tourist with a backdrop of the Virgin of Guadalupe. Jameson said, "Watch that third lady in line. She's pretty plump." I told Jameson that he wasn't being nice, but we couldn't keep our eyes off the booth. The woman finally started the short ascent, with men on either side of her. They had to help get her leg over the donkey, and as soon as she got seated there was a terrible

The King Montezuma Trilogy

cracking noise. The woman and both men fell as the donkey broke in half. Jameson couldn't help himself, and he was laughing so hard that he nearly fell off his seat. Needless to say, the owner of the booth was angry, as a crowd gathered around to see what was going on. The tourist finally got to her feet and said, 'Sir. Your donkey is an ass! And I didn't even get my picture!'"

After we got back to our spot, and settled down from the laughter, Geraldo continued. "About a month later, the Mexicans incurred yet another invasion, this time from the Ecuadorians. Luis gathered his people and launched an unexpected attack in the early morning light. He drove them off the Promised Land, and the people cried out, 'Today the LORD has brought deliverance to Mexico.' The people confessed their sin to Salvador about demanding a king, and he said to them, 'Fear the LORD, and serve him faithfully with all your heart. Do not chase after idols. For it has pleased the LORD to make you a people for himself. Furthermore, I shall pray for you without ceasing, and I will instruct you in the good and right way.' Nobody knows how old Luis was when he began his reign as king and nobody knows how long he served.

"One day Luis acted foolishly when he did not keep the commandment of the LORD. Salvador said to him, 'Your Empire will not continue, so the LORD has sought out a man after his own heart.' Another day Luis committed a very rash act when he told his troops, 'Cursed be anyone who eats food before it is evening.' Luis' son had not heard the charge, so he ate. A soldier told him, 'Your father strictly charged the troops that anyone who eats food this day will be cursed.' His son then convinced the troops to join him in eating, which brought about another breaking of a commandment.

The King Montezuma Trilogy

"Luis called his leaders together and said, 'Let us find out who has brought this outrage upon us.' They pointed at his son, and Luis called for his own son's death, but the people denounced Luis. After that, Salvador reminded Luis that, 'The LORD sent me to anoint you king over his people, but you have failed. Now let me tell you what the LORD said to me last night. 'I anointed Luis king over Mexico, but because he has rejected my word, I also reject him from being king.' And the LORD was sorry that he had made Luis king over Mexico.

"The LORD said to Salvador, 'Fill your horn with oil and go to Cuernavaca, for there you will find the next king. Do not look upon his stature, because the LORD looks on the heart.' Then Salvador came to the village and heard about a young ranchero, and told the people to bring him. Now he was ruddy, and had beautiful eyes, and was handsome. The LORD said, 'Rise and anoint him, for this is the one. His name is Montezuma, and he is a great mix of the Mexica and Aztec people.' Then Salvador anointed Montezuma in the presence of the townsfolk, and the spirit of the LORD was mightily with the man from that day forward.

"Now the spirit of the LORD departed from Luis, and an evil spirit tormented him. His servants offered to find a musician to play for him when he was tormented, and they ended up bringing Montezuma to him. The music was greatly useful and Luis grew to love Montezuma. Whenever he suffered, Montezuma would play his flute and Luis would feel better.

"Now the Colombians made another attack on Mexico, and they gathered on opposite sides of the valley of war. This time they brought a gigantic Columbian with them who said, 'Choose a man to meet me in the valley. If he kills me, we will be your servants, but if I win, you shall be our servants. Montezuma told

The King Montezuma Trilogy

Luis that he was willing to fight, but Luis said, 'You are just a boy, and this giant Columbian has been a lifelong warrior.' But Luis relented, and said, 'Go, and may the LORD be with you!'

Luis tried to dress Montezuma in heavy armor, but it weighed him down too much. Instead, he picked up his macuahuitl and headed into the valley. The Colombian said, 'Am I a dog that you come to me with a stick?' But Montezuma said, 'You come to me with sword and spear, but I come to you in the name of the LORD.' When the Colombian drew near, Montezuma threw his macuahuitl, and the obsidian blades struck him in the eye. As the giant of a man fell down and was writhing in pain, Montezuma ran up to him and slit his throat. When the Colombians saw that their champion was dead, they fled. Luis put Montezuma in charge of his army, and the women came out from all over Mexico, singing and dancing and praising Montezuma. This made Luis very angry, so he decided to keep an eye on this young ranchero.

"The next day Luis' spirit was tortured, so Montezuma played his flute. This time he was not soothed, but instead tried to kill the young man. Luis was well enough to understand that the LORD was no longer with him, but was with Montezuma. So Luis sent Montezuma on many military expeditions, in hopes that he would die, but his victories only made him more popular. When Luis saw Montezuma's great success, he stood in awe of him, and all of Mexico loved him.

"Again there was war, and after Montezuma returned victorious, Luis tried to kill him so he fled. Soon he came upon Salvador and told him the problems he was having with Luis. When Luis heard they were together, he went there, but the spirit of God protected Montezuma by distracting Luis. Montezuma fled once again and came across Luis' son and

The King Montezuma Trilogy

asked, 'What is my sin against your father that he is trying to take my life? If there is guilt in me, kill me yourself.' His son knew nothing of his father's anger toward Montezuma, so he went and talked to his father. Then Luis' anger was kindled against his own son and he said, 'I wish you had never been born!' Then Luis asked his son to bring Montezuma to him, and he replied, 'Why should he be put to death? What has he done?' Then Luis tried to kill his own son, so he got up and left.

"Montezuma went to Guadalajara to be near the Ark of the Covenant. He was hungry and asked for five loaves, but the priest said, 'I only have the holy bread.' It was close enough to the time to replace it, so the priest gave Montezuma the Bread of the Presence. He then requested a sword, and the priest gave him the sword of the gigantic man he had killed. From there Montezuma fled to a cave and many of the discontented of the area gathered there. Then a shaman said, 'Do not remain here. Go near to Tenochtitlan,' so he did.

"Luis became obsessed with finding Montezuma, and even decided his own tribe was conspiring against him. Luis heard that Montezuma had gone to Guadalajara, so he chased after him there. When the priest who helped Montezuma was of no help to Luis, he ordered the priest's death. Now Luis was told where to find Montezuma, and he ordered the closing of the gates of that city, but Montezuma escaped. Montezuma went into the wilderness, and Luis sought him every day, but the LORD did not give him into his hand.

"It was in the wilderness when Luis' son came to Montezuma. He said to him, 'Do not be afraid; for my father shall not find you. You shall be king over Mexico and my father also knows this.' Then Luis was told where Montezuma was hiding, and he graciously accepted this information. He said, 'Go and

The King Montezuma Trilogy

make sure where he is, for I am told he is very cunning.' Luis then went to one side of the mountain, and Montezuma and his men were on the other. As they were closing in to capture Montezuma, Luis was told the Colombians had made a raid on the country. So Luis reluctantly stopped the pursuit and returned to fight the Colombians.

"When Luis returned from battle, he heard that Montezuma was at Cuernavaca. He went there and Montezuma cornered him, but he decided to let the king go free. He asked, 'Why do you listen to those who say that I seek to do you harm? I spared your life because you are the LORD's anointed. Therefore, I shall not be against you. May the LORD be the judge, and give sentence between you and me, and I will plead my cause and expect vindication.' He responded with, 'You are more righteous than I. So may the LORD reward you with good for what you have done for me this day, and now I know that you shall surely be king.'

"About that time, Salvador died and all Mexico assembled and mourned for him, but it didn't stop Luis. He set off again in search of Montezuma, who heard about Luis' arrival. Montezuma went to Luis' camp at night, but was still unwilling to kill Luis, and instead, took several spears around Luis and left. The next morning Montezuma called from across the valley to the king and showed him the items he took. Luis said, 'I have done wrong, so I will never harm you again. I have been a fool, and have made a great mistake.' So Montezuma went his way and Luis returned to his place.

"After the death of Salvador, Luis expelled the mediums from the land, but the Colombians returned. In great fear, Luis turned to the LORD and got no answer, so he sought out a medium. His servants said, 'There is a medium at Guadalajara.'

The King Montezuma Trilogy

Luiz went to her and asked her to conjure up the spirit of Salvador. Right then a divine being came up out of the ground wearing a robe, and Luis knew it was Salvador. He said, 'I am in great distress for the Colombians are warring against me, and God has turned from me. So I have summoned you to tell me what I should do.' Salvador said, 'It is over for you. Tomorrow you will be with me.'

"Now the Colombians were winning the battles in Mexico, and came upon the king. They killed his son and badly wounded him, so Luis told his servant, 'Draw your sword and thrust it through me.' But his servant was unwilling, so Luis took his own sword and fell upon it. When the Mexicans heard what happened, they fled their towns and the Colombians occupied them.

"Break time," requested Jameson.

"Yes. We have done well. Let's take a taxi back to the hotel, get some dinner and a good night's sleep and return tomorrow to hear about the development of King Montezuma."

The next morning, as they returned to the site of Tenochtitlan in the middle of Mexico City, Geraldo set the stage. He said, "The original twelve tribes of Mexica had settled into their areas, but they were slowly becoming divided between north and south. After Montezuma properly mourned the death of Luis, the LORD told him to go to Guadalajara, where the Ark of the Covenant was at. Then the people of the southern tribes came and anointed Montezuma king over southern Mexico. In response, the people of the northern tribes anointed their own king.

"After all the fighting the people of Mexico did to ward off outside invaders, they were now spending their time fighting each other. The northern tribes were becoming weaker and

The King Montezuma Trilogy

weaker as the southern tribes were becoming stronger and stronger. When Montezuma heard of the death of a man who could help unify the northern and southern tribes, he and the people wept. Montezuma offered a poetic eulogy at the gravesite:

> 'Should this man die as a fool dies?
> His hands were not bound,
> his feet were not tied,
> and his desires were sound.'

"After that another battle broke out, and ended in Montezuma's favor, and he celebrated, 'The LORD has redeemed my life out of every adversity.' Then all the tribes of Mexico came to Montezuma at Guadalajara and said, 'We are your bone and flesh. When Luis was king over us, it was you who led out Mexico and brought it in. The LORD said to you, "it is you who shall be ranchero of my people Mexico, you who shall be ruler over Mexico." So all the elders of Mexico came to the king at Guadalajara, and King Montezuma made a covenant with them. There they anointed Montezuma king over all of Mexico. He was thirty years old when he began to reign, and he reigned forty years. The year he started was CE 1481.

"The king and his men marched to Tenochtitlan, and took over the marshland of their destiny. Tenochtitlan had already been discovered, and much development was happening on the island in what was then called Lake Texcoco. Montezuma continued building the city all around, and he became greater and greater, for the LORD was with him. Friends sent wood, and carpenters, and masons to build him a house. Montezuma perceived that the good things happening were God's way of

The King Montezuma Trilogy

exalting Mexico. When the Colombians heard that Montezuma had been anointed king over all of Mexico, they launched an attack that Montezuma easily repelled. Frustrated, they attacked again, but God was with Montezuma and they were struck down.

"Montezuma decided it was time to solidify a political, military, and religious function in his new capital city of Tenochtitlan. He gathered his men and went to Guadalajara to retrieve the Ark of the Covenant. They built a new cart for the ark, and had a festive parade on the return trip. So Montezuma and all the house of Mexico brought up the ark of the LORD with shouting, and with the sound of the trumpet. They brought the ark of the LORD and set it in its place, inside the tent Montezuma had pitched for it. Montezuma then blessed the people and distributed food, and the people returned to their homes.

"Now the king was settled in his house, and the LORD had given him rest from all his enemies. He said to his shaman, 'See now, I am living in a fine house, but the ark of God stays in a tent.' His shaman said, 'Go do all that you have in mind, for the LORD is with you.' But that night his shaman received a word from the LORD: 'Is Montezuma the one to build me a house to live in? Have I ever asked any of the ancestors to build me a house? Go tell Montezuma that when he dies, I will raise up his offspring to build a house in my name.' When his shaman told Montezuma what God had to say, he understood it as God's promise to Mexico.

"Montezuma went to the tent and sat before the Ark of the Covenant. He said, 'O LORD God, you established your people Mexico for yourself to be your people forever, and you became their God. As for the house I wanted to build for you, do as you

The King Montezuma Trilogy

have promised, and your name will be magnified forever. Now I ask that you bless the house of your servant, and may it be blessed forever.' Sometime afterward, Montezuma attacked the Colombians and subdued them. He also defeated others and made them his servants. Still others came to him and congratulated him about his victories. Montezuma was making a name for himself and the LORD gave victory wherever he went.

"So Montezuma reigned over all Mexico and administered justice and equity to all. He even befriended those who had been loyal to Luiz and restored land to them. They said, 'According to all that my lord the king commands his servant, so your servant will do.' Sometime afterward, the king of Ecuador died, and his son succeeded him. The Ecuadorians came to Mexico for battle, and the men of Mexico arrayed themselves against the Ecuadorians. They moved forward into battle against the Ecuadorians, who fled. When kings of other countries heard about the defeat, they made peace with Mexico.

"Well, not everyone. It was spring, the time when kings go out to battle. So Montezuma sent his troops into battle while he stayed at Tenochtitlan. Then it happened. Montezuma was walking about on the roof of his house, and he saw a beautiful woman across the way. He sent someone to inquire about her, and discovered she was the wife of one of his elite officers. Unfortunately, that didn't stop him, because his loins burned for her. He sent word that the king wanted to see her, so she dutifully went. And became pregnant.

"When Montezuma found out that she was with child, he sent for her husband. He asked, 'How is the war going?' He then told her husband, 'Go home and have sex with your wife.'

The King Montezuma Trilogy

Montezuma was wanting to cover up his indiscretion, but her husband was committed to his job. He didn't even go home. When his servants informed Montezuma of the man's loyalty, he summoned his return, and said, 'You have come from a journey, why did you not go home? The man replied, 'The ark is in a booth, and my fellow soldiers are camping in a field. I could not possibly go home to eat and drink and lie with my wife. What kind of a person do you think I am?'

"It turned out that was the wrong thing to say to the king. Montezuma wrote a letter and sent it by this man to his leader in the field. It said, 'Set this man in the forefront of the hardest fighting, and then draw back from him, so that he may be struck down and die.' The ploy was successful and Montezuma was informed by a messenger. Montezuma said to the messenger, 'Tell them to not trouble themselves over this matter. War kills. Be encouraged in your task.' When the woman heard of her husband's death, she mourned, then Montezuma married her and she bore their child.

"But the thing Montezuma had done displeased the LORD. Montezuma's shaman felt inspired, so he shared a story for the king. 'A rich man had a visitor, but he didn't want to offer any of his food, so he sent a servant to steal food from a poor man.' Then Montezuma got angry and said, 'The man who has done this deserves to die!' After a pause for effect, his shaman said, 'You are the man!' While in a state of shock, the shaman continued, 'Thus says the LORD, who anointed you king over Mexico, and rescued you from the hand of Luis, "Why have you despised me and done evil in my sight? You had a man killed so you could have his wife." Then Montezuma said to his shaman, 'I have sinned against the LORD,' and he responded, 'Because of your sin, the child that is born to you shall die.'

The King Montezuma Trilogy

"Indeed, the child became very ill, and Montezuma pleaded with God for the child. On the seventh day the child died, and Montezuma went to the tent where the Ark of the Covenant was, and worshipped. Then Montezuma consoled his wife and lay with her, and she bore him a son and named him Santiago.

"Now Montezuma had another son who garnered much attention in the capital city of Tenochtitlan. He was exceedingly attractive, and Montezuma was jealous of him. So his son lived two full years in Tenochtitlan without coming into the king's presence. Finally, his son sent a question to the king, 'Why have I come here? It would be better for me to never have come to Tenochtitlan.' When the king got the message, he sent for his son who said, 'If there is guilt in me, then kill me!' He then knelt by the king and bent his head to the ground, exposing his neck. And Montezuma pulled out a sword, touched his son's neck with it, then leaned over and kissed his son.

"This gave Montezuma's son an advantage. He went to the gates of Tenochtitlan, and when someone would bring a suit before the king for judgment, he would say, 'Your claims are good and right, but my father has failed to appoint someone to hear you. If only I were judge in the land, I would hear and give justice.' Whenever people came to him, he would take their hand and kiss them. So the king's son stole the hearts of the people of Mexico. He then went to Cuernavaca and told people to shout, 'The king's son has become king at Cuernavaca!' and the conspiracy grew in strength.

"A messenger came to Montezuma, saying 'The hearts of the Mexicans have gone after your son.' Then Montezuma said, 'Let us flee, or there will be no escape for us.' The king's officials said, 'Your servants are ready to do whatever our lord the king decides.' As they left, the king saw a Colombian with them, and

The King Montezuma Trilogy

he asked, 'Why are you coming? You are a foreigner, and also an exile from your home.' The man answered, 'Wherever my lord the king may be, whether for death or for life, there also your servant will be.'

"Then two men came carrying the Ark of the Covenant. Montezuma said to them, 'Carry the ark back into the city. If I find favor in the eyes of the LORD, he will bring me back. So they carried the ark back to Tenochtitlan and remained there with it. Montezuma went part of the way up Monte Tlaloc to mourn, and all the people went with him, weeping as they went. When the king came to the summit, he was inspired to have some of his priests become spies. He told one of them, 'Go into the city and report back to me everything you hear.' So the priest went, and just as he entered the city, the king's son was also entering Tenochtitlan.

"When the king came down from the mountain, a man started throwing stones at him, saying, 'Murderer! Scoundrel! The LORD has avenged on all you the blood of the house of Luis, in whose place you have reigned. And the LORD has given the empire into the hand of your son. See, disaster has overtaken you, for you are a man of blood.' A friend said to the king, 'Why should this dead dog curse my lord the king? Let me go over and take off his head.' Montezuma said, 'If the LORD has told him to curse me, perhaps the LORD has bidden it. And I pray the LORD will repay me with good for this cursing of me today.'

"Montezuma was soon warned to leave the area, so all the people set out with him, and by daybreak not one was left who had not gone with him. His son encamped nearby, but friends brought Montezuma's troops beds, basins, vessels, and food because his troops were hungry and weary and thirsty in the

The King Montezuma Trilogy

wilderness. Then the king divided his army into three groups and offered to go with them, but the men said, 'you are worth ten thousand of us, therefore it is better that you stay.' As the troops marched forth, the king said to his leaders, 'Deal gently with my son.'

"So his army went out into the field, and some of the king's servants happened to meet his son, whose mule tried to go under a thicket. As his mule went under, the son's head got wedged between a limb and a trunk. The mule continued on and he was left hanging. The men knew they were to deal gently with the man, but another soldier took a spear and thrust it into the king's son's heart, while he was still alive. Now Montezuma was waiting to hear word about his son when he saw a man running to the city. A sentinel informed the king, and he said, 'I pray he comes with good tidings.'

"When the man arrived he said, 'Good tidings for my lord the king! For the LORD has vindicated you this day, delivering you from the powers of all who rose up against you.' The king asked, 'Is it well with my son?' He answered, 'May the enemies of my lord the king, and all who rise up to do you harm, be like him.' The king was deeply moved and went to his bedroom and wept, saying, 'O my son! If only it could have been me who died instead of you.'

"Meanwhile, all the Mexicans had fled to their homes, disputing throughout all the tribes. Those who had followed the king's son were having second thoughts, and the king's supporters were swaying the hearts of all the people as one. They sent word to the king, 'Return, both you and all your servants.' So the king came back to Tenochtitlan and met some worried people. 'May my lord not hold me guilty or remember how your servant did wrong on the day you left.' Some of his

The King Montezuma Trilogy

servants called for their death, but Montezuma said, 'Shall anyone be put to death in Mexico this day? For do I not know that I am this day king over Mexico?' He then looked at the guilty ones and announced, 'You shall not die. You have my oath.'

"Now that Montezuma was back on his throne, he spoke to the LORD the words of this song:

> 'The LORD is my rock,
>   my fortress,
>   and my deliverer.
>
> My God is my rock,
>   in whom I take refuge.
>   My shield and the horn of my salvation,
>
> You are my stronghold
>   and my refuge,
>   my savior.
>
> You save me from violence.
>   So I call upon the LORD,
>   who is worthy to be praised,
>
> And I am saved from my enemies.'

"Montezuma also wrote down some thoughts on what he had learned in life:

> 'One who rules over people justly
> ruling in the fear of God,
> is like the light of morning,

The King Montezuma Trilogy

like the sun rising on a cloudless morning,
gleaming from the rain on the grassy land.

Is not my house like this with God?
For he has made with me an everlasting covenant,
ordered in all things and secure.
Will he not cause to prosper
all my help and my desire?

But the godless are all like thorns that are thrown away,
for they cannot be picked up with the hand.
To touch them one uses an iron bar
or the shaft of a spear.
and they are entirely consumed in fire on the spot.'

"The anger of the LORD was kindled against Mexico, and he incited Montezuma against them, saying, 'Go, count the people of Mexico. So the king said to his commanders, 'Go through all the tribes of Mexico, and take a census of the people, so that I may know how many there are.' So they went about to the twelve tribes of Mexico to accomplish their assignment. And when they had gone through all the land, they came back to Tenochtitlan, and reported to the king.' But afterward, Montezuma was grieved. He said to his shaman, 'I am in great distress. Let us fall into the hand of the LORD, for his mercy is great. But let me not fall into human hands.'

"That day Montezuma's shaman came to him and said, 'Go up and erect an altar to the LORD.' Montezuma rose and when people saw him coming, they prostrated themselves before him. They asked, 'Why has my lord come here?' Montezuma said, 'I need to buy land to build an altar to the LORD.' One man said,

The King Montezuma Trilogy

'You may have my land, and offer up what seems good to you.' But the king said, 'No, but I will buy it from you for a price,' and so he did, and Montezuma built there an altar to the LORD.

"Wow!" exclaimed Geraldo. "That was a long time with no interruptions."

Jameson said, "It was great storytelling. Thanks." I agreed, and thanked him for all he had done for us.

He was quick to ask, "Okay, now for my favorite part of the tour. What did you learn?"

"I had no idea," began Jameson, "that the capital of the Aztec/Mexican Empire was founded right here, in the middle of what's now Mexico City. I mean, you told us that at the beginning, but somehow it's different being here with all the loud noises and bold colors. And being surrounded by all of the modern day busyness, you can look down at the archaeological site and see back into history. I love it."

That brought a smile to my face, then I said, "I knew the importance of Abund for the exodus from Guatemala, and Geovanni for the claiming of the Promised Land in Mexico, but I was surprised about the importance of Salvador for the founding of the Empire."

"Great!" exclaimed a rather jubilant Geraldo. "It's been a wonderful day. Time to taxi back for dinner and the hotel, and tomorrow we begin the last set of stories."

The King Montezuma Trilogy

SCENE TWO
The Fall of the Empire

    We all agreed to get up early and drive northeast of the city to see Teotihuacan. Geraldo and I decided to stay at the base of the famous Pyramid of the Sun, but Jameson climbed up with exuberance. When he got back down, he teased us mercilessly about it being the best thing he had done on the whole trip. With a wry smile, we returned to the hotel to leave our car and catch a taxi back to the Plaza de la Constitucion. It was a bright and blue day with pleasantly cool temperatures.

    "Montezuma was old and advanced in years, and his oldest living son believed himself to be the heir apparent. He exalted himself, declaring 'I will be king,' and garnered support, but the king's priest and shaman and troops did not side with him. So the king's shaman went to Montezuma's wife and asked, 'Have you heard that your husband's oldest son thinks he's now king? Go to Montezuma and remind him that he swore to have his son Santiago as his successor.' After she told him, his shaman came to the king and said, 'The eyes of all Mexico are on you to tell them who shall sit on the throne.' The king dismissed his shaman and said to his wife, 'Your son Santiago shall succeed me as king.' The king then told his priest and his shaman to, 'Take your servants and have my son Santiago ride with you. Take him to the main spring outside Tenochtitlan and anoint him king over Mexico, and say "Long live King Santiago." Then return him and have him sit on my throne.' When it was done, all the people said, 'Long live King Santiago!'

    "When the king's oldest son heard what happened, his friends departed in fear. He then sought asylum, desiring an

The King Montezuma Trilogy

unconditional pardon, but Santiago said, 'If you prove to be a worthy man, not one of your hairs shall fall to the ground. But if wickedness is found in you, you shall die.' The eldest son then bowed to the king, and King Santiago said to him, 'Go home.'

"When Montezuma's time to die drew near, he charged his son Santiago, saying, 'Be strong, be courageous, and keep the charge of the LORD your God, walking in his ways and keeping his statutes, so that you may prosper in all you do.' Then Montezuma died and was buried in Tenochtitlan.

"Wait!" requested a puzzled Jameson. "That's it for him?"

Geraldo asked, "What do you mean?"

"Well," explained Jameson, "Abund had a big long story, as well as Mexica, but Montezuma's story didn't seem to last that long. So why is Montezuma the central character of the Aztec Scriptures?"

"Best question yet!" exclaimed Geraldo. "I believe it is because the Mexicans treat Montezuma in the same fashion as we Caldwellians treat Jim Caldwell."

"In what way?" inquired Jameson.

Geraldo smiled and said, "Jim Caldwell united all those who believed in his stories and resurrection, while Montezuma united the Empire."

Jameson shook his head thoughtfully, and then I decided to add my two cents worth. "There are so many characters in what some people call the Old Testament and the New Testament, but I think the central character of the Bible is God. That would give a chance for uniting both faiths."

Then Geraldo continued. "So Santiago assumed the throne and the empire was firmly established. Then the oldest son went to his mother and said, 'You know that the empire was mine, and that all Mexico expected me to reign.' When the king

The King Montezuma Trilogy

heard this, he said, 'My older brother is devising a scheme against me, so he shall be put to death. And he was.'

"One night the LORD appeared to Santiago in a dream. God said, 'Ask what I should give you,' and Santiago said, 'You have shown great and steadfast love to my father, and now you have made me the new king of Mexico. So I ask you to give me an understanding mind to govern your people, able to discern between good and evil.' God said, 'Because you have unselfishly asked for this, I will now give you a wise and discerning mind. No king shall ever compare with you. If you walk in my ways, keeping my commandments, then I will lengthen your life.'

"Later, two women came to the king. One said, 'This woman and I live in the same house, and I gave birth. Three days later, this woman gave birth, then her son died. She got up in the middle of the night and took my son, and left her dead son beside me. When I woke up, I looked closely at him and realized it was not my son. Then this woman said that the living son was hers and the dead son was mine.' So they argued before the king. He said, 'Bring me a machete. I'll divide the living boy and give you each one half.' But the woman whose son was alive said, 'Please, my lord, give her the living boy.' Then the other woman said, 'Divide it.' Then the king responded, 'Give the first woman the living boy. She is the mother.' All Mexico heard of the judgment and perceived that the wisdom of God was in him.

"Santiago was sovereign over all Mexico, and the people brought tribute and served him all the days of his life. God gave him great wisdom, and his fame even spread throughout all the previously invading nations, and they came from all over to hear his wisdom. Soon people were offering help in any way, so he said, 'My father could not build a house for the LORD because

The King Montezuma Trilogy

of the constant warfare, but now the LORD has given rest on every side. So I intend to build a house for the LORD. Send your best materials, and my servants will join your servants, and they will all be paid well.'

Jameson interjected, "Sounds like corporations could learn something today from Santiago!"

Geraldo brushed off the comment and continued. "In the four hundred and eightieth year after the Aztecs came out of the land of Guatemala, in the fourth year of Santiago's reign over Mexico, he began to build Templo Mayor. Thousands of laborers quarried out great, costly stones in order to lay the foundation. So Santiago built the Temple, and finished it in seven years. Then he assembled the elders of Mexico and all the heads of the twelve tribes, and had the priests bring the Ark of the Covenant. They placed it in the inner sanctuary, the most holy place, and it still contained the two tablets of stone that Abund had carried down from Cerro Raxon many years ago.

"Then the king blessed all the assembly of Mexico and gave a speech. After that Santiago stood before the altar of the LORD and spread out his hands to heaven. He said, 'O LORD, God of Mexico, there is no God like you in heaven. But will you indeed dwell on the earth? Even heaven cannot contain you.' He then dedicated the Temple and blessed the people: 'The LORD our God be with us, as he was with our ancestors. May he not leave us or abandon us, but incline our hearts to him, so that all the peoples of the earth may know that the LORD is God. There is no other.'

"When the queen of Panama heard of the fame of Santiago, she came to test him, but instead was amazed and breathless. She said, 'The report was true about your accomplishments, but I did not believe the reports. Your wisdom and prosperity far

The King Montezuma Trilogy

surpass the reports I had heard.' In one year, Santiago amassed twenty five tons of gold. Thus he excelled all the kings of the earth in riches and in wisdom. But not all was right with the king. He had a weakness for foreign women, and ultimately violated portions of the Laws of Abund. The time that Santiago reigned in Tenochtitlan over all Mexico was forty years, then he died and was buried near his father.

"Sure seems to me," suggested Jameson, "that kings were dying all the time."

"That's because," countered Geraldo, "that we are covering a lot of history in a short period of time. But here's the interesting thing. The united Empire split in half after that. The northern tribes named their own king, and the southern tribes, which included the city of Tenochtitlan and Templo Mayor, chose a king for themselves. The northern tribes chose Monterrey as their capital, but their king was concerned that his empire would continue to observe Templo Mayor as the place to offer sacrifices. He said to his people, 'You have gone down to Tenochtitlan long enough. Here are two calves of gold which will serve as our altar.' He also made houses on high places, and appointed priests from among all the people, then created a new calendar for religious festivals.

"A man of God then came from Tenochtitlan in the Southern Empire, to Monterrey in the Northern Empire. He said to the king, 'Your altar shall be torn down,' and it was. The works of God were so evident that the king said to the man of God, 'Come home with me and dine, and I will give you a gift.' He responded, 'I will not go with you, even if you give me half of your empire.' But the king did not turn from his evil ways. He consecrated more priests for the high places, and his actions became sin for his dynasty, and his ultimate demise. The time

The King Montezuma Trilogy

that the first king of the Northern Empire reigned was twenty-two years, then you know what happened?"

"He died!" Jameson and I said in unison.

"Now the son of Santiago reigned over the Southern Empire in Tenochtitlan, the city that the LORD had chosen out of all the tribes of Mexico. But the people did what was evil in the sight of the LORD. They also built sites to worship the old gods of their Aztec ancestors, and the kings of the north and south were at war with each other continually. When the southern king died, his son reigned, but only for three years because he committed all the sins his father did, then he died. His son succeeded him, and he reigned over the Southern Empire for forty-one years, because he did what was right in the sight of the LORD. Then he also died. Back in the Northern Empire, the king's son reigned for two years. Any idea why it was such a short reign?"

Jameson immediately spoke up and asked, "Was it by any chance that he did what was evil in the sight of the LORD?"

We all laughed as Geraldo said, "Of course! However, his demise came at the hands of his successor. This third king of the Northern Empire reigned twenty-four years, even though he too was evil. The fourth king lasted two years, while the fifth king only reigned an astonishing seven days. The sixth king continued the evil ways of his predecessor, but the seventh king did more evil than all the kings before him."

"It seems like it didn't matter if the kings were good or evil," complained Jameson.

"Yes, but listen to this one. Now a shaman came to this seventh king and said, 'As the LORD lives, there shall be neither dew nor rain, except by my word.' That night, the shaman heard a word from the LORD to leave. He was told

The King Montezuma Trilogy

where to hide and that God would care for him during the drought. Next, the LORD told him to go to a certain town where a widow would take care of him. That widow's son became ill and died, so the shaman cried out, 'O LORD my God, let this child's life come into him again.' And it did."

I spoke up again and said, "That sounds like some stories from the New Testament. Do you think they were true?"

"Ooh," groaned Geraldo. "Stories don't have to be true or false, but they do have to carry meaning." Without giving a chance for discussion, he said, "In the third year of the drought, the LORD told the shaman, 'Go to the king, and I will send rain.' When the king saw him, he said, 'is it you, you troubler of the Northern Empire?' and the shaman answered, 'It is not I who has brought trouble, it is you. You have forsaken the ways of the LORD. Now therefore have your empire assemble with all of your gods.' And it was done. The shaman came to them and said, 'If the LORD is God, follow him, but if you prefer other gods, follow them. I will make two shrines and we will put a lame person on each shrine. Then you call upon your god and I will call upon the LORD, and we will see which one is healed.'"

"I've got a clue which person will be healed," smiled Jameson.

"The people of the Northern Empire called upon their gods to heal the lame man on their shrine, but it was to no avail. Then the shaman said, 'Surely your gods are away, or perhaps they have fallen asleep.' Then he cried out, 'O LORD, God of Aapo, Hugo, and Mexica, let it be known this day that you are God in Mexico, that I am your servant, and that I am doing this in your name.' He then looked at the lame man on his shrine and said, 'Stand up and walk!' to which the lame man jumped down and walked. As the crowds looked on in astonishment, the shaman

The King Montezuma Trilogy

said, 'You have turned your hearts from the only God.' When the people saw it, they fell on their faces and said, 'The LORD indeed is God!'

"The shaman then said to the king, 'The drought has ended.' He was deeply impressed, so he went home and told his wife everything the shaman had done. His wife was angered because she made money selling idols of the gods, so she sent a messenger to the shaman, saying, 'May the gods do to me, and more also, if I do not have you killed by tomorrow.' When the shaman got the message, he got up and fled for his life. He sat down by a tree and asked that he might die, then fell asleep. An angel woke him and provided him sustenance, saying, 'You will need strength to travel forty days and forty nights.'

"At the end of his journey, he found himself at Cerro Raxon, the place Abund received the commandments. He stood on the mountain, and there was a great wind, but the LORD was not in the wind. Then there was an earthquake, but the LORD was not in the earthquake. Next was a fire, but the LORD was not in the fire. As the shaman stood there, in this holy place, he heard the sound of sheer silence. Have either of you ever heard that?"

Again I was motivated to share a story. "The time I heard it most clearly was on a tour of Mammoth Cave in Kentucky. The guide turned out the lights and it was the darkest I had even seen. Then he said, 'Can you hear the sound of silence?' I wasn't sure what he was talking about, but in this moment of absolute silence, I began to hear a ringing."

"Was it your tinnitus, Dad?"

"No, this was before I got that, but it was quite profound. I remember thinking that this must be somehow instructive about prayer."

Geraldo said, "Tell us more."

The King Montezuma Trilogy

"Maybe we need to shut everything else out so we can listen for the voice of God."

"I like that," said Geraldo, then went on. "After a while, the LORD gave him a mission to anoint another king over the Northern Empire, and another shaman to take his own place. So he set out from there and found his replacement. The man was a farmer, but the shaman threw his sarape over him, and he responded, 'Let me kiss my father and my mother, and then I will follow you.' Then he set out and followed the shaman and became his servant. Later the following three events took place:

1) A man had a vineyard next to the king's summer palace. The king audaciously said, 'Give me your vineyard. I will give you a better one, or I will give you its value in money.' But the owner said, 'No. I will not give you my ancestral inheritance.' The king went home and threw a fit. His wife asked, 'Why are you so depressed?' When he told her his problem, she said, 'Get up and be cheerful. I will get this vineyard for you.'

2) His wife then wrote a letter in the king's name, and sealed it with an official royal seal, and sent it to the elders. It said, 'Bring the owner of the vineyard to an assembly, and have him brought up on charges of cursing God and king. Then take him out and stone him to death.' When it was done, the elders sent a note back to his wife to let him know the owner was dead. She then told the king, and they went to the vineyard and took possession of it.

3) The shaman then told his new apprentice to join him in an errand for the LORD. They went to the vineyard,

The King Montezuma Trilogy

saw the king, and the shaman said, 'You have killed, and also taken possession? You have sold yourself to do what is evil in the sight of the LORD.' When the king heard these words, he tore his clothes and put sackcloth on his head, and went about dejectedly. Then the LORD told the shaman, 'The king has humbled himself before me. He shall not have disaster visited upon him.'

"There was calm in Mexico for the next three years, then the kings of the Northern and Southern Empires got together for the first time since the division. They discussed the country of Belize, saying, 'Let us take it for the glory of Mexico.' Even though this had little impact on the Northern Empire, it was decided to go to battle. First they inquired of a shaman, who announced, 'Go to Belize and triumph. The LORD will give it into your hands.'

"The kings lived with many superstitions, so they summoned another shaman. When he arrived, he said, 'As the LORD lives, whatever the LORD says to me, that I will speak.' A little while later, the shaman returned and said, 'The LORD has put a lying spirit in the mouth of your shaman. The truth is that the LORD has decreed disaster for you.' The king's shaman slapped the shaman who was summoned and said, 'Who died and put you in charge?' to which he replied, 'You will find out on that day when you have to flee for your life.' The king then ordered this new shaman to be imprisoned until his victory is achieved, to which he replied, 'If you return in peace, then the LORD has not spoken through me.'

"So the two kings went to Belize. The northern king said, 'I will disguise myself and go into battle, but you wear your robes,'

The King Montezuma Trilogy

then the northern king disguised himself and went to fight. Now the king of Belize had commanded his troops to combat with no one except the king, and when they came across the two kings, someone pointed an arrow at the one in his robes. He cried out and they realized he was the wrong king, so they aimed again and shot the northern king. The king struggled for quite a while, but was dead by evening. His body was brought to Monterrey and buried, and his son succeeded him.

"The king of the Southern Empire was thirty-five years old when he began to reign, and he reigned twenty-five years in Tenochtitlan. He walked in the way of this father, by doing what was right in the sight of the LORD. Except that he allowed the worship of gods. The good that he did was to make peace with the king of the Northern Empire, and when he died, he was buried with his ancestors. And his son succeeded him. The king of the Northern Empire reigned for two years, but did evil in the sight of the LORD, and provoked God to anger.

"I could easily be provoked to anger if we don't stop soon for lunch!" quipped Jameson.

"Okay," said Geraldo. "You two have done very well. Let's take a lunch break before I get in trouble."

We hailed a taxi, and asked the driver to take us to his favorite restaurant. The man smiled and said, "I know just where you should go. It's one of the top ten restaurants in the world. It's named Pujol, but you'll never get in."

Jameson said, "The Saint Louis Cardinals first baseman has a restaurant down here?"

"No, no, no," said Geraldo. "But it's pricey. Reservations are needed about five to seven weeks in advance, however I just happen to know the owner. Enrique Olvera is a world-famous chef, and he married one of my nieces."

The King Montezuma Trilogy

As we pulled up to the restaurant, Geraldo went in to see what he could do. It was early for lunch on a week day, so he was hopeful. The taxi driver wasn't, so he happily waited, knowing that the meter was running. After a fairly long time, Geraldo opened a back door and waved us in. I paid the taxi driver, and pretty soon we were seated. Sure, it was next to the bathroom, but we were there.

We all three ordered the tasting menu, consisting of six courses. We started with street snacks, then followed with scallops, softshell crab, chayote squash, duck, grilled fish, mole nuevo, and unpronounceable desserts. We all shared the food, had great drinks, and incredible service. I couldn't believe it when we were done, and saw that it had been three hours. Geraldo made an executive decision to take the rest of the day off, so we taxied back to our hotel and enjoyed the evening.

In the morning, we returned to the zocalo, and I realized that the Templo Mayor archaeological site was beginning to make sense. Frankly, it was hard to imagine much more than a hole in the ground, but the stories Geraldo shared about the capital of the Empire, were starting to come alive. We settled back into a spot, and Geraldo proceeded.

"The next king of the north injured himself, so he inquired of the gods about whether he would recover. The LORD told the southern king's shaman to deliver this message to the northern king: 'Is it because there is no God in Mexico that you are going to inquire of the lesser gods? Here's your answer. You shall not leave the bed to which you have gone, but you shall surely die.' Then the shaman departed.

"The king sent troops after him, but God would not allow them to intervene. More troops were sent, then the LORD told the shaman to not be afraid, but go back with them. When they

The King Montezuma Trilogy

returned, the shaman said to the king, 'Because you have inquired of the lesser gods, you certainly don't believe in the LORD. Therefore, the LORD says as before, you are going to die,' and he died. Having no children, the king's brother succeeded him."

"Remember the shaman's apprentice?" asked Geraldo.

Jameson and I said, "Yes."

Geraldo said, "His name was Elisha, and he was about to become the new shaman, because his mentor was going to die that day. They came to a river, and his mentor took off his sarape. He rolled it up and touched the water, it parted, and the two men crossed on dry ground."

"Sounds familiar," smiled Jameson.

"Which is a sign that something important is going to happen. As they continued walking and talking, a chariot of fire and horses of fire separated the two of them, and Elisha's mentor ascended in a whirlwind into heaven. Elisha then picked up the sarape and touched the water in the river, and again it parted and Elisha went back. He came to a city that had bad water, so he threw salt in it and it became good."

"Again," said Jameson, "this reminds me of Abund, as he wandered in the wilderness."

Geraldo agreed. "I think the author of this story is trying to make those connections. Meanwhile, the kings of the Northern and Southern Empires came together to fight off yet another war. They inquired of Elisha about their possibility of success, and he said, 'The LORD says he will help you in victory.' The enemy approached, but the kings of the Empires took them by surprise and defeated them, so they withdrew from the area and returned to their own land.

"One day when Elisha was passing through a town, he

The King Montezuma Trilogy

heard of a woman in dire need of a son. He prophesied that she would give birth within a year, and it happened. When the child was older, something happened to him and he died. His mother took her son's dead body to where Elisha was, and he found no sound or sign of life. Elisha looked the boy straight in the face, and his eyes opened, then the woman took her son and left.

"Another time a man came to Elisha, bringing twenty tortillas and some grain. Elisha said, 'Give it to the people and let them eat.' But the man said, 'How can I set this paltry amount of food before a hundred people?' Elisha said, 'Because it is what the LORD said to do.' So the man set it before them, they ate, and had some left."

"Wait," said Jameson, "now it's starting to sound like stories from our Caldwellian faith."

"No disagreements from me," announced Geraldo. "After all, the Mexican people are Jim Caldwell's heritage. Now there was a commander of the army of the king of Guatemala. He was in high favor with the king because the LORD helped him to deliver victories."

"Hold on, again," requested Jameson. "Now God is giving victories for the Guatemalans?"

"I know, right?" said Geraldo, "and just when you think you have God figured out. Anyway, the man had a skin disease, and his wife suggested he request a healing from Elisha. The commander agreed to try this, so he traveled to the shaman's home. Elisha told him to go to the nearby stream and wash in it seven times, 'and your flesh will be restored and you will be clean of this disease.' The commander was incensed, saying, 'I thought for sure you would just wave your hand over my skin and it would be healed.' So he turned around and left.

"Those who accompanied him said, 'If the shaman

The King Montezuma Trilogy

commanded you to do something difficult, would you not have done it?' The commander looked a bit embarrassed and said, 'of course.' They said, 'How much more amazing would it be if all you have to do is wash and be cleaned?' The commander agreed with this thought, so he went to the nearby stream, immersed himself in it seven times, and his flesh was restored. The commander returned to Elisha and announced that he had converted to the God of Mexico. Then Elisha's servant decided to try to get something from the commander. He ran after him and asked for money and received it. When he returned, Elisha asked where he had been, and he lied, so Elisha cast the skin disease upon him.

"Now the king of Guatemala was becoming very interested in his victories with the God of Mexico, so he decided to try an attack on the Northern Empire. Elisha got word of this and warned the northern king. When the Guatemalan king discovered his plans were being made known, he became greatly perturbed. He said, 'Who among us is siding with the northern king?' One of his officers said, 'It is the shaman Elisha.' He sent a great army by night and surrounded the city where Elisha stayed.

"Elisha's new attendant rose the next day and saw the army. He told Elisha that he was scared, so Elisha said, 'O LORD, please open his eyes that he may see.' When the servant looked again, he saw chariots of fire all around them. When the army attacked, Elisha prayed that they would be stricken with blindness, and they were. When they regained their sight, they found themselves surrounded by troops of the Northern Empire. The king ordered their execution, but Elisha convinced him to give them food and water and have them return with an amazing story. It was so life-changing, that the

The King Montezuma Trilogy

Guatemalans never again raided into the Empire.

"As for the Southern Empire, the fifth king began his reign. He was thirty-two years old when he became king, and he reigned eight years in Tenochtitlan. And yes. He did what was evil in the sight of the LORD."

"Imagine that!" snarked Jameson.

"When he died, his son succeeded him. He was twenty-two years old when he began to reign, but he only lasted one year. Then the shaman Elisha told his servant to anoint the commander of the army of the Northern Empire as their tenth king. After it was done, the people proclaimed him as their king."

"Wow!" said Jameson. "This is all rather dizzying."

Geraldo said, "I think that's the point, because things were out of control. So the tenth king of the Northern Empire lasted for twenty-eight years, and when he died his son succeeded him. Then something interesting happened in the Southern Empire. Remember that their king only lasted one year, so his mother killed all the remaining male members of the royal family, except for one. The one spared was hidden in a bedroom for six years, while the marauding female killer became queen."

"A female king?" joked Jameson.

I piped up and said, "don't forget that female judge, Debora."

Jameson followed with, "What's this world coming to?"

We all said, "Equality. Hopefully."

After a few smiles, Geraldo continued. "But in the seventh year, the existence of the royal child was made known. The high priest brought the male child out, put the crown on him, and they proclaimed him king. The priest anointed him and the people shouted, 'Long live the king!' When the queen heard the noise, she went there, and saw the king. She cried, 'Treason!' but she was taken outside and put to death. The child king was seven years old when he began to reign, and he served for forty years in Tenochtitlan.

"Back to the north. The eleventh king of the Northern Empire reigned seventeen years, but he was evil. Most importantly, Elisha became sick at that time. The king went to him and wept, then Elisha died and was buried. This eleventh king of the north suffered many problems, but the LORD was gracious to him. Back to the south. The ninth king reigned twenty-nine years in Tenochtitlan and he was twenty-five years old when he began.

"Um," announced Jameson, "I'm a little bored with the king stories."

"So glad you said that," agreed Geraldo. "Let's move on to the impactful stuff. The Northern Empire was in trouble. The Colombians who didn't return to Colombia had settled in the state of Sinaloa. There they became powerful, and during the reign of the sixteenth king, the Colombians demanded money or they would overthrow him. They even fashioned a cart and went to the wealthy to exact money from them. They called it their cart of God, which became known as the cart-el. When everyone complied, they took their booty and returned to Sinaloa, due west of Monterrey.

"Likewise, the twelfth king of the Southern Empire was confronted by the Colombians, who were now working with the Northern Empire. This alliance was surprisingly defeated by the south, but it became known that it was because the king completely submitted to the authority of the Colombians. The king of the Southern Empire went to Monterrey, which means king of the mountain, and saw the cart-el was serving as an

The King Montezuma Trilogy

altar. Everyone knew that offerings were to be made into this cart, and now the kings of both Empires were owned by the leaders of the cart-el.

"The nineteenth king of the Northern Empire became their last king. He chose to be disobedient to the 'cartel,' which is what they now were being called, so he was imprisoned. The cartel then invaded all of the Northern Empire and besieged Monterrey for three years. Totally defeated, the people of the Northern Empire were carried away, and never heard from again. People were brought in to the Northern Empire to resettle it, and the cartel was the new king of the mountain in the capital city of Monterrey.

"Even though the Southern Empire had one of its better kings at this time in history, things were understandably uncomfortable. The king felt the support of the LORD God, so he rebelled against the cartel, which helped for a while, but a new problem was on the horizon. His name was Hernando Cortés de Monroy y Pizarro Altamirano, and he was a Spanish explorer. Cortés first landed in Cuba, with the secret agenda of appropriating new land for the Spanish crown. After gathering a rogue crew of conquistadores, he arrived on the Yucatan peninsula, and started traveling through the region.

"When Cortés arrived in Tenochtitlan, he was initially welcomed by the king who had gotten used to trying to pay people off people to get what he wanted. Cortés had bigger ideas. He surprised everyone by taking the king as a prisoner, and even more surprising when the people of Mexico turned on the king. Together, they plundered Templo Mayor, and ultimately all of the Southern Empire.

"Okay, stop," requested Jameson. "I'm suspicious about surprises. Surely there was some sort of secret to help make

The King Montezuma Trilogy

sense of this loss. Especially considering Mexico was their God-promised land."

Geraldo said, "I seem to recall you asked that question when we first started this tour back at Tikal in Guatemala. So yes, it's called the secret of the empire, but that's for another time. As for now, we have ended the stories from Genesis 12 through 2 Kings from the Aztec Scriptues, with the fall of the Southern Empire. And now it is time for me to ask what you two have learned the past couple of days."

"I was shocked," exclaimed Jameson, "about the intensity of sibling rivalry."

"Say more," requested Geraldo.

"When Montezuma was ready to die, it was time to name his successor, and I kind of side with the oldest brother. Maybe he shouldn't have just declared himself the new king, but it seems to me that Montezuma robbed him of his rightful crown."

"So what's your shock concerning the rivalry?"

"Poor guy had to grovel at his younger brother's feet for a pardon, so I get it when he went behind his brother's back to get their mom on his side."

"Still not getting why you're shocked."

"Because Santiago responded by ordering the death of his brother! I'd call that a pretty shocking rivalry."

"Okay. Thanks Jameson. What about you, dad?"

"Wait a minute, I'm not done with this topic."

"Go ahead."

"When Montezuma was close to the end, he charged his son Santiago to walk in the ways of God. Am I right?"

"You're remembering the stories very well. Yes."

"What I don't understand is that one of the first things he does as the new king is put his brother to death. How is that

The King Montezuma Trilogy

walking in the ways of God?"

"Great question," said Geraldo. "I get a feeling that none of the three of us would say he was following God."

Jameson then asked, "So why did God grant Santiago a wise and discerning mind, just because Santiago was unselfish in his request? Seems like the request was a little late for his brother."

Geraldo agreed and said, "It's very good to ask questions about the Bible. Ultimately, you'll need to find your own answers. Okay, now let's hear from your dad."

"Let me see. I just love sitting here, looking at Templo Mayor, or at least its ruins. And I had never picked up on the idea that Montezuma couldn't build it because he was too busy fighting wars. I always thought it was because of his infidelity."

"Or at least," suggested Geraldo, "that's how the author of this book in the Aztec Scriptures chose to report it."

I then continued, "Your bringing the stories alive through storytelling has really brought out for me the boldness of the shamans. I still can't believe a shaman from the south went to the north and demanded they tear down their altars. Another pronounced a drought on the land. At least that time he was so bold that the LORD told him to get out of there. Then when the LORD told him to return, the northern king called him a trouble maker, and he brilliantly said, 'It is not I who has brought trouble, it is you.' I know places around the world today that would not take kindly to this sort of self-reflection. One other thing. I never caught the fact that when Elisha was chosen to replace the current shaman, he said, 'Let me kiss my father and my mother, and then I will follow you.'"

"And your point, dad?"

"Sounds like a story from Jim Caldwell, when he asked

The King Montezuma Trilogy

people to follow him, and one said, 'I will follow you, Lord; but let me first say farewell to those at my home."

"Ooh. Good pick, dad! Here's something else I noticed. Santiago had a weakness for foreign women."

"Not sure where you're going with that one, son."

"Mom is of Mayan descent, so I'm sure you can relate!"

"Pretty good," laughed Geraldo. "Anything else?"

Continuing on a lighter note, Jameson said, "I get a feeling from these stories that it's not good to do…"

The other two joined him in saying, "…what's evil in the sight of the LORD!"

After we all had a good laugh, I brought us back to a serious note. "It really bothered me that Elisha seemed to need to do so many miracles. I grew up on the idea of letting your actions speak louder than your words, but few people can perform miracles. On the good side, I was delighted that the Southern Empire had a queen. Sure, she was evil, but the way we demean women today is evil, too."

"Here's one last thing I learned," announced Jameson. "God's promised land of Mexico had way more battles than realized. Oh, and thanks for not going through all the kings of the Northern and Southern Empires."

"Thanks for requesting," said Geraldo. "It's time to get back to the hotel, so you two can get ready for your flight home tomorrow."

Frankly, we didn't want to leave. It had been an experience beyond anything we could have hoped for, so I started thinking. Perhaps I'll figure out some way to bring the stories of the shamans alive. Come to think of it, Jameson keeps asking about the secret of the empire, so why did the Southern Empire fold so easily to the Spanish Conquistadors? I think my next trip

The King Montezuma Trilogy

will be a time to look more closely at the shamans, and see if we can come up with an answer.

As for now, I couldn't help but think about our incoming flight to Mexico City, on our way to Guatemala. We came in for a landing hot and sideways, and sometimes God's Word does that to the reader. Along about the time you think you understand God, you find yourself looking ahead at the runway and realize you're seeing things from the wrong viewpoint. It also crossed my mind that our plane lurched back into position when the tires gripped the tarmac. This trip lurched me into better understandings of Scripture, from gripping the fascinating experience of being there. The journey proved to be memorable, and now I can't stop thinking about that secret.

Perhaps I'll start planning that next trip as soon as we get home.

The King Montezuma Trilogy

THE SECRET OF THE EMPIRE
A King Montezuma Story – Book 2

The King Montezuma Trilogy

PREFACE
A Border Crossing

    The front door suddenly swung open, and there stood our son Jameson, fresh home from his first year of college. "Long time, no see!" I said with my usual silly flair. "Dad! Arizona State is only a few miles away," Jameson volleyed back in his equally teasing way. He really was a chip off the old block, so it was good to have him home for the summer. He was serious about staying away most of his first year, so he could focus on his studies, but we at least kept in touch every week. We were quite close, though truth be known, he was closer to his mother. The Mexican culture puts family first, and I often put wo rk first.

    "Hijo!" screamed his mother, as she came running to greet him. I could see tears falling from her eyes as they hugged, and it rather choked me up, too. Soon we settled into the kitchen and chatted while she cooked some tortillas on the placa. The aroma immediately got the hunger pangs stirring, so we nibbled on some fresh fruit and Oaxaca cheese. Mom learned her cooking skills from her mother, and Jameson was so spoiled on his mother's food that he hated all the Mexican restaurants in town. He always said that nothing compared to Mom's food. When dinner was served, the conversation steered toward Jameson and he excitedly shared about his most recent class.

    The religion course was livelier than I could have expected, after touring Mexico with you last summer, Dad." It did my heart good to know it had been worthwhile. It was his eighteenth birthday present from me and his mother, and we all knew it was as much for me as it was for him. "The class was 'The Pentateuch and the Deuteronomistic History,' and everything

The King Montezuma Trilogy

the professor talked about became more than words on paper. I couldn't believe how powerfully the stories came alive from having been there. I could see the sights, and hear the sounds, and smell the aromas as the text was discussed.

"Anyway, I was thinking." About that time his mother folded her arms and had a small scowl on her face. She usually was one step ahead of us, and once again she was right. "To begin my second year of college, I would love to take a class on the Prophecies of the Shamans. So, if there is any chance at all, I would love to return to Mexico this summer with you, Dad, and experience the context of those books."

Mom unfolded her arms and surprised us by saying, "Only if I can join you."

Jameson and I looked at each other and were beyond delighted, so I said, "Let me think about how we might make this thing happen, not to mention the cost involved." As a High School history teacher in the inner city of Phoenix, I never made much money, but had the summers off. My wife is a Social Worker for the Poor People's Campaign, and both of our jobs were influenced by the ethical teachings of Jim Caldwell.

As I prepared for the trip, I made a phone call to Geraldo, the tour guide from last year's trip. He couldn't help us because he recently broke his foot in a farming mishap, but he gave me some great advice. When I told him what we wanted to do, he said, "The shamans prophesied from Tenochtitlan in the Southern Empire, and Monterrey in the Northern Empire. Since you've been to Tenochtitlan, you can talk about those prophecies without returning there, so I would recommend traveling to Monterrey and sharing from that context."

Geraldo had been a great asset, so I really had to think about a trip without him. I was quite familiar with the prophecies,

The King Montezuma Trilogy

so I decided to spend some time at the library and polish up on my understandings. When I told Jameson the news about Geraldo, and that I was planning on being the guide this time, he said, "Dad, you don't look Mexican enough." His wry smile set me at ease that he was happy with the plan, and having his mother with us would be a wonderful benefit in many ways. After thinking about the cost, I decided to drive there and see if we could keep the trip down to two weeks or less.

My wife had plenty of paid time off piled up, so she put in her request for some vacation time and got approved. We spent the next several days packing and buying a few snack items. Well, actually, I used that time to do a little more study at the library. My wife seems to think that I always have something to do instead of help with chores. Soon after we were married, I did some laundry and ruined her expensive cashmere sweater, which resulted in my being banned from doing laundry. I also cooked her an omelette one morning and creatively added vanilla extract, resulting in my being expelled from cooking duties. One can always hope for more disqualifications.

We packed the car and headed out early the following morning. We had a nineteen-hour drive ahead of us, so we planned to get halfway on the first day, stopping at Fort Stockton, Texas.

"So, what way are we going, Dad?" Jameson inquired from the back seat.

"Thought we'd take I-10 all the way to Fort Stockton."

Jameson quickly pulled out his phone and opened the 'maps' ap. "So, we won't be doing the border crossing at El Paso?"

"No. I've always wanted to see southern Texas."

"So, are we going to cross at Ciudad Acuña?"

The King Montezuma Trilogy

"No, again. I want to follow along the Rio Grande, then cross the border at Laredo, Texas." Jameson seemed content with the plan, so he settled in to enjoy his phone as we first headed to Tucson. I glanced over at my wife in the passenger seat, and my heart was full, because I was so happy to have her join us. Her given name is Solana, meaning sunshine, but she always went by 'Sol.' She certainly was my heart and soul, and we did some enjoyable reminiscing as we traveled through southeastern Arizona.

When we passed by the turn to Tombstone, she said, "Remember that family trip to see some of the history from our Caldwellian faith?"

"I do," said a cheery Jameson. "Pretty cool to see where Wyatt Earp and Doc Holliday took on the Clanton Gang at the O.K. Corral. Was that before Wyatt was called up to Phoenix to arrest Jim Caldwell or after?"

"After," Sol and I said in harmony.

"On that trip," said Sol, "we also visited the little mining town of Bisbee. That's where my ancestors arrived in the United States to work the copper mines, after leaving Oaxaca, Mexico."

"I loved the train ride into the Copper Queen Mine," said Jameson. "I can't believe they used to mine by candlelight!"

"They were a hearty group, for sure," I said. Before long we crossed the state line into New Mexico and finally stopped in El Paso for lunch. We wanted some Mexican food and hoped that being so close to Mexico we might find something good. We passed dozens of possibilities on the I-10 corridor through the middle of the city, but finally chose Taquizas Los Pistoleros. We discovered that if you pull up to a restaurant, and find all out of license plates on the cars are out of state, you should just keep going. But if you find all local plates, the food will probably be

The King Montezuma Trilogy

good. Something seemed strange when we stopped, then Jameson laughed and announced that it was a catering service only.

Not just a little bit frustrated, we continued, and next found Julio's Mexican Food. Couldn't possibly be as good as Sol's, but we were hungry and ready to eat. The menu looked great, so we were hopeful. I ordered Chicken Tampiquena, Sol ordered Chiles Rellenos, and Jameson ordered Julio's Mexican Plate. When the food came out, Sol did her usual thing of spreading the food around and lightly sampling from the interior. To our great surprise, she smiled and said, "Not bad." Don't get me wrong, that in no way implies it was good. It just meant that it was edible. Meanwhile, Jameson and I loved our orders.

After leaving El Paso, the interstate paralleled the Rio Grande for a while, then turned east. Fort Stockton didn't come soon enough, because we were getting tired of traveling, and checked into the Fairfield Inn & Suites. Since Fort Stockton was a small town, the prices were very reasonable, and the accommodations were pleasant. We like staying at the Marriott Bonvoy brand of hotels when traveling, and when one is available. In the morning, we enjoyed the free hot breakfast buffet, then checked out and loaded up the car. Jameson asked if he could drive, so I looked at Sol, who agreed. She then volunteered to sit in the back, and we were on our way.

The I-10 interstate continued on to San Antonio from historic Fort Stockton, but we angled south onto US 285. I would have loved to pay a visit to San Antonio, since I've never been there, but this wasn't the time. Jameson did a great job of driving, so we passed on through the Ciudad Acuña area and had lunch at Eagle Pass, just across the river from Piedras Negras. It ended up being a good call to wait so long for lunch,

The King Montezuma Trilogy

because the border crossing at Laredo proved to be more challenging than I would have preferred.

Jameson eased our SUV up to the Columbia Bridge crossing, because it accesses the divided, multi-lane Monterrey Highway. This is the fastest of the five Ports of Entry, one of which is a railroad crossing. Traffic was moving through quite well, considering other crossings can take an hour or two. When it was our turn, Jameson put the window down and gave a nice greeting. The border agent asked, "Do you have any weapons?" and to my utter shock and disbelief, Jameson said, "Yes." Before the agent could say anything, I nearly yelled, "What are you talking about?" Jameson explained, "You have a pocketknife to cut salami and cheese during our trip."

I put my head down and shook it back and forth as the agent asked, "And who's in the backseat?" I responded, "That's my wife, Sol." That seemed to be sufficient to detain us. He asked Jameson to pull the car over to a parking spot ahead on the left, then told us to get out of the car and sit on the bench. It was all very disturbing, as another agent approached and told us to get out our passports and driver's licenses. He then opened the back of our car and pulled out all three suitcases, leaving the three carry ons in place. As he started going through our luggage, another agent came up to us and asked for our passports. When he walked over to a building with them in hand, that sinking feeling in the pit of my stomach started. I couldn't help but think that if the person in the backseat was another white male, this wouldn't be happening.

We nervously sat there for about twenty minutes, feeling rather violated, particularly because there was nothing we could do. Sol suggested it was a bad idea for her to come, and I quickly put that thought to rest. The agent rummaging through

The King Montezuma Trilogy

our belongings put them back in the trunk and closed it. Soon after that, the agent with our passports returned them and said, "You're good to go."

We got back in the car, and Jameson announced that he didn't feel much like driving. I took over, and we finally continued our journey. Sol hoped this wasn't a harbinger of things to come, so she said, "My culture certainly has its share of superstitions. I'm praying things start going better." Meanwhile, Jameson settled into the back seat and wrapped his mind around being busy on his phone. The final leg of this trip was a little over three hours, and it went uneventfully. We pulled into town just before dark and checked into Quinta Real Monterrey.

All three of us were amazed at the beauty of the hotel, and Jameson quickly retorted, "Hey Mom, you should've seen some of the dumps Geraldo had us stay in last year."

As I laughed, to make sure Sol knew it was a joke, I realized this place really was magnificent, and I couldn't believe the great price. Once we got to our room, we quickly settled in, then went downstairs for dinner. After the meal, I said, "It's been a great day."

"You enjoyed the border crossing?" asked Sol.

"Sorry, you're right. Let's just get a good night's sleep, so we're ready to begin hearing about the prophetic books of the shamans."

The King Montezuma Trilogy

ACT I
Before the Exile

The King Montezuma Trilogy

SCENE ONE
Isaiah 1-39

It was an absolutely glorious morning in Monterrey. The sun glinted off the Sierra Madre Oriental Mountains, as we were getting ready to begin this new experience. I was pleased to find that despite Monterrey being one of the largest cities in Mexico, it was also considered one of the safest. It seemed like everyone we passed by had a friendly greeting, which added to our feeling of comfort. After checking with the concierge for a good spot to talk, we headed to the downtown Macroplaza. It had plenty of green space, fountains, gardens, benches, and museums, with City Hall on one end and the Governor's Palace on the other. We chose a great spot, with spectacular views of the mountains, and I was hoping Jameson and Sol were excited to get started. I stepped out in front of the two of them sitting on the wood and iron bench, and opened my copy of the Aztec Scriptures.

"Really, Dad?"

I asked him, "What?"

"Geraldo never had to open the scriptures. He just told the stories."

I was a bit flustered because I wasn't sure if Jameson was teasing, so I simply continued. "This is not where Isaiah prophesied." That got their attention. "He was a shaman from the capital city of Tenochtitlan, and he was prophesying to the king of the Southern Empire."

"So why aren't we there?" Jameson asked, but quickly realized that last year's trip brought the context of the Southern Empire alive, so we didn't need to revisit. Then he said, "But I

The King Montezuma Trilogy

feel bad for Mom, since she wasn't with us."

"Mi hijo," spoke up Sol. "What you don't know is that I was there several times through my childhood, and I am very well acquainted with what it is like."

Jameson looked surprised and asked, "Did you see the ruins of Templo Mayor in the middle of Mexico City?"

"Of course, now let's listen to your father."

"The first thing to understand about the prophecies of Isaiah is that the scriptures we have today are edited. Actually, the book of Isaiah is a combination of three different shamans over two hundred years of time. The first thirty-nine chapters are called First Isaiah, and they take place before the exile. Chapters 40-55 share stories from the exile, and 56-66 take place after the exile. That is critically important to properly understand the prophecies of the shamans. Also, these prophecies can be referred to as oracles.

"So, imagine Isaiah standing before the king in front of the Templo Mayor, when he delivers this word from God. Since Isaiah was a local shaman, the king knew him and was ready to listen. Isaiah took something from his pocket and chewed on it, then went into a trance and shared the vision that came to him. It was not one the king wanted to hear, because it was about God taking the Southern Empire to court. Here's how the oracle went:

'The LORD said, I reared children and brought them up, but they have rebelled against me. Mexico does not know me. My people do not understand me. They are a sinful nation, laden with iniquity. They despise me! Remove the evil of your doings from before my eyes. Cease to do evil, learn to do good, seek justice, rescue the oppressed, defend the orphan, and plead for the widow. If you refuse and rebel, you shall be devoured by the

The King Montezuma Trilogy

sword; for the mouth of the LORD has spoken.'

"The shaman continued in a rather unexpected way. The vision became a lament for a while, then he offered a promise of restoration: 'Therefore says the Sovereign, the LORD of hosts, the Mighty One; I will pour out my wrath on my enemies. I will turn my hand against you. Then I will purify you with fire. And I will restore your judges as at the first, and your counselors as at the beginning. Afterward you shall be called the city of righteousness, the faithful city.'"

"Wow!" exclaimed Jameson. "I wonder how the king and his people took that."

"We'll never know for sure," I said. "It was great being at Templo Mayor, to get the context of the environment, but we don't know how the people responded. We can guess, and that's part of what Bible Study is all about. So, what's your guess?"

Jameson was the first to respond, saying, "It was a good news, bad news oracle. I guess the people responded out of their own context. If they were having problems, they probably heard the bad news, while those not having difficulties probably paid more attention to the good news."

"I'm impressed, Jameson," added Sol, "but I personally suspect that the Mexican culture would tend to notice the bad news. That's just me speaking, as a Mexican living in America, so take it for what it's worth."

Jameson laughed and said, "Ah, yes. And I notice your 'suspecting' is suspiciously like suspicion. I suppose you can take the Mexican out of Mexico, but you can't take Mexico out of the Mexican."

"Of course," said Sol, "I was born in the United States, making me Mexican-American, but I appreciate the sentiment."

The King Montezuma Trilogy

I said, "We don't know how much later it was before Isaiah offered his next oracle, but it was a vision of the near future. That makes me think they might have been more intrigued with the good news. Anyway, there's a verse in the second chapter of Isaiah that became so famous, it was included on a sculpture that was given to the United Nations by the USSR on December 4th, 1959:

> 'they shall beat their swords into plowshares,
> and their spears into pruning hooks;
> nation shall not lift up sword against nation,
> neither shall they learn war any more.'

"So that's where that came from!" exclaimed Jameson, with a raised eyebrow and a grin of learning something new.

"The rest of the chapter was about judgment against arrogance. This oracle was undoubtedly received well because it was against the Northern Empire."

Even Sol laughed at that one, then said, "You might speak lower, since we are currently in what was the Northern Empire."

Looking around with that realization, I soon calmed myself and said, "Not to worry. The next chapter returns to judgment against the Southern Empire. That oracle personifies the capital city of Tenochtitlan as a woman. Here's an example: 'Instead of perfume there will be a stench; and instead of a sash, a rope; and instead of lovely hair, baldness; and instead of a rich robe, a binding of sackcloth; instead of beauty, shame.'"

"That sounds horrible," complained Sol. "What does it mean?"

"It was a cultural nod back then to women and their role in mourning, while using them as a metaphor for condemnation.

The King Montezuma Trilogy

Then there's a series of oracles denouncing social injustice. The first lament is over those who amass wealth at the expense of others. The second one is about drunkenness and the third is about persistent sinners and skeptics. The fourth is about fake news." Jameson complained that I was going too fast, then requested a sample. I opened my Bible and read Isaiah 5:20: 'Ah, you who call evil good and good evil, who put darkness for light and light for darkness, who put bitter for sweet and sweet for bitter!'"

After quick nods from both Jameson and Sol, I continued. "Just two more laments. The fifth is about self-righteousness: 'Ah, you who are wise in your own eyes, and shrewd in your own sight!'

"I had a professor like that this past year," said Jameson with a frown.

"The sixth is about drunkenness and the perversion of justice: 'Ah, you who are heroes in drinking wine and valiant at mixing drink, who acquit the guilty for a bribe, and deprive the innocent of their rights!'"

"I ran into a few college students like that, too," said Jameson.

"Stay away from them," counseled Sol, and I mentioned that you can find those types anywhere.

"Interestingly, the next chapter is a flashback to Isaiah's call to be a prophetic shaman. He saw the LORD in the Templo Mayor and said, 'Woe is me! I am lost, for I am a man of unclean lips; yet I have seen the LORD of hosts! Then a supernatural being touched my mouth with a burning coal and said, "Your guilt has departed and your sin is blotted out." Then I heard the voice of the Lord saying, "Whom shall I send?" And I said, here am I; send me!'"

The King Montezuma Trilogy

"So that's where the song comes from," smiled Jameson.

"The next chapter has a great illustration of the challenge of hearing prophecies today. Let me just read it. 'Therefore the Lord himself will give you a sign. Look, the young woman is with child and shall bear a son, and shall name him Manuel.'"

"Hey, that's familiar!" testified Jameson. "Our pastor always read it at Christmas because it's a prophecy about the advent of Jim Caldwell, who was God with us."

"Okay, let's look at that. First of all, prophecies were always offered about the near future. If the vision is about war, it would be difficult to get the people concerned about something that was hundreds of years away."

"Okay. So far I'm following you," said Jameson, but Sol folded her arms as if to say she was closed to my thoughts.

"This prophecy is about war, and remember what I said about the importance of context. The king of the Southern Empire experienced an attempted attack on Tenochtitlan by the king of the Northern Empire and the king of Guatemala. Even though it was thwarted, it left the king and his empire in fear. That's when the LORD sent Isaiah to say to the southern king, 'Do not fear, and do not let your heart be troubled. If you do not stand firm in faith, you shall not stand at all.'

"Then the LORD spoke to the southern king, saying 'Ask a sign of the LORD your God.' But the king said, 'I will not ask, and I will not put the LORD to the test.' Then Isaiah said, 'Is it too little for you to weary mortals, that you weary my God also? Therefore the Lord himself will give you a sign. Look, the young woman is with child and shall bear a son, and shall name him Manuel.'

"Whoa!" said Jameson. "Is that true?"

"It's scripture, and our task is to understand it."

The King Montezuma Trilogy

"So this isn't about Jim Caldwell?" asked Jameson. Sol was beginning to squirm on the bench, but I pressed on.

"That's the great thing. Once we understand the prophecy for who it was spoken to, and what it meant at the time, we can then say, 'Hey! I can also learn something about Jim Caldwell.' The point is, we must not ignore its original meaning. Here's the most important thing I'm going to say on this whole trip."

> The Caldwellian Scriptures
> (known as the New Testament)
> can learn from the Aztec Scriptures
> (known as the Old Testament),
> but
> the Old Testament
> can't learn from the New Testament.

"Break time," requested Jameson. "I'm going to need to think about that one for a while."

We agreed, and headed off for a little stroll. The Macroplaza, or La Gran Plaza, is the fifth largest plaza in the world. We soon came to a spectacular fountain and decided to settle in there to hear more.

"Honestly, Dad. I'm struggling with the last idea."

"Let me put it this way. The present can learn from the past, but the past can't learn from the present."

"I think that's better, but I'm still going to need more time to think."

"Try this. When it comes to the first part, about the present learning from the past, Winston Churchill said it best. 'Those who fail to learn from history are doomed to repeat it.'

"So why is it bad to see Isaiah's prophecy being about Jim

The King Montezuma Trilogy

Caldwell?"

"It isn't. As long as we first acknowledge that we have learned what it meant in its historical setting, and then learn how we might use it for fresh understandings in the New Testament."

"Then what about the second part, that the past can't learn from the present?"

"That's akin to fortune telling. The prophets were simply sharing about the near future. That a young woman would soon bear a child, who would signify God's presence, which was meant to convince the king that God was with the Southern Kingdom and Tenochtitlan. There was no implication about a future child named Jim Caldwell."

"But then we can say, 'Wow, Jim Caldwell was like that too, because he signifies God's presence in our life. Right?" asked Jameson.

"I think you've got it. What do you think, Sol?"

"I'm where Jameson was earlier, when he said he needed to think about it for a while."

"Fair enough. Are we ready to continue?" They nodded their heads, and I started into another misunderstood prophecy, hoping I had set the stage properly. "I'm sure this one is familiar, from the second verse of Isaiah 9:

> The people who walked in darkness
> have seen a great light;
> those who lived in a land of deep darkness—
> on them light has shined.

"So, that's not about Jim Caldwell either?" asked Jameson with a bit of intrigue, mixed with a minor sense of loss.

"The Caldwellian tradition sees it as a description of the

The King Montezuma Trilogy

coming Messiah, but actually it is a celebration of the coronation of a new king of the Southern Empire. It was particularly hopeful because the Northern Empire had already been overthrown, and the people needed a good word. Isaiah comes along and offers the positive idea that this new king would have a glorious reign, and the two empires would reunite."

"So, if it's okay to learn from the Old Testament, how was Jim Caldwell similar to that verse?" inquired my properly inquisitive son.

"Great question! In my opinion, the Wild West that Jim Caldwell came to in 1881 was full of darkness. It had constant Indian raids, rampant gambling, alcoholism, prostitution, and of course, the Russian Invasion. The good news that Jim Caldwell brought was that we could love one another in spite of the challenges all around. His stories and miracles became a light that shined in the darkness."

Sol spoke up at that point, saying, "I'm still thinking about all of this, but most importantly I am beginning to see that this new way of understanding prophecy could enhance my belief."

I've got to admit, I was glad to hear that. Sol had been so kind to let us go to Mexico last year, and it is great having her with us now, so I relaxed a bit as I continued. "Just a few verses later, in verse six, we get another example of how Caldwellians have misappropriated an ancient text:

> For a child has been born for us,
> a son given to us;
> authority rests upon his shoulders;
> and he is named
> Wonderful Counselor, Mighty God,
> Everlasting Father, Prince of Peace.

The King Montezuma Trilogy

"Don't take that away from me!" announced Sol with furrowed eyebrows. "Jim was born for us, was given to us, has authority, and lived like those titles. And that ends it."

Maybe it was time for me to soften things. Sol was raised in the Catholic faith, then became an evangelistic Caldwellian, and knows her Bible. "I'm not trying to take anything from you. It is fine to hold on to your understandings. The purpose of this trip is to see the places where the shamans delivered their oracles and appreciate what they meant then. Let me repeat. We can learn from the Old Testament. It is fine to say that Jim Caldwell was just like that ancient oracle."

"Don't sugar coat it, Dad. Remind us what it is that's not fine to do."

Sol remained quite emphatic that she wanted this prophecy to be about Jim, so I proceeded, well, how shall we say it? Lovingly. "The past doesn't know the future any more than we do." I looked at my wife and said, "Honey, just let the Holy Bible say what it means."

"Still going to need some time," Sol said earnestly.

"That's fine."

"So," asked Jameson, "what does Isaiah 9:6 mean?"

"Back then the people believed that the king was reborn as God's son at the time of his coronation. Wonderful Counselor, and the other names, were titles given to the king of Guatemala at his coronation, so Isaiah appropriated those titles. This verse is an ecstatic celebration of hope in difficult times. Isaiah went on to describe the destruction of the Northern Kingdom, as a warning that the Southern Kingdom needed to change its ways." Jameson looked happy, but Sol didn't. I had to accept that not everyone likes serious bible study. Taking scripture at surface level is much easer.

The King Montezuma Trilogy

"Isaiah went on with an oracle against Colombia. Here's an example: 'When the Lord has finished all his work on Tenochtitlan, he will punish the arrogant boasting of the king of Colombia and his haughty pride.' He then shares a promise that a remnant of the people of the Northern Kingdom will be saved. After that, he shares an oracle about what the ideal king would be like:

> A shoot shall come out from the stump of King
>   Montezuma, and a branch shall grow out of his roots.
> The spirit of the LORD shall rest on him,
>   the spirit of wisdom and understanding,
>   the spirit of counsel and might,
>   the spirit of knowledge, and the fear of the LORD,
>   which shall be his delight.

"See!" Sol said with a smile. "Jim's ancestor was King Montezuma."

"Yes!" I said with a similar smile. "We can learn from the Old Testament. That's great. So what do you think Isaiah was meaning for the people of his time?"

"You already told us, Dad. He painted a picture of what a great king would be like."

"Thanks, Jameson. I think the ideal king was Montezuma's son. Then, in 11:6, Isaiah paints a picture of what peace and harmony would like, once an ideal king was crowned:

> The wolf shall live with the lamb,
>   the coyote shall lie down with pups,
> the calf and the mountain lion will be together,
>   and a little child will lead them.

The King Montezuma Trilogy

"Yes", said Sol, "and the little child became Jim Caldwell."

"And just maybe," I said softly, "this oracle could be about hope in a king at that particular time. Of course we see the ideal way things could have worked out for Jim, but they didn't. The sheriff and Russian overlord won with their evil."

"And Jim taught us to be peacemakers," responded Sol.

"Okay," I suggested, "maybe we're ready for lunch."

Jameson immediately spoke up and said, "I was checking on Tripadvisor this morning and found a great spot. Fonda El Limoncito. Travelers say the food is delicious, the place is comfortable, the service is impeccable, and Chef Juan Pablo even comes out to greet his customers."

"Okay," announced Sol, "but how far away?"

"That's the best thing! It's only about three blocks away," said Jameson with a huge smile.

We set off for a pleasant walk, but it turned out to be more than three blocks, because we were quite a bit north in the Macroplaza. First we passed the Faro de Comercio monument, then angled through several busy city streets before getting there. It was in a century-old house, with bare stone walls and a tall ceiling, in the heart of the Old Town. To say the least, we had a great experience, and sure enough the happy Chef passed by with a friendly welcome. On the way out, I was anxious to hear what Sol thought, and was delightfully surprised when she said it was reminiscent of her mother's home cooking.

The weather was a stunning 77 degrees, and no wind. For the afternoon we settled in across the street from the Archdiocese of Monterrey Catholic Church, mainly because there was a public restroom nearby. After the c-section birth of Jameson, Sol had a prolapsed bladder and needed bathroom breaks more often. I stepped out in front of them, and began.

The King Montezuma Trilogy

"The next eleven chapters of Isaiah consists of oracles against the countries that fought wars with Mexico, but I want to deal with chapter 14. It has another one of those highly misunderstood verses. Its verse 12, and here it is: "How you are fallen from heaven, O Day Star, son of Dawn!"

Sol had a rather visceral reaction to this verse. Her arms quickly went back to a folded position, and her whole body screamed of a lack of interest. She finally spoke up, saying, "Why would you want to talk about the devil?" Talk about thin ice. I'd never really shared any of my biblical understandings with Sol before, but I guessed her Catholic background was speaking louder than me.

Jameson was understandably intrigued, so I proceeded carefully. Admittedly, I felt about as clumsy as a bull trying to make its way through a china shop. "When the Caldwellian Scriptures were translated into Spanish, this verse used the word '*angel caido*,' for 'fallen from heaven,' meaning fallen angel. What's worse is when 'Day Star' was translated into Spanish it became '*lucifero*,' meaning light-bearer. Soon after that, Caldwellian fantasy ran wild about a 'Lucifer' falling from heaven."

"That's because we know our Holy Scriptures," scowled Sol. She then grabbed my Bible and turned to Revelation 12:7-9 and read, 'And war broke out in heaven; Michael and his angels fought against the dragon. The dragon and his angels fought back, but they were defeated, and there was no longer any place for them in heaven. The great dragon was thrown down, that ancient serpent, who is called the Devil and Satan, the deceiver of the whole world—he was thrown down to the earth, and his angels were thrown down with him.'" She then slapped the book back into my hands in a triumphant gesture.

The King Montezuma Trilogy

"Okay, yet again, let me say that I'm not trying to change your understandings of the Bible. I'm just giving you possibilities to consider." I then cupped my hand to target my voice to Jameson and whispered, "Not very considerate if you ask me." Without hesitation she responded, "I heard that!" I wasn't sure how to proceed at that point, because I love studying the book of Revelation, but the focus of the trip was to hear the prophets in their context.

"Let me take a moment to say what I think Isaiah 14:12 was about. No matter how much one might want that verse to be about Lucifer falling from heaven, it simply wasn't, for two reasons. First, remember that the Old Testament can't learn from the New Testament. Second, let Isaiah speak for himself, because he tells us who this verse is about. Verse 4 says 'You will take up this taunt against the king of Spain.' See. It's not about Lucifer at all. God gave this oracle to Isaiah about the downfall of the King of Spain. The place where God's children were treated so poorly, before they escaped and began their journey to the Promised Land. Verse 12 was almost like a laughter about how far the King had fallen from his heavenly heights of power."

"Wow!" exclaimed Jameson. "I love that."

Sol wasn't affected quite the same way, but I went on. "The oracles from Isaiah came in fast and furious after that. He pronounced prophecies against Belize, Honduras, El Salvador, Nicaragua, Costa Rica, Panama, and Colombia, ending with a warning of destruction of Tenochtitlan. That last oracle was spoken to the people of the Southern Empire. The caution was about being sure the people didn't get too happy, because their exultation could be premature. That twenty-second chapter ends with a denunciation of ego: 'On that day, says the LORD

The King Montezuma Trilogy

of hosts, the peg that was fastened in a secure place will give way; it will be cut down and fall, and the load that was on it will perish, for the LORD has spoken.'

"Chapters 24-27 contain what is known as 'The Isaiah Apocalypse.' The material is very different, because it is not a prophetic speech. The lengthy oracles against nations that just concluded, give way to announcements about the whole earth and all who live in it. It is a proclamation of the final drama of history, dealing with the last things. People who study the Bible are beginning to see that it isn't an apocalypse in the truest sense. It doesn't give a detailed revelation of the future. In my opinion, the difference between prophecy and apocalypse is that prophecy is about the near future, and apocalypse is about the distant future. They are similar in that they both concern revelation from God."

"How do you know so much?" asked Jameson.

"I love the Bible and I love to study. That said, please remember that I'm no expert. These are thoughts from scholars, put in the best way I know how." I then opened my copy of the Bible and said, "Here's some thoughts that Isaiah shared:

- See, the LORD is going to lay waste the earth and devastate it; he will ruin its face and scatter its inhabitants...The earth will be completely laid waste and totally plundered. The LORD has spoken this word.—Isaiah 24:1, 3.
- On this mountain he will destroy the shroud that enfolds all peoples, the sheet that covers all nations; he will swallow up death forever. The Sovereign LORD will wipe away the tears from all faces; he will remove the disgrace of his people from all the earth.

The King Montezuma Trilogy

The LORD has spoken.—Isaiah 25:7-8.
- Open the gates that the righteous nation may enter, the nation that keeps faith.—Isaiah 26:2.
- In days to come the Southern Empire shall take root, the Northern Empire shall blossom and put forth shoots, and fill the whole world with fruit.—Isaiah 27:6.

"It does seem a bit disjointed," Jameson observed.

"I liked it," added Sol.

I announced that I was ready to move on to chapters 28-33, and having no objections, I started. "This is really the final section of First Isaiah. It leads up to the time of the fall of the Southern Empire to Cortés and the Spanish Conquistadors, but begins with an oracle about the fall of the Northern Empire. Verse 7 basically says that the South needs to learn from the North. Isaiah castigates the priests and prophets who 'reel with strong drink,' and scolds them with, 'they err in vision, they stumble in giving judgment.'

"Isaiah goes on in the 16th verse to give hope to the Southern Empire: 'therefore thus says the Lord GOD, See I am laying in Tenochtitlan a foundation stone, a tested stone, a precious cornerstone, a sure foundation: "One who trusts will not panic."' Chapter 29 describes the siege of Tenochtitlan. He says that God will encamp against them, just as King Montezuma originally did to capture the city."

"Okay," said a frustrated Jameson, "I'm lost. Is this oracle about hope or despair?"

I said, "Yes. The despair is about the overthrow of Tenochtitlan, and the hope is about its ultimate salvation."

Sol spoke up at that point and said, "Sounds like Good

The King Montezuma Trilogy

Friday and Easter."

"Thanks," I said. "I kind of like that. It even fits with verse 18, 'On that day the deaf shall hear the words of a scroll, and out of their gloom and darkness the eyes of the blind shall see.'"

Sol then said, "Sounds like the Old Testament was learning from the New Testament." Her arms were again folded and a mild scowl crept across her face.

"I know what you mean, honey, and you may be teaching me something here. Let's go on."

"Okay," said Jameson, "but I hope this gets less tedious."

At first I was offended, then I decided to try to learn something from my son. "In what way is it tedious?"

"Probably because Geraldo just told the stories."

"Good point. The difference might be that the first part of the Aztec Scriptures is simply stories. So now I'm trying to think about why the prophetic stories aren't the same." I paused for a while and saw blank stares from Jameson and Sol. "Maybe it's because I'm explaining them, while Geraldo told them." Jameson then suggested that I quit explaining them, and just let the stories speak for themselves. It took me a while to respond to that one, but I finally spoke up and said, "I'll try, but to be honest, explanation is sometimes needed to keep the story from being misunderstood. The good thing is that the other prophets aren't as long as Isaiah."

"I agree," said Jameson, and Sol almost simultaneously said, "that's a very good thing." Jameson and Sol smiled at each other and winked.

"Then let me wrap up this first part of Isaiah as fast as I can. As the story goes," I said with a mild smirk of my own, "Isaiah warned the Southern Empire not to work with Guatemala to fight off Colombia."

The King Montezuma Trilogy

"Why?" inquired Jameson.

"Because it would be the LORD who would deliver Tenochtitlan from a Colombian attack. After that, a king would arise and reign in righteousness. The prophecy then closes with an oracle against Colombia."

"Wait," announced Jameson. "What chapter is that?"

"Good catch. It's only chapter 33. Chapters 34-39 have long been debated by biblical scholars, and many believe they are sufficiently different from First Isaiah."

"In what way?" asked Sol. I was surprised but pleased with her question.

"It's in both style and substance."

"How can that be?" she continued.

"Okay. Here's a big picture of the Aztec Scriptures. It all started with the stories of Aapo and Abund being told from generation to generation. After Geovanni led God's people out of Guatemala and into the Promised Land of Mexico, the verbal Aztec language learned writing. The stories were written down and edited, to get to the Old Testament we know today. My point is that Chapters 34-39 appear to be later edited additions, so I'm just going skip to them." I was mildly surprised when they had no problems with my plan, so I happily went on.

"We've completed the first of fifteen prophets, and I'm pleased about how it's gone." I then looked at Jameson and asked, "Remember when Geraldo would from time to time ask what we've learned?" Jameson nodded, so I said, "Let's try that. What have you learned so far, even though we're standing in the place of the capital of the Northern Empire, while mostly hearing stories about the capital of the Southern Empire?"

Sol was quick to respond. "I was impressed how brave Isaiah must have been to offer a gloom and doom prophecy to

The King Montezuma Trilogy

the king. I guess I was thinking of medieval times, when the court jester could lose his head if he didn't humor the king."

Jameson immediately spoke up and said, "I had no idea the book of Isaiah contained prophecies of three different people from three different times."

"I liked," Sol offered, "that the young woman bore a son and named him Manuel, which means God with us. It is wonderful to have my understandings of the Bible confirmed because Jim Caldwell became God with us."

A little smoke must have been noticeably rising from the top of my head, so Jameson tried to lighten up the situation. "I loved it that Isaiah induced his visions by chewing on something. Maybe peyote buttons?"

I said, "Probably."

Jameson then Googled it and said, "Hey, cool. It says here that Mexican peyote has been used from earliest recorded time by indigenous peoples in northern Mexico and the southwestern part of the United States."

Sol was next. "I liked confirming that the Old Testament can learn from the New Testament."

"Jeez, Mom. Give it a break." I glared at Sol, when I probably should have been upset with my son.

"Maybe Jameson has something worthwhile to say," I suggested.

"Okay. I'm ready," he said. "I really liked the story of Isaiah's call, since I'm thinking about going into ministry, I loved that he heard the voice of God asking who he could send. Then Isaiah's response was almost life changing for me: 'Here I am; send me!'"

I got a bit choked up and noticed a tear falling down Sol's cheek. "Anything else?"

Jameson said, "I loved learning that the New Testament can learn from the Old Testament, but…"

Sol interrupted with, "You can have your opinion, mi hijo. Meanwhile, I hated the Lucifer story you told."

My eyes must have widened a bit, then I said, "Let's call it a day. Thanks for your attention. I'm ready for dinner and a good night's sleep."

Jameson asked, "What's on the agenda for tomorrow?

"We'll discuss four more of the shamans who prophesied before the exile."

The King Montezuma Trilogy

SCENE TWO
Amos, Hosea, Micah, Zephaniah

The morning brought an unexpected rainstorm, so I went downstairs to talk to the concierge. She said it was a passing storm, and would be fine by late morning, so I told her I would like a conference room for the morning if one was available. She very kindly offered to go check, then came back and said that room 137 could be used. I thanked her for her hospitality and headed back upstairs to share the good news. After breakfast, we made our way to the room and got settled in.

It was a pleasant room with plenty of chairs, but we were first attracted to the window. Not for the view of downtown, but to watch the storm for awhile. The clouds billowed in dark shapes, as the rain came down quite hard. Flashes of light off in the distance told me it was already in the moving on stage. The mild thunder was so muffled that it really was no problem for our morning session, so I pulled up a chair toward the front and decided to relax while talking. Sol and Jameson pulled up chairs and we sat in a circle.

Amos

"We'll begin with the prophecy of the shaman Amos. What makes him unique is that he was from the Southern Empire, yet God called him to offer his prophecies to the Northern Empire."

Jameson seemed a bit disappointed, so I asked what was on his mind. He said, "It's just that yesterday we had to remember the context of the Southern Empire, while we heard

The King Montezuma Trilogy

the prophecies of Isaiah to the capital city of Tenochtitlan. Finally, here we are for today's prophecy to the Northern Empire, and we're still not outside to soak up the context of the capital city of Monterrey."

"I really appreciate that! Just remember we're going to be here for about a week, so we'll have plenty of time to enjoy the city. Besides, there are no ruins here. Nothing historical to see, or at least with respect to the ancient northern capital."

"Why is that?" asked Sol.

"Nobody knows for sure, but it probably has something to do with the secret of the empire."

"Which is?" inquired Jameson.

"No, no, no. Not yet. We're here to enjoy the full experience, so I'll leave that for later. So, back to the shaman. Amos was prophesying while the popular sentiment was that their status as God's people gave them assurance of forgiveness. Amos had an uphill battle because his message was that their special status gave them responsibility, holding them to a higher standard. Amos got started with his drug-induced vision by condemning the nations that went to war against the Mexican Empire."

Jameson interrupted with, "Wait a minute, please. Did Amos share his prophecy to the Northern Empire while he was there, or did he say his words from the safety of his Southern Empire?"

"Great question, as always. Later in his book it becomes evident that he was right here in Monterrey, possibly during a cultic celebration. Amos even used that moment to offer a short prophecy against the Southern Empire for rejecting God's laws."

Sol smiled and said, "I'll bet that was easy for the

The King Montezuma Trilogy

northerners to hear."

"Sure, but Amos quickly turned his judgment back on the north. He first chastises them for ignoring what all God had done for them in the past, including raising up 'some of your children to be prophets.' Then God's punishment is predicted: 'So I will press you down in your place. Flight shall perish from the swift, and the strong shall not retain their strength, nor shall the mighty save their lives…says the LORD' (Amos 2:13-14).

"He continues with this. 'Hear this word that the LORD has spoken against you, O people of the Northern Empire, against the whole family that I brought up out of the land of Guatemala: You only have I known of all the families of the earth; therefore I will punish you for all your iniquities.' Amos then envisions the destruction of the sanctuary at Monterrey: 'Hear, and testify against the Northern Empire, says the LORD. On the day I punish the north for its transgressions, I will punish the altars of Monterrey. I will tear it down and it will come to an end, says the LORD' (Amos 3:13-15).

"Amos goes on in chapter 5 to say 'Fallen, no more to rise, is the Northern Empire; forsaken on her land, with no one to raise her up' (vs. 2). The LORD then offers a way for them to change: 'Seek me and live' (vs. 4). He then offers a warning: 'or he will break out against you like fire, and it will devour Monterrey, with no one to quench it' (vs. 6). After that Amos offers another way out of their problems: 'Seek good and not evil, that you may live' (vs. 14). He then takes direct aim at their problem: 'I hate, I despise your festivals, and I take no delight in your solemn assemblies' (vs. 21)."

"Why are they so despicable?" asked Jameson.

"I know that one!" exclaimed Sol. "Confession without repentance is meaningless."

The King Montezuma Trilogy

"Tell me more, Mom," requested Jameson.

"These were people who confessed their belief in God. That's why they went to the sacred festivals and worshiped, but God didn't like it because they were speaking out of both sides of their mouth. They didn't live a life of repentance. One can't change on the Sabbath, then be evil the rest of the week."

"Got it," announced Jameson. "It reminds me of a lot of people who follow the Caldwellian faith, but one would never know it."

I chimed back in with, "The good news is that Amos didn't just name problems, he offered a solution. Here's probably the best known verse from Amos, in chapter 5, verse 24:

> But let justice roll down like waters,
> and righteousness like an ever-flowing stream.

"How did that work out for Amos?" asked Jameson.

"As you obviously suspect, it got difficult. First of all, Amos had a huge confrontation with the priest of Monterrey, who sent word to the king of the Northern Empire, saying, 'Amos has conspired against you in the very center of Monterrey. He said that you would die by the sword, and the Northern Empire must go into exile away from this land.' A stern response came to Amos from the king: 'O seer, go back where you came from, but never again prophesy at Monterrey, for it is the king's sanctuary, and it is a temple of the kingdom.'

"Then Amos answered the king: 'I am no prophet, I am a herdsman from the Southern Kingdom. But the LORD said to me to prophesy to his people in the Northern Kingdom, so here it is: Your wife shall become a prostitute in the city, and your sons and your daughters shall fall by the sword, and your land

The King Montezuma Trilogy

shall be parceled out. You yourself shall die in another land, and the Northern Kingdom shall surely go into exile away from this land.'"

"Wow!" exclaimed Jameson. "Talk about gutsy!"

Sol suggested, "I suppose if the LORD gives you a job to do, you ought to do it."

"Well, Amos still wasn't done. In chapter 9 he shares a final vision of the LORD himself standing on the altar in Monterrey and commanding its destruction. Amos then shares imagery depicting no place for the people to hide: not in the depths of Sheol, nor the heights of heaven, nor the tops of mountains, nor the bottom of the sea. He then closes this vision with, 'And though they go into captivity in front of their enemies, there I will command the sword, and it shall kill them; and I will fix my eyes on them for harm and not for good' (vs. 4)."

"Dang!" exclaimed Jameson. "Maybe they should have stayed on God's good side."

We laughed, but it was no laughing matter for the people of the Northern Empire. "While the prophesied exile didn't happen immediately, it happened about twenty years later."

"Can't say they weren't warned," exclaimed Sol.

"Hey, did you hear that?" asked Jameson. I mentioned that I didn't hear anything, and Jameson said, "That's because the storm has passed outside." We all three went to the window and saw the clouds parting and the sun beginning to shine, then Jameson said, "Too bad the people of the Northern Empire couldn't get away from their storm, but then again it was a storm they brought upon themselves."

The telling of the prophet Amos couldn't have gone better, but we were ready to get outside. While Sol and Jameson went to our room to get a few towels to dry off the bench, I headed

The King Montezuma Trilogy

back to the concierge to get a weather report. I was delighted to hear that it was going to be great for the rest of the day, so when they came back down, we headed for the Macroplaza.

Hosea

Since the green space was so wonderfully large, we looked around for a while, then chose a bench in a new location. We used one towel to dry it off, then put down two others to sit on. As Sol and Jameson settled in, I got ready to talk. Right then the sun cleared from behind a cloud and made an almost eerie spotlight, which didn't go unnoticed by my family. I cleared my throat as I thought about this rather strange prophecy, then prepared to talk.

"The king of the Northern Empire was surely glad when Amos finally went back home, but next up was the shaman Hosea. At least he was a hometown boy, and his vision was ultimately an appeal for the Northern Empire to return to the LORD. The shaman was angry with the alliance the north had with Colombia, because he considered it a rejection of the LORD, and viewed it as idolatry.

"Hosea was a compassionate man who loved his people and was aware of their sin. To symbolize the north's unfaithful relationship with God, the LORD told Hosea to, 'Go, take for yourself a wife of whoredom and have children of whoredom, for the land commits great whoredom by forsaking the LORD.'

"I don't like that," announced Sol.

"It's pretty rough," I agreed, "but here's the point. Amos offered a solution to their problems, while Hosea lived an example of redeeming love. He married the harlot Gomer…"

The King Montezuma Trilogy

"Yuck!" Sol just couldn't help from sharing her surprise.

"They then had children and gave them symbolic names."

"Okay," complained Sol, "you just don't do that. Names are everything!"

"This probably won't help, but it was a metaphor for the bad relationship the people of the north had with God."

"Correct, as usual," Sol said curtly, "but not helpful."

"I think it's time to check out Hosea's speeches against the north. They were designed to get the Northern Empire to repent of their ways. Hosea basically asks his people to learn from him, with this: 'She shall pursue her lovers, but not overtake them, and she shall seek them, but shall not find them. Then she shall say, "I will go and return to my first husband, for it was better with me then than now" (Hosea 2:7).

"I get it!" said Jameson. "Hosea wants his people to see that they are like harlots who have run off with other men, but they would be better off by being faithful to the LORD." I smiled, and Sol folded her arms.

"Verse 13 get less symbolic and more direct. 'I will punish her for the festival days of the gods, when she offered incense to them and decked herself with her ring and jewelry, and went after her lovers, and forgot me, says the LORD.' After that, the speech moves on to Hosea trying to win his wife back. Unfortunately, Sol, chapter 3 turns bad again." I could barely bring myself to look at her, but the story must go on. "The LORD told Hosea to love an adulterous woman."

"That's it!" exclaimed Sol. "You just keep right on talking while I take a restroom break. Maybe by the time I get back, the story will be better, or maybe even finished."

As she left, I was a bit uncomfortable because we were out of the country. The restroom was within eyesight, but I just

The King Montezuma Trilogy

didn't feel like continuing. Jameson understood, so we started chatting about last year's tour. The great memories just came flooding back, and I was so happy that event happened. I was also hopeful that this event would prove useful.

"Here she comes," whispered Jameson in an almost scared tone.

I looked at him, shook my head and said, "No, we have to be honest with her."

As she settled back onto the bench next to Jameson, she said, "I hope you've made good progress."

When I assured her we had, Jameson shot me a look that made it obvious I failed the test of honesty. "Anyway, Hosea shared the thought that the Northerners would indeed return and seek the LORD. In chapter 4 he shares the word of the LORD; 'for the LORD has an indictment against the inhabitants of the land. There is no faithfulness or loyalty, and no knowledge of God in the land' (vs. 1). He then points the finger at the priesthood for failing to hold the people accountable to the covenant.

"Next, Hosea moves into lengthy oracles against the north. In 5:6 he says, 'With their flocks and herds they shall go to seek the LORD, but they will not find him; he has withdrawn from them.' Hosea gives an extended speech from God, mainly explaining that their punishment is due to the alliance the Northern Empire made with Guatemala and Colombia. In chapter 6 he says, 'Come, let us return to the LORD; for it is he who has torn, and he will heal us; he has struck down, and he will bind us up. After two days he will revive us; on the third day he will raise us up, that we may live before him' (vss. 1-2).

"Wonderful!" celebrated Sol. "Jim Caldwell was raised on the third day, so it sounds like the Old Testament is once again

The King Montezuma Trilogy

learning form the New Testament."

"That's fine," I said. "We all understand scripture in whatever way speaks best to us." It was obvious Sol was done thinking about it, so I went on. "Next the oracle complains about impenitence. Isaiah reports that God says to the Northern Empire, 'Your love is like a morning cloud, like the dew that goes away early.' (6:4). In the following chapter he says, 'the Northern Empire's pride humbles them; yet they do not return to the LORD their God, or seek him' (7:10). God even says, 'Woe to them, for they have strayed from me! Destruction to them, for they have rebelled against me! I would redeem them, but they speak lies against me' (7:13). God then levels his charge against both empires: 'The north has forgotten his Maker, and built palaces; and the south has multiplied fortified cities; but I will send a fire upon his cities, and it shall devour his strongholds' (8:14).

Jameson broke into the story and said, "Is that God speaking or Hosea?"

"Yes. The words alternate between the messenger and the message so much, that sometimes it's difficult telling the difference. This verse seems to be an interesting combination: 'The days of punishment have come, the days of recompense have come; the Northern Empire cries, "The prophet is a fool, the man of the spirit is mad!" Because of your great iniquity, your hostility is great' (9:7).

"So," continued Jameson, "Hosea was complaining about how he was being treated, while his task was to let the people know that the LORD was being mistreated."

"Yes! Very good. It's hard to not take things personally, even if you have a divine task. Here's Hosea's next response: 'Because they have not listened to him, my God will reject them;

The King Montezuma Trilogy

they shall become wanderers among the nations' (9:17).

Sol said that she heard one of her Caldwellian Church pastors talk about this verse. "He used the image of 'the wandering Aztec' to justify persecution of today's Mexicans when they don't accept Jim Caldwell."

Jameson asked her, "How does that make you feel as a Mexican, Mom?"

She responded with, "It seems to me to be stereotyping, and prejudice, and discrimination, and hatred, all rolled into one." Her body told the same story as she folded her arms and crossed her legs.

I said, "It sounds like we have to be careful with the way we interpret scripture."

She shocked me when she replied, "Maybe sometimes we shouldn't try to make the Old Testament learn from the New Testament." Jameson's jaw dropped and he gave her a spontaneous hug.

When we were ready to proceed, I said, "All I know is that I love the Bible. Its difficult trying to understand what it says, and even tougher to interpret what it means. But spending time with it is time well spent." They both nodded, then I went on. "Check this out. 'When the Empire was a child, I loved him, and out of Guatemala I called my son' (11:1)."

Sol said, "Okay, now that one's about Jim!"

Jameson and I just looked at each other, then I said, "Sure, hon, if that's what you need, just stick with it. I just love it when Hosea's prejudice creeps in, like in 11:12, he seems to offer God's complaint that the North is lying and deceitful about God, but the South 'still walks with God, and is faithful to the Holy One.' Chapter 13 recalls the exodus and the wilderness wanderings to show God's original good intentions toward the

The King Montezuma Trilogy

North, while chapter 14 is a plea for repentance.

"The book concludes with an assurance of forgiveness, if they reject their idolatrous ways. The final verse is a call to understand God's righteousness: 'Those who are wise understand these things; those who are discerning know them. For the ways of the LORD are right, and the upright walk in them, but transgressors stumble in them' (vs. 9). Okay. That's gotten us through the first two prophets. Let's go to lunch, then this afternoon we'll tackle Micah and Zephaniah."

Micah

The afternoon turned into a gorgeous day, as the sun shone bright and glistened off the tall downtown buildings. Even though the temperature was in the high eighties, the mild breeze made it feel cooler and the humidity was thankfully low. Being from Arizona, my family struggles with any muggy environment. We settled into yet another location in the Macroplaza and prepared for the next shamanic vision.

"Micah prophesied the fall of Tenochtitlan, and the destruction of Templo Mayor. What made him unique was that he was a commoner from the south, speaking to the people of the capital city, and he was prophesying at the edge of the north's demise. Here's how it starts: "The word of the LORD that came to Micah of San Miguel Ajusco in the days of three kings of the Southern Empire."

"Ah, yes. I remember it well," exclaimed Sol. We looked at her with confused expressions, so she said, "Another reference to Jim." When that didn't bring clarity, she said, "Don't you remember the three kings from the birth story of Jim?" I muddled

The King Montezuma Trilogy

out the words, "maybe we find what we're looking for," but that went about as well as running over a skunk.

"Maybe we should just continue," I offered. To be honest, I was surprised that Sol and I had never discussed these things. Our faith is very important to us, but I think our upbringing had an even bigger impact on our theology. "Micah's vision called for the people to hear and listen. I kind of like that. Its one thing to hear someone, and a totally different experience when one listens. Anyway, his vision was not easy to hear, so they really needed to listen. The LORD said through his prophet, 'I will make Tenochtitlan a heap in the open country' (vs. 6). Micah then shared that he would mourn for them, and that they should mourn for themselves.

"He goes on to denounce their wickedness, saying, 'They covet fields, and seize them; houses, and take them away' (2:2). The people don't like what they are hearing, so they disagree: 'one should not preach of such things; disgrace will not overtake us' (2:6). Next the prophet turns his attention to the leaders: 'Hear this, you rulers who abhor justice and pervert all equity' (3:9), 'because of you the Temple shall be plowed as a field; Tenochtitlan shall become a heap of ruins, and the mountain of the house a wooded height' (3:12).

"At that point the vision turns to hope. 'In days to come the mountain of the LORD's house shall be established as the highest of the mountains, and shall be raised up above the hills. Peoples shall stream to it, and many nations shall come and say: "Come, let us go up to the mountain of the LORD, to the house of the God of Mexica; that he may teach us his ways and that we may walk in his paths"' (4:1-2). Those days would come, but the sinful people are still going to have to endure exile: 'for now you shall go forth from the city and camp in the open

The King Montezuma Trilogy

country; you shall be conquered by the Spanish, but you shall be rescued' (4:10).

"Here the vision turns again, talking about the siege of Tenochtitlan. 'Now you are walled around with a wall, siege is laid against us; with a rod they strike the ruler of the Southern Empire upon the cheek.' (5:1)."

"Wait a minute," requested Jameson. "Did Micah just include himself as part of the ones who will be sieged?"

"Yes. Remember that he was from there. He was one of them. He just had a task to do as called upon by God. I don't really want to read the next verse, but I will. 'But you, O Texcoco de Mora, who are one of the little clans of the Southern Empire, from you shall come forth for me one who is to rule in Mexico, whose origin is from of old, from ancient days' (5:2)."

"Thanks," said a grinning Sol. "We all know that's about Jim Caldwell. Case closed."

First I caught myself folding my arms, but quickly unfolded them. Knowing that rebuttal would be futile, I continued on. "Chapter 6 shifts back to the present day, with God taking the people to a metaphorical court: 'O my people, what have I done to you? In what have I wearied you? Answer me!' (vs. 3). There is no answer, because they were wrong. They just needed a solution to their problem, and they got a good one.

> 'He has told you, O mortal, what is good;
> and what does the LORD require of you
> but to do justice, and to love kindness,
> and to walk wisely with your God' (vs.8).

"I have a question," mentioned Jameson with a quizzical look.

The King Montezuma Trilogy

"Of course, go ahead."

"This great verse is something even some of the college kids talk about, but it never hit me until now. Since this was a prophecy of gloom and doom, I think it would be much tougher to practice if you're being told a disaster was looming."

"My son!" exclaimed Sol. "That's a great point. Its one thing to live a proper life, but I think God is very interested in how we react in the midst of problems."

Great comments from my wife and son caused us to pause for a bit. The beautiful weather, friendly people, and lovely views were certainly a blessing, so we chatted for a while about living Micah 6:8 when life wasn't so good. Sol offered a dramatic example. "When I was in high school, my class visited Cartolandia, on the southwest side of Mexico City."

"What's that?" asked Jameson.

"Literally a city of houses made from cardboard boxes, usually with a tin roof over it. It was the poorest of the poor who lived there, but it wasn't heartbreaking. The people were full of joy and hope. We visited on a Saturday, and several people invited us to come to church the next morning. After the teacher figured out how to adjust his agenda, we went. That church was filled with more praise than any place I've ever been."

"Wow! Thanks Mom, that's inspiring."

Finding good in challenging times was a truth to savor. I wanted to bask in this moment, but my agenda-driven personality forced me to move on. The final chapter shares the prophet's anger: 'The faithful have disappeared from the land, and there is no one left who is upright' (7:2). He then shares his personal response: 'But as for me, I will look to the LORD, I will wait for the God of my salvation; my God will hear me' (7:7).

"Micah closes with making sure that listeners understand

The King Montezuma Trilogy

God as the compassionate one:

> 'Who is a God like you, pardoning iniquity
>   and passing over the transgression
> of the remnant of your possession?
>   He does not retain his anger forever,
> because he delights in showing clemency.
>   He will again have compassion on us;
> he will tread our iniquities under foot.
>   You will cast all our sins
> into the depths of the sea.
>   You will show faithfulness to Mexica
> and unswerving loyalty to Aapo,
>   as you have sworn to our ancestors
> from the days of old' (7:18-20)."

The Fall of the North to the Colombians

"Remember when I talked about a time when the Colombians lost a war against Mexico?"

"No," answered Sol.

A bit puzzled, I thought maybe my wife wasn't listening very well. Then Jameson said, "That was from last year's trip, Dad."

Relieved, I said, "A quick refresher. Not all of the Colombians returned to Colombia. Some took their boats north and settled in the state of Sinaloa. There they became powerful, and started demanding money from the King of the Northern Empire. They became known as The Cartel, and when the Northern king disobeyed them, they imprisoned him. The Cartel went on a rampage against the entire Northern Empire, and

The King Montezuma Trilogy

besieged Monterrey for three years. The Northern Empire only lasted two hundred years in total, but its defeat served warning to the Southern Empire.

Hezekiah's Reform

"Something needed to be done. The Northern Empire was lost, and cultic worship was rampant in King Hezekiah's Southern Empire. He knew the problem was that his people were no longer acting like God's people, so he set out to do massive reforms. 'He did what was right in the sight of the LORD, just as his ancestor Montezuma had done. He removed the high places, broke down the pillars, and cut down the sacred pole. He broke in pieces the bronze serpent that Abund had made, for until those days the people of Mexico had made offerings to it' (2 Kings 18:3-4).

"I'm not sure I understood any of that," complained Jameson.

Sol said, "I'm with you, mi hijo."

"Fair enough. All we need to know is that Hezekiah's Reform was about getting back to following the LORD."

Zephaniah

"Even though the prophet Zephaniah came along after Hezekiah's Reform, there was still plenty of trouble. He had given up on the hierarchy of the day, and turned his attention to preparing the humble so they might avoid God's vengeance. The first verse says he worked as 'the son of Hezekiah, during

The King Montezuma Trilogy

the reign of Josiah.' Being of royal lineage, it seems somewhat surprising that his efforts went unheeded. Perhaps his job was more about planting seeds, because it wasn't long before the successful, sweeping reforms of Josiah took place.

"Isn't that what ministry is about?" queried Sol.

Jameson looked confused and asked, "What do you mean, Mom?"

"I've heard several pastors say that their job seemed unfruitful, only to remember that it takes a long time from planting seeds to growing fruit."

"Maybe that's why Zephaniah comes across so harsh. He's planting a seed for those who are open to the message, in hopes they will work to avoid God's judgment. Like verse 9: 'On that day I will punish all who leap over the threshold, who fill their master's house with violence and fraud.'"

"Oh, I get it," exclaimed Jameson. "Don't be like the bad guys!"

"The rest of chapter 1 gives chilling details of the great day of the LORD, but the prophet's real reason for sharing his words comes in the third verse of chapter two: 'Seek the LORD, all you humble of the land, who do his commands; seek righteousness, seek humility; perhaps you may be hidden on the day of the LORD's wrath.'"

Sol said, "Sounds persuasive to me!"

"The third chapter offers a picture of an idyllic future: 'On that day you shall not be put to shame because of all the deeds by which you have rebelled against me; for then I will remove from your midst your proudly exultant ones, and you shall no longer be haughty in my holy mountain. For I will leave in the midst of you a people humble and lowly' (3:11-12). What's even better is that the book closes with a song of joy: 'The LORD has taken away the judgments against you, he has turned away your enemies. The king of Mexico, the LORD, is in your midst; you shall fear disaster no more' (3:15).

"Once again I'm very pleased. Let's collect up your thoughts of what was learned, then head back to the hotel for the evening."

"Can we take the car out tonight" requested Jameson, "and look around the city?"

"Sure, and let's do dinner out." I suggested. "Tomorrow we'll cover Jeremiah, Habakkuk, Nahum, and Ezekiel 1-32. Now, who wants to go first?"

"I learned that there are no ruins here in Monterrey," complained an obviously disappointed Jameson.

Sol spoke up next and said, "Who was the first prophet you talked about at the hotel?" I told her it was Amos, and she said, "I was impressed. It couldn't have been easy for a southerner to go to the north and speak against them."

Jameson suggested, "The overall theme I got from the prophets seems to be about how easy it is to forget, with respect to keeping God's Law."

"To me," offered Sol, "the theme seems to be that we first need to remember, but then we have to obey."

I nodded affirmatively, then Jameson said, "I was kind of shocked how easily God seemed to talk about prostitutes."

Sol reverted to her favorite theme next. "I learned that Hosea prophesied about Jim Caldwell's resurrection."

"It was very intriguing to me," explained Jameson, "that the wonderful Micah 6:8 passage about what the LORD requires, was said as part of an imagined trial."

"Say more," I requested.

"Even though Micah was offering the verse as a solution to

The King Montezuma Trilogy

the people's problem, it was done at a trying time. Get it? A trial."

"Son," Sol said. "You are too young for Dad jokes." After we all laughed, she continued. "I learned that it was The Cartel who overthrew the Northern Empire."

Jameson got a bit more serious and said, "I had always heard about Hezekiah's reform, but never really understood what happened. From what you said Dad, it seems it was simply about doing what was right in the sight of the LORD."

"Great! Any learnings about Zephaniah?"

Sol smiled and said, "I can now relate more to his book. He seemed frustrated that he was planting seeds to help the humble, and I'm guessing his frustration was about wanting to enjoy a harvest."

"Okay," I said, "that's a wrap. Let's have a good evening. We've earned it."

The King Montezuma Trilogy

ACT II
The Fall of the Empires

The King Montezuma Trilogy

SCENE ONE
The North—Jeremiah, Habakkuk, Nahum

In the morning we decided to get a little more creative. We took a taxi to Alameda Marino Escobedo, a beautiful park with lots of trees, green space, and benches. Another glorious day awaited us, as birds chirped, squirrels skittered by, and walkers enjoyed the many sidewalks.

Josiah's Reform

"Josiah was considered the greatest king in biblical history. When his father was assassinated, he ascended the throne, even though he was only eight years old. Nineteen years into his reign, the High Priest 'found the book of the law in the house of the LORD' (2 Kings 22:8). Once Josiah heard about it, he said, 'Go, inquire of the LORD for me, for the people, and for all of the Southern Empire, concerning the words of this book that has been found; for great is the wrath of the LORD that is kindled against us, because our ancestors did not obey the words of this book' (2 Kings 22:13).

"The King and the people established a covenant promising to obey the laws of the LORD. Josiah then enacted the covenant by destroying the idols that were being worshiped. He continued his reforms by expelling the idolatrous priests and demolishing the places dedicated to sacred prostitution. He was following this newly discovered book of Deuteronomy, which had been lost and forgotten. It directed the people to bring sacrifices to the one, true, approved sanctuary, which was Templo Mayor at Tenochtitlan. This was particularly useful for

The King Montezuma Trilogy

Josiah, since the temple in Monterrey was no longer in existence, due to its demise at the hands of The Cartel.

Jeremiah, which means 'Jeremy the Mayan'

"This book begins with a surprising thought. It says that Jeremiah prophesied over a 40-year period, from the time of King Josiah to the fall of Tenochtitlan. With that sobering thought in mind, the book continues with his call:

> 'See, today I appoint you over nations and over kingdoms,
> to pluck up and to pull down,
> to destroy and to overthrow,
> to build and to plant' (1:10).

"After that, Jeremiah offers a verse that has meant a lot to me:

> 'For my people have committed two evils:
> they have forsaken me,
> the fountain of living water,
> and dug out cisterns for themselves,
> cracked cisterns
> that can hold no water' (2:13).

"As you say, Dad, tell me more."
"I sense great anger in this text. Jeremiah was offering a vision of God being appalled at the abandonment of his people. After God called Abund from Guatemala, made the Aztecs his

The King Montezuma Trilogy

people, and gave them the Promised Land of Mexico, this was their thanks? After God provided living water from a rock and sustained them as they wandered through the wilderness, they choose stagnant water that leaks through cracked cisterns? It reminds me of our idolatrous worship of money and power today. Why do people choose to forsake God, which Jeremiah calls evil, and instead select worthless idols which cannot refresh? Not to mention that the prophet also calls that evil."

"Whoa! I didn't expect a sermon there Dad, but thanks. That was pretty good."

Sol smiled approvingly and I went on. "Jeremiah continues sharing God's anger: 'You have played the whore with many lovers; and would you return to me? Says the LORD' (3:1).

Jameson asked, "What is this obsession God has with whores?"

"I think it is because God doesn't want these polluted people back," I suggested.

"And learn from God, my son. Stay away from prostitutes!" demanded Sol.

"You and Dad have raised me well. No worries."

"Jeremiah then issues a call to repentance, suggesting they should surely learn something from the infidelity of the Northern Empire. Knowing it won't happen, a vision of destruction is shared."

"You mean," asked Jameson, "they were hopeless?"

"Not really. The problem was that their hope wasn't in God. 'At the noise of horseman and archer every town takes to flight; they enter thickets; they climb among rocks; all the towns are forsaken, and no one lives in them' (4:29)."

Jameson seemed really intrigued. "And that wasn't enough to scare them into submission?"

The King Montezuma Trilogy

"No. The problem was they didn't believe Jeremiah. They had become a faithless people. Listen to this one: 'They have made their faces harder than rock; they have refused to turn back' (5:3). Here's the clincher: 'But even in those days, says the LORD, I will not make a full end of you. And when your people say, "Why has the LORD our God done all these things to us?" you shall say to them, 'As you have forsaken me and served foreign gods in your land, so you shall serve strangers in a land that is not yours' (5:18-19).

"Increasing urgency is created by Jeremiah envisioning the plan of attack. 'Prepare war against her; up, and let us attack at noon!' (6:4).

Jameson asked, "So that vision was about Hernando Cortés and the Spanish Conquistadors?"

"Yes, but the people didn't know it. Cortés first landed in Cuba, with the secret agenda of appropriating land for the Spanish crown. He put together a crew of conquistadors and arrived on the Yucatan peninsula, and slowly worked his way to Tenochtitlan. At first he was greeted by the southern King, and slowly began to show his true colors. It was a brilliant way to conquer, because it was bloodless at first."

"That's the Secret of the Empire?" asked Jameson.

"Certainly part of it, but we still have to hear from Habakkuk, Nahum, and Ezekiel 1-32. Next, Jeremiah continues to explain the problem of the Southern Empire. 'From the least to the greatest of them, everyone is greedy for unjust gain; and from prophet to priest, everyone deals falsely' (6:13). He then offers a heartfelt plea, followed by a warning that deeply reveals the Secret of the Empire. 'Thus says the LORD of hosts, the God of Mexico: Amend your ways and your doings, and let me dwell with you in this place. Do not trust in these deceptive words:

The King Montezuma Trilogy

'This is the temple of the LORD' (7:3-4)"

"Gotta ask, Dad. How is that the secret?"

"Another part of it, because they believed they could never lose their God-promised Land, let alone the holy Templo Mayor. Here's how Jeremiah put it: 'Here you are, trusting in deceptive words to no avail. Will you steal, murder, commit adultery, swear falsely, make offerings to gods that you have not known, and then come and stand before me in this house and say, "We are safe!"—only to go on doing all these abominations? Has this house become a den of robbers?' (7:8-11).

"Shades of Jim Caldwell!" claimed a rather ebullient Sol.

"Correct!" I countered. "Because Jim was quoting this Old Testament passage. Jeremiah then prophesies a desperate people: 'Why do we sit still? Gather together, let us go into the fortified cities and perish there; for the LORD our God has doomed us to perish, and has given us poisoned water to drink, because we have sinned against the LORD. We look for peace, but find no good, for a time of healing, but there is terror instead' (8:14-15)."

Jameson then said, "I'll bet God's response to that soliloquy would have been, 'Correct!'"

Sol and I smiled at first, then frowned, then weren't sure what to say, so I just went on. "The shaman turned to a collection of dialogues about grief, like 'Why is the land ruined and laid waste like a wilderness, so that no one passes through? And the LORD says; Because they have forsaken my law that I set before them, and have not obeyed my voice, or walked in accordance with it' (9:12-13)."

"You'd think they would get it after a while," suggested Jameson.

"This makes a great case study in how deeply we can get

entrenched in the wrong, believing it's okay. This first large part of Jeremiah's book, the first ten chapters, ends with poetic warnings, and this final plea:

> 'I know, O LORD, that the way of human beings is
> > not in their control,
> that mortals as they walk cannot direct their
> > steps.
> Correct me, O LORD, but in just measure;
> > not in your anger, or you will bring me to
> > > nothing.
>
> Pour out your wrath on the nations that do not
> > know you,
> and the peoples that do not call on your
> > name;
> for they have devoured the North;
> > they have devoured him and consumed him,
> and have laid waste his habitation' (10:23-25).

"The next ten chapters are full of laments. He starts with the curses the people have brought upon themselves for disobedience to God's ways. Then he shares a personal complaint: 'It was the LORD who made it known to me, and I knew; then you showed me their evil deeds. But I was like a gentle lamb led to the slaughter' (11:18-19)."

"Amen," Sol suddenly said with surprising strength. "Yet another prophecy of Jim!"

"Nope," I said plainly. "This was simply Jeremiah confessing that he isn't particularly enjoying his task. Once that's said, sure, the same can also be said about Jim

The King Montezuma Trilogy

Caldwell." I glanced quickly at Jameson and he didn't want to have anything to do with it.

"I love you guys," volunteered Jameson, "but it seems like I'd get triangulated into your argument. Hey, wait a minute. Maybe that's how Jim felt, being triangulated by the Russians and clergy."

"Not bad, son. In fact, Jeremiah grieved this so much that he proceeded to complain against God."

"That's pretty daring," offered a frowning Sol.

"Interestingly, God follows with God's own lament. 'I have forsaken my house, I have abandoned my heritage; I have given the beloved of my heart into the hands of her enemies' (12:7). Jeremiah then threatens exile: 'But if you will not listen, my soul will weep in secret for your pride; my eyes will weep bitterly and run down with tears, because the LORD's flock has been taken captive' (13:17).

"After a great drought is prophesied, Jeremiah offers a vision of the people's plea for mercy: 'Have you completely rejected us? Does your heart loathe the Southern Empire? Why have you struck us down so that there is no healing for us? We look for peace, but find no good; for a time of healing, but there is terror instead' (14:19)."

Sol said, "Reminds me of the two criminals hung from a noose next to Jim."

"What do you mean, Mom?"

"One of the criminals who were hanged there kept deriding Jim, saying, 'Are you not the Messiah? Save yourself and us!' while the other just asked Jim to 'remember me when you come into your kingdom.'"

"Thanks, Mom. You always give me new ways of seeing things."

The King Montezuma Trilogy

"You'll like this one, honey. The next thing Jeremiah does is complain to his mother." Sol indeed had a happy smile spread across her face. "He said, 'Woe is me, my mother, that you ever bore me, a man of strife and contention to the whole land! I have not lent, nor have I borrowed, yet all of them curse me' (15:10)."

"No, that makes me sad."

"Same as God. Here's what God had to say, 'Therefore I am surely going to teach them, this time I am going to teach them my power and my might, and they shall know that my name is the LORD' (16:21). That paves the way for God to launch into more threats of punishment, followed by the famous potter and clay story at the beginning of chapter 18. It's a wonderful way to symbolize repentance. God calls Jeremiah to go to a potter's house and watch him work. The point is that a potter can take a vessel that comes out poorly, and reshape it. That's what God is offering, one last time: 'Turn now, all of you from your evil way, and amend your ways and your doings' (18:11)."

Jameson asked, "So, they are called to reshape themselves?"

"No, of course not. God is the potter, we are the clay, and pots can't form themselves. God is saying that the decision is not fixed. If they change their ways, God would still be willing to reshape them back into being God's people. In the next chapter, Jeremiah shares God's word about their refusal to change: 'Thus says the LORD of hosts, the God of Mexico: I am now bringing upon this city and upon all its town all the disaster that I have pronounced against it, because they have stiffened their necks, refusing to hear my words' (19:15).

"That concludes the laments. The next five chapters are about how the people will be after the coming invasion. Shall

The King Montezuma Trilogy

we take a quick break?" Sol answered by heading off for the nearest restroom.

When we got resettled, I returned to the story. "We are already to the last King of the Southern Empire, before the invasion. The King said, 'Please inquire of the LORD on our behalf, for Cortés and the Spanish Conquistadors are making war against us; perhaps the LORD will perform a wonderful deed for us, as he has often done, and will make them withdraw from us' (21:2)."

"How did that go?" asked Jameson with an impish grin.

"The answer was no. Then the prophet offers a vision from God of restoration: 'I myself will gather the remnant of my flock out of all the lands where I have driven them, and I will bring them back to their fold, and they shall be fruitful and multiply' (23:3). Then God expressed anger at lying prophets: 'Am I a God near by, says the LORD, and not a God far off? Who can hide in secret places so that I cannot see them? Says the LORD. Do I not fill heaven and earth? Says the LORD. I have heard what the prophets have said who prophesy lies in my name' (23:23-25).

"God is obviously angry, but now it is turned toward the shepherding kings: 'Wail, you shepherds, and cry out; roll in ashes, you lords of the flock, for the days of your slaughter have come—and your dispersions, and you shall fall like a choice vessel. Flight shall fail the shepherds, and there shall be no escape for the lords of the flock. Hark! The cry of the shepherds, and the wail of the lords of the flock! For the LORD is despoiling their pasture, and the peaceful folds are devastated, because of the fierce anger of the LORD. Like a lion he has left his covert; for their land has become a waste because of the cruel sword, and because of his fierce anger' (25:34-38).

The King Montezuma Trilogy

"The next seven chapters deal with conflict and comfort. God tells Jeremiah to deliver this message to King Zedekiah, who represented the beginning of the end for the Southern Empire. 'It is I who by my great power and my outstretched arm have made the earth, with the people and animals that are on the earth, and I give it to whomever I please. Now I have given all these lands into the hand of Cortés, my servant' (27:5-6)."

"I'll bet that was a shock!" exclaimed Jameson.

"It helped to explain why many of the southerners were being exiled to Spain. After that, Jeremiah sent a letter to the exiles. 'Thus says the Lord of hosts, the God of Mexico, to all the exiles whom I have sent into exile from Tenochtitlan to Spain. Build houses and live in them; plant gardens and eat what they produce. Take wives and have sons and daughters; take wives for your sons, and give your daughters in marriage, that they may bear sons and daughters; multiply there, and do not decrease. But seek the welfare of the city where I have sent you into exile, and pray to the LORD on its behalf, for in its welfare you will find your welfare' (29:4-7)."

"I guess they realized they were going to be there for a long time," said a rather subdued Jameson.

"Yes, but right away Jeremiah offers a vision of hope: 'the days are surely coming, says the LORD, when I will restore the fortunes of my people, the Northern Empire and the Southern Empire, says the LORD, and I will bring them back to the land that I gave to their ancestors and they shall take possession of it' (30:3). After that, Jeremiah offers a vision of restoration: 'Thus says the LORD: I am going to restore the fortunes of the tents of Mexico, and have compassion on his dwellings; the city shall be rebuilt upon its mound, and the citadel set on its rightful site' (30:18). Then Jeremiah shares three poems celebrating

The King Montezuma Trilogy

the journey home from exile. That brings us to one of my favorite passages in the Aztec Scriptures:

> 'The days are surely coming, says the LORD, when I will make a new covenant with the Southern Empire and the Northern Empire. It will not be like the covenant that I made with their ancestors when I took them by the hand to bring them out of the land of Guatemala—a covenant that they broke, though I was their master, says the LORD. But this is the covenant that I will make with Mexico after those days, says the LORD: I will put my law within them, and I will write it on their hearts; and I will be their God, and they shall be my people. No longer shall they teach one another, or say to each other, "Know the LORD," for they shall all know me, from the least of them to the greatest, says the LORD; for I will forgive their iniquity, and remember their sin no more' (31:31-34).

Sol was grinning from ear to ear. "Jim Caldwell became the new covenant!"

Returning to my gentle style I said, "When Jeremiah speaks of the new covenant, he is thinking about a renewed relationship between Mexico and God."

"You think your way. I'll think mine," suggested Sol as she settled back into her bench.

"What I find interesting is that Jeremiah also became imprisoned during the time Cortés was sending the southerners into exile in Spain. 'The word of the LORD came to Jeremiah a second time, while he was still confined in the court of the guard' (33:1). Then Jeremiah was told to let King Zedekiah know that he too would be captured, sent to Spain, and die there (34:5). For what its worth, here's another thing I find interesting.

The King Montezuma Trilogy

Jeremiah had a scribe: 'Then Jeremiah called Baruch and Baruch wrote on a scroll at Jeremiah's dictation all the words of the LORD that he had spoken to him' (36:4).

"They had secretaries way back then?" asked Sol.

"No, Mom," claimed a smiling Jameson. "They had administrative assistants."

After a good-natured bit of laughing, including Sol, I got back to the story. "The next nine chapters are about the last days of the Empire, and may have been written by Baruch. Even Cortés and the Conquistadors withdrew from Tenochtitlan at the approach of the Guatemalan army. Jeremiah was leaving for a different reason, but when he was seen, he was believed to be deserting with Cortés. He was arrested, beaten, and imprisoned (37:15).

"Next up is the fall of Tenochtitlan. After the Guatemalans left, Cortés and his Conquistadors returned and besieged the capital city. King Zedekiah tried to escape, but he was pursued and overtaken. Cortés sentenced him, put out his eyes, and then bound him for exile in Spain (39:7). Cortés then turned to Jeremiah."

Jameson was listening intently and said, "I'll bet that made him nervous."

"You would think, but here's what happened. Cortés said, 'Take him, look after him well and do him no harm, but deal with him as he may ask you' (39:12). Jeremiah decided to stay in the Promised Land, and others were slowly allowed to return, as long as they served Cortés. Slowly, the remnant gathered and sought advice from Jeremiah about what they should do. He prayed for ten days, and delivered this message from God: 'If you will only remain in this land, then I will build you up and not pull you down; I will plant you, and not pluck you up; for I am sorry for the disaster that I have brought upon you' (42:10)."

"God apologized?" Jameson asked with incredulity. Then he asked me to wait while he googled it. "Wow! There's a lot, so here's some. Just before the flood, God said 'I am sorry that I have made them,' (Genesis 6:7). When God got mad at his Aztec people wandering in the wilderness, the Bible says, 'And the LORD changed his mind about the disaster that he planned to bring on his people' (Exodus 32:14). Jeremiah prophesied, 'Now therefore amend your ways and your doings, and obey the voice of the LORD your God, and the LORD will change his mind' (Jeremiah 26:13).

"Very interesting. Thanks, mijo."

"Yes, and getting back to the story, God said in the very next verse, 'Do not be afraid of the king of Spain, as you have been; do not be afraid of him, says the LORD, for I am with you, to save you and to rescue you from his hand.' The divine response continued with, 'Just as my anger and my wrath were poured out on the inhabitants of the Tenochtitlan, so my wrath will be poured out on you when you go to Guatemala' (42:18). An insolent remnant called Jeremiah a liar, telling the crowd that Jeremiah wanted them handed over to the Spaniards, 'in order that they may kill us or take us into exile in Spain' (43:3).

"So the survivors who had returned to the Promised Land, along with Jeremiah and Baruch, 'came into the land of Guatemala, for they did not obey the voice of the LORD' (43:7). After they arrived, the remnant confronted Jeremiah, saying, 'As for the word that you have spoken to us in the name of the LORD, we are not going to listen to you' (44:16)."

"How did that go for them?" inquired Jameson.

"The LORD said, 'I am going to watch over them for harm and not for good; all the people of the Southern Empire who are

The King Montezuma Trilogy

in the land of Guatemala shall perish by the sword and by famine, until not one is left' (44:27).

"Guess that explained that!" said Jameson with widened eyes.

"But the point is not that God brought on their problems, it is that they brought on their own problems by refusing to listen."

Jameson solemnly added, "And not too easy to learn from your mistakes when you're dead."

Sol then said, "Sounds like something my father would say," and we all laughed.

After a short pause, I continued. "The next six chapters are oracles against nations. The first concerns Guatemala, using the Motagua River, the longest in the country, as a symbol of Guatemala's own rise and fall: 'Who is this, rising like the Motagua, like rivers whose waters surge? Guatemala rises like the Motagua, like rivers whose waters surge' (46:7-8)."

"Why do they surge?" asked a curious Jameson.

"Because it rushes out of the mountains, and drains into the Gulf of Honduras. It was also important in the Pentateuch, because it flows by Cerro Raxon, where the Ten Commandments were given, and Lake Izabal where the Aztecs famously crossed on its east end, on dry ground. After prophesying that Cortés would also attack Guatemala, Jeremiah envisions hope for the remnant of Mexico: 'I am going to save you from far away, and your offspring from the land of their captivity. Southerners shall return and have quiet and ease, and no one shall make them afraid' (46:27).

"After that, Jeremiah declares judgment on six more nations, then settles in on Spain. There is no longer the need to explain why the Southern Empire fell, so the judgment on Spain is about the injustices that were committed against them. 'Thus

The King Montezuma Trilogy

says the LORD of hosts: The people of the Northern Empire were oppressed, and so too were the people of the Southern Empire; all their captors held them fast and refused to let them go. Their Redeemer is strong; the LORD of hosts is his name. He will surely plead their cause, that he may give rest to the earth, but unrest to the inhabitants of Spain' (50:33-34).

"As if that weren't enough, the LORD says through his prophet, 'I will stretch out my hand against you, and roll you down from the crags, and make you a burned-out mountain. No stone shall be taken from you for a corner and no stone for a foundation, but you shall be a perpetual waste' (51:25-26). Then Jeremiah tells Baruch's brother to perform a symbolic against Spain: 'Jeremiah wrote in a scroll all the disasters that would come on Spain, all these words that are written concerning Spain. And Jeremiah said to Baruch's brother: "When you come to Spain, see that you read all these words, and say O LORD, you yourself threatened to destroy this place so that neither human beings nor animals shall live in it, and it shall be desolate forever. When you finish reading this scroll, tie a stone to it, and throw it into the sea, and say, 'Thus shall Spain sink, to rise nor more, because of the disasters that I am bringing on her' (51:61-64).

"The final chapter is a review of the destruction of Tenochtitlan, and it serves as the fulfillment of Jeremiah's prophecies. Let's take a lunch break, then return to hear about the prophecies of the shaman Habakkuk, and conclude our day by sharing our new learnings from these experiences of hearing the story in the setting of Mexico."

"I'm choosing the restaurant this time," announced Sol, and we were happy to accommodate. The clouds came in and a pleasant breeze made for a relaxing break.

The King Montezuma Trilogy

Habakkuk

After a very satisfying meal that even Sol approved of, we found a new bench in the park and got comfortable. "The shaman Habakkuk is thought to have prophesied during the reign of the final Kings of the Southern Empire. He begins his oracle with a complaint about theodicy."

"What's that?" asked a puzzled Jameson.

"It's the study of the problem of evil. Listen to how Habakkuk addressed it: 'O LORD, how long shall I cry for help, and you will not listen? Or cry to you "Violence!" and you will not save? Why do you make me see wrongdoing and look at trouble? Destruction and violence are before me; strife and contention arise. So the law becomes slack and justice never prevails. The wicked surround the righteous—therefore judgment comes forth perverted' (1:2-4)."

"Pretty bold, I'd say!" exclaimed Jameson.

"Then listen to this one, 'Why do you look on the treacherous, and are silent when the wicked swallow those more righteous than they?' (1:13)."

Sol looked solemn, then said, "I agree with Habakkuk. Where was God during the Holocaust of the Aztecs that happened in just the last century?"

We all sat silently in response to that painful question, then I said, "Nobody knows, but here was God's response. 'Look at the proud! Their spirit is not right in them, but the righteous live by their faith' (2:4)"

"Wait a minute," requested Jameson. "Why does that sound familiar?"

"Because Pablo used it in the Caldwellian Scriptures," announced Sol, "to support his doctrine of justification by faith."

The King Montezuma Trilogy

"Whoa!" said Jameson with genuine surprise. "What makes you say that?"

Sol immediately said, "Pablo quoted it in his letter to the Caldwellian Church of San Francisco."

"I'm impressed! Yes, this is an important verse for all of God's people. There was even a Dominican friar named Las Casas who said that this verse was a summary of all 613 commandments. And here's just a silly little point that I personally like. Habakkuk 2:14 says 'the earth will be filled with the knowledge of the glory of the LORD, as the waters cover the sea.'"

"Okay," offered Jameson, "and why do you like that verse?"

"Because it is the first time that scripture is quoted in scripture."

Jameson looked mildly confused, so Sol said, "Your father is easily amused."

"Habakkuk 2:14 is a direct quote from Isaiah 11:9. Why I like it is because it lets you know that scripture has been around long enough by this time, that the community is starting to accept certain scrolls that later became finalized as part of the Aztec Scriptures."

After some shrugged shoulders, I got back to the text. "Habakkuk is a short book, so we're ready for the final chapter. It's a psalm that was written for use in worship, and employs exodus imagery like, 'Was your wrath against the rivers, O LORD? Or your anger against the rivers, or your rage against the sea, when you drove your horses, your chariots to victory' (3:8). It closes with words of hope that the LORD will deliver: 'Though the fig tree does not blossom, and no fruit is on the vines; though the produce of the olive fails, and the fields yield no food; though the flock is cut off from the fold, and there is no

The King Montezuma Trilogy

herd in the stalls, yet I will rejoice in the LORD; I will exult in the God of my salvation. God, the Lord, is my strength; he makes my feet like the feet of a deer, and makes me tread upon the heights' (3:17-19). Thanks again, for a nice session. Let's see what we've learned."

Sol spoke excitedly, "I loved that not only was Josiah a great king, but he began at age 7!"

"Well, he was actually 8," I corrected, "but who's counting?"

"That king caused me to be a little frustrated," announced Jameson.

His mother asked, "How's that?"

"Because he was the one who was reigning as king when the book of the law was found. For one thing, it's kinda sad that the law had become so unimportant to the people, that nobody even had a copy anymore. For another thing, he got credit for 'Josiah's Reform' when it didn't really seem to change the people too much. After all, they still never paid attention to the prophets, and ultimately lost their land."

"Nice. Very nice," I offered, complementarily.

Sol commented that, "I didn't like Jeremiah's call to prophesy destruction."

Not wanting to correct my wife again, I simply added, "and he was called to prophesy about rebuilding."

Jameson got one of those impish looks on his face, then said, "I liked the cistern thing."

"Thanks, son. Maybe I shouldn't have mentioned that Jeremiah 2:13 is very meaningful to me."

We laughed, then he got serious. "I really loved the bit about writing the law on their hearts."

"Even though Jeremiah 2:13 bears a lot of meaning for me, Jeremiah 31:31-34 is one of my favorites."

The King Montezuma Trilogy

"Mine, too," responded Sol. "At least now, since I realized that Jim Crawford was the new law on their hearts."

I really tried to hold back, but finally said, "Jim Crawford wasn't even a gleam in anyone's eyes at that time, let alone being the one who the Mexican people were talking about."

She dismissively waved me off, then said, "I also liked the den of robber's quote they got from Jim Caldwell."

"To be honest, Jim Caldwell got it from Jeremiah, and it is found in 7:11."

Jameson couldn't help himself, so he asked, "Why am I all of a sudden thirsty?"

Sol got that implication, and again rather dismissively said, "Dad jokes!" as she shook her head back and forth. Then she offered that she was still surprised that Jeremiah had a secretary. At first I was ready to shake my head too, then I realized that it really was a great thing to learn.

Jameson said, "I learned a new word: theodicy."

"Yeah, and that's a tough one. The most detailed discussion about the source of evil is in the book of Job."

"Are you going to talk about Job?" inquired Jameson.

"You know what? Last year we experienced the Law through the book of Kings. Right now we're trying to gain knowledge about the Prophets. That's two of the three parts of the Aztec Scriptures. Job is in that last section called the Writings."

"Sounds like another trip!" exclaimed a jubilant Jameson.

As Sol crossed her arms, I said, "We'll need to think about how that might be done. Right now I'm ready to get back to the hotel and get ready for dinner. Tomorrow we'll consider Nahum and the first thirty-two chapters of Ezekiel."

The King Montezuma Trilogy

SCENE TWO
The South—Nahum, Ezekiel 1-32

We looked out our bedroom window and saw another sunny day. When we went downstairs, the concierge mentioned it would be in the low 80's, and Jameson and I gave one another high fives. Sol was happy, too, but she was generally above silly behavior. This time I decided to drive, and Sol had chosen Parque Roma for the day. She found it on Trip Advisor, but later admitted it was because there was a nearby Mexican restaurant. As usual, we found a pleasant park bench on a tree-lined sidewalk, with a view of the mountains.

Nahum

"This book is surprisingly mean-spirited. It's a celebration of vengeance, but little is known about the author. The focus is a vision of the destruction of Bogota, the capital of Colombia."
"Why would that be?" asked a surprised Jameson.
"Well, remember, it was the Colombians who had stayed in Sinoloa and became The Cartel that conquered the Northern Empire."
"And?"
"Not only did it feel good to envision punishment to the people of Bogota, but maybe Nahum was pointing to the past, to suggest the same could happen to the Southern Empire if they didn't change. Anyway, let me get started. Here's the first three verses: 'An oracle concerning Bogota. The book of the vision of Nahum of Elkosh. A jealous and avenging God is the

The King Montezuma Trilogy

LORD, the LORD is avenging and wrathful; the LORD takes vengeance on his adversaries and rages against his enemies. The LORD is slow to anger but great in power, and the LORD will by no means clear the guilty.'"

"I like it!" announced Sol.

"What?" asked Jameson with astonishment.

"They deserve punishment for not turning to Jim Caldwell."

A look of near horror went across my face before stating, "I'm lost."

She replied, "So were they?"

I took a minute to compose myself. My wife is absolutely the best, but I couldn't make heads or tails out of this comment, so I nurtured her along with, "Tell us more."

"Jim has been around since the beginning of time, so they had plenty of time to live the Good News. Don't you know it was Jim who appeared in the Aztec Scriptures as King Melchizedek? Who was from Salem, which means peace? Who brought out bread and wine? Who was a priest of God Most High? Who blessed Aapo? And Aapo gave him one-tenth of everything? Maybe you should read the Old Testament. That's from Genesis 14:18-20." She then folded her arms and was done.

"Pretty interesting, hon," I offered, then got back to the story. "Let's see. Oh, wow. The next part is about good news to the Northern Empire." After scratching my head for a moment, I read it: 'Look! On the mountains the feet of one who brings good tidings, who proclaims peace! Celebrate your festivals, O Southern Empire, fulfill your vows, for never again shall the wicked invade you; they are utterly cut off' (Nahum 1:15)."

Even Jameson was shocked when Mom said, "See," and then made a motion like dropping a microphone.

The King Montezuma Trilogy

"Next is a vivid description of the attack against Bogota. Here's a sample: 'Devastation, desolation, and destruction! Hearts faint and knees tremble, all loins quake, all faces grow pale!' (2:10). But it gets worse: 'I will throw filth at you and treat you with contempt, and make you a spectacle. Then all who see you will shrink from you and say, "Bogota is devastated; who will bemoan her?" Where shall I seek comforters for you?' (3:6-7). Nahum closes his oracle with the Southern Empire rejoicing the destruction of Bogota: 'Your shepherds are asleep, O king of Colombia; your nobles slumber. Your people are scattered on the mountains with no one to gather them. There is no assuaging your hurt, your wound is mortal. All who hear the news about you clap their hands over you. For who has ever escaped your endless cruelty?' (3:18-19).

"Okay, we're done with that prophet. Let's take a short break before we get into the first thirty-two chapters of Ezekiel."

"None too soon, Dad. None too soon," he said with his first sense of boredom since the trip began.

Ezekiel 1-32

"Ezekiel was deported to Spain after the invasion of The Cartel, and before the fall of the Southern Empire. His book begins with a vision that is very important, because God had a home at the Temple in Tenochtitlan, yet the LORD shows up over in Spain! Get it? Even though God's people are absent from Templo Mayor, the LORD was still present in their new surroundings. They surely needed some assurance that the LORD wasn't just a local god, and that was the purpose of this vision.

The King Montezuma Trilogy

"What Ezekiel saw was indescribable, so he used terms he was familiar with from scripture about God's presence, like storms and fire. In the middle of the fire was something like four living creatures, then wheels beside the living creatures, followed by something like a dome over their heads.

"Oh, I remember that story!" announced Jameson. "Some of my friends at college call it the first UFO sighting."

"Wow!" I replied. "Talk about finding what you're looking for! All you have to do is read the next verse for a proper explanation, 'Like the bow in a cloud on a rainy day, such was the appearance of the splendor all around. This was the appearance of the likeness of the glory of the LORD' (1:28). Ezekiel then hears God speaking to him, so he falls on his face, but God says to stand up, 'and I will speak with you' (2:1). The LORD told Ezekiel that he was going to have a difficult mission of prophesying to a rebellious people. He then saw a scroll with words of lamentation and mourning and woe, and the LORD said, 'Eat this scroll that I give you and fill your stomach with it' (3:3). Then God said, 'Go to the exiles, to your people, and speak to them. Say to them, "Thus says the Lord GOD"; whether they hear or refuse to hear' (3:11).

"After some words of warning, the spirit bore Ezekiel away from that place to the exiles at Toledo, who lived by Rio Tajo. 'And I sat there among them, stunned for seven days' (3:15). After receiving more instructions, Ezekiel was driven by the hand of the LORD into another deserted region to prepare for his ministry."

Sol smiled and said, "That's how Jim Caldwell started his ministry."

"True, and thanks, but this ends differently for Ezekiel, because he is told not to speak. 'But when I speak with you, I

The King Montezuma Trilogy

will open your mouth, and you shall say to them, "Thus says the Lord GOD"; let those who will hear, hear; and let those who refuse to hear, refuse' (3:27).

"I think I like this guy," pronounced Sol. "He followed what God said, and Jim said the same thing, 'Let anyone with ears to hear listen!' (Matthew 13:9)."

"The next several chapters share the prophecy of the siege, fall, and final deportation of the Mexicans to Spain. It begins with God telling Ezekiel, 'You shall set your face toward the siege of Jerusalem, and with your arm bared you shall prophesy against it. See, I am putting cords on you so that you cannot run from one side to the other until you have completed the days of your siege' (4:7-8). The vision turns violent in God's actions against Mexico, 'therefore thus says the Lord GOD: I, I myself, am coming against you; I will execute judgments among you in the sight of the nations' (5:8).

Chapter 6 offers judgment on 'the mountains of Mexico' (vs. 2)."

"What does that mean?" asked a confused Sol.

"Good question. When I was preparing for this trip, I discovered that the expression 'the mountains of Mexico' shows up nowhere else in the Aztec Scriptures. It must be important because it shows up seventeen times in Ezekiel. The point appears to be that the judgment was about more than just the mountain that Tenochtitlan was on, but all of the high places where idolatry was practiced. 'I will spend my fury upon them. And you shall know that I am LORD, when their slain lie among their idols around their altars, on every high hill, on all the mountain tops, under every green tree, and under every leafy oak, wherever they offered pleasing odors to all their idols' (6:12-13).

The King Montezuma Trilogy

"The next chapter seems to be a sermon, designed to show his fellow exiled Mexicans, that Cortés and his Conquistadors will bring a decisive end to the Promised Land. That is such an unbelievable consequence, that Ezekiel takes four full chapters to share the divine vision of the desecration of the Temple. Ezekiel is escorted by an angel, reminiscent of Jacob Marley and Ebeneezer Scrooge in *A Christmas Carol*. They first come to the entrance, where God says, 'do you see what they are doing, the great abominations that the house of Mexico are committing here, to drive me far from my sanctuary?' (8:6). Then God said to enter and see what the ruling elders of Mexico are doing in the dark. Next God took him to the entrance of the north gate of the house of the LORD, and he saw women weeping over the departure of a fertility god. Finally, Ezekiel was brought into the inner court, where twenty-five men had their backs to the temple. They were worshiping the sun god, rather than the Almighty. 'Therefore I will act in wrath; my eye will not spare, nor will I have pity; and though they cry in my hearing with a loud voice, I will not listen to them' (8:18).

"Hey, Jameson. Your friends who thought chapter one was about a UFO sighting would be intrigued with this. Chapter ten features a return of the dome thingy, and now it is specified as a description of the indescribable: 'the glory of the LORD' (vs. 4)."

"I'll be sure to mention that when I get back to school this fall," said Jameson in a weirdly snarky way.

"The point of this story, which is known as a theophany…"

"Wait," requested Sol. "What is a theophany?"

"Thanks for asking. *Theo* means 'God' and *phonos* means 'light,' so a theophany is a visible representation of God to humankind."

The King Montezuma Trilogy

"Didn't help," frowned Sol.

"Now where was I? Oh yeah, the point of the story is that the LORD was preparing to leave the Temple, which the Aztecs thought was his home. What Ezekiel was sharing with his fellow exiles, was that the LORD was not confined by space or time."

"I like that," said Sol. "Wish you would have started with it."

After a quick nod of understanding I said, "Then Ezekiel announces that he was lifted up by the spirit and taken to the house of the LORD, and told to prophesy, 'You shall fall by the sword' (11:10). When Ezekiel asked God if that included the exiles, God said that even though he removed them far away, 'I will gather you from the peoples and assemble you out of the countries where you have been scattered, and I will give you the land of Mexico' (11:17).

"Yay!" announced Sol.

"But there was one caveat, that if they don't keep the statutes, woe is them. Then the Temple vision ended, Ezekiel was lifted again by the spirit, returned to the exiles, and there he told them all he had seen."

"Break time," requested Jameson, so we took a quick break. As we settled back in, I told them that the next thirteen chapters were oracles anticipating Tenochtitlan's destruction.

"The problem Ezekiel is having is that the people won't listen. They are an obstinate group, so God continues to call them, 'a rebellious house' (12:2, 3), and then shows them their rebelliousness in a visual of carrying their bags out in the dark. The LORD then instructs Ezekiel to explain that this oracle concerns the King of Mexico and all his tribes: "they shall go into exile, into captivity" (12:11). This was to have a two-fold purpose: 1) the people were to acknowledge their guilt, and 2) they were to recognize God's sovereignty. Then the LORD told

The King Montezuma Trilogy

Ezekiel that the Mexicans would say, 'The vision that he sees is for many years ahead; he prophesies for distant times. Therefore say to them, Thus says the Lord GOD; None of my words will be delayed any longer, but the word that I speak will be fulfilled' (12:27-28)."

Jameson immediately said, "Isn't that what you've been saying, Dad, about prophecy, that it is always about the near future?"

"Thanks, son. It is difficult to inspire people past their own lifetime. Again, let me say that prophecy is the most misunderstood part of the Bible. And it becomes more difficult when Caldwellians see prophecy about the distant future."

"Next," complained Sol with her arms firmly folded.

"Okay. God then went after those who prophesy with fake news. God called them, 'jackals among ruins' (13:4) because they were liars in a losing war. God pledged to be against them, 'because they have misled my people' (13:10), and God's rage will be spent on 'the prophets of Mexico who prophesied concerning Tenochtitlan and saw visions of peace for it, when there was no peace' (13:16)."

"Men!" exclaimed Sol.

"Not so fast! The women also got in on the action. Here's what God had to say to them: 'You have profaned me among my people for handfuls of barley and for pieces of bread, put to death persons who should not die and keeping alive persons who should not live, by your lies to my people, who listen to lies' (13:19)."

"Okay, move your story along again." said Sol with great annoyance.

"This is where it gets interesting. Certain elders of Mexico went to Ezekiel and sat down, and God told him what to say,

The King Montezuma Trilogy

'Any of those who take the idols into their hearts and place their iniquity as a stumbling block before them" (14:4) will be ignored because God wants to recover the hearts of the entire exilic community. For those who don't repent, 'I will set my face against them' (14:8)"

"Just like his son did," explained Sol.

"What?" asked a bewildered Jameson.

"Mi hijo. If you are thinking about going into the ministry, you need to read your Bible more. Listen to this about Jim Caldwell: 'When the days drew near for him to be taken up, he set his face to go to Phoenix' (Luke 9:51)."

"Interesting comparison, hon, but let me continue to chapter 15. It's a short metaphor about the value of Mexico, comparing the nation to wood. Ezekiel's point, which of course is claimed to be inspiration from the LORD, is that wood is valuable when it is used for its purpose. Mexico's purpose was to be the Promised Land that held God's People, but they have forgotten their calling, so God is acting accordingly. 'I will make the land desolate, because they have acted faithlessly' (15:8). This was virtually impossible for them to believe. How could God go back on a promise?"

"Is that the secret of the empire?" asked Jameson.

"A very large part of it, but we'll get into the rest of it later. As if the metaphor of a desolate land wasn't enough, the next chapter offers an allegory. It uses a courtroom setting to indict God's faithless bride Mexico, and is set up in four parts:

1. The indictment.
2. The sentencing.
3. A renewed indictment.
4. Covenant renewal.

The King Montezuma Trilogy

"So God gives them hope?" asked Jameson.

"Absolutely. Even in their total depravity they find that their hope isn't in themselves but in God. Kind of like what Pablo wrote in the Caldwellian Scriptures that faith isn't about us, it's about God. Here's what Ezekiel said: 'I will deal with you as you have done, you who have despised the oath, breaking the covenant; yet I will remember my covenant with you in the days of your youth, and I will establish with you an everlasting covenant. Then you will remember your ways, and be ashamed' (16:59-61). The next chapter is a political fable."

"Uh-oh," complained an alarmed Sol. "Politics and religion mix about as well as oil and water."

"We were certainly raised with the idea that you can't talk about politics or religion without a fight, but this chapter might give us some fresh insights. The first ten verses share what the LORD has told Ezekiel: "propound a riddle, and speak an allegory to the house of Mexico" (17:2). The metaphor is about two eagles and a vine, but the explanation comes in the next eleven verses. It explains to the exiles that they need not hold out hope that King Zedekiah's revolt would be successful. The last three verses is a poetic celebration that Mexico would ultimately be restored:

> 'All the trees of the field shall know
> That I am the LORD.
> I bring low the high tree,
> I make high the low tree;
> I dry up the green tree
> And make the dry tree flourish.
> I the LORD have spoken;
> I will accomplish it' (17:24)."

The King Montezuma Trilogy

"Sorry," claimed Jameson, "but what were these fresh insights you promised?"

"Well, first of all, I said we *might* get some fresh insights," to which both Sol and Jameson offered a wry smile. "My thought was that discussing politics and religion as a fable was designed to soften the blow. So, my insight was that we need to talk about politics and religion, but we need to learn how to do it with respect."

"I agree," said a smiling Sol. "Relationships are everything. If we can't get along, there must be something wrong with our relationship with God. I remember at our premarital counseling the pastor said that communication is the key to success. And if we communicate with respect, we have a better chance than when it's all about anger and frustration."

"I like that," said Jameson, "and now I would respectfully ask that we go to lunch."

That got three confirming votes so we headed to Sol's choice of Las 3 Abuelas. That means "The Three Grandmothers," and the restaurant was subtitled Cocina Tradicional Mexicana which means "Traditional Mexican Kitchen." It turned out to be a breakfast & brunch place that also handled special events, but we were lucky on both counts. We weren't too late to eat and no special events were happening. Jameson ordered a Combination Plate, Sol tried the Chile Relleno, and I had the Huevos Benedictinosa la Mexicana. As we left, we all agreed that the food was wonderful, but Sol said, "My culture is all about hospitality, and it was disappointing to have such slow service." Returning to our bench at Parque Roma, we settled in with pleasantly full stomachs.

"Next, God refutes negative ideas behind how God governs the moral order, and calls the exilic community to have a stand-

The King Montezuma Trilogy

up type of character. If a person is righteous, 'he shall surely live, says the Lord GOD' (18:9). If he has a son who practices violence, 'he shall surely die; his blood is upon himself' (18:13)."

"I'm not following," mentioned Sol with a furrowed brow.

"The point is that the popular belief of the day was that God was judge and we had no say in the matter. Ezekiel continues with an example of a grandson. If he sees the error of his father's ways and does not do likewise, 'he shall not die for his father's iniquity; he shall surely live' (18:17). This was a monumental change for God's people because they had fallen so far away from God's ways. Here's the point: 'The person who sins shall die. A child shall not suffer for the iniquity of a parent, nor a parent suffer for the iniquity of a child; the righteousness of the righteous shall be his own, and the wickedness of the wicked shall be his own' (18:20).

"Maybe," said Sol, "this passage was on Jim's mind when his Hole in the Rock Gang saw a man blind from birth. They asked Jim, 'Teacher, who sinned, this man or his parents, that he was born blind?' Jim answered, 'Neither this man nor his parents sinned'" (John 9:2-3)."

"Very nice, Sol, thanks. Here's how the chapter ends. God says, 'Repent and turn from all your transgressions; otherwise iniquity will be your ruin. Cast away from you all the transgressions that you have committed against me, and get yourselves a new heart and a new spirit! Why will you die? For I have no pleasure in the death of anyone, says the Lord GOD. Turn, then, and live' (18:30-32). For what it's worth, that's what I believe. Just like a judge in court doesn't really judge anyone, it's that persons actions that brings judgment upon them. Likewise, when we die and stand before the judge, judgment day becomes about our actions. We need not worry about God

The King Montezuma Trilogy

being corrupt, just us."

"And just us," suggested Jameson, "is proper justice. I guess we have no one to blame but ourselves."

"That's what God was trying to get his people to understand. They had gone so far astray that they lost their Promised Land."

"Is that the secret of the empire?" asked Jameson.

"A very large part of it, indeed. Now let's hear about the next chapter. It's simply a lament about the politics of power going to the head. The secret of the empire is that Zedekiah lost control of the Promised Land. 'And fire has gone out from its stem, has consumed its branches and fruit, so that there remains in it no strong stem, no scepter for ruling' (19:14).

"Ooh!" proclaimed Jameson. "Now you're offering answers to the secret of the empire."

"That's exactly it. There are many answers and many secrets, and more will be shared later. The story in Ezekiel takes an abrupt change in chapter 20, and some call it a revisionist history. The exilic community needs to understand that Tenochtitlan's judgment was inevitable and a just action from God, and they needed to see God's vision. Ezekiel then retells salvation history with an emphasis on Aztec idolatry. With this new vision of their sinful past, the LORD says: 'As a pleasing odor I will accept you, when I bring you out from the peoples, and gather you out of the countries where you have been scattered; and I will manifest my holiness among you in the sight of the nations' (20:41).

"Next, Ezekiel's attention is drawn to the people remaining in Mexico. The LORD told him to, 'set your face toward Tenochtitlan and preach against the sanctuaries; prophecy against the land of Mexico' and let them know that, 'I am coming against you, and will draw my sword out of its sheath, and will cut off from you both righteous and wicked' (21:1-3). The book continues with a poem about God's sword, interpreted as Cortés coming against Zedekiah. It ends with 'I will pour out my indignation upon you, with the fire of my wrath I will blow upon you. I will deliver you into brutish hands, those skillful to destroy. You shall be fuel for the fire, your blood shall enter the earth; you shall be remembered no more, for I the LORD have spoken' (21:31-32)."

"I was hoping we would be past all those old stories of bloodshed," complained Jameson.

"I liked," said Sol, "that Ezekiel was told by the LORD to 'set your face toward Tenochtitlan.'"

"Why do you like that, Mom?"

"Because when Jim Caldwell came down from the Hole in the Rock, he set his face toward Tenochtitlan, and ultimately the noose that took his life."

"Nice connections, hon. I like it, and now for chapter 22. It is about shedding blood and making idols. The point is to show the rapid disintegration of those remaining in Mexico. Chapter 23 is an allegory that shows the deviant behavior of the Mexicans, by talking about them as prostitutes and adulterers. 'She did not give up her whorings that she had practiced since Guatemala...Therefore I delivered her into the hands of her lovers, into the hands of the Spanish Conquistadors' (23:8-9)."

"Can we move on?" requested Sol. "This is pretty intense to have to listen to in the presence of my husband and son."

"We're moving to the unspeakable conclusion of the end of the Holy City, so just hang in there. Chapter 24 begins with the date when Cortés started his siege of Tenochtitlan. It is described in yet another metaphor."

The King Montezuma Trilogy

"Not more prostitutes, I hope," said Jameson.

"No. This time it's the image of a boiling pot."

"What would that signify?" asked Sol.

"Sadly, it's the bloody city, and the Lord GOD says, 'Woe to the bloody city!' (24:9). The story continues with, 'when I cleansed you in your filthy lewdness, you did not become clean from your filth; you shall not again be cleansed until I have satisfied my fury upon you. I the LORD have spoken; the time is coming, I will act. I will not refrain, I will not spare, I will not relent. According to your ways and your doings I will judge you, says the Lord GOD' (24:13-14).

"At this point in Ezekiel's prophecy, things turn personal. The LORD tells him his wife will die and he is not to mourn. 'So I spoke to the people in the morning, and at evening my wife died. And on the next morning I did as I was commanded' (24:18).

"I don't get that at all," said a shocked Sol.

"Neither did the exilic community. They asked, 'Will you not tell us what these things mean for us, that you are acting this way?' (24:19). Ezekiel explained that they needed to lose their understanding of God being present in the temple, and imitate Ezekiel's lack of grief. "And you, mortal, on the day when I take from them their stronghold, their joy and glory, the delight of their eyes and their heart's affection, one who has escaped will come and report to you the news. On that day your mouth shall be opened to the one who has escaped, and you shall speak and no longer be silent. So you shall be a sign to them; and they shall know that I am the LORD' (24:25-27)."

"Surely that means break time for us," suggested Jameson, so we took a silent stroll through the park and thought about the profound secret of the empire. It was a lovely walk through wooded paths with statues and memorials, playgrounds and beautiful views of the mountains. It crossed my mind that it would have been an almost incomprehensible thing to be in captivity and hear about the loss of your homeland. Tears started to well up in my eyes as I thought about the death of Ezekiel's wife and how blessed I was to have Sol by my side. She saw my tears and simply nodded. It was really quite profound that many years together could allow unspoken understandings.

"When we got back to our park bench I mentioned that the next seven chapter were oracles against Mexico's neighbors, then I would follow with a story about the final fall of the Southern Empire."

"Hope the next seven chapters go fast," said a gloomy Sol.

After ignoring that understandable comment I said, "Ezekiel had a pattern for what he wrote next. He prophesied, on the LORD's behalf, about seven nations. The seventh was Guatemala, and it alone got seven oracles. Any idea why Ezekiel used seven?"

"Dad! You act like we don't listen. We know that seven is the number of wholeness, but in what way does that make them whole?"

"It doesn't. Seven can also mean "complete," and I suspect Ezekiel was saying that the LORD's anger toward the nations was whole."

"Maybe," said Jameson, "but doesn't sound very holy."

"Ah, you touch on a touchy subject there. Some biblical scholars suggest seeing the same God in the Old Testament as you notice in the New Testament. Which means that some of the authors might be adding their perspective."

"Move it along," Sol said with indignation.

The King Montezuma Trilogy

"Okay. The first was Belize: 'Because you have clapped your hands and stamped your feet and rejoiced with all the malice within you against the land of Mexico, therefore I have stretched out my hand against you' (25:6-7). Next was Costa Rica and the LORD complained that they didn't find anything special about Mexico. Third was Panama, indicted for being vengeful, then Nicaragua was in trouble for the same reason.

"Fifth up for God's wrath was Honduras, and it was a big one. Chapter 26 brings us ever closer to the end of the Promised Land, because it talks about Cortés and his Spanish Conquistadors being used to fight against Honduras. Chapter 27 offers a lament over Honduras for its pride, while the next chapter offers an oracle against the King of Honduras for his pride. Chapter 28 continues with a lamentation over the King of Honduras, then takes aim at Colombia: 'I will send pestilence into it, and bloodshed into its streets; and the dead shall fall in its midst, by the sword that is against it on every side. And they shall know that I am the LORD' (28:23).

"Before moving into the seven oracles against the seventh nation, Ezekiel shares a word of hope for Mexico from the LORD: 'When I gather the house of Mexico from the peoples among whom they are scattered, and manifest my holiness in them in the sight of the nations, then they shall settle on their own soil that I gave to my servant Tobillo' (28:25).

"Now we're in the final four chapters of Ezekiel, before we look at the fall of the Southern Empire and the devastating destruction of Templo Mayor. In the coming days, we'll discuss the life of the Aztecs in the Exile, followed by the prophets who spoke upon returning home after the Exile. Meanwhile, chapters 29-32 share the seven oracles against the seventh nation: Guatemala.

The King Montezuma Trilogy

1. Chapter 29:1-16. This oracle is against the king's pride for saying, "Lake Izabal is my own; I made it for myself" (vs. 3). God is mad, and continues with judgment against the whole land: "they shall never again be the reliance of the house of Mexico; they will recall their iniquity, when they turned to them for aid. Then they shall know that I am the LORD God" (vs. 16).
2. Chapter 29:17-21. This is an oracle against Guatemala: "I will give the land of Guatemala to Hernando Cortés of Spain; and he shall carry off its wealth and despoil it and plunder it; and it shall be the wages for his army" (vs. 17).
3. Chapter 30:1-19. This is a lamentation of God's judgment against Guatemala: "the day of the LORD is near" (vs. 3), because "its proud might shall come down" (vs.6), so the "most terrible of the nations, shall be brought in to destroy the land" (vs.11). Ezekiel polishes this off with a list of cities that will be in trouble.
4. Chapter 30:20-26. This is a proclamation against the King: "I am against the King of Guatemala, and will break his arms, both the strong arm and the one that was broken; and I will make the sword fall from his hand" (vs.22), then the LORD will "scatter the Guatemalans among the nations and disperse them throughout the countries" (vs. 26).
5. Chapter 31:1-18. In this oracle Ezekiel returns to allegory, using a cosmic tree that is nourished by deep waters (vs. 4). The problem was that "its heart was proud of its height" (vs. 10), so God "closed the

The King Montezuma Trilogy

deep over it and covered it" (vs. 15). It closes with a question: "Which among the trees of Eden was like you in glory and in greatness? Now you shall be brought down" (vs. 18).

6. Chapter 32:1-16. This is followed by a lamentation over both the King and Guatemala. It starts with an accusation: "You consider yourself a lion among the nations, but you are like a dragon in the seas" (vs. 2). Verses 3-10 are reminiscent of the Mayan creation myth of Guatemala called the Popol Vuh, while the ending says, "This is a lamentation; it shall be chanted" (vs. 16).

7. Chapter 32:17-32. This final oracle against Guatemala is a dirge about its descent to the Mayan Underworld called Xibalba, which means "The Place of Fright." The LORD said, "wail over the hordes of Guatemala, and send them down to the world below, with those who go down to the Cave" (vs. 18).

"This was the preparation for the Exile. The fall of King Hezekiah and the Southern Empire, to Cortés and the Conquistadors was brutal and final. We'll look at some of the sparse understandings we have in the Aztec Scriptures, then spend some time debriefing our learnings of the day.

"The destruction occurred in two parts: 1) the holy city, Tenochtitlan, and 2) the house of the LORD, Templo Mayor. First of all, it wasn't Montezuma who lost the city to Cortés, as is the popular belief, it was Zedekiah."

Jamesons asked, "So why do people believe these kinds of things?"

The King Montezuma Trilogy

"It's more about it being tradition because Montezuma was the Aztec King that the story surrounds, but it definitely was Zedekiah. Montezuma died before the Empire divided. The final problem began when Zedekiah rebelled against Cortés who 'came with all his army against Tenochtitlan, and laid siege to it; they built siege-works against it all around' (2 Kings 25:1). Being cut off from the world, the residents had no food and a famine set in. Cortés and his army made a breach in the wall, so Zedekiah and his soldiers fled by night. Cortés' army pursued them and overtook them, and Zedekiah's army deserted him. He was brought to Cortés 'who passed sentence on him. They slaughtered the sons of Zedekiah before his eyes, then put out the eyes of Zedekiah; they bound him in fetters and took him to Spain' (2 Kings 25:6-7).

"The next thing they needed to do was destroy the holy city. The captain of Cortés' army came to Tenochtitlan and 'burned down the house of the LORD, the king's house, and all the houses' (2 Kings 25:9). They broke down the walls around the city and 'carried into exile the rest of the people who were left in the city...But the captain of the guard left some of the poorest people of the land to be vinedressers and tillers of the soil' (2 Kings 25:11-12).

"After this they destroyed Templo Mayor. Jeremiah had warned the people that they had broken their relationship with God and would lose their land, but they refused to believe. He prophesied the word of the LORD: 'Amend your ways and your doings, and let me dwell with you in this place. Do not trust in these deceptive words: "This is the temple of the LORD, the temple of the LORD, the temple of the LORD" (Jeremiah 7:3-4). The promise to God's people turned out to make them arrogant, and they paid the price. The conquistadors took the bronze pillars and broke 'them in pieces, and carried the bronze to Spain' (2 Kings 25:13).

"After that, the conquistadors 'took away the pots, the shovels, the snuffers, the dishes for incense, and all the bronze vessels used in the temple service, as well as the firepans and the basins. What was made of gold the captain of the guard took away for the gold, and what was made of silver, for the silver' (2 Kings 25:14-15). In other words, they plundered the holy temple in the holy city, and legend says that the amount of bronze that was taken was beyond weighing. Okay. Let's all take a deep breath, then share what learnings we've had today."

After a long pause, Jameson said, "I hated Nahum. You guys taught me to never gloat when troubles happen to those who don't like us."

"It certainly comes from the teachings of Jim Caldwell, but thanks for the kudos to us."

Sol responded with, "I loved Nahum, because Columbia deserved destruction. They were guilty, and those who remained in Mexico stayed in Sinaloa and formed The Cartel. If ever a group deserved destruction, it is them. They are the complete opposite of our Caldwellian faith."

I waited for a moment, then said, "I'm surprised that I found the book consoling. It reminds me that God can be counted on to destroy enemies of people who trust in God."

"I had terrible troubles with a boss one time," announced Sol, "and I really wanted vengeance. That anger in me never resolved, but I think good old Nahum helped me. God will take care of things in the long run."

"Good to hear, dear."

After giving me a hug, she said, "I liked how Ezekiel

prepared for his ministry, just like Jesus did."

All of a sudden, Jameson had a burst of energy, and said, "I loved the UFO story at the beginning of Ezekiel!"

I frowned and said, "I trust you're joking." Jameson gave an impish smile and shrugged his shoulders, then I said, "I enjoyed how Ezekiel's prophecy came true."

"Please explain that one, Dad"

"Only the prophecies that came true were the ones that made it into the Bible. It makes me wonder what the prophecies that didn't make it were all about."

Sol then volunteered, "I found it interesting that Ezekiel was lifted by the spirit to see his homeland, and then returned spiritually to the exiles. I had an out-of-body experience when I was a child. I received terrible burns on my legs and was in the hospital for a long time. Early on I heard the doctors say that I wouldn't make it, and my spirit was lifted up so that I was able to look down on the scene. I found myself sitting on a shelf next to a doll and the doll said, 'The doctors don't know what they are talking about. You're going to make it.'"

"Wow! What a great story. I mean, sorry that happened to you, but I guess it feels pretty good to be alive and to tell the story."

"Yes it does, son, because now I have you and your father in my life."

We all got choked up a bit, then Jameson asked me, "Didn't you say something about hope?"

"Yes. What the exiled community learned was that hope is in God, not themselves."

Next, Sol said, "I could have done without the last half of what we heard today. Oracles, and allegories, and visions, and

The King Montezuma Trilogy

metaphors, and laments probably have their place, but I prefer the Good News of Jim Caldwell."

"Just remember that it's all 'God's Word.' What I love about that thought is, knowing the authors offered their perspective, means it's not all 'God's words.' Now let's pack up, head for the car, be thankful for a beautiful day in Parque Roma, get a nice dinner and a good night's rest. Tomorrow we will hear about the experience in exile."

The King Montezuma Trilogy

ACT III
During the Exile

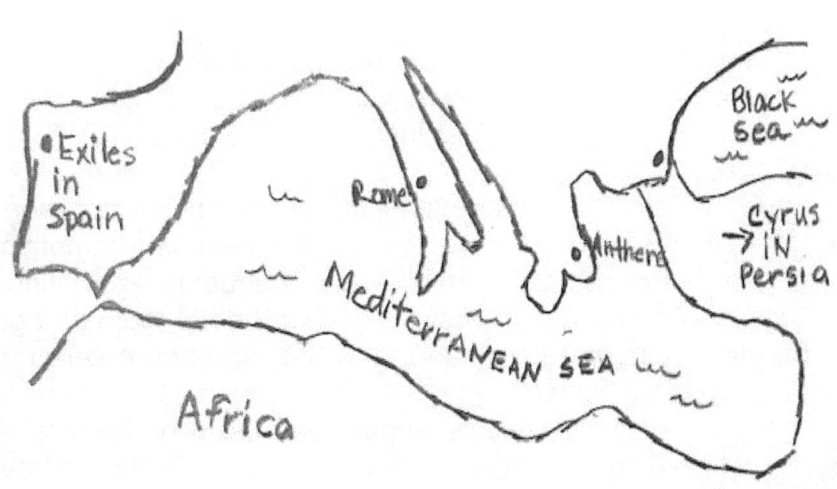

The King Montezuma Trilogy

SCENE ONE
Ezekiel 33-58

It was a gorgeous day outside, but Sol and Jameson knew I was up to something.

"Okay," announced Sol, who probably knew me better than I knew myself. "What's going on?"

"What?" I asked sheepishly.

"Come on, Dad. You should never gamble because you can't hide excitement."

"Okay, I admit it. Something pretty cool is going to happen."

"What is it?" asked Sol, who can't ever wait for surprises.

"Nope. Not this time. Let's just go downstairs and get in the car."

"But we haven't had breakfast yet!" complained Jameson.

"Ah, the glint in your father's eyes tells me it has something to do with breakfast, but I can't imagine that being so exciting."

We finally headed downstairs from our hotel room and got in the car. I plugged my phone in to the map and entered an address, and off we went.

Jameson was in the passenger seat and was desperately trying to figure out the mystery when he asked, "Does this have anything to do with the secret of the empire?"

I just laughed and left them in the void of unknowing. Sol was enjoying being in Mexico, so she spontaneously broke into one of her favorite songs, La Bikina, by Luis Miguel. Soon we were in the suburb of Santa Catarina, then headed northwest to the city Garcia. From there we headed out of town to the northeast and my fellow passengers started getting pretty frustrated. When we passed a sign that said Xenpal, Jameson

The King Montezuma Trilogy

looked it up and said, "We're going to a zoo?" We drove right past and both of them were now getting exasperated.

Next we went past a campground and Sol sarcastically said, "I hope you haven't taken us out here for breakfast!"

The scenery was fantastic, with craggy mountain crests constantly getting closer, but we continued on. At this point the road came to an end with a loop for the return trip.

"You're lost, aren't you!" demanded Sol.

I then turned on to a singular road that went back to an old farmhouse, and Jameson said, "Kinda' creepy, Dad. Did you ever read *In Cold Blood*?"

It was an old farmhouse on a large expanse of land with lots of farming equipment, and I opened my door and got out. It took a bit of coaxing to get them to cooperate, but soon enough I was knocking on the front door. When it creaked open, a rather scary looking, short and stocky Mexican man with a long beard was standing there with his leg bent on a knee scooter.

Jameson nearly screamed, "Geraldo!" who almost tipped over when Jameson ran up to give him a hug.

After lots of laughter, I finally introduced him to Sol who was quite astonished at the developments. "Geraldo was our tour guide last year."

After I introduced Sol, Geraldo's wife came to greet us all and said, "I have the best breakfast you'll ever have. It's all ready to go. My name is Rivera."

Jameson couldn't miss the chance to say, "So together you are Geraldo Rivera?"

Geraldo tried to act hurt for a moment but couldn't keep the laughter at bay. Then Rivera said, "Actually my parents were big fans of Frida Kahlo, but they didn't like either of her names, so they chose her husband's last name of Rivera."

The King Montezuma Trilogy

We had much to talk about, so Rivera suggested we continue the conversation over breakfast. We happily took a seat at their kitchen table with its sumptuous spread of homemade tortillas made fresh on a placa, huevos rancheros, and an amazing bean skillet like I had never seen. To the side was an array of homemade jams and jellies and salsas, and by each plate was a glass of atole. Geraldo offered grace and Rivera began passing the food around.

"Okay, Dad, so how did you know Geraldo lived here?"

"Remember sitting at the Great Pyramid of Cholula?"

"How could I forget?" Jameson said with a huge smile.

"That's where Geraldo told us about the Aztec people getting organized into twelve tribes."

"Okay."

"And you got excited about the most well-known cities currently in each tribal area, like Puerto Vallarta, Acapulco, and Oaxaca."

"I hope you're going somewhere with this."

"Then Geraldo asked if we knew what Monterrey was well-known for."

"Vaguely familiar, but what was the answer?"

Geraldo then beamed as he reminded, "Because it is where I was born!"

All five of us laughed heartily for a while, then Jameson asked, "So how did you know he lived here?"

I pointed at the knee scooter next to Geraldo and asked, "Remember when I said Geraldo couldn't be our guide this time because he had a farming accident?" Jameson and Sol both acknowledged, then I said, "We've kept in touch."

The conversation continued while eating great food, and when we were done Sol offered to help Rivera clean up so "the

The King Montezuma Trilogy

boys" could finish their conversation. It was certainly a visit to remember and we hated to go, but before long my agenda orientation took over. We said our fond farewells then I said "adios" as we got in the car. Geraldo said "adios" back to us and Jameson seemed a bit confused, so Sol explained as we went down the driveway, "it simply means 'go with God.' It's a great word for hello and goodbye, just like the Hawaiian word 'aloha.'"

As we drove down the long driveway, Jameson said, "That was the best! Thanks, Dad." Even Sol said it was a great idea and she was glad it worked out. Soon we made our way to Parque Fundidora, got out of the car, and found some benches facing the Rio Santa Catarina.

Another wonderful day of sunshine and shade awaited us as we settled in for a day of learning. A gentle breeze rose from the river and refreshed us as I began. "Ezekiel's story continued with a discussion of how God would hold him accountable to warn the wicked ones. 'But if you warn the wicked to turn from their ways, and they do not turn from their ways, the wicked shall die in their iniquities, but you will have saved your life' (33:9).

"The problem was that the demoralized exiles were concerned for their own lives. God told Ezekiel to tell them, 'I have no pleasure in the death of the wicked, but that the wicked turn from their ways and live; turn back, turn back from your evil ways; for why will you die, O house of Mexico?' (33:11)."

Jameson said, "Not sensing much comfort."

"Then listen to what God had to say next: 'None of the sins that they have committed shall be remembered against them; they have done what is lawful and right, they shall surely live' (33:16). This was to prepare the exilic community for the fall of the Southern Empire, where someone who had escaped from

The King Montezuma Trilogy

Tenochtitlan came to Ezekiel and said, 'The city has fallen.' This must have come as a crushing blow. They lost their Promised Land because they quit following God's commandments, but if they returned to being God's People by following the commandments, they could hope to get back their Promised Land. I'm a very visual person, so let me draw this:

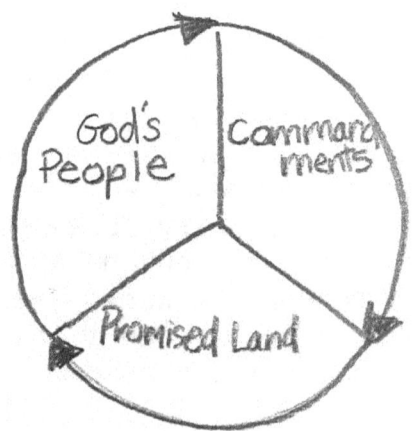

"Not bad," said Jameson with a chuckle, "but let's just say drawing isn't your strong point."

"Actually, I like it," offered Sol. "If God's People move back to following the Commandments, they could regain the Promised Land."

"Great! Maybe that college class I took on geometry paid off!" Both of them looked confused, so I moved on. "In the next chapter Ezekiel says the first step in the right direction is to understand that the leadership back in Mexico was corrupt. God

The King Montezuma Trilogy

chose to use the image of sheep and shepherd, but it wasn't about having the leaders become better shepherds. 'For thus says the Lord GOD: I myself will search for my sheep, and will seek them out' (34:11)."

"Yep," agreed Sol. "Jim was willing to do anything to find the one lost sheep."

"And that was a parable, where Jim Caldwell probably got inspiration from this chapter, and Jim also called himself the good shepherd in John 10:11."

Sol spoke up again and said, "Don't forget Montezuma saying that 'The LORD is my shepherd,' in Psalm 23:1."

"Wait," complained Jameson, "this is getting rather dizzying, so what's the point?"

"Try this," I offered. "God says, 'I will seek the lost, and I will bring back the strayed, and I will bind up the injured, and I will strengthen the weak, but the fat and the strong I will destroy. I will feed them with justice' (34:16). To me this emphasizes that we need to turn to God, then, now, and always."

"Amen!" exclaimed an almost jubilant Sol with both arms raised in the air.

"From here it gets a bit strange, because the LORD pronounces an oracle against Panama in chapter 35."

"I'll pass," frowned Jameson.

"Me, too. After all, we're people of the Good News. Which is where chapter 36 turns. After the LORD spends some more time denouncing Panama, we hear, 'But you, O mountains of Mexico, shall shoot out your branches, and yield your fruit to my people Mexico; for they shall soon come home' (36:8). Rather than being against his people, God is planning to be on their side. 'I will multiply human beings and animals upon you. They shall increase and be fruitful; and I will cause you to be inhabited

The King Montezuma Trilogy

as in your former times, and will do more good to you than ever before. Then you shall know that I am the LORD' (36:11).

"The Lord God continues offering this vision to Ezekiel to prophesy to the people: 'On the day that I cleanse you from all your iniquities, I will cause the towns to be inhabited, and the waste places shall be rebuilt...And they will say, "This land that was desolate has become like the garden of Aztlan"' (36:33, 35)."

"Been there, done that!" claimed a smiling Jameson.

"What do you mean?" asked Sol.

"That's where dad and I started last year's adventure, sitting at the Tikal Temple in the jungles of Guatemala," as Sol looked on approvingly.

"Next comes one of the more memorable chapters in Ezekiel, known as *The Valley of Dry Bones*. To do it justice, let me just read the vision offered in the first six verses:

> The hand of the LORD came upon me, and he brought me out by the spirit of the LORD and set me down in the middle of a valley; it was full of bones. He led me all around them; there were very many lying in the valley, and they were very dry. He said to me, "Mortal, can these bones live?" I answered, "O Lord GOD, you know." Then he said to me, "Prophesy to these bones, and say to them: O dry bones, hear the word of the LORD. Thus says the Lord GOD to these bones: I will cause breath to enter you, and you shall live. I will lay sinews on you, and will cause flesh to come upon you, and cover you with skin, and put breath in you, and you shall live; and you shall know that I am the LORD."

The King Montezuma Trilogy

"I know what happened next!" said a captivated Jameson. "The bones came together, and the renewed people stood on their feet. It's a great vision of hope for people who are down and out."

"Very good, son. Very good. The rest of chapter 37 uses the image of two sticks to represent the Northern Empire and the Southern Empire. God tells Ezekiel to 'join them together into one stick' (vs. 17), signifying their ultimate unification. God finishes this story with, 'Then the nations shall know that I the LORD sanctify Mexico, when my sanctuary is among them forever' (vs. 28). Next the story takes a strange turn to 'Gog, of the land of Magog' (38:2)."

"I know all about that!" said Sol with a huge frown. "That's from the Book of Revelation."

"You got that right," I cautioned, "because the Revelation story was adapted from these two chapters. It was a vision about feeling secure once they return to the Promised Land. The point was that nobody can thwart God's ultimate plans. The word from God was 'I will turn you around and put hooks into your jaws, and I will lead you out with all your army' (38:4). The LORD continues with, 'and I will not let my holy name be profaned any more; and the nations shall know that I am the LORD, the Holy One of Mexico. It has come! It has happened, says the Lord GOD. This is the day of which I have spoken' (39:7-8). Here comes another seven, concerning the burial of Gog. 'Seven months the house of Mexico shall spend burying them, in order to cleanse the land' (39:12)."

"Oh, I get it," announced Jameson. "The death of God's enemies means a complete cleansing of the land."

"And for the apocalypse!" proclaimed Sol.

"Sounds like a good time to take a lunch break." They both

The King Montezuma Trilogy

agreed and Sol mentioned that she saw a nearby store where she would like to shop, then Jameson said that he would like to find a baseball cap with the word Monterrey on it. We agreed to take thirty minutes and meet back at the El Lingote restaurant. When we regathered, we found out that they didn't open until one, so we had thirty more minutes to kill. We then agreed to take a stroll around the park. Jameson checked the map on his phone and said there was a short round trip on the walkways. We paused for a moment at Canal Santa Lucia, then headed north past Casa Rosa. The weather was beginning to warm up, so we took the next path to the right and stopped at Conarte, an Arts pavilion. After a brief visit, we headed back south and the path took us straight to El Lingote just as they opened.

"Hey, Dad. I saw some great seats with views if we sit out on the terrace."

"Okay, I'll check." It turned out to be a much fancier restaurant than I expected, but since we were there right at opening time, we got our choice of seats. The terrace was amazing with beautiful views of the mountains in the distance, but it turned out that the service and food was even better. We were treated exceptionally well, and I wondered if having Sol speak Spanish to the server was part of the reason. Let me just say that I ordered Pulpo Norestense, and here is how it was described in the menu: Pulpo a la parrilla en adobo de chiles secos, con risotto de asado de Puerco, chicahrron de pork belly, garbanzo y salsa macha.

Sol laughed when I tried to pronounce it, but at least I could understand about half of what was in it. Far more importantly, it had a heavenly fragrance and out-of-this-world flavor. I don't even know what Sol and Jameson ordered because I was too entranced by my gastronomic experience. We all three enjoyed

The King Montezuma Trilogy

a classic margarita, but Sol struggled a bit with the idea that her son was growing up. After lunch, we decided to relax a bit to let the meal settle, then slowly made our way back to the bench by the river to hear the final nine chapters of Ezekiel.

"Chapters 40-48 envision a new social order of God's people again living on their God-promised land. God will be the new king and the Temple will need to be restored. They will need to relearn how to live with the divine presence, and the land will need to be rid of violence and injustice. To accomplish this, the first thing God does is transport Ezekiel to the land of Mexico and sets him down on a mountain. Again he has an experience with a Jacob Marley type of guide who tells him to 'look closely and attentively' (40:4). The purpose of this visit was to encourage fellow exiles to believe that they will become the house of Mexico. The guide went about doing lots of measuring, but I'll spare you the details."

"Thanks, Dad!" Even Sol looked relieved.

"In the big picture, the guide measured the exterior of the temple, then did the same for the interior. After that, the guide showed the sanctuary and the altar and the inner court, in his tour for Ezekiel. Finally the guide spoke again, saying, 'The north chambers and the south chambers opposite the vacant area are the holy chambers' (42:13). But here's the important thing. The guide took Ezekiel to the gate, and there, 'the glory of the God of Mexico was coming from the east' (43:2)."

"Obviously," said Jameson, "this is important, but specifically, why?"

"It's because it is a vision of the reversal of the LORD's departure from the temple and the city. The departure was frightening enough, so the exilic community needed this vision to give them hope. Then a voice came from the temple and said,

The King Montezuma Trilogy

'this is the place of my throne and the place for the soles of my feet, where I will reside among the people of Mexico forever' (43:7). The voice then told Ezekiel to tell his people the plan of the temple, and said, 'This is the law of the temple: the whole territory on the top of the mountain all around shall be most holy. This is the law of the temple' (43:12).

"What comes next is a reordering of life toward holiness, purity, justice, and economic equity. It begins with seven days of consecration of the altar."

"Wait a minute," requested Jameson. "Is the exile over?"

"No, but the practical applications sure sound that way, don't they?" Jameson looked mildly embarrassed, so I assured him it was a good question. "Here's what was said next: 'When these days are over, then from the eighth day onward the priests shall offer upon the altar your burnt offerings and your offerings of well-being; and I will accept you, says the Lord GOD' (43:27).

Sol seemed intent on helping to alleviate Jameson's embarrassment, so she said, "Sure sounds to me like everyone is back in Mexico."

Jameson smiled and said, "I'm alright, mom. Thanks."

"Next, the LORD said to Ezekiel, 'This gate shall remain shut; it shall not be opened, and no one shall enter by it; for the LORD, the God of Mexico, has entered by it; therefore it shall remain shut' (44:2).

"And the purpose of that?" asked Jameson.

"I think it means that the LORD will never again depart from the Temple. God then told Ezekiel that the Levites who had gone astray would serve a purpose. 'I will appoint them to keep charge of the temple, to do all its chores, all that is to be done in it' (44:14)."

The King Montezuma Trilogy

"Ooh," said Jameson. "A bit of vengeance. Cool."

"But the Levitical priests who stayed faithful while Mexico went astray would be assigned to minster to God."

"How would they do that?" inquired Jameson.

"By not shaving their head, nor drinking wine when they enter the inner court. They are also not to 'marry a widow, or a divorced woman, but only a virgin of the stock of the house of Mexico, or a widow who is the widow of a priest' (44:22)"

"I hope you are listening, Jameson," exclaimed Sol in an almost scolding voice.

"Mom!"

Quickly getting back to the task at hand, I said that they were to teach, act as judges as needed, and follow proper procedures toward the dead. The attention then turned to the area outside the temple. A portion was to be set aside as a holy district, followed by an area for the city. Then Ezekiel is told to have them observe honesty in weights and measures, and make offerings so that the LORD would also not be defrauded. Next was a discussion of festivals, concentrating on the reestablishment of Passover.

"Chapter 46 talks about the Sabbath and some miscellaneous regulations, then chapter 47 shows the effects of having the divine presence in the land. 'Then he brought me back to the entrance of the temple' there, water was flowing from below the threshold of the temple toward the east (for the temple faced east); and the water was flowing down from below the south end of the threshold of the temple, south of the altar. Then he brough me out by way of the north gate, and led me around on the outside to the outer gate that faces toward the east; and the water was coming out on the south side' (47:1-2).'"

The King Montezuma Trilogy

"Sorry," said Jameson. "What is that all about?"

"It's to set up contrast. The next several verses talk about the guide leading Ezekiel through the water. At first it is ankle-deep, then knee-deep, then waist-deep, then deep enough to swim."

"So?" asked a mildly perturbed Jameson.

"It is to show the beauty of God's presence, and here's how. 'On the banks, on both sides of the river, there will grow all kinds of trees for food. Their leaves will not wither no their fruit fail, but they will bear fresh fruit every month, because the water for them flows from the sanctuary. Their fruit will be for food, and their leaves for healing' (47:12). After that the land was equitably divided among the twelve tribes. The Lord GOD said, 'you shall divide this land among you according to the tribes of Mexico' (47:21). The city itself does not belong to any particular tribe, so it is renamed: 'And the name of the city from that time on shall be, The LORD is There' (48:35), which later became Mexico City.

"That ends the book of the prophet Ezekiel. Time to share your learnings."

"Not so much a learning," said a thoughtful Jameson, "but I have a question."

"Of course!"

Jameson thought for a moment to formulate his question, then asked, "Why does God seem to be evil sometimes?"

Sol looked shocked, and turned to her body language of folded arms, then I said, "I thought that question might come up. I did some research this past year, and found that what you're talking about is sometimes referred to as divine justice, but then it gets a bit trickier." All of a sudden Sol perked up with obvious intrigue, and I continued. "You have to start with the idea of justice. Now wait a minute, I want to check a note on my phone to give you the correct quotation." After a brief pause, I said, "Okay, here it is: 'Justice is a philosophical concept of rightness in ethics and is part of the central core of morality.'"

Sol threw her hands in the air and said, "Sounds like what some haughty professor would say!"

"I don't disagree. It needs to be more practical to be useful. Try this. Some scholars say that justice is whatever God says it is."

"That's more like it!" beamed Sol. "God is sovereign!"

"All I know is that the Bible oftentimes says the righteous will be rewarded and the wicked will be punished."

"Tell us more about that, Dad."

After thumbing through my phone, I found several characteristic verses. "Remember when Geraldo was talking about Sodom and Gomorrah?" Jameson nodded, then I continued. "It is a classic story of crime and punishment, and says, 'keep the way of the LORD by doing righteousness and justice' (Genesis 18:19).

"What about the punishment part?" asked a mildly frustrated Sol.

"Well, here's a setup story from the book of Judges. 'It is not I who have sinned against you, but you are the one who does me wrong, by making war on me. Let the LORD, who is judge, decide today' (11:27)."

"Ready for the knockout punch," said a now exasperated Sol.

"Okay, here it is. My point is that concentrating on bad news might cause us to miss out on the good news." Sol again folded her arms, then I went on. "We recently dealt with the book of Amos, where with the famous quote, 'But let justice roll down like waters, and righteousness like an ever-flowing stream' (5:24)."

Jameson then said, "So maybe our task is to let God do the justice part, and let us do the righteousness part."

"Didn't hear a knockout punch," complained Sol.

"Okay, so try this. I already highlighted it a few days ago when we were talking about Micah, but it is certainly worth repeating. 'He has told you, O mortal, what is good; and what does the LORD require of you but to do justice, and to love kindness, and to walk humbly with your God?' (6:8).

"That's great Dad, but it still doesn't explain why God was so mean to the chosen ones."

"Well, that's easy. They quit following God's ways. God's commandments. God's promises. Now, can we get back to your learnings?"

Jameson spoke up first and said, "I love Dickens' *A Christmas Carol*, so I found it pretty neat that the guy who led Ezekiel around the vision of a newly restored Tenochtitlan was like the Jacob Marley character."

"Yes," agreed Sol, "and I loved the part of the prophecy, right after that, when God returned to the Temple."

"I make no bones about it, that one of my favorite stories is the Valley of Dry Bones."

"It's kinda sad, Dad, how you can't keep away from dad jokes."

"To each their own," I said with a big smile. Next, Jameson said that he enjoyed learning where Geraldo lived. "Not exactly a learning about the Bible, but, yes, it was great."

Next, Sol volunteered that she hated that business about Gog. "The Book of Revelation scares me enough that I don't need some Old Testament prophet reminding me of the end

The King Montezuma Trilogy

times."

"Okay. That's just not it at all. Gog exemplifies the forces of violent domination, and that they will be destroyed. Even in that story we find good news, for those who are looking for it." I quickly turned in my Bible to Ezekiel 37 and read, 'I will make a covenant of peace with them; it shall be an everlasting covenant with them; and I will bless them and multiply them, and will set my sanctuary among them forevermore. My dwelling place shall be with them; and I will be their God, and they shall be my people. Then the nations shall know that I the LORD sanctify Mexico, when my sanctuary is among them forevermore' (vv. 26-28).

"A bit heavy for me," announced Jameson, "so let me say that I loved the restaurant."

I had a huge smile and agreed. "I have no idea what you two had, but my meal was spectacular."

"We know you were oblivious," said Sol. "The food was dripping out of both sides of your mouth."

After some uncomfortable laughter, I said, "I loved that the city of Tenochtitlan was renamed, 'The LORD is there.'"

"Why?" inquired Jameson.

"Because it makes me think that when I was renewed in God's grace, I was renamed a 'Caldwellian.'"

That drew smiles from both of them, then Sol asked, "What did Ezekiel say about turning your life around?"

"Let me look it up." I somehow found it intriguing that I was turning the pages to find about turning life around, but I wasn't about to mention it. "Here it is. 'Now you, mortal, say to the house of Mexico, Thus you have said: "Our transgressions and our sins weigh upon us, and we waste away because of them; how then can we live?" Say to them, As I live, says the Lord

The King Montezuma Trilogy

GOD, I have no pleasure in the death of the wicked, but that the wicked turn from their ways and live; turn back, turn back from your evil ways; for why will you die, O house of Mexico?'"

"Aren't we right back to that righteousness and justice stuff? asked Jameson.

"Well, yes. Didn't I say it was pervasive? But try these verses: 'If the wicked restore the pledge, give back what they have taken by robbery, and walk in the statutes of life, committing no iniquity—they shall surely live, they shall not die. None of the sins that they have committed shall be remembered against them; they have done what is lawful and right, they shall surely live' (Ezekiel 33:15-16)."

"Okay," announced Sol, "I'm ready to move on. I really did like the drawing you did today, about God's People moving back to following the Commandments, and then they could regain the Promised Land. Mexico is too precious to lose for any reason."

Taking an opportunity to balance the compliments, Jameson said, "I learned that the last nine chapters of Ezekiel are amazingly boring."

"Good one, son," I said with a smirk. "Ending on a positive note, let me lift up these verses: 'But you, O mountains of Mexico, shall shoot out your branches, and yield your fruit to my people Mexico; for they shall soon come home. See now, I am for you; I will turn to you, and you shall be tilled and sown; and I will multiply your population, the whole house of Mexico, all of it; the towns shall be inhabited and the waste places rebuilt; and I will multiply human beings and animals upon you. They shall increase and be fruitful; and I will cause you to be inhabited as in your former times, and will do more good to you than ever before. Then you shall know that I am the LORD' (Ezekiel 36:8-11).

The King Montezuma Trilogy

"It's been a great day. Thanks for your attentiveness and interest. We're done a little early, so let's celebrate with a bit of exploring Monterrey." We headed back to the car and drove for a long time, enjoying the culture and creativity of this marvelous city. The one stop we made was to take in an up-close view of the Palacio del Obispado, a Baroque palace that housed a regional museum.

Soon Jameson was on his phone looking for a place to eat. "The hotel is terrific, but I'd to take in more of the local color." We all agreed so he kept looking. "How about seafood?" Again Sol and I were favorable so in very short order he said, "Let's try El Camaron."

When we got there, the place was filled with music. A mariachi band was playing, then a soloist and a guitar player took over. During break time, a server stepped up to the microphone and announced that they would have an open mic time next. I looked at Sol and said, "You've got to do this!"

She smiled and said, "I think I will. There's nothing better than being a Mexican in Mexico singing a Mexican song."

Waiting for the music break to be over, we ordered an appetizer of scalloped octopus and a large shrimp cocktail. As we waited for our dinner, I mentioned that tomorrow we will hear about Isaiah 40-55. Not only is it more of the brief information we have about the exile, but it also is one of my favorite sections of the Bible.

Pretty soon the waiter returned to the microphone and said, "Okay, who wants to come up and sing?"

Sol immediately stood up and made her way to the front. Jameson and I were grinning and applauding because we were so happy for her to get this opportunity. She has a wonderful voice, but only sings special music from time to time at church.

The King Montezuma Trilogy

"Gracias," she said to the waiter, then turned to the dining audience. They were mostly eating, but she went ahead and said, "I'd like to sing a favorite song of my mother's called Estrella." Several people looked up as she began singing, and it was almost magical. Not only was she doing a wonderful job, but many in the restaurant joined in. The colorful restaurant, fabulous food, and great music made for a memorable evening. All of a sudden, Jameson became more interested in his Hispanic roots.

The King Montezuma Trilogy

SCENE TWO
Isaiah 40-55

We were blessed this morning with a refreshing rain, which left the birds chirping and an occasional rooster crowing. Jameson requested Parque San Nicolas for our talk, so we drove northwest from our hotel and quickly found a park bench near the Museo de San Nicolas. We brought some towels from the hotel, dried the bench off, and I was pretty excited to get started.

"One reason I love this book, sometimes called Second Isaiah or Deutero-Isaiah, is because this prophet wasn't about gloom and doom. Isaiah was all about liberation, restoration and salvation."

"What makes you think Isaiah wasn't written by one prophet?" asked Sol.

"Thanks. Questioning is always a good thing. One reason scholars today believe Isaiah 40-55 was written 200 years after Isaiah 1-39, is the way chapter 40 begins. 'Comfort, O comfort my people, says your God. Speak tenderly to Tenochtitlan, and cry to her that she has served her term, that her penalty is paid, that she has received from the LORD'S hand double for all her sins' (vv. 1-2)."

"Sorry," exclaimed Jameson, "but I don't get it."

"First Isaiah began his prophetic work before the Northern Empire fell to The Cartel, and well before the Southern Empire fell to the Conquistadors. So what's the business about Tenochtitlan's penalty being paid? It makes sense if you let Second Isaiah be written during the exile."

"Still not there," informed Sol.

"Let me try better. Later, the LORD says of Cyrus, 'He is

The King Montezuma Trilogy

my shepherd, and he shall carry out my purpose'; and says of Tenochtitlan, 'It shall be rebuilt,' and of the temple, 'Your foundation shall be laid' (44:28)."

"I get it," announced Jameson. "Cyrus wasn't even around during First Isaiah, and the temple wasn't destroyed."

"Great! Next I want to mention that Isaiah 40-48 is about promising liberation to the exiles in Spain, and Isaiah 49-55 anticipates the restoration of Tenochtitlan back in Mexico. The first eleven verses of chapter 40 record the commissioning of Second Isaiah. Try to imagine the task he had to bring good news to these beleaguered people. Their world collapsed when the Conquistadors defeated them, destroyed the temple, and exiled them to Spain. For nearly 50 years this group of Aztecs lived in defeat. Their hope was waning, and they were dying in a foreign land.

"Then along comes Isaiah. He sensed that God was ready to do great things again for the Aztec people, so he used imagery from the Exodus. To inspire them, Isaiah's message was going to be filled with joy, so he begins like a general getting stationary troops ready to move. Encouragement comes from a voice crying out from the heavens:

> 'On the ocean prepare the way of the LORD,
>   make straight a shipping lane for our God.
> Every valley of water shall be lifted up,
>   and every swell shall be made low;
> the uneven water shall become level,
>   and the rough places made smooth.
> Then the glory of the LORD shall be revealed,
>   and all people shall see it together,
> for the mouth of the LORD has spoken' (40:3-5).

The King Montezuma Trilogy

"I remember glory," said Sol.

"What do you mean?" asked Jameson.

Sol quickly opened her Bible and read, "'Like the bow in a cloud on a rainy day, such was the appearance of the splendor all around. This was the appearance of the likeness of the glory of the LORD.' That's from Ezekiel 1:28, saying that we can see the glory of the LORD, so Isaiah was prophesying that the presence of God would be so strong it would be visible."

Jameson and I looked at each other a bit stunned, then I smiled, thanked her for a great observation, and continued. "Another voice cries out from the heavens and tells Isaiah to preach. After he expresses despair at his challenging task, he digs deep and comes up with the essence of what he has to say to his fellow exiles. 'The grass withers, the flower fades; but the word of our God will stand forever' (40:8)."

"Amen," said a smiling Sol.

"I like it," said Jameson, "especially that verse eight is a one sentence sermon, but just exactly how does that help them?"

"Because it instills the hope they needed that the Promised Land would again be theirs. Even though God's promise seemed to be gone for now, its eternal nature would shine through. The final inspiration Isaiah received was to imagine the exiles returning and give them the good news that God intends to deliver them: 'He will feed his flock like a shepherd; he will gather the lambs in his arms, and carry them in his bosom, and gently lead the mother sheep' (40:11).

"The next section is a hymn that celebrates God as the almighty creator by asking a series of rhetorical questions. The point is that even the captors in Spain are little more than dust. Isaiah increases his boldness by referring to the sun, the moon, and the stars as meaningless in God's much larger universe.

The King Montezuma Trilogy

This is so bold because Spain worshipped them as gods. Can you imagine proclaiming God's superiority while you are still in Spain?"

"Pretty cool," proclaimed Jameson.

"Then Isaiah really gets down to business with the intention of removing the stumbling block of hopelessness. Here's how he puts it:

> 'Why do you say, "My way is hidden from the LORD,
>   and my right is disregarded by my God?"
> Have you not known? Have you not heard?
>   The LORD is the everlasting God,
> the Creator of the ends of the earth.
>   He does not faint or grow weary;
> his understanding is unsearchable.
>   He gives power to the faint,
> and strengthens the powerless.
>   Even youths will faint and be weary,
> and the young will fall exhausted;
>   but those who wait for the LORD
> shall renew their strength,
>   they shall mount up with wings like eagles,
> they shall run and not be weary,
>   they shall walk and not faint' (40:27-31)."

"Now that's one of my favorite Aztec scripture passages," announced Sol.

I agreed, then said, "Isaiah was trying to help his people see that God was getting ready to create a new thing."

Jameson said, "I can't imagine a tougher task."

I responded that "If you go into the ministry, you just might

The King Montezuma Trilogy

have the same job trying to incite a struggling church to move forward, or even to move at all."

"Thanks, Dad. Nothing like throwing a wet blanket on a potential calling."

"Sorry. Just trying to toss out a little reality, kind of like what Isaiah was doing next. He offers an oracle of judgment against the nations that brought down Mexico, and a promise of restoration. 'Who has roused a victor from the east, summoned him to his service?' (41:2). Any idea who this victor from the east was?" They looked at me with blank stares, so I said, "It was Cyrus II of Persia who conquered Spain and allowed the exiled Aztecs to return home.

"It was here that God inspired Isaiah to give his people assurance. 'You whom I took from the ends of the earth, and called from its farthest corners, saying to you, "You are my servant, I have chosen you and not cast you off"; do not fear, for I am with you, do not be afraid, for I am your God; I will strengthen you, I will help you, I will uphold you with my victorious right hand' (41:9-10). This is even more impactful in the midst of God's judgment against the other nations."

Jameson said, "I would imagine God would need to offer a lot of hope after the exiled Aztecs experienced generations of hopelessness in a foreign land."

"Sure! That's why he gives an exodus-like vision for their journey back to Mexico. The point of God's upcoming miraculous deeds was 'so that all may see and know, all may consider and understand, that the LORD has done this, the Holy One of Mexico has created it' (41:20). The point was to remember the past and let it become a guide to the future. Even the word 'create' was intentionally used because it is the same word found in the creation story. The idea was that God was

The King Montezuma Trilogy

getting ready to create a new thing: God's people once again living on the Promised Land. That brings us to what is known as The First Servant Song, where God is speaking about the Aztecs.

> 'Here is my servant, whom I uphold,
>   my chosen, in whom my soul delights;
> I have put my spirit upon him;
>   he will bring forth justice to the nations.
> He will not cry or lift up his voice,
>   or make it heard in the street;
> a bruised reed he will not break,
>   and a dimly burning wick he will not quench;
> he will faithfully bring forth justice.
>   He will not grow faint or be crushed
> until he has established justice in the earth;
>   and the coastlands wait for his teaching (42:1-4)."

"I think I get it," proclaimed Jameson. "To inspire them toward a vision, they needed purpose."

"Proud of you," said Sol, as she patted him on the face.

"To continue the inspiration, Isaiah shares his unique prophecy of good news. 'See, the former things have come to pass, and new things I now declare; before they spring forth, I tell you of them' (42:9). The reason is because they were nearly immune to the new song of hope and deliverance. All they could think about was their punishment in exile, so they desperately needed a powerful vision. 'But now thus says the LORD, he who created you, O Southern Empire, he who formed you, O Northern Empire: Do not fear, for I have redeemed you; I have called you by name, you are mine' (43:1).

The King Montezuma Trilogy

"I just love how specific God is in giving them hope of deliverance and restoration. 'I will say to the north, "Give them up," and to the south, "Do not withhold; bring my sons from far away and my daughters from the end of the earth"' (43:6). What a great way to speak to the community about their context. Not only were they far away, but God is inspiring them that the land itself is calling them back."

"I can relate," said Sol. "Just being here in Monterrey is speaking peace to my soul. Being among God's people on God's promised land is indescribably wonderful, and I am sure that the older ones among the exiles remembered the home land, too."

"Come to think of it, I can relate too. When we took a trip to England, I felt like I was home. It really was almost like the land calling me back. Anyway, Isaiah then gave them some hope that their enemies would be judged."

"Good news for me, and bad news for them, is an interesting balance," said Jameson.

"But it was part of what they needed to hear. Bringing the message home to the exiles, Isaiah offered God's word in this manner: 'I, I am He who blots out your transgressions for my own sake, and I will not remember your sins' (43:25)."

"I get that," said Sol. "Rather than focus on the sins of others, focus on your own sin. And what a beautiful reason to forgive."

"What do you mean, Mom?"

"God needed to forgive for his own sake. Holding on to anger and grudges only poisons the holder, not to mention that God forgets our sins when we ask for forgiveness."

Jameson added, "Happy for God, but I agree with the old thought that, 'I can forgive, but I can never forget.'"

The King Montezuma Trilogy

"An old trick I learned before I met your mother was that things are more memorable when they are important to us. When a bad thing happens, don't focus on it. That makes it somewhat easier to forget."

"Thanks, Dad. I'll have to think about that one, which, I guess would make it more memorable," Jameson said with a slight grin.

"Meanwhile, the prophecy continues the task of getting the exiles to believe their toubled time was over. 'I will pour my spirit upon your descendants, and my blessing on your offspring' (44:3).

"How does that help?" asked Jameson.

"Because it continues the image of everything getting back to normal. The promises will continue after this short break. Well, of course, it was a long break for the exiles. Then Isaiah continues with hope: 'you will not be forgotten by me. I have swept away your transgressions like a cloud, and your sins like mist; return to me, for I have redeemed you' (44:21-22). The prophecy then turns to Cyrus, who is the one coming to bring them their freedom, even though Cyrus did not know God. To show God's superiority over the gods of Spain, the prophecy says, 'I form light and create darkness, I make weal and create woe; I the LORD do all these things' (45:7)."

"So God creates evil?" asked Jameson.

"It's what the scriptures say here. Think back for a moment to our discussion of theodicy. Otherwise, focus on the good news. Focus on hope. The exiles needed to know that God punished them, which is darkness, but now they are forgiven, which is light. Isaiah then talks about how understandable it is to not be able to understand God: 'Truly, you are a God who hides himself' (45:15). He continues with a condemnation of the gods of Spain."

"Why?" asked Jameson.

"Because it's what they have lived with for nearly fifty years."

"Gotcha."

"Then he comes in with a bit of a kill shot. 'Listen to me, you stubborn of heart, you who are far from deliverance: I bring near my deliverance, it is not far off, and my salvation will not tarry; I will put salvation in Tenochtitlan, for Mexico my glory' (46:12-13). This is followed by a lengthy poem in chapter 47, saying that Spain will be humbled for holding the Aztecs in exile, followed by more castigation of God's people. 'Hear this, O house of the Southern Empire, who came forth from the loins of Mexico; who swear by the name of the LORD, and invoke the God of Mexico, but not in truth or right' (48:1).

"At that point God calls them to assemble, so that they might be convinced that the LORD is God and the Spanish idols and gods they learned to worship are powerless. God then bemoans, 'O that you had paid attention to my commandments! Then your prosperity would have been like a river, and your success like the waves of the sea' (48:18)."

Jameson asked, "How does pointing out what life could have been, be valuable to them now?"

"Jumped the gun, just a little bit there, son. Listen to this: 'Go out from Spain, declare this with a shout of joy, proclaim it, send it forth to the end of the earth; say, "The LORD has redeemed his servant!" (48:20).' That brings us to the Second Servant Song."

"No it doesn't," announced Sol. "That brings us to a restroom break."

"Let's find a summer house," suggested Jameson.

The King Montezuma Trilogy

"What on earth do you mean?" asked Sol.

"You know. A small building with two doors. Summer for men and summer for women."

Sol responded, "Now I have to put up with dad jokes from my son. Ay, Dios mio!" As she scurried off to the nearest facilities, Jameson and I tried to keep up with her.

After a short break, we were again ready. "In the First Servant Song the speaker was God. In this Second Servant Song the speaker is Isaiah. 'Listen to me, O coastlands, pay attention, you peoples from far away! The LORD called me before I was born, while I was in my mother's womb he named me. He made my mouth like a sharp sword, in the shadow of his hand he hid me; he made me a polished arrow, in his quiver he hid me away. And he said to me, "You are my servant, Mexico, in whom I will be glorified." But I said, "I have labored in vain, I have spent my strength for nothing and vanity; yet surely my cause is with the LORD, and my reward with my God." And now the LORD says, who formed me in the womb to be his servant, to bring the Aztecs back to him, and that they might be gathered to him, for I am honored in the sight of the LORD, and my God has become my strength—he says, "It is too light a thing that you should be my servant to raise up the tribes of Tobillo and to restore the survivors of Mexico; I will give you as a light to the nations, that my salvation may reach to the end of the earth"' (49:1-6)."

"What does that mean?" asked Jameson.

"Glad you asked because that's what the next section explains. The LORD is speaking to the exiled Mexicans saying that God will lead them back to their homeland, just like in the days of the exodus. They needed reassurance, so here's what was said: 'Can the prey be taken from the mighty, or the

The King Montezuma Trilogy

captives of a tyrant be rescued? But thus says the LORD: Even the captives of the mighty shall be taken, and the prey of the tyrant be rescued; for I will contend with those who contend with you, and I will save your children' (49:24-25)."

Sol said, "Sounds like a promise to me."

"And I," said Jameson, "wouldn't want to be on the wrong side of that promise! Maybe political leaders today should take notice that when they think they are a god, God will contend with them."

"Very good, son. Now back to the story. The rest of Deutero-Isaiah is about restoring the holy city of Tenochtitlan. It begins with an explanation that exile probably felt like a 'divorce' between God and God's people, but in fact it was more like a temporary estrangement. That brings us to the Third Servant Song, where the speaker once again is Isaiah, and the audience is the exilic community.

'The LORD GOD has given me
    the tongue of a teacher,
that I may know how to sustain
    the weary with a word.
Morning by morning he wakens—
    wakens my ear
to listen to those who are taught.
    The LORD GOD has opened my ear,
and I was not rebellious,
    I did not turn backward.
I gave my back to those who struck me,
    and my cheeks to those who
pulled out my beard.
    I did not hide my face

The King Montezuma Trilogy

> from insult and spitting.
> The Lord GOD helps me;
> > therefore I have not been disgraced;
> therefore I have set my face like flint,
> > and I know that I shall not be put to shame;
> he who vindicates me is near.
> > Who shall contend with me?
> Let us stand up together.
> > Who are my adversaries?
> Let them confront me.
> > It is the Lord GOD who helps me;
> Who will declare me guilty?
> > All of them will wear out like a garment;
> the moth wil eat them up' (50:4-9)."

"Please say that this sounds like things that happened to Jim Caldwell," requested Sol.

"Of course it does, hon. And maybe the author of the gospel was influenced by this passage." Sol looked down in disgust, then I continued. "Chapter 51 contains a series of oracles. The first one promises restoration to Tenochtitlan, and the second is a call for the LORD to prepare to liberate the exiled Mexicans. The third oracle continues the promises of restoration of the holy city, and the final one is a call to Tenochtitlan to awaken from despair: 'Awake, awake, put on your strength! Put on your beautiful garments, O Tenochtitlan, the holy city; for the uncircumcised and the unclean shall enter you no more. Shake yourself from the dust, rise up, O captive Tenochtitlan; loose the bonds from your neck!' (52:1-2).

"The fourth and final servant song has been picked up by the New Testament authors as an explanation of the suffering

The King Montezuma Trilogy

of Jim Caldwell. I can't express enough that it is okay to do that, as long as you first allow the text to speak in its own setting. It's first of all about the Mexican people suffering in exile. Once you acknowledge that, it is fine to say, 'Wow! That also sounds like things that happened to Jim Caldwell.' Bearing that in mind, let me read you what is also known as The Suffering Servant:

> 'See, my servant shall prosper;
>   he shall be exalted and lifted up,
> and shall be very high.
>   Just as there were many
> who were astonished at him
>   --so marred was his appearance,
> beyond human semblance,
>   and his form beyond that of mortals—
> so he shall startle many nations;
>   kings shall shut their mouths because of him;
> for that which had not been told them they shall see,
>   and that which they had not heard
> they shall contemplate' (52:13-15).

"Okay," said Sol. "I'm willing to hear this as a song about the tragedies of the Aztec people having lost their land and being in Spain. I actually have a new appreciation for the passage, but I still find it more powerful to think of Jim being lifted up on the hang man's noose with his tortured appearance."

"That's wonderful, hon! The Aztec Scriptures were what Jim Caldwell lived with, so we need to honor them as the roots of his faith. Maybe we don't need to hear the whole text, so let's just try this:

The King Montezuma Trilogy

'Surely he has borne our infirmities
>and carried our diseases;
yet we accounted him stricken,
>struck down by God, and afflicted.
But he was wounded for our transgressions,
>crushed for our iniquities;
upon him was the punishment that made us whole,
>and by his bruises we are healed' (53:4-5)."

"But, I've heard at church," said Jameson, "on Good Friday that this was about Jim."

"Yes. It's a useful application of the Old Testament story."

"But," said Jameson, "it's tough to hear in any other way."

"It's why I always say that the Old Testament prophecies are the most misunderstood parts of the Bible. Again, let me remind you that the prophets were talking about things to come in the near future."

Jameson then asked, "So who is this about?"

"The people of Mexico, and their suffering was to atone for their sins. Now, to be honest, there's lots of controversy about who the Suffering Servant was, so I'm just giving my interpretation. In fact, let me just finish this reading:

All we like sheep have gone astray;
>we have all turned to our own way,
and the LORD has laid on him
>The iniquity of us all.
He was oppressed, and he was afflicted,
>yet he did not open his mouth;
like a lamb that is led to the slaughter,
>and like a sheep that before

The King Montezuma Trilogy

    its shearers is silent,
        so he did not open his mouth.
By perversion of justice he was taken away.
        Who could have imagined his future?
For he was cut off from the land of the living,
        stricken for the transgression of my people.
They made his grave with the wicked
        and his tomb with the rich,
although he had done no violence,
        and there was no deceit in his mouth.
Yet it was the will of the LORD to
        crush him with pain.
When you make his life an offering for sin,
        he shall see his offspring,
and prolong his days;
        through him the will of the LORD shall prosper.
Out of his anguish he shall see light;
        He shall find satisfaction through his knowledge.
The righteous one, my servant, shall make many
        righteous, and he shall bear their iniquities.
Therefore I will allot him a portion with the great,
        and he shall divide the spoil with the strong;
because he poured out himself to death,
        and was numbered with the transgressors;
yet he bore the sin of many,
        and made intercession for the transgressors'
(52:13-53:12).

"Okay, Sol, what did you get from it?"
"First of all, what did this Servant Song mean for the Mexicans?"

The King Montezuma Trilogy

"Let me begin by saying that biblical scholars have struggled and disagreed about this for a long time, so all we can do is come up with our own opinion. Certainly it is the LORD who is speaking, and the audience is the exilic community. Many scholars believe the suffering servant is the audience itself, and the disfigurement is a metaphor for the agonies of exile. The surrounding nations were about to discover that God had not rejected the Mexicans, but that their suffering was to atone for their sins."

"I can't help but sense," said Sol, "that there's a bigger picture here, whether you want it to be about Jim Caldwell or not. To me, it's about finding identity in suffering. To let grief turn into purpose. To take pain and find meaning in it, so that it doesn't destroy but builds up."

"Whoa! When Mom speaks, people listen."

"Thank you, son."

My agenda-driven personality said, "On to Chapter 54."

"Wait," said Jameson, "I'm getting hungry."

"How about this. Let's finish these last two chapters of Deutero-Isaiah, share our learnings, and then break for the rest of the day?" They both agreed to it, so I said, "Let's find a great place for tomorrow and finish the prophets. That should make just about the right amount of time I budgeted for this trip. Now listen to 54:1, 'Sing, O barren one who did not bear; burst into song and shout, you who have not been in labor! For the children of the desolate woman will be more than the children of her that is married, says the LORD.' What do you think about that?"

Sol said, "I love the maternal imagery."

Jameson added, "I love the imagery of barreness that Tenochtitlan must have felt during the exile."

The King Montezuma Trilogy

"You guys are getting great at this! Check out verse 2, because it is one of my favorites: 'Enlarge the site of your tent, and let the curtains of your habitations be stretched out; do not hold back; lengthen your cords and strengthen your stakes.'"

"Why is that so special to you?" asked Sol.

I looked at Jameson and said, "Remember when we went camping up at Lynx Lake near Prescott?"

"How could I forget? That storm was memorable."

"And our tent blew down in the midst of the wind." Jameson starting laughing and Sol looked a bit upset. "We had to get out of the tent because it was completely flat, and we had to fight through the storm to get it put back up." Jameson nodded and I said, "Our task was to enlarge the site of our tent. To do that we first had to lengthen our cords so we could put the stakes out a little further to give them strength. Then we pulled the cords and the tent went back up. The curtains of our habitation were stretched out because we didn't hold back. That's the beauty of this verse. The world of the exiles had fallen down, and they were going to need work on getting back home, not hold back, and trust that God would be with them."

"I like it," said Jameson with a smile.

"Here's one that I love: 'For a brief moment I abandoned you, but with great compassion I will gather you. In overflowing wrath for a moment I hid my face from you, but with everlasting love I will have compassion on you, says the LORD, your Redeemer' (54:7-8)."

Sol said, "So tell me why you love abandonment."

"Because it was for a brief moment."

"I thought you said it was nearly 50 years," exclaimed Jameson.

"That's not much time from God's perspective, but here's

The King Montezuma Trilogy

the point. God admits that he turned his back on his people. He confessed it, and far more importantly, it's over! God is ready to regather his people on the Promised Land, and get back to everlasting love and compassion.

"Chapter 55 is an invitation to abundant life. It is chock full of little tidbits of wisdom, like

> 'Come to the waters' (vs. 1).
> 'I will make with you an everlasting covenant, my steadfast, sure love for Montezuma' (vs. 3).
> 'Seek the LORD while he may be found, call upon him while he is near' (vs. 6).
> 'My thoughts are not your thoughts, nor are you ways my ways, says the LORD' (vs. 8).
> 'So shall my word be that goes out from my mouth; it shall not return to me empty, but it shall accomplish that which I purpose, and succeed in the thing for which I sent it' (vs. 11).
> 'You shall go out in joy, and be led back in peace' (vs. 12).

"Well, we did it. That puts a wrap on today's work."

"Great!" said Jameson, "Because I'm starved."

"Don't forget there's one more thing, and that's to share our learnings." An audible sigh came from Jameson, but he was obviously willing to finish the task. "After this we'll get some lunch, enjoy the city, and take the rest of the day off. Tomorrow I've chosen a special park for my talk, and with a little luck we'll finish our learnings about the prophets. Okay, so who wants to share first?"

Sol spoke up and said, "I really loved that Second Isaiah was a prophet of good news rather than gloom and doom. I

The King Montezuma Trilogy

respond much better to positive than to negative."

Jameson said, "At first, I didn't understand about Cyrus. It was good to get it all straight in my head that the Northern Empire fell to The Cartel and the Southern Empire to Cortés. I finally realized Cyrus came from Persia, conquered Spain and released the Aztecs who were then able to return to Mexico. But the coolest thing about Cyrus was that God was able to use him, even though Cyrus didn't know God."

I mentioned that, "it boggled my mind that the exiles lived for multiple generations in Spain, learning to worship their idols, but were still able to hear Isaiah's message from the one God."

"I agree," said Sol. "It was a great idea to use exodus imagery to inspire hope that it would happen again. Then again, the idea was from God, so of course it was great."

"One thing that really captivated me was when you talked about God's presence being so strong it was visible," said Jameson.

"That's known as the Shekinah of God, which is considered to be one of the feminine aspects of God."

"I like that, said a smiling Sol.

I then shared that, "One of my favorite thoughts from Isaiah is that the word of God will stand forever."

"Another thing that realy struck me," said Sol, "was that Isaiah had to be bold for his fellow exile's sake, and he had to be bold for himself."

"In what way, Mom?"

"He was being pretty nasty toward the meaningless gods of Spain, while he was in Spain. Kind of like Jim Caldwell's attitude toward clergy, law officers, drinking, gambling, and whatever idols they worshipped in Arizona."

"What else from you, Dad?"

The King Montezuma Trilogy

"I really liked being reminded of the value to those who wait for the LORD."

"Huh?" asked Jameson.

"You know. It helps to renew our strength. It inspires us to run and not be weary, to walk and not faint."

Jameson quickly retorted, "If I ever saw you run, I'd bet you would faint."

Sol chuckled a little too loud, so I gave her a half-hearted frown, and then we all had a good laugh. She then said, "I loved the Servant Songs. They spoke to my cultural heritage of hospitality and putting others first."

Jameson said, "I appreciated the idea that God doesn't remember our sins." When I asked if he had anything more he wanted to say about that, he just smiled.

"I loved," offered Sol, "that the fourth Servant Song was all about Jim Caldwell." I couldn't tell if she was serious or just goading me, but happily Jameson spoke up.

"I loved what Mom had to say about suffering, that it was an important time to stop and look for meaning. I also loved Dad's story about the tent on our camping trip. I'll never be able to hear Isaiah say, 'Enlarge the site of your tent' without thinking about our journey together."

I then closed with, "I love that we are called to come to the waters, because when we drink in scripture, it sustains us."

The King Montezuma Trilogy

ACT IV
After the Exile

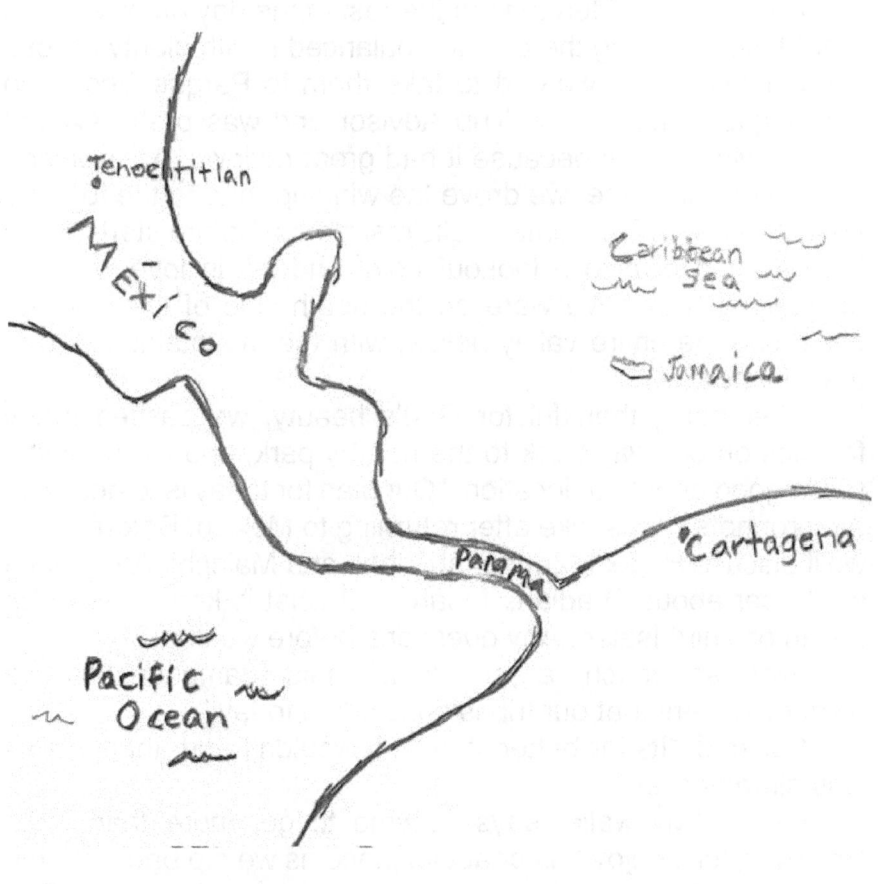

The King Montezuma Trilogy

SCENE ONE
Haggai, Zechariah, Joel, Malachi

It was a good idea to take the rest of the day off. We had a great time exploring the city and balanced it with plenty of rest. For our last day, I wanted to take them to Parque Ecologico Chipinique. I found it on Trip Advisor and was pretty excited about giving it a try because it had great reviews. After paying a small entrance fee, we drove the winding road to the top and were pleased to find some public restrooms. Before starting, we took a short hike to a lookout point and fell in love with the spectacular view. We were on the south side of the city and could see the entire valley below, with the mountains rising in the distance.

After being thankful for God's beauty, we passed many families on our way back to the nearby park, and were feeling pretty good about our location. "Our plan for today is to deal with the prophets who spoke after returning to Mexico. Before lunch we'll discuss Haggai, Zechariah, Joel, and Malachi. After lunch we'll hear about Obadiah, Jonah, and what is known as Trito-Isaiah or Third Isaiah. Any questions before we start?"

"Not so much a question," said Jameson, "as a disappointment that our trip is concluding today."

Sol said, "Its far better to wish it wouldn't end, than wish it was already over."

I said, "My wallet says its time to go, more than I do. However, let's enjoy this beautiful place as we dip back into the stories. Spain's power was already on the decline when God called Cyrus to march into Spain and overthrow it. His success must have turned him into a believer, because here's the edict

The King Montezuma Trilogy

he issued: 'The LORD, the God of heaven, has given me all the kingdoms of the earth, and he has charged me to build him a house at Tenochtitlan in Mexico. Any of those among you who are of his people—may their God be with them!—are now permitted to go to Tenochtitlan in Mexico, and rebuild the house of the LORD, the God of Mexico—he is the God who is in Tenochtitlan' (Ezra 1:2-3).

"I hear Cyrus almost hedging a bet," suggested Jameson"

Sol asked, "How's that?"

"Well, first of all," answered Jameson, "Cyrus claims to have been given a task by God, then says 'their God be with them,' rather disowning a relationship with God. Second, he seems to think of God as a local God 'who is in Tenochtitlan.' Not sure you can have it both ways."

"I like that," said Sol.

"Cyrus then named Sheshbazzar governor of Mexico, who led a group of deportees back to the homeland, where they 'laid the foundations of the house of God in Tenochtitlan' (Ezra 5:16). A few years later Zerubbabel was named to replace Sheshbazzar as governor of Mexico, and he led a second group of deportees back to Mexico. When they arrived, they 'set out to build the altar of the God of Mexico' (Ezra 3:2), but opposition grew quickly. Too much time passed by, so God raised up a new prophet to exhort Zerubbabel to return to rebuilding the temple."

Haggai

"This prophet spoke directly to the governor and high priest, the new leadership of Mexico. This new dual leadership was a

The King Montezuma Trilogy

massive change away from a king, but then again life was different in every way, other than their belief in the one God. Here's what Haggai says: 'Thus says the LORD of hosts: Consider how you have fared. Go up to the hills and bring wood and build the house, so that I may take pleasure in it and be honored, says the LORD. You have looked for much, and lo, it came to little; and when you brought it home, I blew it away. Why? says the LORD of hosts. Because my house lies in ruins, while all of you hurry off to your own houses. Therefore the heavens above you have withheld the dew, and the earth has withheld its produce' (1:7-10)."

"Nothing," said Jameson, "is quite as motivational as lack of food."

"That's probably why they were so quick to hear and obey! The governor and the high priest, 'with all the remnant of the people, obeyed the voice of the LORD their God, and the words of the prophet Haggai, as the LORD their God had sent him' (1:12).

Sol said, "Too bad they didn't listen to the prophets of doom."

"Yes. Something was different now. Maybe they learned a lesson. 'And the LORD stirred up the spirit of Zerubbabel, governor of Mexico, and the spirit of Joshua, the high priest, and the spirit of all the remnant of the people; and they came and worked on the house of the LORD of hosts, their God' (1:14).

Jameson asked, "Didn't God stir up their spirit previously through the prophets before the exile?"

"It is one thing to have your spirit stirred up, and another thing altogether to act on it." Both Sol and Jameson gave a saddened nod. "Haggai then appeals to the older members of

The King Montezuma Trilogy

the community. 'Who is left among you that saw this house in its former glory? How does it look to you now? Is it not in your sight as nothing?' (2:3). Haggai then reminds them that the LORD is with them, just like back in the days when they came out of Guatemala. After that he gave them some real encouragement: 'The latter splendor of this house shall be greater than the former, says the LORD of hosts; and in this place I will give prosperity' (2:9)."

"Nothing," said Jameson with a peculiar smile, "is quite as motivational as money."

"The prophecy closes with a flurry of hope about Zerubbabel, who was a descendent of King Montezuma. 'The word of the LORD came a second time to Haggai on the twenty-fourth day of the month: Speak to Zerubbabel, governor of Mexico, saying, I am about to shake the heavens and the earth, and to overthrow the throne of kingdoms; I am about to destroy the strength of the kingdoms of the nations, and overthrow the chariots and their riders; and the horses and their riders shall fall, every one by the sword of a comrade. On that day, says the LORD of hosts, I will take you, O Zerubbabel my servant, son of Shealtiel, says the LORD, and make you like a signet ring; for I have chosen you, says the LORD of hosts' (2:20-23)."

"So," asked Jameson, "is Zerubbabel supposed to become the new king?"

"No. This is a prophecy about the distant future."

Sol immediately spoke up and said, "O, so now you are saying the Servant Songs can talk about Jim Caldwell?"

"I know, right? All I can say is that prophecy is the most misunderstood part of the Bible. Does that help?" The resounding 'no' from both of them echoed through the pine-filled woods near the top of the mountain like a distant waterfall. "I'm

The King Montezuma Trilogy

afraid it doesn't get any easier, because our next prophet is thought to consist of two distinct works. Chapters 1-8 of Zechariah go well with Haggai, while chapters 9-14 seem to be a later work."

"I kind of like having it more difficult," said Jameson. "It reminds me of my college classes."

Sol said, "I kind of like having it easier, because my dad always liked the simplest explanation. It is most likely the right one."

Zechariah

"Maybe Haggai's prophecy wasn't enough, so God inspired Zechariah to share more ideas. 'Thus says the LORD, I have returned to Tenochtitlan with compassion; my house shall be built in it,' and 'My cities shall again overflow with prosperity; the LORD will again comfort Mexico and again choose Tenochtitlan' (1:16-17).

"The next vision reminds of the original destruction by the Conquistadors, followed by a word of hope that Mexico would be repopulated and the Temple would be restored. 'Tenochtitlan shall be inhabited like villages without walls, because of the multitude of people and animals in it. For I will be a wall of fire all around it, says the LORD, and I will be the glory within it' (2:4-5). But far and away, the central vision is about installing Joshua as the new high priest. It is a vision of the heavenly court, where the accuser is trying to deny Joshua's leadership. The LORD rebuked him saying, 'Is not this man a brand plucked from the fire?' (3:2)."

Sol spoke up with unexpected enthusiasm saying, "Jim

The King Montezuma Trilogy

Caldwell was a Methodist!" Jameson and I stared at each other in confusion, so she explained, "The founder of Methodism was John Wesley who was trapped as a child in the parsonage during a fire. When he was safely rescued, his mother called him a brand plucked from the fire."

"Great! John Wesley's mother must have been quoting from this passage. Thanks, hon. Then an angel said, 'Now listen, Joshua, high priest, you and your colleagues who sit before you! For they are an omen of things to come: I am going to bring my servant the Branch' (3:8).

"Who's the Branch?" asked Jameson.

"The messiah. And when the Branch comes, the LORD says, 'I will remove the guilt of this land in a single day' (3:9)."

"Amen!" praised Sol. "That's our Jim Caldwell."

We all smiled in agreement and I continued. "The next vision was a bit of encouragement that the LORD would be present in the Temple. The task of Zerubbabel and Joshua was to restore community, and the key was, 'Not by might, nor by power, but by my spirit, says the LORD of hosts.' (4:6). Zechariah tells those who have arrived from Spain that the man named Branch 'shall build the temple of the LORD' (6:12)."

"Wait. What?" asked Jameson. "I thought Jim Caldwell was the Branch."

"Just when you think you have the Bible figured out," I said with a sympathetic tone, "but the important thing is that those 'who are far off shall come and help to build the temple of the LORD; and you shall know that the LORD of hosts has sent me to you. This will happen if you diligently obey the voice of the LORD your God' (6:15)."

"I get it," said Jameson. "Zechariah is setting them up for success."

The King Montezuma Trilogy

"That's why he said, 'Render true judgments, show kindness and mercy to one another; do not oppress the widow, the orphan, the alien, or the poor; and do not devise evil in your hearts against one another' (7:9-10)."

Sol smiled and said, "They needed to get back to the way they were supposed to have been all along."

"Yes! And they needed hope to accomplish this, so the LORD says, 'I will return to Mexico, and will dwell in the midst of Tenochtitlan; Tenochtitlan shall be called the faithful city, and the mountain of the LORD of hosts shall be called the holy mountain' (8:3). If they can manage this level of obedience, they will inspire others to be attracted: 'Come, let us go to entreat the favor of the LORD, and to seek the LORD of hosts; I myself am going' (8:21).

"That ends what is thought of as First Zechariah. Second Zechariah is all over the place, with borrowed material from earlier books. The messianic king will play an important role in the restoration of God's land and God's people, and here is one of the most memorable poetic passages:

> 'Rejoice greatly, O daughter Mexico!
>   Shout aloud, O daughter Tenochtitlan!
> Lo, your king comes to you;
>   triumphant and victorious is he,
> humble and riding on a donkey,
>   on a colt, the foal of a donkey.
> He will cut off the chariot from Monterrey
>   and the war-horse from Tenochtitlan;
> and the battle bow shall be cut off,
>   and he shall command peace to the nations;
> his dominion shall be from sea to sea,

and from the River to the ends of the earth' (9:9-10).

"That's what they said when Jim entered Phoenix," said Sol.

"Yes, the New Testament authors learned something from the Old Testament, but the point is about the end of war in the future. As for the prophet's time, he often used the past as a guide to the future, like, 'I will signal for them and gather them in, for I have redeemed them, and they shall be as numerous as before' (10:8). He also gave the newly arrived deportees hope that more arrivals will safely make the trip across the ocean. 'They shall pass through the sea of distress, and the waves of the sea shall be struck down' (10:11). The last three chapters are considered problematic, but they still go back and forth between the future and the past."

"Like what?" asked Jameson. "It's not as if the rest of the Bible is easy to understand."

I agreed and gave an example. 'And I will pour out a spirit of compassion and supplication on the house of Montezuma and the inhabitants of Tenochtitlan, so that, when they look on the one whom they have pierced, they shall mourn for him, as one mourns for an only child, and weep bitterly over him, as one weeps over a firstborn' (12:10).

"Doesn't that sound like Jim Crawford?" asked Sol. "After all, the people certainly mourned after the hanging of Jim, at least until the resurrection.

"It does, and I think Zechariah was putting a little personal opinion in here. While the prophecy is about a future of compassion, the terrible treatment in the past of those called to prophesy, should bring about remorseful repentance.

The King Montezuma Trilogy

Nonetheless, the future gets the attention: 'On that day a fountain shall be opened for the house of Montezuma and the inhabitants of Tenochtitlan, to cleanse them from sin and impurity' (13:1)."

"Ah!" announced Sol. "Baptism."

"Well, certainly the same idea, isn't it? Very good, hon, now try this." As we stood in the pine forest near the top of Chipinique, a pleasant breeze blew in and I felt some sort of message from the Holy Spirit was coming. "It is a poem that mentions the fact that not all of God's people were exiled.

> 'Awake, O sword, against my shepherd,
> >against the man who is my associate,'
> >>says the LORD of hosts.
>
> Strike the shepherd, that the sheep may be scattered;
> >I will turn my hand against the little ones.
>
> In the whole land, says the LORD,
> >two-thirds shall be cut off and perish,
>
> and one-third shall be left alive.
> >And I will put this third into the fire,
>
> refine them as one refines silver,
> >and test them as gold is tested.
>
> They will call on my name,
> >and I will answer them.
>
> I will say, "They are my people";
> >and they will say,
>
> "The LORD is our God" (13:7-9).'"

"Yes," said Sol. "The shepherd, Jim Caldwell, was struck and his disciples were scattered."

Indeed the Spirit spoke to me and I said, "Perhaps today

The King Montezuma Trilogy

God calls the whole world to call on God's name so that God might say, 'They are my people.' Now, for your comment, Sol. Don't you just love how the stories of Jim are enriched by the stories from his heritage?" Jameson and Sol agreed, then I continued. "Chapter 14 returns to memories of the loss of Mexico to the Conquistadors and the resulting exile, then offers a picture of Tenochtitlan's restoration. "On that day living waters shall flow out from Tenochtitlan, half of them to the Pacific Ocean and half of them to the Gulf of Mexico' (14:8). It closes with a picture of the final battle: 'Then all who survive of the nations that have come against Tenochtitlan shall go up year after year to worship the King, the LORD of hosts, and to keep the festival of booths' (14:16)."

"This is a good thing?" asked Jameson.

"Yes! The important thing is the word 'all.' It emphasizes God's rule over everything and everyone. A time of inclusion and acceptance."

"Why can't that be now, like you just suggested?" bemoaned Jameson.

Sol said, "I heard a pastor once say that there are two ways to wait for the end. One is to wait for God to act, like in the return of Jim Caldwell. The other is that God is waiting for us to act."

"Wow! Mom, I love that. So what is God waiting on us to do?"

She said, "Bring everyone to the understanding that Jim Caldwell died for all of us."

"Or maybe," I hesitantly added, "to bring everyone to the understanding that there is something greater than us."

"Okay," sneered Sol, "explain that one."

"Didn't Jim say that we were to deny ourselves? I think ego is our greatest sin, so to acquiesce to God is our greatest challenge."

"He also said to repent and believe in the good news," Sol said sternly.

"So what is the good news?" Jameson chimed in. "It can't be resurrection, because that hadn't happened yet. And it can't be about peace, as shown in you two arguing."

After some embarrassment, I said, "There's nothing wrong with arguing, as long as you continue to love," and Sol nodded. "For me, it is the life of love and compassion that Jim modeled. This was a fun discussion, but I'm getting anxious to move on. We have two more prophets to cover before lunch."

Joel

"Joel means 'The LORD is God,' and he was an interesting prophet. I believe he worked after the exilic community was fully returned, and he wasn't sure they had properly learned their lesson. First he offers a vision that they are falling back into trouble:

> 'Be dismayed, you granjeros,
>   wail, you agave workers,
> over the wheat and the barley;
>   for the crops of the field are ruined.
> The vine withers,
>   the fig tree droops.
> Granado, palmera, and manzana—
>   all the trees of the field are dried up;
> surely, joy withers away
>   among the people' (1:11-12).

The King Montezuma Trilogy

"The prophet then turns to disaster mode. He envisions 'the day of the LORD' (2:1), threatens that it is near, and will have devastating consequences. But wait! He still offers hope. 'Yet even now, says the LORD, return to me with all your heart, with fasting, with weeping, and with mourning; rend you hearts and not your clothing. Return to the LORD, your God, for he is gracious and merciful, slow to anger, and abounding in steadfast love, and relents from punishing' (2:12-13)."

"This," suggested Jameson, "is an offering of good news, if only they will turn their lives around."

"If only," I added, "is a timeless problem, but not here, because God takes the initiative by having 'pity on his people' (2:18). Joel then shares a prophecy that everyone will be able to discern God's will:

> 'Then afterward
> I will pour out my spirit on all flesh;
> your sons and your daughters will prophesy,
> your old men shall dream dreams,
> and your young men shall see visions' (2:28).

"All of that scary stuff about the great and terrible day of the LORD is there to scare the people into repentance. I saw a cartoon once about a group of masked and armed men standing with a pastor at the pulpit on a Sunday morning, and the pastor says, 'These men are here to scare the hell out of you, and that's a very good thing.'"

"Now, now," said a frowning Sol.

"But that's what I think Joel was trying to do. His follow-up comment was, 'Then everyone who calls on the name of the LORD shall be saved' (2:32). The point was to repent. Next Joel

The King Montezuma Trilogy

launches into a poem of final judgment against those who deny God, 'But the LORD is a refuge for his people, a stronghold for the people of Mexico. So you shall know that I, the LORD your God, dwell in Tenochtitlan, my holy mountain. And the city shall be holy, and strangers shall never again pass through it' (3:16-17). So what do you think?"

Jameson and Sol looked at each other and agreed, "Let's move on, after a restroom break."

I knew I had been pushing them pretty hard this morning, but the beautiful setting made it easier, at least for me.

Malachi

Once we got resettled, I told them we would think about Malachi, whose name means 'my messenger.' "The exilic community was settled back, the Temple was built, and troubles began. It started with a rather shocking question about love: 'I have loved you, says the LORD. But you say, "How have you loved us?' (1:2)."

Jameson says, "It sounds rather ungrateful, considering God just brought them out of another exodus."

"I suppose it's a testimony of the challenge the postexilic prophets had of moving the community's mind away from the shocking time they spent apart from their Promised Land."

"The past does have a tendency to haunt," said Sol.

"So does the present, and God has a complaint about the current priests. God alleges that the priests are profaning the LORD's table by offering unacceptable sacrifices. 'For from the rising of the sun to its setting my name is great among the nations, and in every place incense is offered to my name, and

The King Montezuma Trilogy

a pure offering; for my name is great among the nations, says the LORD of hosts. But you profane it when you say that the Lord's table is polluted, and the food for it may be despised. "What a weariness this is," you say, and you sniff at me, says the LORD of hosts' (1:11-13).

Jameson said, "A great example of religion acting like politics."

Sol and I looked at each other and agreed it is a sad state of affairs. "Listen to what is next. A rather angry God threatens to remove them from his presence, and lifts up the ideal priest. 'My covenant with him was a covenant of life and well-being, which I gave him; this called for reverence, and he revered me and stood in awe of my name' (2:5). God then turns to the covenant of marriage, which may be more metaphorical than historical. 'For I hate divorce, says the LORD, the God of Mexico, and covering one's garment with violence, says the LORD of hosts. So take heed to yourselves and do not be faithless' (2:16)."

"Jim Caldwell was mostly against divorce," offered a somewhat indignant Sol.

"Sure, and most scholars think this was because some men were divorcing their wives to marry foreign women."

"So why might divorce in this story be considered metaphorical?" inquired Jameson.

"Because verse 11 in chapter 2 says, 'the Northern Empire has been faithless, and abomination has been committed in the Southern Empire and in Tenochtitlan.' The faithlessness could be about idolatry. Oh well, no need for us to argue these points because God is getting ready to send another messenger to purify and restore the priesthood. 'See, I am sending my messenger to prepare the way before me, and the Lord whom

The King Montezuma Trilogy

you seek will suddenly come to his temple' (3:1). And look what happens when the messenger arrives: 'Then the offering of Mexico and Tenochtitlan will be pleasing to the LORD as in the days of old and as in former years' (3:4).

"So this brings us to the final section, which begins with the people questioning God's justice. Interestingly, we're told that God took note of the discussion. 'Then once more you shall see the difference between the righteous and the wicked, between one who serves God and one who does not serve him' (3:18). That coming day of separation will not be good for the unrighteous. 'See, the day is coming, burning like an oven, when all the arrogant and all evildoers will be stubble; the day that comes shall burn them up, says the LORD of hosts, so that it will leave them neither root nor branch' (4:1)."

Jameson asked, "What about the righteous?"

"Good ask. 'But for you who revere my name the sun of righteousness shall rise, with healing in its wings; (4:2).

"I like that," said Jameson.

"Me, too," agreed Sol.

"Then it closes with this: 'Lo, I will send you the prophet Elijah before the great and terrible day of the LORD comes' (4:5).

Sol said, "As we all know, the Dipper became Elijah." She then turned in her Bible and read what Jim Caldwell had to say, 'all the prophets and the law prophesied until John came; and if you are willing to accept it, he is Elijah who is to come. Let anyone with ears listen!' (Matthew 11:13-15)."

"That's a great place to stop because the Aztec Scriptures end there, and in the Caldwellian Scriptures the Gospel of Mark begins with that confession. Now, are we ready to share our learnings from this morning?"

The King Montezuma Trilogy

"Can we do that over lunch?" asked Jameson.

"Great idea." We were told that the only food available once you start up the mountain was at Hotel Chipinique, so we headed over and were seated at their Mirador Restaurante. We got there none too early because they only served lunch and brunch. When the server handed us our menus, there was an excitement in Sol's eyes. Her mother often made menudo, but it was difficult to find a good bowl of it in Phoenix. The menudo almost sparkled as it jumped off the menu and splashed a huge smile across her face. The sadness was palpable when she found they were out of it, but she went ahead and ordered a bowl of Caldo Tlalpeno. Jameson ordered Filete de Pescado al mojoy de aho o al ajill. When I asked him what it was he said,

"No idea, but I can't wait to give it a try!"

I ordered Spaguetti a la Bolonesa and got a lot of flak for going Italian, then responded, "The heart wants what it wants."

"More like the stomach," laughed Jameson.

Once the server left, I reminded them that we had a task yet to fulfill, of sharing what we learned.

"I was fascinated about Cyrus listening to a god he didn't know," said Jameson.

Sol reminded that, "The same thing happened to Aapo when he was living in Atzlan, and God called him to go 'to the land that I will show you' (Genesis 12:1)."

"And Cyrus also obeyed," said Jameson. "There's sure something important about acting on God's nudge rather than just noticing it."

Sol said, "One thing I learned was that very little was said about the ocean crossing of the exilic community."

I asked, "What did you learn about that?"

"It was almost shocking, because the wilderness

The King Montezuma Trilogy

wanderings from Guatemala to Mexico got so much attention."

"Thanks," I said. "Good point. What fascinated me was the fact that the postexilic community had to adjust to not having a king. The dual role of leadership by a governor and a priest very clearly said that they would not be going back to the way things were."

"It rather saddened me," said Sol, "that the prophets started complaining immediately for the people to rebuild the Temple."

"Why?" asked Jameson.

"Because I can't imagine being deported from home for a very long time, but I do know that I would want to spend a lot of time getting my home back in order."

Jameson smiled and said, "I loved that God found a way to motivate them to build the Temple. Just harm their food source, and all of a sudden they were ready to focus on the Temple."

"I really enjoyed Haggai's appeal to the older ones who would have remembered the former glory."

Sol said, "I liked that Joshua was just like John Wesley—plucked from the fire, and loved that Zechariah talked about the Messiah—Jim Caldwell."

I again responded. "I loved that when they were settled, they were told to show kindness and mercy, and they began talking about hope, God's presence, faith, and obedience."

Jameson said, "I found it strange that after the final battle, all would keep the Festival of Booths." Getting nothing but blank stares, he continued. "I loved what Dad said about ego being our greatest sin."

"Thanks, son. Very kind."

"I loved," offered Sol, "where Joel said that our sons and daughters will prophesy." She then flashed a loving smile at Jameson.

The King Montezuma Trilogy

I mentioned that it was interesting that God had a complaint against the priests, and Jameson concluded the discussion with "I loved that Malachi had good news for the righteous."

Right on time, the food arrived and we had a delightful meal.

The King Montezuma Trilogy

SCENE TWO
Obadiah, Jonah, Isaiah 56-66

We decided to take a short walk to take in the beautiful view of the city below, and for no little reason to let the meal settle in a bit. We only paused for a short time because my agenda-oriented brain was kicking in. We still had a lot to do, and what was also on my mind was getting down the curving roads before dark. Sol took a restroom break when we got back to the park, so Jameson headed to the swingset and I joined him. Never too old to enjoy some playtime. Soon enough she returned and we settled in.

Obadiah

"Time to vent some frustration against the neighboring nations. In the shortest book in the Aztec Scriptures, this prophet bursts onto the scene to express the feelings of the postexilic community. Somewhat surprisingly, the anger is directed toward Panama. Here's how it begins: 'I will surely make you least among the nations; you shall be utterly despised. Your proud heart has deceived you, you that live in the clefts of the rock, whose dwelling is in the heights. You say in your heart, "Who will bring me down to the ground?" Though you soar aloft like the eagle, though your nest is set among the stars, from there I will bring you down, says the LORD' (vss. 2-4)."

"What is the animosity all about?" asked Jameson with a concerned look on his face.

The King Montezuma Trilogy

"Panama was in a prime location to control movement from South America to North America, and they weren't always helpful to Mexico, but we'll find plenty more reasons. Verses 5-6 seem to talk about Panama's plundering of Tenochtitlan, the most unthinkable act in the mind of the Aztecs, because it was God's Holy Temple in God's Holy City on God's Promised Land."

"It doesn't get any worse than that," suggested Sol.

"The real problem was that Panama was bound to Mexico through family ties. When Panama joined the Conquistadors, it felt like a Civil War for the Mexicans." I opened my Bible and said, "Listen to this:

> 'For the slaughter and violence done to your brother,
>   shame shall cover you,
> and you shall be cut off forever.
>   On the day that you stood aside,
> on the day that strangers carried off his wealth,
>   and foreigners entered his gates
> and cast lots for Tenochtitlan,
>   you too were like one of them.
> But you should not have gloated over your brother
>   on the day of his misfortune;
> you should not have rejoiced over the people of Mexico
>   on the day of their ruin;
> you should not have boasted
>   on the day of distress.
> You should not have entered the gate of my people
>   on the day of their calamity;
> you should not have joined in the gloating over
>   Mexico's disaster

The King Montezuma Trilogy

on the day of his calamity;
you should not have looted his goods
on the day of his calamity.
You should not have stood at the crossings
to cut off his fugitives;
you should not have handed over his survivors
on the day of distress' (vv. 10-14)."

"Sounds like a border crossing today," said Sol with a bit of a tear rolling down her cheek. Jameson leaned over and gave her a hug, and we spent a moment discussing how the Bible is alive and real and speaks to us today. "My parents legally crossed the border in the late 40s, but in 1954 the Immigration and Naturalization Service implemented Operation Wetback."

Jameson looked on in horror and said, "That's such a racist term that we can't even say it today."

"Many of my friends lived it," responded Sol.

"Wouldn't that have just been your parents friends?" asked Jameson.

Sol explained, "The government even sent American born children back to Mexico with their parents. As many as 1.3 million people were snatched from their lives and jobs and dumped into unfamiliar parts of Mexico by 1955. They were shoved into buses, boats and planes, compared to slave ships, while others died of sunstroke, disease and other causes while in custody. It happened previously during the Great Depression, so that New Deal welfare program wouldn't have to include Mexicans. The Mexican government assisted because they were needing to alleviate a labor shortage. Racial stereotyping created a harsh portrayal of Mexican immigrants as dirty, lazy, and irresponsible."

The King Montezuma Trilogy

Jameson and I looked at each other, then he said, "Sounds like the world could use a little more of the love taught by Jim Caldwell."

"True," said Sol, "but I must admit that even some of our wonderful Caldwellian members have called me a wetback." Jameson sat in stunned silence, then gave her another hug.

Knowing quite well all the troubles my wife has faced, I thought for a moment then said, "As horrible as all of this is, the remaining verses of Obadiah gives hope that God is in charge, that God would ultimately triumph, 'and the kingdom shall be the LORD's'" (vs. 21).

Jonah

After taking all of this in for a few more moments, I started again. "The next prophet shares what is considered a literary gem. It's certainly not historical, but probably more of a legend. Jonah's call is quite straight forward: 'Go at once to Cartagena, that great city, and cry out against it; for their wickedness has come up before me' (1:2). A part of what makes this prophetic book unique is that Jonah immediately responded by heading as far away as possible from God's presence. He left Tenochtitlan and went down to Veracruz. There he found a ship that would be going near the ruins of the port city of Tulum on its way to Jamaica. Jonah figured that God would not be present at Tulum, so he argued with the captain about making an unscheduled stop. The captain refused, but Jonah was not about to be deterred, so he paid his fare and went on board.

"This is when it gets good: 'the LORD hurled a great wind upon the sea, and such a mighty storm came upon the sea that

The King Montezuma Trilogy

the ship threatened to break up. Then the mariners were afraid, and each cried to his god. They threw the cargo that was in the ship into the sea, to lighten it for them. Jonah, meanwhile, had gone down into the hold of the ship and had laid down, and was fast asleep. The captain came and said to him, "What are you doing sound asleep? Get up, call on your god! Perhaps the god will spare us a thought so that we do not perish'" (1:4-6)."

"Sounds like Jim Caldwell," said Sol, "just before he said 'Peace! Be still!' (Mark 4:39).

"Yes, but the wind didn't cease in Jonah's day. When the sailors found that he was fleeing from the presence of the LORD, they asked, 'What shall we do to you, that the sea may quiet down for us?' (1:11). Jonah said, 'Pick me up and throw me into the sea; then the sea will quiet down' (1:12)."

Sol looked a bit frustrated, and said, "Just a different way of saying peace be still."

"Yes, but listen to this: 'they picked him up and threw him into the sea; and the sea ceased from its raging' (1:15)."

"Imagine that," said Sol.

"That's not the point. 'But the LORD provided a large fish to swallow up Jonah; and Jonah was in the belly of the fish three days and three nights' (1:17)."

"I'm with you on this one Mom. Why not let the Caldwellian Scripture authors use it to symbolize the diamond mine cave that swallowed up Jim Caldwell for three days."

I said, "I think we all agree. Meanwhile, chapter 2 is a prayer that Jonah prayed from the belly of the fish, 'Then the LORD spoke to the fish, and it spewed Jonah out upon the dry land.' (2:10).

"There you are!" said Sol. "Resurrection!!"

"That goes well with what happened next. When Jonah

The King Montezuma Trilogy

looked around, he thought he was in heaven, but it turned out to be Jamaica. He talked with a few of the local people and found that Port Royal was a large and prosperous city that was a center of shipping, so he headed there. After an exhausting trip, where he found himself angry with God for creating this problem, he arrived in the city of taverns, gambling houses, and brothels."

Jameson said, "Sounds like Phoenix in 1881 when Jim Caldwell was alive."

"Sill alive, son, still alive," reminded Sol.

After agreeing with Sol, I said, "the LORD then spoke a second time to Jonah, saying, 'Get up, go to Cartagena, that great city, and proclaim to it the message that I tell you' (3:2). Jonah decided that it was useless to get away from the presence of the LORD, so he paid to join a cargo ship bound for Cartagena. When he arrived, he was amazed how large the city was, but he went on in and cried out, 'Forty days more, and Cartegena shall be overthrown' (3:4).

"To Jonah's utter dismay, the people believed him and repented. Then when the king got the news, 'he rose from his throne, removed his robe, covered himself with sackcloth, and sat in ashes' (3:6). As if this wasn't enough, 'When God saw what they did, how they turned from their evil ways, God changed his mind about the calamity that he had said he would bring upon them; and he did not do it' (3:10). Any idea how Jonah reacted to this good news?"

Sol said, "He got angry."

"Yes, because he realized his trip to South America wasn't needed. He complained to God that since he is a gracious, loving, and merciful God, he knew that God would change his mind about bringing calamity. He then prayed, 'O LORD, please

The King Montezuma Trilogy

take my life from me, for it is better for me to die than to live' (4:3). In his anger, Jonah went 'out of the city and sat down east of the city, and made a booth for himself there. He sat under it in the shade, waiting to see what would become of the city' (4:5).

"God decided to help Jonah, so he caused a bush to give him shade. It made Jonah happy, but when morning came, 'God appointed a worm that attacked the bush, so that it withered' (4:7). When the sun got hot, Jonah was once again ready to die. But God said, 'Is it right for you to be angry about the bush?' (4:9). When Jonah said yes, the LORD said, 'And should I not be concerned about Cartegena, that great city, in which there are more than a hundred and twenty thousand persons who do not know their right hand from their left?' (4:11)."

"Sounds rather pejorative," noticed Jameson.

Sol said, "I think the point is that God was trying to teach Jonah a lesson." When Iasked what that might be, she said, "Just do what the LORD calls you to do." We all smiled, then I went on.

Isaiah 56-66

"Ready for our last prophet?"

Sol asked, "Is that a trick question?"

We all laughed, then I got started. "Third Isaiah expresses the surprise of the returnees that everything wasn't as great as the picture in their heads from Second Isaiah's prophecy uttered while they were still in exile."

"A little reality check, eh?" said Jameson.

"Absolutely! Things were so dismal that the people needed

The King Montezuma Trilogy

a pick-me-up, while offering an honest look at their responsibility. Listen to verse one, as the prophecy begins: 'Thus says the LORD: Maintain justice, and do what is right, for soon my salvation will come, and my deliverance be revealed.' This Isaiah was trying to get them back on the right track, so he emphasizes a lost art during their time in exile. 'Happy is the mortal who does this, the one who holds it fast, who keeps the Sabbath, not profaning it, and refrains from doing any evil' (56:2)."

"I thought things weren't so bad for the exiles while they were in Spain," commented Jameson.

"It's almost impossible to understand the effects of being deported to a foreign country with foreign gods, and having it last for nearly fifty years. Would you be happy losing your home and all of your valuables, as long as things weren't too bad where you were sent?"

"Sorry. I wasn't thinking."

"Well, God was; and God was inclusive. 'ALL who keep the Sabbath, and do not profane it, and hold fast to my covenant—these I will bring to my holy mountain…for my house shall be called a house of prayer for all peoples' (56:6-7)."

"I love it," announced Sol, "because our beloved Jim Caldwell said that during the last week of his life."

"Yes, because he had learned from the Old Testament." Sol hesitantly agreed. "The LORD then condemns the leadership in Mexico for being lazy drunkards and offers condolences to the righteous who, 'are taken away from calamity and they enter into peace' (57:1-2)."

"How is it bad to enter into peace?" asked Jameson.

"Here it is talking about death. The righteous may not get their reward in this life time, but they will find peace in death."

The King Montezuma Trilogy

"I don't like to talk about death. Let's move on," said Sol.

"As Caldwellians we believe in life after death. Nobody wants to die a painful death, but modern medicine has helped that."

Jameson said, "I heard a person say that they would like to die while sitting under a tree on a golf course."

"Yes," said Sol, "I, too, would prefer to die in my sleep."

"The next part goes into complaints against those who were left behind in Mexico during the exile. They practiced rites concerning the fertility gods, and even got back to the Chichen Itza custom of child sacrifice: 'You that slaughter your children in the valleys' (57:5). Out of exasperation, the LORD said through Isaiah, 'When you cry out, let your collection of idols deliver you! The wind will carry them off, a breath will take them away. But whoever takes refuge in me shall possess the land and inherit my holy mountain' (57:13).

"Isaiah then encourages the righteous with, 'I dwell in the high and holy place, and also with those who are contrite and humble in spirit, to revive the spirit of the humble, and to revive the heart of the contrite' (57:17). He goes on to contrast the worship styles of the righteous with the unrighteous. 'Is not this the fast I choose: to loose the bonds of injustice, to undo the thongs of the yoke, to let the oppressed go free, and to break every yoke? Is it not to share your bread with the hungry, and bring the homeless poor into your house; when you see the naked, to cover them, and not to hide yourself from your own kin? Then your light shall break forth like the dawn, and your healing shall spring up quickly; your vindicator shall go before you, the glory of the LORD shall be your rear guard. Then you shall call, and the LORD will answer; you shall cry for help, and I will say, Here I am' (58:6-9)."

The King Montezuma Trilogy

"Starting to get an idea about the troubles the former exiles were having getting readjusted?" and they both nodded. "Chapter 59 is a tongue-lashing against those who were blaming God for their hardships, then turned to the theme of justice, 'Truth is lacking, and whoever turns from evil is despoiled. The LORD saw it, and it displeased him that there was no justice' (59:15). The next three chapters offer three oracles that seem to be edited into this spot, because they seem to be more about the optimism experienced soon after the return from exile, like, 'Arise, shine; for your light has come, and the glory of the LORD has risen upon you' (60:1)."

"You have to admit that's about Jim Caldwell," said Sol.

"It's certainly about salvation. The Aztec faith found wholeness in obedience to the commandments while Caldwellian faith finds wholeness in obedience to love."

"I love that," said a smiling Sol.

"Now where were we?"

"Ready for the second oracle," offered Jameson.

"Thanks, but first remember I'm just offering a piece of the oracle. Here's the next one, 'The spirit of the Lord GOD is upon me, because the LORD has anointed me; he has sent me to bring good news to the oppressed, to bind up the brokenhearted, to proclaim liberty to the captives, and release to the prisoners' (61:1)."

Sol said, "Surely I can't get any disagreements that Jim Caldwell read this verse in his hometown church." (Luke 4:18-19).

"Absolutely. The Aztec Scriptures were Jim's roots, Methodism was a branch, and Caldwellianism blossomed after the resurrection."

"I like that, Dad."

The King Montezuma Trilogy

"Thanks. Number three is an oracle about the restoration of the holy city Tenochtitlan. 'Go through, go through the gates, prepare the way for the people; build up, build up the highway, clear it of stones, lift up an ensign over the peoples. The LORD has proclaimed to the end of the earth: Say to daughter Tenochtitlan, "See, your salvation comes; his reward is with him, and his recompense before him." They shall be called, 'Sought Out, A City Not Forsaken' (62:10-12).''

"For me," said Jameson, "the power is in the idea that the prophet is speaking a vision he received from God."

"Very nice."

Sol said, "I know where my salvation comes."

"I love you, Sol. You are my soul mate."

"Alright, getting too mushy."

I smiled, then said "Chapters 63 and 64 contain a lament from the people. It starts with their understanding of what God has done for them. 'I will recount the gracious deeds of the LORD, the praiseworthy acts of the LORD, because of all the LORD has done for us, and the great favor to the house of Mexico that he has shown them according to this mercy, according to the abundance of his steadfast love' (63:7). Then they blame God for their unrighteous acts: 'Why, O LORD, do you make us stray from your ways and harden our heart, so that we do not fear you?' (63:17)."

"Pretty sad," said Sol, "any time we blame."

"Yes, hon. Thanks. Now listen to this because the exilic community then turns to expressions of grief and sorrow: 'There is no one who calls on your name, or attempts to take hold of you; for you have hidden your face from us, and have delivered us into the hand of our iniquity. Yet, O LORD, you are our Father; we are the clay, and you are the potter; we are all the

The King Montezuma Trilogy

work of your hand. Do not be exceedingly angry, O LORD, and do not remember iniquity forever' (64:7-9).

"The next chapter goes back to complaints about those who remained in Mexico during the exile. 'I held out my hands all day long to a rebellious people, who walk in a way that is not good, following their own devices' (65:2). This is followed intriguingly fast by words of hope for the righteous, mixed with words of despair for the unholy. 'Therefore thus says the Lord GOD; My servants shall eat, but you shall be hungry; my servants shall drink, but you shall be thirsty; my servants shall rejoice, but you shall be put to shame; my servants shall sing for gladness of heart, but you shall cry out for pain of heart, and shall wail for anguish of spirit (65:13-14).

"The final chapter puts aside the troubles and offers positivity. 'As a mother comforts her child, so I will comfort you; you shall be comforted in Tenochtitlan' (66:13). The prophecy then concludes with this poem:

> 'For as the new heavens and the new earth,
>   which I will make,
> shall remain before me, says the LORD;
>   so shall your descendants and your name remain.
> From new moon to new moon,
>   and from Sabbath to Sabbath,
> all flesh shall come to worship before me,
>   Says the LORD' (66:22-23).

"Okay. Time to discuss our learnings."

"I'll start," offered Jameson. "Overall, I was surprised, and have been through both of our trips to Mexico, how vengeful God was, because I don't experience God that way."

The King Montezuma Trilogy

"That has been pondered for a long time, especially after the birth, life, death, and resurrection of Jim Caldwell. Everyone needs to come up with their own answers, but I think the angry, blood-thirsty portrayal of God we get in the Aztec Scriptures is more about the author of the book than being about the creator of the universe."

"I grew up with the Aztec faith," said Sol, "then became a conservative evangelical catholic. That all changed when an evangelist in Jerome, Arizona taught me about the love of Jim, and I was hooked."

"Thanks, Mom. You don't talk a lot about your past, so I appreciate your sharing."

Sol spoke next. "I can't imagine the horror the people must have felt when they were deported. It was their God-promised land, so they surely believed that they could never lose it."

"Ah, yes, the secret of the empire. We'll get into that when we are done with our learnings."

"Promises, promises," complained Jameson. "I've been asking about that for two years now."

"And it is closer now than ever before," I said with an impish grin. "One thing I learned was that the Mexicans had blood relatives in Panama. All of a sudden the story of the battle for Tenochtitlan became very real to me. I always thought it was the conquistadors who pillaged the sacred city, but to find out the Spaniards were aided by Panamanians who were cousins and such, made it even worse."

Jameson said, "Again, a general learning for me, is that the Bible comes alive today when we let it come alive back then."

"I love it. Books by biblical scholars often say that the Bible is a living and breathing thing. That's why it has, can now, and will in the future, come alive for every new generation."

The King Montezuma Trilogy

"I didn't like," said Sol, "the thought that Jonah was a legend rather than a story from history."

"The Bible has legends and history and laws and poems…"

Sol interrupted with, "…and the Gospel."

"Yes! And all of it is open to how the Holy Spirit moves an understanding of the story within you."

"You mean," asked Jameson, "like a song speaks to me differently than you?"

"Thanks, mi hijo. I love that!"

"What I liked was how Jonah got his call and tried to distance himself from it."

"Why would you like that, Dad?"

"Because I can relate."

"Sorry. You have to say more."

"I'm what's known as a frustrated pastor wannabe. I sensed a call to go into ministry, but I turned and went the other way."

Jameson asked, "Why?"

"I also felt a call to teach, then realized that teaching would be my ministry."

Jameson then said, "If I end up going into ministry, please don't try to live vicariously through me." I gave a half-hearted nod of agreement, then he continued. "The story of Jonah showed me that God has a tendency to get what God wants. You might think about that one, Dad."

Sol interrupted with, "I loved all of the allusions Jonah had to Jim Caldwell."

Almost in unison, Jameson and I said, "The Old Testament can't learn from the New Testament."

Sol replied, "That's why I said allusions, not learnings."

"I think we are all growing through this experience," offered Jameson.

The King Montezuma Trilogy

I said, "Here's one way I grew. The conversion of all of Cartagena, because Jonah told them they would be overthrown in forty days, solidifies in my mind that this book is not historical."

"Yah, pretty far-fetched," agreed Jameson, "but what intrigued me was that Jonah got mad about God repenting from the calamity he planned for Cartagena."

"That's not what made Jonah mad," explained Sol. "He was mad because it was an unnecessary trip. If God was willing to be forgiving, why not do that before Jonah's trip?"

Jameson said, "Even though this is not historical, I don't like it that Jonah wanted to take his own life. A student at college killed himself last semester, and I just think we need to speak more about living than dying."

"I loved the point God made to Jonah about being angry at a bush, while he didn't care about the people of Cartagena."

"So," said Jameson, "legends have value beyond the story itself."

Sol then offered that, "I really liked something early on in Third Isaiah. Now what was it?" She grabbed her Bible, turned to Isaiah, and quickly found it. "It's 56:2, which says, 'Happy is the mortal who does this, the one who holds it fast, who keeps the Sabbath, not profaning it, and refrains from doing any evil.'" Jameson asked why she like it, and she said, "It reminds of a blend of Jim Caldwell's beatitudes and the Ten Commandments."

"I learned that good doesn't make bad go away," said Jameson. When I asked him to say more, he said, "Mom's comment about the exiles not having it too bad in Spain, really opened my eyes because at the same time they were forcibly taken away from their homes and their God-promised land."

The King Montezuma Trilogy

Sol said that she learned about peace in the Aztec Scriptures, as a metaphor for death, then said, "but more importantly I love God's steadfast love."

"I loved," said Jameson, "what Dad said about the Aztec Scriptures being Jim's roots, Methodism being his trunk, and Caldwellianism blossoming after the resurrection. I do have one other question."

"Fire away."

"What is the secret of the empire?" he asked with quite a bit of exasperation.

"Why don't you start first?"

"Okay. I think the secret is that the Empire was lost to the Spaniards because they believed they could never lose their God-promised land."

"Certainly a part of it. What about you, hon?"

"I think it was because they quit following God's laws."

"I agree."

"What about you, Dad?"

"I think it came from infighting."

"A little more, please," requested Jameson.

"Just look at the different civilizations of Mesoamerica. The Olmecs lasted 800 years, but what happened to them? Nobody knows. They just died off. The Mayans were active from 1000 B.C. to A.D. 1521, a very successful run all over the Yucatan Peninsula, but most of their pyramids and cities are nothing more than ruins. The Zapotecs had a 1,500 year run in the area of Oaxaca, and now they are gone. The incredible city of Teotihuachan only lasted 650 years, and even though it was one of the largest cities in the world, it now lies in ruins. Then you have the Aztecs from A.D. 1200-1521. I don't think Cortés ended the Aztecs, when there is a pattern of not being able to

The King Montezuma Trilogy

last in Mesoamerica."

"So infighting ended them all?" asked Jameson.

"I don't know, but when you have many people competing for sometimes limited resources, bloodshed tends to happen sooner or later."

"So, you're exhonerating Cortés in the fall of the empire?" asked Sol.

"Partly, because history is remembered mostly from the winner's perspective."

"What do you mean?" asked Jameson.

"It's just like the prophets we've considered this week. There were many prophecies in Aztec times, but only the ones that came true were canonized in scripture. It's kind of like the loudest voice gets heard."

"That makes sense," agreed Sol. "As a Mexican-American, I can testify that my opinions are often drowned out when a person of the majority culture speaks."

"Sorry, Mom. That's sad. When has that happened?"

"Sure. Just last week at a church meeting, the pastor asked what we thought about the music. I mentioned that I didn't care for contemporary, but my opinion was quickly dismissed. A little later, several Caucasians spoke against contemporary music and all of a sudden the concern was heard."

"Wow," said Jameson, "I guess even the church needs the equality teachings of Jim Caldwell."

"History remembers the Aztecs willingly surrendering, because that's what the Spanish wanted to have happen. What actually happened was the horrific destruction of Tenochtitlan. The sands of time have whitewashed the story for the last 500 years, but the Aztecs were supposedly given a choice to submit to Spain or be killed. The Dominican friar Bartolomé de Las

The King Montezuma Trilogy

Casas thought this story was absurd because it was simply the majority voice that history wanted to hear."

"I get it," said Jameson. "Maybe the conquering of Mexico wasn't a simple surrender."

"Perspective is everything when it comes to history. I think about the Gospels. Matthew, Mark, Luke, and John all share the same story in very different ways, based on their theology, context, audience, and such."

"Those are the kinds of things I'm learning in college," said Jameson.

"There are two other things biblical authors used to make their point: legitimization and aggrandizement."

"What are those about?" asked Sol.

"Aggrandizement is about making something appear greater than it is, and legitimization is about exercising control over others by virtue of authority."

"Okay," said Jameson, "but what's your point?"

"Even though it is remembered as a conquest moment for Cortés, an example of both aggrandizement and legitimization, it will mostly be remembered as a surrender.'"

"So you're saying," asked Jameson, "King Zedekiah was not defeated by the Conquistadors?"

"Well, not exactly. Old lies die hard, like meteorologists telling us every day when the sun sets."

"How is that a lie?" asked Sol.

"The sun doesn't set. The earth rotates."

"I like that," offered Jameson.

"The Spanish–Aztec War wasn't a momentary event. It started in 1519 and lasted three years, from 1519-1521. I think the secret is that the Aztec Empire was tragically invaded by Cortés, then infighting among the Aztecs helped to burn it down.

The King Montezuma Trilogy

As for now, its starting to get dark and we have a winding road to drive down from the mountain."

As we got back in the car, Jameson said, "Last year you explained the Law through the book of Kings, and now we've gone through the Prophets of the Aztec Scriptures. There are other books in the Old Testament, so what about them?"

It was a tantalizing question, so I said, "They're called the Writings. Interested?"

"Sure," said Jameson.

"Let me think about it. At least we can try to address that next summer."

"Fair enough," said a smiling Jameson, but Sol was less enthusiastic.

As we settled in for our trip back to the hotel and our final night, I couldn't help but think the impending darkness was a metaphor for many people's attitude about the Old Testament. My heart was strangely warmed to realize my son was open to learning about the Aztec Scriptures. So often our fellow Caldwellians are so mesmerized by the New Testament, that they have no interest in learning about the Old Testament. The sun sets every night, but I hope our thirst for knowledge never ends, so that each sunrise would whisper new secrets.

All of a sudden I got excited about studying the Writings part of the Aztec Scriptures, and couldn't wait to figure out how to share them next year.

The King Montezuma Trilogy

THE VALUE OF THE EMPIRE
A King Montezuma Story – Book 3

The King Montezuma Trilogy

PREFACE
An Aztec Synagogue

A phone call last week to the docent at the local Aztec synagogue went better than I could have hoped. Her name is Maria, and she told me that she is a Mexican of the Aztec faith, while most of her family became Catholic, so I immediately made an appointment to visit her on Saturday. I told her that I had been to Guatemala and Mexico to hear stories in context about the Law portion of the Aztec Scriptures. I somewhat did the same the next summer for the Prophets, but only experienced them from Monterrey, Mexico. I then explained that I was low on money, so now I needed to get creative with ways to experience the Writings section of the Aztec Scriptures. She was delighted with the request, because she said she loves to share about her faith and her synagogue. "I will look forward to meeting you," said Maria, "and will get started right away gathering ideas that might help you."

The week passed quickly because I was very busy with my job as a High School history teacher. On the day of the trip, Phoenix hit a balmy 100 degrees Fahrenheit for the first time this year. Hard to believe it's only April 21, but the record earliest 100-degree day was March 26, 1988. I haven't even opened my pool yet, because it's not about how hot it gets during the day, it's about how cool it gets overnight. Once the temperature stops dropping below 70, the pool becomes tolerable. Most people think I'm crazy for living here, but the pool makes a huge difference, and finding shade and a breeze are the other keys to a successful life in the desert. Sipping a coconut-lime drink doesn't hurt either.

The King Montezuma Trilogy

As I got ready for the short excursion downtown, I realized how fortunate I was to have a job that gave me the summer off. Sometimes I get so caught up in work that I don't notice the wonderful things around me. This morning I was noticing. The saguaros were beginning to bloom, but they were all over the main body rather than confined to the crown. I heard this unique phenomenon was due to the stress of drought and heat, but had never seen it. The West Indian Lantana was blossoming, an emerald green and scarlet red Elegant Trogon was sharing its song, and a coyote walked across my front yard. All in all, I thought it was a pretty hard day to beat.

The appointment with Maria was for 10 a.m. The traffic on the 101 was surprisingly heavy, and got worse on I-17 as I headed downtown. To be honest, I had never been in an Aztec synagogue, so I was mildly uncomfortable. After parking, I went in and was cheerily greeted at the front desk, then mentioned my appointment with Maria. The woman picked up a telephone and let Maria know I was there, so I took a seat, feeling much more relaxed.

A few minutes later a bubbly woman in her fifties, although I'm a terrible judge of age, came out and greeted me. "I was delighted with your call last week, and have some thoughts about how I can help." She then invited me to her office, and I followed her down a short hallway to a small room with a desk, two chairs, and lots of bookshelves. She sat at her desk and asked me to be seated. "So, first of all," she began, as she looked at her notes, "was your first trip to Mexico an attempt to hear all of the stories from the Law part of our Bible, while in their proper setting?"

"No, no," I said with a smile. "We just focused on some of the stories from Genesis 12 through 2 Kings."

The King Montezuma Trilogy

"So, who is 'we'?"

"Wow! Sorry. Guess I'm getting ahead of myself. Two years ago was the first trip. It was actually my son Jameson's 18th birthday gift, but I accompanied him. He is thinking about going into ministry, and my wife and I wanted him to see the origins of our Caldwellian faith. I hired Geraldo, a Mexican guide, who met us in Guatemala, and told us the stories where they took place, as we traveled to Mexico City.

"Thanks," she said. "That makes sense. I love it that you focused on the Law and the Former Prophets, because they tell a complete story from the forming of the empire to the exile."

"I'll have to give credit to our guide Geraldo. I just asked for the stories from the first five books, but he insisted that we cover the first nine books. I thought his plan would cover eleven books, but Geraldo explained that Samuel and Kings were originally two books, not four. The next summer, my wife joined the two of us for a trip to Monterrey, Mexico, where I shared the stories from the Prophets. Since Jameson and I already knew the sites of the former Southern Empire, we just needed to experience the former Northern Empire."

"Those remaining prophets," she explained, "are called the Latter Prophets. Isaiah, Jeremiah, and Ezekiel are further designated as the Major Prophets and the remainder are the Minor Prophets, also known as the Book of the Twelve." A smile grew across my face as I realized that Maria was just the person I needed to help plan the final experience.

"That's what brings me here. I'm looking for ideas about how to present the Writings section of the Aztec Scriptures to my son."

"Okay. Well, I think you'll be happy with my ideas. There are twelve books that are officially listed as Writings, and I've

The King Montezuma Trilogy

broken them into four categories: poetry, wisdom, stories, and liturgies. Among the most famous poems in the world are those by King Montezuma. They have all kinds of classifications, but they are all called Psalms. To enrich your appreciation of poetry, I would recommend traveling to the Universtiy of Arizona in Tucson. Call Paola Valenzuela, she's the Event Coordinator for their Poetry Center, and see if you can lead a one day workshop on the Psalms."

"Oh, my heavens! Not sure I'd feel comfortable doing that."

"When you called me last week, didn't you mention you're a high school teacher?"

"And?" I asked, while feeling a bit caught.

"If you love the Aztec Scriptures and you love teaching, you'll get over yourself."

After I laughed uncomfortably, she continued. "It really is a great place. Over a thousand poets have been invited to read their work at the center since opening in 1960, and the Dedication Ceremony featured a reading by Robert Frost."

"Okay, now you're just trying to scare me!"

"Not at all. I'm trying to motivate you. Besides, you wouldn't be teaching your poems, because they are Montezuma's." Then, looking mildly perturbed, she said, "Next I would recommend going to the small, historical town of Tubac. Have lunch at Wisdom's Café and soak up the conversations of the eclectic group that eats there. Try to engage some of them in conversation, because that's where I think you could discuss the books of Proverbs and Job."

"Love that idea. It seems much more natural."

"Good. Then I would visit the Nature Conservancy right here in Phoenix. They started in 1966 and have protected more than 1.5 million acres of Arizona land. They thrive on the power

The King Montezuma Trilogy

of story to get their message out, so that's where you could find a kindred spirit. There I would share four stories: Ezra, Nehemiah, Chronicles, and Daniel."

"How would I go about it?"

"That, my friend, is on you. Finally, I would go to Flagstaff and visit their Aztec Synagogue."

"Why not here?"

"This last part of the Writings have become liturgy for worship, and the Flagstaff synagogue has some wonderful copies of the original five: Lamentations, Ecclesiastes, Solomon, Esther, and Ruth."

"Wow. I can't thank you enough."

"Hold on. I'm not done." She then handed me a copy of Don Miguel Ruiz' book *The Four Agreements: A Toltec Wisdom Book: A Practical Guide to Personal Freedom*."

"I like that book."

"I don't want you to like it, I want you to live it. It will help you on this final leg of your journey."

As I graciously took this gift, I shook her hand warmly and thanked her profusely. Walking back to the car I hoped to focus on driving, because so many things were going through my head. It will be exciting when Jameson returns home after his second year of college, and by that time I hope to have everything lined up for this summer's experience.

When I got home, I handed my wife the book. She smiled and said, "He's a favorite of my people. He's a *nagual*, who shared in this book the teachings of the Toltecs. It's a way of life that shows how to find happiness and love."

I sat down and started reading the book in earnest. It wasn't long until I realized why Maria gave me the book. The four agreements amount to a code of conduct that frees one up from

The King Montezuma Trilogy

wasting time on unnecessary things. They are:

> 1. Be impeccable with your word.
> 2. Don't take anything personally.
> 3. Don't make assumptions.
> 4. Always do your best.

    As I contemplated the meaning of these words, and their application to the Writings section of the Aztec Scriptures, something important dawned on me. I realized that the book was about me, so that's how I could attempt to live the book, as Maria suggested. If I was going to lead Jameson through this final part of the Old Testament, I needed the rules to apply to myself. To be honest, it's much easier to impose the agreements on an inanimate object like the Bible, but Maria wanted me to live what it said. As a Caldwellian, I have always been focused on the teachings of Jim Caldwell, so my appreciation for the roots of his faith needed to be owned. This turned me to a study of the Toltec wisdom. If I could manage to understand how its wisdom guided the Writings, perhaps I could let the Aztec Scriptures speak fresh and new to both Jameson and myself.

    Toltec wisdom is about knowledge. Those who practiced it came together as masters and students at Teotihuacan. Jameson and I visited those pyramids on our first journey to Mexico, to experience the sights and sounds of the stories from the Law and the Former Prophets. I also went online to www.am-innovations.com which says, "The Toltec System of Knowledge is a Practical Exploration of the Great Spiritual and Physical Universes, and as such is a Facet of the Diamond of the One Life." That thrilled me because Jim Caldwell is referred

The King Montezuma Trilogy

to as the Diamond. He rose from the dead from an old diamond mine, giving that dual message of love and eternal life. That said, Toltec knowledge didn't form a religion. Its practitioners appreciate all spiritual teachings which leads to happiness, and they practice it as a way of life.

Now I have one month to finish planning these outings. They will involve four, mid-week day trips to the locations Maria recommended. My first task was to call Paola at the Poetry Center and see if I could schedule a time to teach the Psalms. Even though their mission is to "advance a diverse and robust literary culture that serves a local-to-global spectrum of writers, readers, and new audiences for poetry and the literary arts," I didn't hold out much hope. To my surprise, and no little amount of fear and trepidation, she said "yes." June 18 was open, and before I knew it, Paola put my workshop on their calendar.

The trip to Tubac would be much more relaxed. I've been to the small, artsy town before, but Wisdom's Café is closed on Sundays and Mondays. They started in 1944 and are famous for their fried, fruit burrito and award-winning margaritas. It's a two-and-a-half hour drive to get there, so I'll plan to leave mid-morning and have lunch on the premises. Once the crowd thins out a bit, I'll see if I can engage some in a discussion of the wisdom of Job and the book of Proverbs. After looking over my calendar, I chose July 10.

The Nature Conservancy in Arizona began in 1966. Although they are undergirded by reports and data, they are driven by the power of story. They tackle climate change, protect land and water, and provide food and water. In Camp Verde, development and water scarcity were threatening a family farm, so the Conservancy upgraded their irrigation infrastructure. I thought it was a long shot to gain their interest

The King Montezuma Trilogy

in hearing four biblical stories, then I realized Ezra and Nehemiah were returning to Mexico after disaster. Chronicles was an intentional effort for denying problems, and Daniel was apocalyptic. Maybe this will work, I thought, so I called Daniel Stellar, the State Director, and he agreed to have a small group of his staff meet with me. He offered July 30 and I accepted.

The final trip would be strictly for learning. Jameson and I will go to the Aztec Synagogue of Flagstaff to hear about the last five books, commonly known as the Megillot. Maria told me that those books are used liturgically in worship for different holidays, and I found myself intrigued. Maria had already called the synagogue and got me lined up to spend the day with Atzi on August 13. Now all I have to do is study the other seven books, to do them justice when presenting, and most importantly wait for Jameson to get home for summer break.

The King Montezuma Trilogy

ACT I
Poetry in Tucson

The King Montezuma Trilogy

SCENE ONE
Psalms 1-72

"Let's get this show on the road!" exclaimed an enthusiastic Jameson, when we were finally ready to go.

His mother, Sol, gave him a kiss on the cheek, and my wife of twenty five years gave me a hug, as we headed to the car in our garage. Of course, we were only going to be gone for the day, but my class at the Poetry Center started at 9 am and the map showed we had a 2 hour and 18 minute trip ahead of us. We left before 6 to help avoid some rush hour traffic on interstate 17, and the trip south happily meant avoiding the bright, Phoenix sun in our eyes.

"Can't believe that cake mom made for me for graduating my sophomore year of college. She always goes above and beyond."

"Of course, but she would say it was from her Mexican culture of hospitality."

"How does that matter?"

"To your mother, she was doing the minimum, she was doing her best. You know, Ruiz's fourth agreement."

Jameson nodded and said, "That book was a fun read. Thanks for loaning it to me."

We cruised through the traffic with no delays, as the navigation system only showed normal slow downs. I just love science, but truth be known, I probably rely on it too much. As we drove past the airport, I noticed visibly fewer planes. Although 200 people are moving here every day, the busiest time is still the winter. That's when snowbirds arrive for a winter of golf, and masses arrive later on for the Cactus League spring

The King Montezuma Trilogy

training games. I must admit I was feeling a little anxious about this first opportunity, when Jameson broke the silence.

"That's a strange place," he said, as we passed the exceedingly strange sign that reads 'Rooster Cogburn Ostrich Ranch' in Picacho, Arizona.

"What's even stranger," I replied, "is that it is billed as 'The Darndest Place You'll Ever Visit.'" We agreed to never visit it.

Tucson was actually busier than Phoenix, but then again we were arriving at peak rush hour. The University of Arizona is in downtown Tucson, and the Poetry Center was easy to find. I was delighted to find a parking spot and before we knew it, Jameson and I were at the front desk. The facility didn't officially open until 9, but the kind woman there was expecting me. She escorted us to our room and said, "You have twelve people signed up for the one day seminar, and it's a great variety of individuals. Enjoy!"

We settled in to the fairly large room, put two 8' x 10' tables next to each other, and set up fourteen chairs around them. Feeling a little unworthy about teaching college students, I pulled the teacher's chair from the front desk and placed it at one end, as a sign of prominence. As the students arrived, and it was time to begin, I looked out and realized these kids were about the same age as my high school teenagers. Soon my anxiety abated and I began with, "Welcome to this seminar about the poetry of the book of Psalms. They were a collection of one hundred and fifty poems, composed from the time of King Montezuma to postexilic Mexico."

"Hey, prof," called out one of the students, "we're poetry students, not Bible scholars. What's postexilic?"

"Great question!" I said. "First of all, let me mention that I'm not a professor. I'm a High School history teacher who loves

The King Montezuma Trilogy

poetry and the Psalms. Also, this isn't a regular class, so feel free to be interactive. It's my hope that we can learn together. Any other questions?"

"Yes," said the same student. "What's postexilic?"

Several sarted laughing, and I felt a need to prove myself, so I said, "When Cortés and the Spanish conquistadors seized Tenochtitlan, which is now Mexico City, they deported the upper class Aztecs to Spain. That's known as the Exile. They were there for forty seven years, then Cyrus of Persia overthrew Spain and allowed the Aztecs to return home. Postexilic poems were those written when they were back in Mexico."

That seemed to help, then another student raised her hand and said, "I heard there were 151 Psalms."

"Very good. The Greek translation of the Aztec Scriptures is called the Septuagint, and it indeed had a 151st Psalm, but it was excluded during the canonization process."

It was surprising that nobody had a question about that statement, then I realized these kids were pretty sharp. I suspected they were simply testing me, and, if so, I think I passed their vetting. "The Psalms were finally written down for use in Templo Mayor, once it was rebuilt, and these poems were of great importance for ritual and liturgy in Aztec worship. As they were sung, they were often accompanied with dancing and music."

"Sounds like a party," suggested another, as the class loosened up with several people laughing in a good way.

"Very much so. To the Aztecs, worship itself was considered a holy day, and experienced as a holiday. The sheer joy of having their Temple rebuilt made for a phenomenal celebration, and that's what worship is. Here's one more comment as a means of introduction. There's a wide variety of

The King Montezuma Trilogy

classifications of the poetic psalms, and they were divided into five books to imitate the Law section of the Aztec Scriptures."

"That sounds like two comments."

There was a brief moment of silence, then we all laughed. It felt like we were off to a great start and I couldn't have been happier. Jameson looked comfortable sitting among students from the 'other' university, but I was glad he wasn't wearing his Arizona State University shirt. No need for in-state rivalry while I'm trying to teach. I then handed out a syllabus for the day so they could know that we wouldn't dwell endlessly on just a few psalms.

"The next chance you get, open a Bible to the first Psalm. In most versions it will start with the title, 'BOOK I: Psalms 1-41,' and the first two psalms introduce the entire book. Psalm 1 distinguishes between righteous and wicked people, while Psalm 2 differentiates between Mexico's king and other rulers. The first psalm is a didactic wisdom poem..."

A student immediately interrupted with, "Now that sounds like something that could be useful in the Poetry Center. What is it?"

"Didactic just means teaching, but the ulterior motive is usually moral instruction."

"Nope," said another. "Probably no value here."

After some mirth, I continued. "Wisdom isn't so much about knowledge, as it is about using experience to make good decisions." A female student suggested that she just might try to write a didactic wisdom poem about avoiding situations that could turn bad. "Wonderful," I said with an approving smile. "Just one other thing about the first two psalms."

"Yeah, right," the class said almost simultaneously.

I flashed a quick smile, then said, "Psalm 1 begins with a

The King Montezuma Trilogy

beatitude, 'Happy are those...' and Psalm 2 ends with a beatitude, 'Happy are all....' These happiness sayings bracket the introduction to the Psalms, and no matter what the political climate might be at any given time, following the LORD is the right thing to do."

A young man raised his hand and said, "I sure wish I had a Bible to follow along as you go."

Embarrassed that it hadn't crossed my mind, I quickly called Jameson over and gave him my credit card. "Please find ten copies as fast as you can." Two of the twelve who signed up for the seminar never came, then the most surprising thing happened. Three of the students pulled out their Bible. "Well, some of you are more prepared than me." As Jameson was going through the door I called to him and said, "Make that seven." I then turned to the class and said, "Let's go ahead with the third Psalm while we wait."

A student asked, "What about the guy who just left?"

"Oh, I'm sorry. That's my son. If you're interested, we'll tell you why he's here during lunch break. Meanwhile, Psalm 3 is a lament. Do you know any lament poems?"

After a short silence, one student said, "*Lament for the Makers* by W. S. Merwin."

"*A Lament* by Percy Bysshe Shelley," said another.

"*A Writer's Lament* by Bill Munn," said yet another.

"Wow! I'm impressed. I actually found that last one when preparing for the class. It ends with, 'who can write again, the Iliad, or Macbeth, or maybe even the Bible.' I love that. Great poetry calls us to emote, and Psalm 3 is about placing one's trust in God in difficult situations."

"What do you call this coincidence?" a female asked as Jameson returned right then with seven Bibles.

The King Montezuma Trilogy

Jameson smiled and said "This Poetry Center is great! The woman at the front desk quickly rounded up all seven."
Responding to the young woman, I said, "I would call it good luck, but you call it whatever you want." Jameson then handed out the Bibles and I had everyone turn to the poem. "There's just one more thing I want to say about Psalm 3. Notice the word *Selah* at the end of each stanza? They all said, "Yes," so I said, "Any idea what it means?"
A young man said, "I heard it means *amen*."
"Yes. That's a very common understanding, but the fact is, it is such a rare word that nobody knows for sure what it means. Any questions before we move on?"
Another young man said, "Not a question, but I'd like to say that I'm inspired to write a poem of grief, because I've never thought of the Bible for source material."
That really did my heart good, so I said, "Thanks, so much! Broadening our horizons is what I think education is all about. Maybe this collaborative effort to teach the Psalms at the Poetry Center will pay off far more than I could have ever expected. Okay, let's turn to Psalm 8 and read it through before we begin discussing it." All but one opened their copy and quickly read the nine short verses. I asked the other young man if there was a problem, and he said he didn't know where to find it. I was delighted that nobody laughed, and simply said, "If you open it in the middle, you'll find it." He looked shocked when that worked, then I continued. "See the tag line 'according to the Gittith'?"
"What's that?" asked a young woman.
"Yeah, I don't git-tith it," said Jameson to a round of groans.
Another suggested, "Maybe it's the King James Version."
Some laughed, and I realized there was a pretty wide

The King Montezuma Trilogy

spectrum of biblical knowledge among this small group. "A gittith is probably a musical instrument," I said, "but scholars have found its identification to be elusive. The reason the psalm needed accompaniment was because it was written as a song. Can songs be poems?"

"Sure!" said another. "Chrissie Hynde wrote 'I'll Stand by You' for The Pretenders, and that song is definitely a poem."

All of a sudden I realized I didn't have names and faces put together, so I asked Jameson to go to the front desk again and see if we could get name tags. He quickly returned, and everyone wrote down their name and put the tag on their shirt. I immediately said, "Thanks Olivia," I know names are important, and since I'm a perfectionist at heart, I'm glad to get that little problem corrected. "Please look at verse 6 and tell me what you think about the word 'dominion.'"

Henry spoke up and said, "Sounds like a trick question."

"Unintentional, but you're probably right, so let me just talk about it for a moment. Many people of my age think it means that humans are to dominate, and have used that as an excuse to plunder the earth through mining. That is not at all what it means. It means that God set humans on the earth to be caretakers, and certainly not to dominate one another."

Emma quickly scribbled a note and said, "That's going to become a poem for me to write, and I hope I can do a reading of it some time here at the Center."

"Great! Here's another poetic song: Psalm 19. Take a few minutes to read through it, then we'll discuss it."

"So that's where that comes from," blurted out Sophia. "My pastor often says 'Let the words of my mouth and the meditation of my heart be acceptable to you, O LORD, my rock and my redeemer,' and now I know its Psalm 19:14."

The King Montezuma Trilogy

I said, "The Bible is probably referenced in every day life far more than most people realize. Now, if you like natural theology, that's what the first six verses are about. 'The heavens are telling the glory of God; and the firmament proclaims his handiwork.' For me, when I look up at the night sky, my mind drifts to thoughts of infinity and eternity. Likewise, this part of the poem celebrates God's glory in creation, but I want to draw your attention to the word 'God.'

Oliver spoke up and said, "If this seminar becomes religious, I'm outa here."

"Fair enough. What I want to point out is that the first six verses use the Aztec word *El* for God, and the next four verses use the Aztec word *YHWH* for God."

"Then who," asked Emma, "is the LORD?"

"When it shows up in capitals, it is giving you the clue that the word behind the translation is *YHWH*."

"I'm lost," complained Oliver.

"When the Aztecs experienced God as transcendent and far away, they used the term *El* for God. When they experienced God as close and personal, they used the term *YHWH* for God, because it was God's own name."

Evelyn said, "Please say more."

"Yahweh comes from Exodus 3:14, when God first reveals the divine name. The Bible is full of examples of God being both transcendent and personal and I think that's the point. God is whatever you need. Whether you need an overseeing protector or a relational God, the Bible has stories to support that."

"Now that sounds more like poetry. Thanks," said Sophia.

I said, "Let's try the 23rd Psalm," and that turned out to be familiar to most of them. After they quickly read it, I said, "It's obviously a very personal poem because it is bracketed with

The King Montezuma Trilogy

LORD at the beginning and the end, and at the very center of the poem are the words, "you are with me" (vs. 4). God's overseeing protection and intimacy combine wonderfully in this poem of trust."

"I've had too many experiences of broken trust to be much of anything but a skeptic," said Mia with a frown.

"Thanks for sharing, Mia. That sounds very painful, so I hope Psalm 23 can inspire a useful poem for you. It involves a beautiful sheep/shepherd metaphor."

Sophia spoke up and said, "It kinda gives me the creeps, because I only hear this psalm read at funerals."

"Good observation. To help us all settle in for an enjoyment of the 23rd Psalm, I see this poem as a way of life more than a solemn song about death." Everyone smiled and nodded in appreciation. "Another great thing is that it's about God and a single sheep, not an entire flock. That's what makes it so personal."

"I don't believe in God," complained a distressed-looking Oliver. "When my parents died in a car crash, there was no magical deity to make a difference." The class sat in stunned silenced. It seemed like forever before Sophia finally got up to go over and give him a hug, but Oliver crossed his arms and would have nothing to do with it.

"I'm sorry," offered a choked up Emma, as Sophia returned to her seat.

"Not your fault that my parents died," responded Oliver in a cold-hearted manner.

After another moment of silence, Henry said, "I don't believe in a magical deity either, but I've got to admit that history has shown a preference for believing in something greater than ourselves."

The King Montezuma Trilogy

Oliver responded, "I only trust myself." The class was quiet yet again, so I finally asked if he had anything more he wanted to share. "Just stay with the poetry. That's why I signed up. I could care less where it comes from."

"Okay," I said, "let's bring the discussion back to poetry. Who is it that said, 'No man is an island?'"

Everyone pulled out their phones and googled it. "John Donne!" called out Noah. "An English poet who wrote it in his devotional book in 1624."

"It's another great metaphor," I said. "It shows what its like to be a human, by comparing a person to an island that's disconnected from other land." Oliver continued to sit with arms rather defiantly folded.

"Yah," said Sophia. "Don't be an island, be a sheep."

All of a sudden, Oliver sat up and said, "Wait a minute. Didn't you say the Aztecs used the term *El* for God, when that thing you call God is experienced as transcendent and far away?" I nodded a yes, and he said, "That's how I experience God. So far away I'm disconnected, or God is disconnected from me. Either way, leave me and my island alone."

"Okay, try this. Psalm 23 is a prayer," I responded.

"How does that make a difference?" Oliver asked.

"When we are in prayer, it's like being alone on an island in a conversation with God." Oliver returned to folded arms, and I went on.

"Now let's take a look at the rest of it. The poem starts with 'The LORD is my shepherd,' and that tells us a lot. Using LORD with all capital letters means Yahweh, which is God's name, and it indicates intimacy."

"Sorry, Dad, but that just seems a little weird," said Jameson, as others squirmed a bit in their seats.

The King Montezuma Trilogy

"I suppose folk of your age think of intimacy in terms of sexuality, but it's simply a feeling of connectedness. It can mean sexual, but here it obviously implies emotional closeness. The emotional closeness comes from the comfort that a personal God cares for an individual. Remember, this is a prayer by King Montezuma, as he celebrates experiencing God looking over him like a shepherd. The first verse ends with 'I shall not want,' which means that the king is content. Somebody want to read verse 2?"

Amelia offered, "'He makes me lie down in green pastures.' Now wait a minute. That sounds like a dominant male trying to force himself on me."

"Whoa, I never read it that way before, but thanks, Amelia. It's good to hear how different generations experience the Bible. Actually, the original Aztec word here is about helping animals lie down, which furthers the sheep-shepherd metaphor."

"Okay, then let me continue", said Amelia. "'He leads me beside still waters.' Even I get that. Some of my favorite memories are sitting by a lake on a calm day with my best friend. I guess it's an image of trust and rest."

Sophia then started to read the next verse. "'He restores my soul. He leads me in right paths for his name's sake.' Yes. I can testify that God has restored my soul, because he led me on the right path to Jim Caldwell."

"You all are about to lose me," said Oliver, in a threatening way, as he sank deeper in his chair..

"Interestingly, the Aztec word here isn't so much religious as it is about life. Oliver, have you ever felt refreshed?" That seemed to settle him down, but he didn't answer. "Now for the all important fourth verse. Let me read it and then we'll talk about it. 'Even though I walk through the darkest valley, I fear no evil; for you are with me; your rod and your staff—they comfort me.'"

"Doesn't happen," said Oliver emphatically.

"Isn't Hell 'the darkest valley'?" asked Sophia.

"Nope," suggested Mia. "I've been to hell, and it was called depression."

Several students agreed with her, then I said, "It's about death, whether you're talking physical, emotional, or spiritual." I then turned in my Bible and said, "Here's how Job described the darkest valley: 'before I go, never to return, to the land of gloom and deep darkness, the land of gloom and chaos, where light is like darkness' (10:21-22)."

"Yep," said Sophia, "that's Hell."

"Nope," said Mia, "that's depression."

Oliver surprised everyone by saying, "It reminds me of a cave."

"What?" questioned Noah, with a bit of intrigue.

"Never mind him," suggested James. "He's into Plato."

Not being very well grounded in philosophy, I turned the discussion back to the Bible. "Truer to the text would be Isaiah 9:2: 'The people who walked in darkness have seen a great light; those who lived in a land of deep darkness—on them light has shined.'"

"Yep," said Sophia, "the light is Jim Caldwell!"

Jameson and I looked at each other for a moment, as if Sol was in our midst. "Let's move on to the 'fear no evil' part. Anyone able to do that?" Nobody spoke up, so I asked what the poem says about keeping fear at bay.

Evelyn, who talked for the first time, said, "'for you are with me.' I believe in God, but fear seems greater than God."

"Nothing is greater than God!" proclaimed Sophia.

The King Montezuma Trilogy

"I'm greater than God," announced Noah.

After a moment of silence, Amelia asked, "What do you mean?"

Noah smiled and said, "Because I'm nothing."

After some confused laughter I said, "Sounds like a Sufi or Rumi poem. Are you of Eastern religion persuasion?"

"Not particularly," said Noah. "I just like to learn from all religions. I believe sacred writings are worthy of study, consideration, and reflection."

"Great! Learning should never be restricted. The rest of verse 4 offers comfort through the sheep-shepherd image. So what do you think about verse 5?"

Mia offered to read: "'You prepare a table before me in the presence of my enemies; you anoint my head with oil; my cup overflows.' Who in their right mind would fix dinner for a bunch of enemies?

"We do that," said Sophia, "at my church. During communion and at pitch-in suppers."

Oliver asked, "So you willingly have enemies at your church?"

"We willingly have room for everyone," she responded.

"So," continued Oliver, "what's that overflowing cup all about?"

"I think it's poetry," said Mia. "It's seems like a metaphor for reconciliation and peace. What do you think, prof?"

I said, "If we let it be poetry, perhaps what it means to you is more important than what it means." After a thoughtful pause, I asked, "Someone want to read the 6th verse?"

Noah surprised everyone by standing up to read. "Surely goodness and mercy shall follow me all the days of my life, and I shall dwell in the house of the LORD my whole life long."

The King Montezuma Trilogy

After he sat back down, Sophia complained. "I though it ended with 'forever,' not 'my whole life long.'"

"That's another one of those pretty famous interpretations, but it certainly does not mean 'forever.' The poem is all about the here and now. That's why he hopes goodness and mercy will pursue him throughout his life, and he especially looks forward to finding security when he's in Templo Mayor in Tenochtitlan. Anything else?"

"No thanks, you pretty much ruined the 23rd Psalm for me," said Sophia, as she sank into her chair and folded her arms. Everyone started to laugh, but I noticed that Sophia was serious. I stole a quick glance toward Jameson, and he saw it, too, so I decided to give her time to recuperate by focusing on the next item.

"Okay," I said, "let's move on to Book II, keeping our back-and-forth discussions lively. That should take us close to the noon hour and then we'll break for lunch. This afternoon we'll wade through the poems of Books III, IV, and V. Book II goes from Psalm 42-72. Why don't you spend about five minutes looking them over and let me know the first one you'd like to discuss?"

After just a few minutes, Henry said, "How about that first one, Psalm 42?"

We all turned to it, and I said, "Interesting. This one was originally with Psalm 43, but they were separated in the canonization process."

"Sounds like my parents," groaned Mia. Shallow laughter disappeared into reality, and we once again moved on.

"This psalm is a lament about being so sick, the author wasn't able to make a pilgrimage to Templo Mayor."

"I thought all the Psalms were written by Montezuma," said

The King Montezuma Trilogy

a mildly annoyed Sophia.

"Some were, maybe even most, but this is a great example of how scholars realized they were not all by him."

"Why?" asked James.

"Oh," said a surprised Noah, "I bet it's because Montezuma wouldn't need a pilgrimage to get to Tenochtitlan. He lived there."

"And why do you think it used to be a part of Psalm 43?" asked Evelyn.

I got up, grabbed a piece of chalk at the blackboard, and drew a quick chart of how scholars think it used to be:

Stanza 1	42:1-4
Refrain	42:5
Stanza 2	42:6-10
Refrain	42:11
Stanza 3	43:1-4
Refrain	43:5

"I'm not sold," announced Mia, our resident skeptic.

"That's fine. I'm just saying what the scholars think, and that certainly doesn't mean it's correct. They further their thoughts with the fact that the two psalms have many linguistic links."

"I'm buying it!" announced Olivia.

"That's fine, too, so let's jump right in. Have any of you hiked Sabino Canyon in the summer?"

"Yah," said Noah, "but its nasty hot."

"Can you imagine being desperate for water, then finding a dry stream bed?"

"That would be awful," said Emma.

"Verse 1 says, 'As a deer longs for flowing streams, so my

The King Montezuma Trilogy

soul longs for you, O God.' As powerful as this kind of suffering is, it's not the point of the verse."

"Okay, I'll bite," said Evelyn.

"This prelude to the psalm represents the author's passionate longing for God."

"Getting too religious, again," complained Oliver, with his arms crossed in the usual manner.

Sophia quickly shot back, "Deal with it!"

Not wanting to lose focus, I said, "Then think of it as poetry. What does your soul long for?"

Noah said, "Learning."

"Yes, thanks. This class is about poetry. We simply use the Psalms as timeless examples of lyrical prose. Someone want to read verse 2?"

Amelia rose her hand and read, "'my soul thirsts for God, for the living God. When shall I come and behold the face of God?'" She then looked up and asked, "What does it mean to behold the face of God?"

"Scholars say it's a technical term for entering Templo Mayor," I said, "but frankly I don't get it."

"I love that," said Emma. "A man who doesn't have all the answers."

"James, would you please read verse 3?"

He quickly said, "My tears have been my food day and night, while people say to me continually, 'Where is your God?'"

"Ooh," said Oliver, "I like that. The people are taunting the author for failing to get help from God! More power to them."

"Please," said Olivia, "if you don't want religious connotations, why are you pushing them now?"

Amelia was getting a little frustrated, and said, "I agree, and because of that, I'm going to work on a poem about tears being

The King Montezuma Trilogy

my food."

"Good stuff," I said. "Verse 4 completes this first stanza with a memory of wonderful pilgrimages of the past. I'm sure you can relate to going home for the holidays." They all nodded, then I said, "Okay, now read the three refrains."

After a few moments, Noah said, "They're the same."

"That's another reason the two psalms are thought to go together. That just leaves us with stanza 2. Please read verses 6-10, then share with me their poetic power."

"Well," said Evelyn, "verse 6 is sad, but I know a lot of college students whose 'soul is cast down.' My roommate got a bad grade yesterday, and she was in a pretty bad funk."

Olivia said, "I just love verse 7, where 'deep calls to deep.' What do others think that's about?"

"Not sure," said Emma, "but I find it interesting that the poem begins with a parched soul, and now deals with thundering waterfalls and billowing waves. Maybe the deep troubles are calling for deep solutions. Just a second." Emma grabbed her pen and notebook and quickly wrote down a few thoughts. She then looked up and said, "I feel another poem coming on."

I then looked to Henry and asked if he had any thoughts. "You guys stop too quick," he said. "The next verse spells out the answer. 'By day the LORD commands his steadfast love, and at night his song is with me, a prayer to the God of my life.' I think religion is interesting, but I find it difficult to put into practice. For me, the psalmist is finding help in his distress. All of a sudden, 'deep calls to deep,' makes sense, because when the depths of my troubles cry out to the depths of the creator of the universe, inexplicably, God is there."

"What about when God isn't there?" asked Mia.

The King Montezuma Trilogy

"Oh, come on!" complained Sophia. "God is always there. Sometimes we just find it difficult to sense God's presence."

Wanting to get back to Henry, I asked, "Do you have any stories about God being there?"

"Really tired of this God talk," grumbled Oliver, but nobody paid attention to him.

"I've never told this story before," responded Henry, "but my first year here at school I thought about taking my life." He paused for a moment, and even Oliver turned to listen. "My parents live in New York, and I had no friends here. I'm an introvert, so it was difficult to get to know people. It was just a dark night, in my dimly lit room, and I was hollowed out with loneliness. School wasn't really working for me, so I started to think about ways I could go about ending it all. About that time there was a knock on my door and a group was going down the hallway inviting everyone to go out for dinner. That's when my 'deep' was unknowingly calling to the depths of God, and God answered. That group that night became the angels I needed." Henry stopped again and choked back some tears along with most everyone else, and then continued. "Verse 8 says, 'at night his song is with me, a prayer to the God of my life.' The song of that story stays with me in a comforting way, and now I'm trying to learn how to pray to the God of my life."

"I think you just did," said Noah, with several others nodding in agreement.

"And wow!" said Olivia, "That song, that prayer, that confession, whatever it was, will become a powerful poem. I can't wait to hear it at some future reading here in the Center."

Henry said, "I'll sure think about it. If it can help others, it would certainly be worthwhile."

"Thank you, Henry, for sharing that very personal story."

The King Montezuma Trilogy

Henry appeared to be uncomfortable, so I decided to move on. I asked, "Any thoughts about verse 9?"

Emma said, "I'll write a poem about God being a rock. That somehow seems to be a nice, genderless way to talk about God."

Henry surprised me by saying, "'Why have you forgotten me?' might be a good way to start my poem. Then the bit about being mournful, 'because the enemy oppresses me,' is a great metaphor for loneliness." I wanted to encourage Henry in his lyrical interests, but Oliver interrupted.

"I can relate to verse 10. My anti-religious stance makes people think I have, 'a deadly wound in my body,' so maybe that's why, 'my adversaries taunt me.' Pathetic!" He then looked back down at the psalm and read the end of the verse, "'while they say to me continually, 'Where is your God?' Taunting people doesn't seem very religious to me."

"Then write a poem!" declared a frustrated Olivia.

"Okay, let's have a look at Psalm 66, then I'll take us all out to lunch." After a surprisingly spirited round of applause I explained, "This poem is about liberation." Emma was pleased to hear this, then I said, "And it was meant to be heard. Someone want to come to the front and read it?" Emma quickly volunteered, and while she came forward I said, "Start with verse 5."

"Come and see what God has done," read Emma. "Sorry, I don't see much liberation going on here."

"Read verse 6," I requested.

Emma looked back down at the page and read, "'He turned the sea into dry land; they passed through the river on foot.' Sorry, I'm not familiar with the Bible. I'm here for the poetry."

James said, "That is the moment in history that all of

The King Montezuma Trilogy

modern day liberation is based on. It's after the Aztec people escaped from Guatemala, and dramatically found themselves caught between Lake Izabal and the approaching Guatemalan army wanting to take them back into captivity."

When James paused for effect, Amelia took the bait. "What happened?" He responded by telling her to reread verse 6. She said, "'He turned the sea into dry land; they passed through the river on foot.' They were set free from captivity, but what happened to the Guatemalans?"

Noah said, "They drowned. Maybe they'll have it better next time around."

Sophia frowned. "I don't believe in that reincarnation stuff."

Emma said, "Hey, I'm a feminist, but let's not deal with our differences. Now, tell me more about liberation."

I said, "Verses 10-12 moves the story from the remote past to the recent past. Would someone please read them?"

Amelia read, "'For you, O God, have tested us; you have tried us as silver is tried. You brought us into the net; you laid burdens on our backs; you let people rise over our heads; we went through fire and through water; yet you have brought us out to a spacious place.' I think I smell a poem coming on."

"In what way?" asked Emma.

"Being tested, going through trials, and getting caught up in a net. Feeling burdened, experiencing snobs who look down on me, getting judged through fire and water, then coming out of it in a spacious place. Yeh, I think I could find a poem in all of that."

"Thanks so much, Amelia. Verses 16-19 celebrate a personal story of liberation. Read it to yourselves, then we'll discuss it."

Very shortly, Oliver uttered a complaint. "'Come and hear,

The King Montezuma Trilogy

all you who fear God.' That's one of the reasons I'm against religion. Why would people want to fear the God they worship?"

"Well, Oliver, that translation has an unexpected twist. The Aztec word translated into English as 'fear,' is better translated as 'reverence' or 'honor,' as we are called to have toward our parents.'

"There you go," stated Oliver with increasing anger. "I don't know how to revere dead parents, and I definitely don't know who God is!"

"Couldn't that at least become a meaningful poem?" asked Henry. He quickly got his answer, as Oliver stood up, flipped his chair over, and shocked everyone by walking out. Sophia wanted to go after him, but several students said that he's angry like that all the time. She couldn't take it, so after a few moments she got up and went after Oliver.

When Sophia got back to the classroom, she told us about the conversation. "He said, 'Leave me alone,' and I responded, 'but I care about you.' He then said, with a surprisingly angry voice, 'No you don't. You don't even know who I am!' I started to reach out to touch him on the shoulder and said, 'But I would like to know who you are.' He brushed my hand away in an almost violent way, and then faced me with an angry look.'" At this point the class was listening intently. "He said, 'I'm warning you. Leave me alone!' He walked on ahead and I reluctantly returned."

"How do you feel about that?" asked Noah.

Sophia said, "Not so good, but at least I feel better about me. The only thing I could think of was Jim Caldwell, and his parable about the lost sheep."

Henry said, "Maybe this is like that moment when the Aztecs made it across the lake, but the Guatemalans drowned."

The King Montezuma Trilogy

"And your point?" asked Emma.

"Some people move on, while others die because they can't escape their pain."

"Astute observation," I said, "but it bothers me that he left. Anyone else have anything to say?"

Sophia said, "I'll grieve our loss. I'm sure Oliver had more to offer us."

"I'm not so sure," suggested Henry. "He's a troubled person. I'm ready for the rest of the psalm."

"Okay," I said. "Well, the rest of the psalm is summed up with, 'and I will tell what he has done for me.' This is your invitation from the poetry of the Psalms to write about the things you have been liberated from. Any ideas what that might be for you?"

"I'm a creative soul," said Olivia, "and I learned as a child that it is okay to color outside the lines."

Henry said, "I'm a cautious type, so I just might pray for God to help me be more open."

"Men," announced Emma. Most people looked confused, so she offered an explanation. "I have been liberated from men telling me what to do."

James said that the experience with Oliver liberated him from needing to change people, while Sophia felt liberated to work harder at evangelism. Evelyn said, "I'm a seeker, and this whole seminar liberated me to work harder at understanding the Bible."

Noah said, "I really like Eastern religions, so I would say I feel liberated to delve deeper into the great unknown."

"I'm an agnostic," said Amelia, "and I feel liberated to question things even more."

After a bit of silence, Mia said, "I'm a skeptic, and Psalm

The King Montezuma Trilogy

66 taught me to look more for the good things in life."

"I'm humbled that the class has gone so well. Now, as I said, lunch is on me. What's your favorite haunt?"

After a little discussion, the class agreed on Graze. Sophia said, "It's really close. Just go west from here on East Speedway Boulevard. Pass North Campbell Avenue, then when you see Himmel Park on your right, make a left U-turn and it'll be on your right. Luckily we're getting there a little early, so the crowd shouldn't be too bad. The burger place is small, and so is the parking lot." Everyone quickly figured out how to carpool, then Sophia said, "See you there."

Jameson and I got in our car and hoped they weren't pulling our leg. After a surprisingly short distance, we found ourselves parked in the right place. It did seem like a hole-in-the-wall kind of dive, but the sign out front was inviting: Graze Premium Burgers & Fresh Cut fries. When we walked in, the class was already ordering their meal, and I was impressed that the staff would believe I was going to pick up the bill. We looked the menu over, and Jameson immediately went with the Graze Double with Cheese. He also ordered a regular size of Fresh Cut Fries and a Chocolate Shake. I've always loved food, but am finding that, as I get older, I can't consume as big of a meal. I ordered a Graze Single, and just as I was ready to order some fries, a gigantic basket of fries was being taken out to a nearby table. I figured I would be able to pilfer some of Jameson's fries, so I just ordered a fountain soda. The bill tallied higher than expected, but this teaching thing was as much for me as for the students who signed up.

Some of the staff had kindly pushed tables together for us, and we gathered for a great meal. The discussion was also enjoyable, and I was pleased how inclusive the class was,

The King Montezuma Trilogy

because Jameson and I really felt like we were a part of them. Sophia reminded that we offered to explain during lunch about Jameson's presence.

"I can handle that one, Dad. For my 18th birthday, my parents gave me a trip to Belize, Guatemala, and Mexico to enliven my understanding of the Aztec Scriptures."

"Wow! That's a great gift," said Sophia.

Jameson continued, "Dad joined me for the trip."

"So much for a great trip," declared Henry, and the class roared with laughter.

When things settled down, Jameson said, "and he hired a Mexican guide named Geraldo to tell the sacred stories at prominent pyramids along the way. We saw Tikal, Monte Alban, Chichen Itza, Tulum, Cholula, and the ruins of Tenochtitlan."

Amelia said, "I have no idea what you just said, but it sounds like fun."

"The best thing was swimming at Tulum."

"Okay," said Olivia, "I've heard of that."

"On that trip, we covered the Law and the Former Prophets, or Genesis to Second Kings. Last year Mom joined us for a trip to Monterrey. Dad told the stories of the Prophets section of the Old Testament, including Hernan Cortés' overthrow of Mexico. Today is the first stop for this third trip, as Dad is working to bring the Writings section of the Bible alive." They seemed impressed, and when we were finished with our meals, we returned to our cars, and looked forward to the afternoon session.

The King Montezuma Trilogy

SCENE TWO
Psalms 73-150

Jameson and I were the first ones back, and I started to get nervous as we waited together in an empty room. I looked at the clock and could tell Jameson was feeling the same way. Finally they all came strolling in and apologized. Sophia said, "We decided to stop for some ice cream." I couldn't believe they were still hungry, but then they thanked me for lunch. This really was a great group of students, but my heart sank a bit realizing Oliver wouldn't be returning. I silently offered a quick prayer that he might find peace, and be liberated from his anger.

"Ready for Book III?" I asked, while strangely feeling like a carnival barker. They all nodded, so I said, "To get a sense of Psalms 73-89, I chose numbers 73 and 80. Let's turn to Psalm 73 to begin, and look at verses 1 and 28." Everyone dug right in and got started. "Notice that this psalm is framed by a confession of God's goodness. I think it's because the poem depends on faith as a means of dispelling envy of evildoers."

"Just a second," requested Noah. "At the beginning of the poem, it says 'A Psalm of Asaph.' What's an Asaph?"

"Not a what, but a who. Asaph is thought to be one of Montezuma's chief musicians," and Noah gave an approving nod. "The issue here is in verse 3, where the poet is envious of the happiness of the wicked."

"I can relate," said Amelia. "I don't know if I believe in God or not, but if there is no God, then why should I bother to be good?"

"The way I answer that question," said Noah, "is that I believe we are called to leave this world in better shape than we found it."

The King Montezuma Trilogy

"Good luck with that one," snarked Mia.

"Why so negative?" asked Sophia.

Mia almost barked back, "Because I'm envious of the happiness of the wicked!"

"Wow," I said. "Perhaps we can look at verses 4-12, and see if we can guide the discussion around the poem."

The class seemed okay with that, then Olivia said, "Looks pretty good to me: verse 4, 'no pain;' verse 5, 'not in trouble;' verse 6...wait a minute. It doesn't seem to fit: 'Pride is their necklace; violence covers them like a garment.'"

"Sure it does," said Sophia. "Just like verses 4 and 5, verse 6 also suggests impunity for their haughty ways."

"Noah smiled and said, "Sounds like inspiration for evil."

"Hey, Noah," called out James. "You fit in with verse 10. 'Therefore the people turn and praise them, and find no fault in them.'"

Reading ahead, Noah replied, "Still sounds good. Look at verse 12, 'Such are the wicked; always at ease, they increase in riches.'"

"So," asked Evelyn, "what's the point of all this?"

I explained that, "There's a famous Old Testament scholar named Walter Brueggemann, who suggests Psalm 73 is the theological center of the Psalms."

"Happy for Walter," said Mia, "but that's no help to me."

"Maybe it could be," I said, "if you let theology be poetic."

"Now we're talking," said Olivia. "That's what I'm here for."

I said, "When something is in the middle, it often has poetic meaning. In this Psalm, the first twelve verses identify the problem. The last twelve verses, 18-28, offer the solution, and the middle, verses 13-17 represent the turning point for the poet."

The King Montezuma Trilogy

"So, you're saying," questioned James, "that the turning point is more important than the solution?"

"Yes. One cannot practice a new way until they have turned from an old way. Just like there's no such thing as multitasking."

"Fake news," suggested Mia.

"Not according to science. Anyway, look at how the poet does it in verse 13, 'All in vain I have kept my heart clean and washed my hands in innocence.'"

"That's what happened at Jim Caldwell's trial," said Sophia. "Dmitri Ivanov washed his hands and claimed to be innocent of Jim's upcoming hanging." Her comment was met with silence, and it seemed everyone else was more interested in the poetics than the spirituality.

"At a deeply human level," I continued, "verse 16 suggests that reason is insufficient for theology."

"Now that has poetic significance," said Emma. "When I can't understand something, I seek something outside of my experience."

"Yes," said Evelyn. "That's when I turn to faith."

Noah said, "That's when I turn to Eastern religions."

I then mentioned, "In verse 17, the poet chose to turn to God, which, in turn helped him understand the problem of the evildoers."

"Which is what turned him around, right?" asked Emma.

"Yes. Then verses 18-20 reveal the divine undoing of the wicked, like verse 18's 'fall to ruin,' verse 19's 'swept away utterly by terrors,' and verse 20's 'on awaking you despise their phantoms.'

"Thanks," said Emma. "Plenty of poetry there."

"Verses 21-28 show the mental, emotional, and spiritual well-being that has come to the poet through this journey. He sums it up for himself in verse 28 that happiness isn't about depending upon oneself, but upon God."

"I find wholeness," said Amelia, "by communing with nature."

Jameson then spoke up for the first time and said, "College brings me wholeness."

Everyone seemed rather shocked to hear him talk. Olivia expressed appreciation for his thought, then asked, "In what way?"

"I find happiness in community, and my classes are doing that for me." Several smiled and nodded affirmatively.

"Let's move on to Psalm 88," I said, with the intention of keeping the focus on the text.

Noah said, "So, it's a 'Prayer for Help in Despondency.' That should be useful in today's world. Personally, I keep from becoming despondent by focusing on Buddhism. It centers me in peace."

"You don't use the Bible?" asked Sophia.

"Sure, but Buddhism isn't so much a religion as a philosophy. I like to learn from all wisdom, and yes, the Bible has some great teachings."

"I have a question, prof," said Mia. "The introduction to this Psalm also says, 'A Song. A Psalm of the Korahites. To the leader: according to the Mahalath Leannoth. A Maskil of Heman the Ezrahite.' What does that mean?" General laughter broke out in agreement.

"I don't know."

After some mildly stunned silence, Mia said, "That's quite refreshing."

"Coming from a place of more experience in life than this class has, I can say that life is better when you don't have all

The King Montezuma Trilogy

the answers."

After another bit of thoughtful silence, Jameson said, "I've never heard him say that in my whole life!" Lots of laughter settled us in, as we got ready to deal with the Psalm at hand.

"I love that it's called 'A Song,'" said Olivia. "Songs are certainly a part of poetry."

"Absolutely," I agreed, "and this is a pretty difficult poem to sing. The first two verses are a cry for help, and verses 3-7 describe how he feels. Verses 8-12 share a complaint, and verses 13-18 contain an urgent appeal for God's help. Let's try to personalize this poem by taking the next 20-30 minutes to write your own poem, as inspired by Psalm 88."

Everyone pulled out their laptops and began the task. I wanted to look outside, but this was an interior room, so I got up and went to God's great outdoors. It was a bit warm and humid for a summer day in Tucson, so I quickly found a bench in the shade. A gentle breeze blew across me, not unlike the way I feel when I'm being inspired by the Holy Spirit. That made me hope that the students would be inspired by this break from our day of learning. My mind quickly drifted off to memories of my last two trips to Mexico, so I pulled my phone out and set an alarm for fifteen minutes. A huge smile crossed my face as I recalled friendly exchanges between Jameson and our guide Geraldo. The traveling was a bit much, but the payoff was beyond anything I expected. Hearing Geraldo tell stories from the Aztec Scriptures while we stood at the very place they happened, was both enlightening and thrilling. Sadness slowly crossed my face as I thought about our second trip. My wife joined Jameson and myself on that journey, but she wasn't interested in this excursion. Sol said she would have been happy to go if we were returning to Mexico, but Tucson just

The King Montezuma Trilogy

didn't intrigue her. A terrible rattling sound pierced my peace enough to bring me back to the present. Reaching down to my phone, I turned the alarm off and headed back inside. About half the class chimed in with, "More time please." They didn't even look up, so I sat down and waited for the first person to finish. About five minutes later, Henry put his pen down.

"My poem is ready, and it's definitely a difficult song to sing. I wrote about that night when I thought about taking my life." His eyebrows furrowed as if to say he wasn't sure he was ready. Finally, he said, "If you want to hear it, I'm ready to read it." Everyone stopped writing, looked up, and listened intensely.

A Poem Inspired by Psalm 88

I cried for help,
    within the emptiness of my soul.
It reverberated like a tree falling in the forest,
    but no one was there to hear.
My soul was deeply troubled,
    because my loneliness had consumed me.
I felt forsaken by life,
    and thought there was nothing left for me.

Overwhelming feelings possessed me,
    like a rogue wave destined for my demise.
I felt shunned,
    but blame was of no use now.
My choice for seclusion was mine,
    and mine alone.

The King Montezuma Trilogy

> Sitting in darkness,
>   my eyes ached with sorrow.
> Then I saw myself sitting in the corner,
>   like a scared little child.
> Inaudibly I formed a question to God.
>   "Aren't you also the creator of night?"
> Deafening silence echoed back
>   my final note of despair.
>
> I wanted to say, "How will my life end?
>   That's all I want to know,"
> but the words just stuck in my throat.
>   That's when unexplained noises
> filtered to my ears.
>   Thank you God for angels unawares.
> They saved my life that night,
>   and I am forever changed.

Henry's sharing was met with silence, and soon I noticed tears falling on several faces.

"So glad they came by," said Sophia. "Thank God."

Those sitting next to him patted him on the shoulder, and I asked if anyone else wanted to share. It became obvious that they were deeply touched by the poem, and just wanted to sit with the moment.

After a little while, Olivia said, "I look forward to sharing my poem sometime here at the Center. I'll need a lot more time to get it done."

"Okay, then maybe we're ready to move on. Book IV covers

The King Montezuma Trilogy

psalms 90-106, and I'd like us to take a look at 95 and 100." The class quickly turned their Bibles to Psalm 95 and read it through. "Let's try something different again. Spend about fifteen minutes preparing a report about the following verses: 1) Sophia, 2) James, 3) Emma, 4-5) Evelyn, 6) Noah, 7a) Amelia, 7b Mia, and 8-11) Henry and Olivia.

"What about me?" asked Jameson.

"Oh, for heaven's sake. How embarrassing. I'm sorry. Why don't you join Sophia for a report on the first verse?"

They all tore into the assignment with great excitement, and I could hardly wait to hear what they had to say. Fifteen minutes seemed like an eternity when just sitting and waiting, so I got up to take a walk around the Center. It really is an impressive building, designed as 'a progression toward solitude.' I moved through the building's meeting rooms, and experienced the intended gradual retreat to the peaceful library collection. There I found the 80,000 items housed in various galleries, and a bust of Robert Frost, who opened the Poetry Center with a reading. It also inaugurated a Reading and Lecture Series that has now heard over 1,000 writers. My head was filling with awe when I realized it was time to get back to my humble seminar.

Walking into the room I was pleased to find everyone still at work. When I asked how much more time they needed, we agreed on ten minutes. Feeling honored to have this unique experience, I walked around the circle and spent some time looking at what they were doing. Taking my seat, I said, "Okay, Sophia and Jameson, what do you have for us from the first verse?"

"Let me read it, because poetry is meant to be heard," said Jameson. I must admit I broke a little smile of pride as he began.

"'O come, let us sing to the LORD; let us make a joyful noise

The King Montezuma Trilogy

to the rock of our salvation!'"

Amelia asked, "How are you going to keep that from being religious?"

"You might be surprised," said Sophia. "It can be about liberation, like when the term was used during the Exodus wanderings."

"But that's still about religion," complained Amelia.

Sophia explained, "God says in Exodus 17:6, 'Strike the rock, and water will come out of it, so that the people may drink.'"

"So how is that not about religion?" asked Amelia, with deepening frustration.

She responded, "Think more about the rock."

"Okay, but how's that about liberation?" asked Henry.

Jameson said, "The world needs more drinkable water. The poetry becomes about ways we today can liberate the thirsty, by striking the rock of our hardened hearts."

"Ooh, he's good," said Olivia. "Hey, prof, your son just might be on his way to becoming an honorary U of A student!" Kind laughter broke out, then Sophia continued.

"Try this one from Job 24:8. 'They are wet with the rain of the mountains, and cling to the rock for want of shelter.' Here I find rock as a metaphor for people who want to fight homelessness."

"We sure have that problem in Tucson," said James.

"But the churches don't care," complained Amelia.

Sophia fired back, "Not all churches. Please don't lump people or churches together like that."

Being a good, agenda-oriented man like his father, Jameson charged ahead. "We just have one more example, and it's from Proverbs 30:18-19, which is itself a poem:

The King Montezuma Trilogy

> 'Three things are too wonderful for me;
> four I do not understand:
> the way of an eagle in the sky,
> the way of a snake on a rock,
> the way of a ship on the high seas,
> and the way of a man with a girl.'

Emma didn't like this one, so she said, "the way of a man with a girl is just like the way of a snake on a rock."

"Great," said Noah. "Sounds like you have a poem that needs written."

Oliva said, "As our favorite poet, Robert Frost, once said, 'Poetry is when an emotion has found its thought and the thought has found words.'"

The class seemed sufficiently satisfied, so I continued. "Thanks, Sophia and Jameson. Now let's hear about verse 2 from James."

Being pro-religion, he was excited to share his findings. "Let me read it first. 'Let us come into his presence with thanksgiving; let us make a joyful noise to him with songs of praise.' What I found was that 'presence' has to do with being face-to-face with someone. This Thanksgiving, I look forward to being face-to-face with my family."

"Sounds like a poem," said Evelyn, "for denigrating social media. There's nothing like being present with someone, and too many of my friends think sending an emoji from time to time is enough."

Henry spoke up and said, "Had I chosen to be present with people, I might not have gotten so depressed." That got a few appreciative nods, then Mia got up, took a piece of chalk, and made a happy face emoji on the blackboard.

The King Montezuma Trilogy

"What in the world do you mean by that?" asked a rather angry Henry.

She responded, "I'm defending emoji's. When I can't be there face-to-face, I find they're better than nothing."

Deciding that this wasn't the time to take on social media, I said, "Emma, what did you find out about verse 3?"

"I hated it, but here it is. 'For the LORD is a great God, and a great King above all gods.' One thing I liked about it was that it acknowledged other gods. What I didn't like was that it sounded like theology, and what I hated was its patriarchy. That said, I could easily write a poem about the evils of men holding power, versus the joy of matriarchy."

"That needs written, Emma," said Noah. "Plenty has been said, but plenty more needs done."

Sophia said, "In my church, we refer to the kin-dom of God, rather than the kingdom of God. Little ways to promote equality helps in this world of division."

"Thanks, Sophia," I said. "Okay, Evelyn, please share verses 4 and 5."

She immediately started reading, "'In his hand are the depths of the earth; the heights of the mountains are his also. The sea is his, for he made it, and the dry land, which his hands have formed.' To me, this is a confession of faith that God is the author of creation. The poetic element would be about protecting this glorious yet fragile environment. Personally, I most easily experience God in nature, so my poem would be a call to activism against the destruction of rain forests for the holy grail of profit."

Olivia said, "So your poem would be prophetic, spelled with a 'ph.'" Some laughed, but they all agreed.

"Looks like you're up, Noah, with verse 6."

The King Montezuma Trilogy

"'O come, let us worship and bow down, let us kneel before the LORD, our Maker!' I see this verse being about humility. While I prefer Eastern religions, I appreciate Jesus' call to deny ourselves. Bowing down before anyone or anything is to affirm something greater. This verse is a call to empty ourselves of self importance, and reach out for something beyond. I'll probably work on a poem about Vishnu, to help people understand a bit more about Hinduism, then Allah, from the Islamic tradition."

"Educational poetry, I like it," said Evelyn.

"Isn't that what Kaepernick was trying to do when he knelt during the national anthem?" asked Mia.

"Nah," said Noah. "He wasn't educating, he was protesting racial inequality."

"See where that got him?" asked James.

"Yes," said Jameson. "A visual poem that's still talked about today."

"Good one, grasshopper," said a smiling Noah.

"Okay," I said. "Amelia, what do you have to say about verse 7a?"

She read, "'For he is our God, and we are the people of his pasture, and the sheep of his hand.' Even though I'm an agnostic, I can appreciate the idea of being cared for. My poem is developing along the lines of our need for one another."

"Why do we need one another?" I asked.

"I'm working on it," she said with an impish grin, "but here at the very beginning, I'd say without friendship and/or fellowship, we can start to feel like Henry did." She then looked at Henry and said, "Hope no offense was taken."

Henry replied, "What I've found is that the lack of community becomes offensive to the soul."

The King Montezuma Trilogy

"Love it," said Sophia.

After a brief pause I said, "Mia, what did you find of interest about verse 7b?"

"O that today you would listen to his voice!" she read. "Sounds like a rather angry rebuke. Religion and politics have a tendency to get out of hand, so I'm working on a poem about listening to whatever voice you want. For me, the problem comes when we expect everyone to hear things the same. I'm thinking about titling it, 'They,' which is the nastiest and most divisive word in our language. We need to let people be, and maybe that could move us toward unity." After a thoughtful applause from the class, I asked Henry and Olivia to finish us up with verses 8-11.

Olivia started by saying, "Verses 8-10 are simply about the Exodus from Guatemala, as the Aztec people journeyed to the Promised Land of Mexico. My interests focused on verse 10 that says, 'They are a people whose hearts go astray.' I'll definitely write a poem about following unhealthy paths, and talk about the values of diet and exercise."

Henry seemed a bit subdued as he began to talk. "It was troubling to me that God would say to his people, who wandered in the wilderness for forty years, that he loathed them. My poem will be about my personal journey to the Promised Land, and my fear that I may not be able to enter when I get there."

Some liked what Henry had to say, and others didn't. I realized he was going in a religious direction, so I said, "We're ready to finish Book IV by first looking at Psalm 100. It's titled 'A Psalm of Thanksgiving,' but more importantly it's categorized as a hymn. We have a chance to let this poem become a song by singing it, so take a few minutes to find our best singer, and we can all sit back and experience it."

The King Montezuma Trilogy

They quickly tackled the assignment, and found two volunteers. Sophia sang in her church choir and had a nice soprano voice, but Noah was a great tenor. As the class tried to decide who should sing the poem for them, I suggested they try a duet. Noah said, "I love to harmonize, so if you," speaking to Sophia, "could make up a tune that goes with the lyrics, I'll follow." They asked to leave for a few minutes to practice, and excitedly walked out. A moment later Noah came back in to get his Bible, saying, "Tough to have a song without the lyrics."

We could hear them practicing down the hallway, and were quite eager to hear how the song would work out. They took much longer than I wanted, but when they walked back in, Noah started with a lot of enthusiasm. He said, "We have titled this song, 'Make a Joyful Noise,' but first we want to teach you the refrain, verse 4. Don't look it up in your Bibles, because we want you to learn it. I'll sing it first, then you try it." After a hit and miss effort, he proceeded a line at a time and the group echoed them back. "Enter his gates with thanksgiving." The class tried hesitantly, so Noah said, "Come on, its just five words." One more try and everyone was loosening up. "The second line is 'and his courts with praise.'" They got that so he shared the third line, "'Give thanks to him, bless his name.'"

Sophia took over and asked if anyone had rhythm. After a bit of laughter, Evelyn said that she would give it a try. "Okay, just drum on your desk as you feel the beat. Everybody else just clap your hands with a joyful noise." Sophia then sang the full refrain with Noah doing harmony, and Evelyn covering percussion. Then they tried it with the class clapping their hands, and a little applause broke out after they successfully completed the refrain.

Sophia continued with, "Noah, Evelyn, and I will do the first

The King Montezuma Trilogy

verse, then you come in with the refrain when I point to you. Actually, we will sing the first two verses, but that's beside the point." They managed it quite well, then Sophia said, "All right, we'll lead the first two verses, then you sing and clap the refrain. We'll sing verse 3, followed by the refrain, then verse 5 and the refrain. Ready?" The class nodded their heads yes and off they went. It really became quite a joyful noise, and the class gave a standing ovation when it ended. That's when I realized poetry was just like music. Notes and letters are little more than symbols on paper. They both needed to be heard to be fully appreciated.

When they were seated, I said, "Now that's what the psalms were written for! They were designed to be music to the ears, so that they might touch the soul." Jameson looked rather proud, as the class just had an unforgettable experience together. When our eyes caught one another, I just knew Jameson was saying, 'and that's community.' Amelia, our resident agnostic, even said that she just found a new appreciation for the Bible.

After relishing the moment, then looking at my watch, I said, "The afternoon is passing quickly, so let's get into Book V. I want to start with Psalm 118 because it's a victory song, and I hear your basketball team is pretty good."

"Woot, woot, woot!" called out several of them, as they churned their firsts in the air.

After smiling, I said, "Look at verses 2-4. Think of them as cheerleaders giving directions to different parts of the arena. Verses 5-9 are like expressing confidence in the coach. Consider verses 10-18 as describing a difficult game that ended in victory, 19 to 25 as a flashback to waiting to get inside the arena, and 26 to 27 as a celebration upon admission. Verse 28

The King Montezuma Trilogy

serves as a closing act of thanksgiving."

Olivia, the creative one, offered to kick it off. "Give me a 'U,'" she said while facing the north, and that part of the class responded with "U." She then turn to the east and said, "Give me an 'of,'" and that part of the class said, "of." Facing south she said, "Give me an 'A,'" and they dutifully echoed it back. Then she said, "What have you got?"

Before she finished the word 'got,' Jameson called out, "No idea. I attend Arizona State," and the class roared with hilarious approval.

After that, Sohpia said, "I'll paraphrase verses 5-9:"

> Coach wasn't happy with his last job,
>   then he found U of A, or U of A found him.
> He said, to allay fear, 'What can they do to me?
>   I will make this a winning team,
> and the students will have confidence in me.'

Something felt wrong, so I cautiously said, "Please remember, this isn't a legitimate interpretation of scripture, but it works to inspire poetry."

They nodded, then Henry said, "I'll give verses 10-18 a try."

> The Wildcats were surrounded,
>   with time running out.
> Then a guard fell from a hard foul,
>   and the free throws fell through the net.
> Victory was assured and new hope was born.

"I'll never forget," said Mia, as she immediately jumped into verses 19-25, "waiting outside McKale Center. We chanted to

The King Montezuma Trilogy

gain entrance, then the doors finally opened. The crowd broke into, 'This is the day that the coach has made; let us rejoice and be glad in it.'"

"Wow!" I said. "That almost returns to interpretation."

The class laughed, then Noah said, "26-27 feels like a benediction, so try this. 'Blessed is the one who comes in the name of the coach. We bless you from McKale Center because Coach has given us hope, so let's party.'"

A round of cheers went up, and I got a little nervous that we might be asked to quiet down. After all, the Poetry Center has a library in it. However, I didn't say anything, because we were having too much fun. "Let's move on to our final psalm, number 133." There was a surprisingly audible sigh of disappointment, which made me feel good and bad at the same time. "It's just three verses long, so will someone please read it for us, to get it off the paper and into our imagination?" James began:

> How very good and pleasant it is
>   when kindred live together in unity!
> It is like the precious oil on the head,
>   running down upon the beard,
> on the beard of Aaron,
>   running down over the collar of his robes.
> It is like the dew of Hermon,
>   which falls on the mountains of Zion.
> For there the LORD ordained his blessing,
>   life evermore.

"I don't get it," complained Amelia, "and the other psalm was much more fun."

After acknowledging what Amelia said, I suggested that we

The King Montezuma Trilogy

just might have to dig deeper to find the treasure in this psalm. Then I said, "The first verse isn't too difficult, because it is simply about community. "Verse 2 harkens back to Exodus 29:7—'You shall take the anointing oil, and pour it on his head and anoint him.' That's a description of the anointing of a new chief priest among the Aztecs, and the overflowing image comes from Psalm 23:5—'You prepare a table before me in the presence of my enemies; you anoint my head with oil; my cup overflows.' All of this is a simile for community."

"Then what's the 'dew' business from verse 3?" asked Noah.

"It," I said, "creates another simile for community, because dew covers everything, same as an anointing. The last part of verse 3 is a reminder of the covenant God made with his people, the Mexicans, for life evermore."

"So how do we use this psalm poetically?" asked Olivia.

"Thought you'd never ask," I said with a smile. "I've compared it to the stages of community-making, developed by M. Scott Peck in his book *A World Waiting to Be Born: Civility Rediscovered*."

"Who's that?" asked Amelia.

To be honest, I was so dumbfounded that it took me a moment to recuperate. "Maybe you know him better from his bestselling book, *The Road Less Traveled*."

"Nope," responded Mia.

Still reeling, I began to think that many in this age group probably had no idea who George Harrison was. "Okay, fair enough. The stages of community-making can be noticed by somewhat discernable movements. Those stages have been given many names, but I like the four-fold evolutionary names Peck prefers of pseudocommunity, chaos, emptiness, and

The King Montezuma Trilogy

community."

"What's that got to do with Psalm 133?" asked Sophia.

"I'm getting there." Something told me that it was probably a good idea to have this be the last psalm, not to mention that I was getting a bit tired. The class had done remarkably well so far, but I could sense we were all just about done for the day. Ignoring this realization, I pushed on with my agenda. "First of all, let me explain the stages:

1) pseudocommunity—this is when people tend to speak in generalities and ignore individuality. It is fine for the short term, but its main purpose is to follow manners. A group can move on to the next stage by personalizing their comments.

2) chaos—this is when people begin to take sides. Group members try to heal or fix each other, and it's a win/lose process that gets nowhere. The only good thing about this stage is that division is better than the pretense of harmony.

3) emptiness—this is when people try to build bridges instead of walls, by letting go of expectations, prejudices, and solutions. It is a stage of very hard work, where the group members empty themselves of everything that stands between them and community.

4) community—this is when people find mutual support for a shared vision. They choose to resolve conflicts rather than avoid them. The shift is momentary, and a sense of peace pervades the room.

"Now I'm going to show how the psalm itself reveals the stages of community-making, and I hope this is where you find

The King Montezuma Trilogy

inspiration for poetry. Verse 1 is pseudocommunity, because unity here is little more than a hope. Verse 2 represents chaos, because finding a new priest/pastor is a challenging process. Verse 3a reveals emptiness, because community can't genuinely form without personal sacrifices. Verse 3b is that elusive thing known as community, because conflict resolution is short-lived. Have any of you ever experienced the peace that comes from the time when genuine community happens?"

"I did," said Sophia, "toward the end of a week of church camp."

"Did it last?" I asked.

"No, and I always wondered why I couldn't keep that feeling."

James said, "I found it after a week of mission work in Mexico, helping to build a home, and no, it didn't last."

"The church tries to build community each year," I suggested, "through the experience of Holy Week."

"I'm intrigued," said Noah.

"Good, but understand that I'm not trying to push my Caldwellian faith on anyone." I looked around, and seeing no objections, I continued. "Pseudocommunity is kind of like Maundy Thursday."

"What's that?" asked Emma.

"It's the night when Jim Caldwell gave the commandment to love one another, and instituted what Caldwellians call The Last Supper."

"So how is that pseudocommunity?" asked James.

"Because the disciples of Jim were willing to be loving, but unbelievably challenging times were ahead. Chaos is represented by Good Friday. The world has rarely known a deeper sense of chaos than the killing of a beloved leader, in

The King Montezuma Trilogy

this instance it was Jim Caldwell."

"Why do Caldwellians call that good?" asked Mia.

"Because it sets up the next stage of community-making, which is emptiness."

"Not seeing the connection," complained Mia.

"Emptiness reveals what Holy Saturday is all about. It foreshadows an empty tomb."

"Ooh," said Olivia, "emptying myself out is how I always prepare myself to write poetry."

"Community is what is found in Easter Sunday. It's an elusive thing, so people gather and sing and experience the mysterious moment when Jim rose from the dead."

Emma then asked, "Can we try to make sense out of the community-making process from this class?"

"Definitely pseudocommunity when we started," said Noah, "because we didn't know one another."

Sophia said, "I felt the chaos stage when Oliver stormed out of the class. As a church-goer, it made my heart ache."

"Emptiness might have been experienced when we returned from lunch," said Henry.

"Say more," I requested.

"If that stage is about building bridges instead of walls, then I saw letting go of the Oliver concern as a way of letting go of solutions."

Evelyn said, "And community happened when we applauded after the basketball-oriented psalm. Which one was that?"

"It's Psalm 118," said Noah. "I'll never forget that one, and I'm guessing that's why sports is so popular. At least when you're winning, because it gives that momentary excitement that 'teach' calls community."

The King Montezuma Trilogy

"Here's another moment," I said. "Class is finished." All of a sudden I thought of Good Friday, but that's beside the point. The class applauded, and one by one they shook my hand and thanked me. I suppose it's because they knew I didn't get any money. When they were gone, Jameson and I picked up our few things and left. We talked a bit on the way home, but somehow the experience just needed to marinate.

The King Montezuma Trilogy

ACT II
Wisdom in Tubac

The King Montezuma Trilogy

SCENE ONE
Proverbs

    The time passed quickly, while I put together some thoughts for our next trip. Finally, we stepped outside into one of those famous 115 degree summer days in Phoenix. Jameson and I said our goodbyes to Sol and headed off. We didn't have any set time for an arrival, because the customers and staff had no idea we were coming. My plan was to enjoy lunch, then see if anyone wanted to discuss the wisdom of Proverbs and Job. Wisdom's Café seemed like the ideal place, and my mind was filled with hope.

    Two hours later, we drove past Speedway Boulevard in Tucson. Jameson and I just smiled at each other from our shared memories of the wonderful time at the Poetry Center. Next, we curved away from I-10, to head south on I-19. It was only about 45 miles further, so we pulled into the little, artsy community by late morning. Jameson committed the cardinal sin when he called it 'Two-Bach,' so I quickly informed him that it was pronounced 'Two-Back,' as in one step forward and two back.

    The town is full of history. Being Arizona's first European settlement, it was established in 1752 as a Spanish Presidio. In 1775, an expedition led by Lieutenant Colonel Juan Bautista de Anza, marched through Tubac on his way to settle Alta California, and founded San Francisco. The Tubac Presidio State Historic Park and Museum does a great job of maintaining the treasured history of this small, unincorporated community.

    "So where's Wisdom's Café?" asked Jameson.

    "A few more miles down the road in Tumacacori."

The King Montezuma Trilogy

"Tuma-what-ori? That's weirder than Tubac."

"It's named after the nearby Tumacacori mountain range, but you can't get there from here." Jameson just shook his head in silence. "Wisdom's Café is on the frontage road, so we have to go past it, get off the interstate, and come back north. The good thing is we'll go past the Tumacacori National Historical Park, which protects the ruins of three Spanish mission communities."

"Great, but I'm ready for some lunch and wisdom."

We pulled into the parking lot and found the place surprisingly busy for a weekday. It hadn't changed since my last visit, and I was looking forward to their always excellent food. Jameson wasn't impressed by the large chicken statue outside, but I calmed him with the thought that this place really was eclectic, and that was why I hoped to find some interesting wisdom. We were seated at a nice table and chairs, and enjoyed viewing the rifles, hats, and guns on the walls.

"This place sure keeps busy," commented Jameson as he looked over a menu. "They have live music every Friday and Saturday, two-for-one margaritas every Tuesday, and a fish and chips special every Friday. They must be doing something right, to keep the customers interested. I'm going to go wander around a bit." I watched him look at antiques, paintings, murals, photos, medals, pottery, and countless treasures. When he got back to the table he said, "Okay, dad. You win. If the customers are half as eclectic as this place, I'm guessing we'll hear some interesting wisdom."

A middle-aged woman, wielding a pen and order pad, arrived and spoke with a detectable Spanish accent. "Can I get you boys an appetizer or something to drink?" We both requested a soda, and I chose a Shrimp Ceviche appetizer to

The King Montezuma Trilogy

share. Jameson mentioned he was pretty hungry, so when she returned he ordered the Combo Plate, and I chose a bowl of Pozole with a side of Mexican Rice. I then asked if I could talk to the manager.

"Something wrong?" she asked, with a bit of a scowl.

"Oh, no. I just want to see about approval to talk to some of the crowd when they begin finishing their meals." She gladly took me back to the kitchen, where I met Herb Wisdom, a stocky guy with a receding hairline and full mustache.

"So that's how this place got its name!" I said with an embarrassingly large amount of shock. Herb smiled and gave me a quick rundown of the five generations of Wisdoms who have run the place since 1944. His short talk showed an equal amount of joy and pride.

"So what can I do for you?"

"I'd like to gather some wisdom from your diners. Is there any place I can engage some in a discussion of the wisdom of the books of Job and Proverbs?

Herb smiled and said, "Sounds just like the kind of thing my diners would like." Herb gave his approval, and said I could lead the discussion from the live music area, since it's only used on Fridays and Saturdays. Returning to my seat, I was beaming, and the food had just arrived.

Jameson said, "You sure seem happy to see the food."

"Well, yes, but even more so because the owner gave me the green light to talk." I then dove into my hominy soup, while Jameson scratched the surface of his gigantic, meaty, Combo Plate. We were eating right along when I noticed the cup of ceviche, and was delighted when I tried it, because it's difficult to get good seafood when you're this far from the coast. I started looking around and noticed a few people finishing their meal. It

The King Montezuma Trilogy

was probably too early, but I wanted people to have time to think about what I wanted them to do.

I stood up and clanged my glass of soda with a spoon. "Excuse me," I called out, with the experience of a high school teacher. When I finally got most of their attention, I said, "Herb Wisdom has given me permission to do something." I thought a pregnant pause here might generate some intrigue, but this eclectic crowd was beyond that. "So I wanted to let you know about it. In about ten minutes, I'll be on the music stage leading a discussion of wisdom, for any who want to participate. It'll take place in two parts, and you are welcome to stay as long as you like. The first part will be about wisdom from popular proverbs and the biblical book of Proverbs. The second part will be a discussion of wisdom that can be gleaned from the biblical book of Job. Thanks for your attention." I then dutifully returned to my seat and everyone went back to dining. Not feeling too sure of myself, I asked Jameson what he thought.

"It was fine, Dad, but do you think anyone will participate?"

"That's the $64,000 question."

"What?"

"Never mind. I think most places would have ignored me altogether, but I have hope for this environment." I started looking around and saw that many people were digging into their desert order of 'The World Famous Fruit Burro.' I was getting a bit anxious about timing, but decided to wait out the full ten minutes. It felt like an eternity, but I finally walked up to the stage. My heart sank as several got up and left, but then I saw a good crowd wiping their mouths and turning toward me.

"What a great place to talk about wisdom. Thanks for staying, and I hope we can all get something out of this." Something I wish I had was my soda. My throat was dry, but I

The King Montezuma Trilogy

decided to wait until break time.

"We need more wisdom these days," called out a short man in a cowboy hat. "But first, whatcha mean by wisdom?"

"Many people think it's about knowledge, so therefore, only well-educated people can be wise. Obviously, that's not true. Sometimes it just boils down to good sense. The wise person puts their experience into practice, from whatever knowledge they have attained."

"Some of the dumbest people I have ever known have doctoral degrees," proclaimed a well-dressed man in the back.

"If it's not too intrusive, may I ask what you do?"

"I'm a professor at the University of Arizona," and the crowd roared their approval.

"Okay, we're off to a great start. Now I'd like someone to call out a popular proverb."

"Many hands make light work," offered an older woman at a table that appeared to be her family.

"She always says that when chores are needed around the house," said a young boy next to her.

I asked, "And where is the wisdom in that proverb?" There was a surprisingly thoughtful silence before one of the servers spoke up.

"I love working here. Its family, and we care about one another. I used to work in Tucson, and somehow I was always the one needing to pick up the slack."

Another older woman said, "There's a four-letter word for that." The crowd showed concern about what she was going to say next, because there were plenty of younger ones in the Café. Then she said, "The word is," spelling slowly, "L- A- Z- Y!" The crowd actually clapped their support.

"Okay, now for a biblical parable. Here's one from

The King Montezuma Trilogy

Proverbs 10:11. 'The mouth of the righteous is a fountain of life, but the mouth of the wicked conceals violence.'"

A man close by said, "I have a problem with that, because I think wickedness is in all of us."

I asked, "And where is righteousness?"

"In all of us," called out the professor.

"So where's the wisdom in this proverb?"

After a useful period of quiet, a younger woman said, "Water is certainly an image of life, so why shouldn't we all choose to follow our righteous life-giving side, rather than our wicked violent side?"

"I'll drink to that!" said a rough looking older man, who then got up, swigged the rest of his beer, and walked out. The crowd seemed happy to see him go, so I went right ahead and asked for another popular parable.

"Don't judge a book by its cover," said a man who had been sitting with the man who left.

"Very good. I suspect you have a reason for saying that one."

The man was hesitant for a moment, then said, "You never know what's going on in a person's life, but I'll tell you that my friend, who walked out, recently lost his wife." This eclectic crowd was hushed from the power of a parable.

After a few moments, I said, "Thanks for sharing that. It's an important thought to remember. Now, here's another biblical parable: 'Where there is no guidance, a nation falls, but in an abundance of counselors there is safety.'"

"Where's that found?" called out a younger man.

"Oh, sorry. It's from Proverbs, chapter 11, verse 14."

"I disagree," said the same man who had a problem with the first biblical parable.

The King Montezuma Trilogy

"That's great!" I exclaimed. "Because I see the Bible as something to interact with, not to force compliance."

"I think I like that," said an older woman in hippie-type clothes.

Looking at the man who disagreed, I said, "Tell us about how the parable affected you."

"My problem is more with the second half. Just because a governing body has an abundance of counselors, doesn't mean everything will be alright. They might have bad advisers."

"I like the first part," said Jameson. I must admit I was a bit surprised to hear him speak up. "Guidance is kind of like a lighthouse. When a boat is near trouble, it has a tendency to sink if there is no help."

"Thanks. Somebody have another popular parable?"

"How about," said a junior high-aged girl sitting with her family, "Actions speak louder than words."

"And why is that important to you?"

"I like to talk, and everybody throws that stupid parable at me at school. It made me so mad that I actually talked to my parents about it." Some careful laughter broke out when the people saw her parents were smiling, then she said, "They cautioned me about talk being cheap. I said that didn't help, so they said something strange about character. That didn't help either, but then Dad said that things don't get done by words. Now that started to make some sense. Getting my bed made in the morning doesn't happen by just saying I will make my bed. Unfortunately, it takes action." The crowd gave a sympathetic 'aww.' She continued, "And then Mom and Dad said that backing your words with action is what develops character."

That was a pretty hard act to follow, but I pushed on with a biblical parable. I had memorized my first two scriptural texts,

The King Montezuma Trilogy

but went ahead and opened my Bible to the bookmark. "Let's try Proverbs 12:22—'Lying lips are an abomination to the LORD, but those who act faithfully are his delight.'"

"Lies are an abomination to me, too," said a man who explained that he was a business owner in Nogales. "I ordered from one particular company, I won't even waste my time mentioning its name, and they lied about the delivery date. I started checking back with them every week, and they kept saying it was delayed. After a couple of months, I asked for the manager, and he said it quit being made last year! To say the least, I was furious. I tried to get somebody, anybody, to be held accountable for the lie, and he just protected his employees."

"Faithfulness is what it's all about for me," said another. "I spent twenty years in the US Marines, and our motto is 'Semper Fi,' which means 'Always Faithful.'" He then looked over at the Nogales business man and said, "You had a tough one. The boss was trying to be faithful to his employees, but they weren't being faithful to the customers. I suppose it's easier in the armed forces, because the commitment to fidelity is based on the assumption that your commander is trustworthy. The idea of 'employees' being unfaithful to the American citizens is unthinkable. So, I kinda like the proverb that, 'those who act faithfully are his delight.'"

"You all are making the Bible shine today," I said with a huge grin. "How about another popular parable?"

"Beauty is in the eye of the beholder," came a voice from the back of the dining room.

A guy with one of Wisdom's award-winning margaritas stood up, lifted his drink high in the air and said, "I always thought that was, 'Beauty is in the eye of the beer holder!'"

Uproarious laughter broke out, interrupted by someone

The King Montezuma Trilogy

yelling, "That's not even a beer!" I waited quite a while for things to settle down, then asked what the parable meant.

Another man stood and said, "I've been to Barcelona, Spain and saw Sagrada Familia. You know what I'm talking about right?" Most in the crowd said, "Sure," then he continued. "Well my wife thought it was the most beautiful thing she had ever seen, but I thought it was gaudy."

I said, "That's a great example of the parable. Now let's try this biblical proverb from chapter 13, verse 16: 'The clever do all things intelligently, but the fool displays folly.'"

"I never equate clever with intelligence," said a middle-aged man. "It was always the clever person at work who was very calculating in what he did, and it was rarely nice."

"That's why," I explained, "intelligence is an important part of the story, but where does wisdom fit in?"

"It fits in," said an older woman, "when you allow intelligence to be more important than cleverness." The crowd was quiet for a bit, then people slowly started standing and clapping. It was a memorable moment that told me we should wrap up our discussion of Proverbs fairly soon.

"Let's try one more proverb, take a quick break, then have a look at the wisdom from the book of Job. Who's got another popular proverb for us?"

An older woman said, "The grass is always greener on the other side of the fence."

"And what is the wisdom of that proverb?"

She said, "I heard a sermon one time that 'twenty percent' was the answer to the question of 'how much more money would you need to be happy?' The answer was the same up and down the economic spectrum. In other words, it didn't' matter how much money you made, it was never believed to be

The King Montezuma Trilogy

enough. I kind of think that's an example of the loss of wisdom we get when we think happiness is external."

"I quit a job one time," said a young man who appeared to be in his late twenties, "because I was attracted to a job a friend told me about where the employees were all very nice. They weren't." A collective 'aww' was made by the group. "I learned right then and there to not go chasing dreams that aren't well researched."

"I learned it," said a middle-aged woman, "from reading Erma Bombeck's book, *The Grass is Always Greener over the Septic Tank*."

"Thanks, now here's a parable from Proverbs 14:29—'Whoever is slow to anger has great understanding, but one who has a hasty temper exalts folly.'"

"Doesn't the Bible say that God is slow to anger?" asked someone hidden in the back.

I said, "Yes, so maybe that's a good plan. At least I can testify, that my sometimes quick temper never paid off. I have a tendency to hold anger in, so when it exits, it surprises people. I had a friend who suggested my pent up anger was like rolling up a tube of toothpaste without taking off the cap. When I do, it almost explodes."

"So how do you deal with that?" asked an older man.

"I've learned to be slow to anger, by letting it out a little at a time," I responded. "Okay, let's finish by simply calling out a few other popular proverbs."

"Strike while the iron is hot," said an old cowboy.

"Honesty is the best policy," said a young man.

"An apple a day keeps the doctor away," called out a man who then identified himself as a doctor, followed by a generous amount of laughter.

The King Montezuma Trilogy

"Better late than never," suggested a person who had walked in about ten minutes earlier.

"Don't bite the hand that feeds you," said a woman as she looked rather scoldingly at her children.

"Rome wasn't built in a day," offered the professor.

"Learn to walk before you run," said a young woman with a cast on her foot.

"Better safe than sorry," said Jameson with a peculiar smile on his face.

"Thanks so much. You seem to have a lot of wonderful parables that easily apply to life, so what is your favorite biblical parable?"

A lengthy and surprisingly uncomfortable silence ensued before somebody said, "I think I'll read the book of Proverbs."

"Okay, let's take a break, and for those who want to continue, we'll chat in ten minutes about the wisdom in the book of Job."

The King Montezuma Trilogy

SCENE TWO
Job

    The bathroom line was a bit longer than I expected, so we didn't get started again for about fifteen minutes. When I finally stepped back up on the music stage, I was delighted to see that more than half of the group stayed. They moved in a bit closer, and seemed eager to gain some wisdom from Job. "Can anyone relate to undeserved suffering," I asked. The question was met with laughter, then people called out several responses.

    "I got laid off about ten years ago, and was without a job for more than a year," and the gathered folks let out a collective sigh.

    "My wife cheated on me." The crowd grew momentarily quiet, and I supposed they were dwelling on his undeserved suffering.

    "My neighbor was involved in a hit and run, and they never caught the guy." I must admit that things were far more painful than I had expected.

    "I stepped on an IED in Vietnam, and lost my leg." At this point, most of the crowd was hanging their heads down in shared grief. Then one more person spoke up.

    "My wife and kids were killed in a head-on collision by a drunk driver." Wow, I thought, are you kidding me? That set an unbelievably heavy tone, so I first expressed my condolences to all who shared their stories. Then, after a considerate pause, I began.

    "The book of Job is the retelling of an ancient folktale, or at least the first two chapters. Scholars call those chapters the

The King Montezuma Trilogy

prologue, while the last eleven verses of the book provide an epilogue. The chapters sandwiched in between are quite different in character. I just love the way the folktale part of the story begins." I picked up my Bible and began reading, "There was once a man in the land of Uz whose name was Job. That man was blameless and upright, who feared God and turned away from evil" (Job 1:1).

"Okay," said a middle-aged man, "that story just got a little harder to relate to."

A few chuckles went around the room, then I continued. "The point of the folktale is that Job falls victim to a heavenly competition." I again looked in my Bible and read, "One day the heavenly beings came to present themselves before the LORD, and Satan also came among them" (1:6).

"There you go! The answer to all of our problems. The devil made me do it."

I wasn't sure if the speaker was referring to Flip Wilson or being serious, but I said, "Well, first, remember that this is a folktale. The word Satan is an Aztec word that means 'the Accuser,' and that character encourages God to see if Job would remain faithful when dealing with adversity. After a series of unfortunate events, Job refuses to curse God, and instead says, 'the LORD gave, and the LORD has taken away; blessed be the name of the LORD' (1:21b). At the end of the folktale, Job says, 'Shall we receive the good at the hand of God, and not receive the bad?'" (2:10b).

"That's the end of it?" asked an older boy.

"No, that's the end of the prologue. It gives a rather simplistic answer to a complicated problem, and then the epilogue gives a happy ending, because Job is restored to even greater fortunes than before."

The King Montezuma Trilogy

"Sounds good to me," said the boy.

I said, "Sure," then looked to the crowd and continued, "but that's why biblical scholars think the prologue and epilogue were originally a story by itself. The problem was that it explained human suffering as a result of divine testing of faithfulness."

"Yep," said an older woman, "That's the story, like it or not."

Starting to feel a bit exasperated, I took a breath and said, "That's why this sandwiched-in material was added. It properly complicated the issue through some friends who show up and say that Job was correct in proclaiming his innocence. They even suggest that God was wrong for allowing the terrible things that happened to Job."

"Whoa, now pardner," said the man in the cowboy hat. "We can't question the works of the Almighty!"

"Yet that's precisely the purpose of the book of Job. So what do you all think is the nature of God?" A series of words then rang out.

"All knowing," said the cowboy.

"All powerful," said a young woman.

"Always present. Always has been and always will be," said the man with the missing leg.

"Holy," said a server.

"Three-in-one," said a young man.

"Good," said the owner, who stepped out of the kitchen to listen to the wisdom discussions of Job.

"Unknowable," proclaimed the professor.

"But that's why Jim Caldwell came along," said an older woman. His words, and God's actions, made God knowable."

I smiled, then said, "One of the questions the book of Job raises is about the origin of evil. If God is nothing but good,

The King Montezuma Trilogy

where does evil come from?" A hush went over the room before I asked, "Do you think God is responsible for human suffering?

"Who else do I blame when my crops fail due to a drought?" asked the farmer.

"Maybe blame the drought," answered the professor with sarcasm in his voice.

"Ya reap what ya sow," said an older woman.

"Say more," I requested.

"Well, I suppose everybody knows the story of Sodom and Gomorrah. Ya sin and ya pay for it."

"So God is responsible for human suffering?" asked the professor, directing his question to the woman.

"Not really. All we have to do is not sin."

"You mean like," continued the professor, "the good Aztecs who were massacred during the Holocaust?"

"Maybe they deserved it," she grumbled, "for not following the teachings of Jim Caldwell."

The professor stood up and prepared to depart before I said, "This is certainly a confusing topic. I would love for you to stay, so here's a text to consider. 'Indeed we call blessed those who showed endurance. You have heard of the endurance of Job.'"

"Where's that from?" asked a young man.

"James 5:11, I replied."

The professor surprisingly sat back down and spoke. "I'll choose patience, because my parents taught me that. But I sure hope we can get back to wisdom."

"Okay, let's get back to the origin of evil. That field of study is called theodicy, which is an attempt to justify God. If God is all-powerful, all-knowing, and all-good, why would evil be created?"

The King Montezuma Trilogy

"Simple," claimed a middle-aged woman. "If evil didn't exist, how would we know if we had it good?"

A round of applause broke out, then I said, "The Bible supports that idea." I opened my Bible and read, "'I form the light, and create darkness: I make peace and create evil: I the LORD do all these things.' That's from Isaiah 45:7. It's actually from the King James Version, but I prefer the New Revised Standard Version."

"So why did you read to us from a version you don't like?" asked the cowboy.

"Well, here it is in the NRSV: 'I form light and create darkness, I make weal and create woe; I the LORD do all these things.'"

"So you pick and choose a Bible that's fits your preference?" complained the cowboy.

"Yes, because 'make peace and create evil' is easier to understand than 'make weal and create woe.' Now, many of you seem to prefer an all-powerful God, and that's why this text might appeal to you. The question you would have to ask yourself is whether or not God is all good, since God creates evil."

"Aha," proclaimed the professor, "a conundrum. Let's see the wisdom you use to pull out of that one."

"Well, there are two answers. Both come from Genesis 1:1, and they depend on how you interpret the verse. The traditional translation is, 'In the beginning God created the heavens and the earth.' This has come to be known as the doctrine of creation out of nothing. If nothing was there, then God also created evil, which answers the question of the origin of evil."

"That's the same answer as the verse you read from Isaiah," said the middle-aged woman. "It sure seems like God created evil, so the case is closed."

"If only it were that easy," I said with an impish grin. "The other translation of Genesis 1:1 supports the doctrine of creation out of chaos. It lets evil be preexistent to creation, and consequently lets God off the hook."

"I'll bite," said the professor.

"Great, then here it is. 'When God began to create the heavens and the earth.'"

"I don't see a difference," said the cowboy.

"The second translation begins with the word 'When.'"

"How could starting with the word 'when' make a difference?" asked the young man.

"And yet it does," I said.

"Wait a minute," called out the cowboy. "You can't just change the words in the Bible to get them to say what you want them to say."

"Very good, but that's not what happened here. Biblical scholars believe both interpretations are legitimate, leaving us to choose what we prefer. So, let's talk about creation out of chaos, because that's where God isn't responsible for evil."

"I kind of like that idea," said a young woman.

"Great. Now let's see the difference this translation makes." I took a brief pause for effect, then said, "It allows us to consider the possibility that other things were going on before God began to create the heavens and the earth. The traditional answer says nothing was there, but this answer lets us think about what might have been happening before this particular creative act. Rather than creating out of nothing, God takes the 'formless void' of verse 2 and creates out of chaos. And what do you think might have been there with God in the midst of the chaos?"

"Evil!" yelled a happy young woman. "That means God

didn't create evil. Wow! I love it."

"And with this interpretation, we can say that God is good."

"All the time!" yelled out a nicely dressed young man.

Confused looks spread across almost everyone's face, so I just continued. "So what do you think, professor? Does that solve the conundrum for you?"

"I'm an agnostic, so I really don't care. I just wanted to see if you could solve it, and I'd say you did a pretty good job."

I smiled, and said, "Now let's delve lightly into that 'sandwiched' material that makes up the vast majority of the book. Remember, our task is to find wisdom, and Job is considered to be the finest wisdom text in the Bible. That part of the story is divided into three sections: 1) a dialogue, 2) an interruption, and 3) a divine encounter, so let's begin with the dialogue. This lengthy part is between Job and his friends. It's difficult to call it a dialogue, because they rarely listen to one another."

"Sounds like my family," said the cowboy, to a round of laughter.

"The scene is set when Job's three friends come to console him. 'They sat with him on the ground seven days and seven nights, and no one spoke a word to him, for they saw that his suffering was very great' (Job 2:13). After that, Job cursed the day he was born. His first friend finally speaks up and suggests that Job has nobody to blame but himself."

"Wow!" said a young woman. "With a friend like that, who needs enemies?"

"I agree, and Job did, too. He called them fair weather friends: 'In time of heat they disappear; when it is hot, they vanish from their place' (6:17).

"Wait a minute!" called out an older man. "That's me. I

The King Montezuma Trilogy

head for Minnesota in the summer."

After some laughter, I said, "The next friend suggests that Job should repent: 'If you seek God and make supplication to the Almighty, if you are pure and upright, surely then he will rouse himself for you and restore to you your rightful place' (8:5-6).

"Yep," said an older woman. "All you need is faith, and God will take care of you."

After a rather uncomfortable silence, I said, "The final friend says that Job's guilt deserves punishment, and encourages him to get right with God: 'If you direct your heart rightly, you will stretch out your hands toward him. If iniquity is in your hand, put it far away, and do not let wickedness reside in your tents'" (11:13-14).

"I ain't touchin' that one," said a man in a cowboy hat.

Several nodded their heads in agreement, then I continued, "This same bit of advice happens in three cycles, before chapter 28 offers a poem about the elusive nature of wisdom. I hope you will read the full chapter some time, because it contains some of the most elegant poetry in the Old Testament. It also has an answer to our question about wisdom. The set up comes in verse 12: 'But where shall wisdom be found? And where is the place of understanding?' The answer is in verse 28: 'Truly, the fear of the Lord, that is wisdom; and to depart from evil is understanding.'"

"That's as good as it gets?" asked a young woman.

Jameson spoke up and said, "It reminds me of something Jim Caldwell said: 'You shall love the Lord' (Matthew 22:37), which is like Job's fear of the Lord, and 'You shall love your neighbor as yourself' (Matthew 22:39), which is like departing from evil."

The King Montezuma Trilogy

"I don't know, young'un," said the cowboy. "Sounds like a stretch to me."

Jameson responded with, "Maybe wisdom calls for us to do some stretching, if we are to understand it."

"I don't know, either," said the professor. "I kind of think that divine wisdom is beyond our grasp, no matter how much we stretch it. We surely understand God about as well as an ant understands us."

"My aunt never understood me," laughed the cowboy in the back.

"Nobody understands you," said a young boy, and the group agreed wholeheartedly.

After the group settled down, I continued. "Getting back to our task at hand, a new character is introduced. This fourth person is said to be 'angry at Job because he justified himself rather than God; he was angry also at Job's three friends because they had found no answer, though they had declared Job to be in the wrong' (32:3). The next six chapters contain this other man's rebukes to Job and his friends. The rest of the story, other than the epilogue, shares the divine encounter. In it, God has some questions that serve to quiet any of us.

> Then the LORD answered Job out of the whirlwind:
> 'Who is this that darkens counsel by words
>   without knowledge?
> Gird up your loins like a man,
>   I will question you, and you shall declare to me.
> 'Where were you when I laid the foundation of the
>   earth?
> Tell me, if you have understanding' (38:1-4)

The King Montezuma Trilogy

"That's exactly how I feel," said the professor. "It's also why I struggle to believe. We have no way of understanding the Almighty. Then again, this is why I'm an agnostic rather than an atheist."

"How's that?" asked Jameson.

"Because that passage sounds very angry," he said.

"But you don't believe?" asked Jameson.

"Well, let's just say I don't disbelieve."

A young woman said, "Sounds like a double negative."

"I'm not trying to be negative at all," said the professor. "The reason I stayed for this discussion was because I like answers."

"Then you won't like what comes next," I said cautiously. "In chapter 40, we get Job's response: 'Then Job answered the LORD: See, I am of small account; what shall I answer you? I lay my hand on my mouth. I have spoken once, and I will not answer; twice, but will proceed no further.' (verses 3-5). God then gets mad at Job who says, 'therefore I despise myself, and repent in dust and ashes' (42:6). It's as if Job accepts that God will never apologize."

"Job sure has some interesting wisdom," said the professor. "Is that the end of the story?"

"Well, don't forget that an epilogue makes things right, but yah, that's as good as it gets about wisdom."

The crowd stood up and most of them came forward and thanked me. A few left looking a bit disgusted, but I was satisfied. I especially thanked the owner, and told him I just might write this up and send him a copy. He said he'd be happy to get one, and thanked me for my time. Jameson then came up and introduced himself to the owner, making me feel terrible that I'd even forgotten to introduce him to the crowd.

The professor was the last to leave. "Thanks for tackling a

tough topic," he said, while shaking my hand. "To be honest, I go round and round on this issue with my pastor."

"So, you go to church?" I said with a surprised look on my face.

"Sure, and to be honest, I kind of like stirring up a little trouble from time to time," he said as he left with a devilish look on his face.

As we prepared to get in the car, Jameson asked, "Can I drive home?" Actually, I was pretty tired, so I was happy to oblige. As we pulled away from the parking lot, I asked Jameson what he thought about our wisdom learnings in Tubac. He said, "It's kind of disappointing that modern proverbs are easier to live by than biblical ones."

"I agree. That was quite the thing to learn. Maybe it's because the instructions are parental in tone, and adults don't like to be told what to do."

"Job was kind of fun," offered Jameson. "I guess it helps to deal with undeserved suffering, but I really like where Job questioned God. Have you ever questioned God?"

"Just about every day," I said, as Jameson's eyes grew large. "My job as a high school teacher in inner city Phoenix offers plenty of opportunity to suffer. I need that Job 28:28 bit about 'departing from evil is understanding."

"Wow," said Jameson. "You live with someone for 18 years and think you know them. May I ask, do you blame God for your troubles?"

"Most people are uncomfortable with that idea, but I have come to think that God has broad shoulders. It's better to blame God than keep anger in, and I suspect God wouldn't be offended." With that, Jameson safely brought us back home, where we were lovingly greeted by Sol.

The King Montezuma Trilogy

I spent the next few weeks preparing for our visit to the Nature Conservancy in Phoenix, for what I hoped would be some good, old-fashioned storytelling.

The King Montezuma Trilogy

ACT III
Stories in Phoenix

The King Montezuma Trilogy

SCENE ONE
Ezra & Nehemiah, Chronicles

A quick call to Dan Stellar, the Arizona State Director of The Nature Conservancy, served as a reminder of my contact earlier this summer. He remembered me, and said he would have 3-4 staff members present on July 30 to listen to my stories. I spent a couple of weeks rereading Ezra, Nehemiah, Chronicles, and Daniel, and decided to make it a rather loose sharing of the texts. Jameson and I didn't need to travel far this time, so when that morning came, we prepared to leave at 9:30 for our 10 a.m. appointment. Sol had already left for work, so we got in the car and headed south. While I drove, Jameson mentioned how much he enjoyed the discussion of the wisdom from Job, and complained a bit about the book of Proverbs. He said that he hoped this trip would be more like Job, and I quickly glanced over to see an impish grin.

To be honest, I was a bit concerned about how this presentation would go, then I remembered my visit to Maria at the Aztec Synagogue in Phoenix. She said that the Nature Conservancy thrives on the power of story to get their message out. What haunted me was when I asked her how the biblical stories could find a kindred spirit with their stories, she said, "That, my friend is on you." I felt prepared to share the stories, but even here at the last minute I was wondering how the connection might happen. That's when I recalled that Ezra and Nehemiah were returning to Mexico after disaster, and climate change is certainly bringing on calamity. Chronicles is an attempt to hide problems, so that would surely speak, and Daniel is an apocalyptic. I think I just talked myself out of worry.

The King Montezuma Trilogy

We parked and walked in to their nicely appointed office, just off East Morten Avenue. It had a great location west of Piestewa Peak, the second highest mountain in the Phoenix area. Dan was waiting for us, and ushered us back to a small conference room where I was delighted to find four staff members. He introduced Diana, Scott, Rebecca, and Sonja to us, then mentioned that the five of them would probably be rotating in and out during the meeting. I told them that I hoped we would find a kindred spirit in storytelling, so asked them to begin by sharing what stories empowered them.

Dan kicked it off by saying, "We are blessed here in Arizona to have the third highest level of wildlife and plant diversity in America. We have been around since 1966, and our mission is, 'To conserve the lands and waters on which all life depends.' We use science to focus our efforts on four themes: 1) conserving our lands and waters, 2) restoring our forests, 3) building healthy cities, and 4) taking climate action. I'll turn it over now to Diana to talk about our first and foremost task."

"Hi," she said as she stood up with an enthusiastic look on her face. "Let me begin by saying that there is a tract of land up north along the Verde River called Otter Waters. In some ways, I'm proudest of what we have done there. Over the years, The Nature Conservancy has developed a strong relationship with the Yavapai-Apache Nation, and in 2023 we turned over the property and water rights for Otter Waters to them. I'm also pleased to be ensuring the following preserves are protected for future generations: 1) Verde River, 2) Patagonia-Sonoita Creek, 3) Ramsey Canyon, 4) San Pedro River, 5) Aravaipa Canyon, and 6) Hart Prairie. I also work to improve the efficiency of irrigation ditches. This is helping to keep farms in production while leaving more water in the river."

The King Montezuma Trilogy

She sat down with a smile on her face, then Scott stood up and introduced himself. "I have been working in the forests of northern Arizona for more the 20 years and have some tremendous accomplishments. My personal favorite is working with the largest continuous ponderosa pine forest in the country. Extending from northern Arizona to New Mexico, it is unfortunately at enormous risk of wildfire and tree mortality. Our Four Forest Restoration Initiative has seen improvements in forest resilience, carbon storage, water availability, growth, regeneration, mortality, and wildfire frequency and severity."

"Wow." I said, "I couldn't even say that sentence, let alone live it." Some mild laughter tottered about.

Continuing with exuberance, Scott explained, "There was a major science study of forest regeneration that followed 334 wildfires across the West. The findings were published in the *Proceedings of the National Academy of Science*, and gained a lot of important coverage, but I really appreciated this." He pulled out a letter from Randy Moore, the USDA Forest Service Chief, and read it. "This type of science collaboration strengthens our efforts to support land managers in designing and implementing effective projects with multiple benefits, making good work even better. It also is key in informing our overall efforts to address the wildfire crisis facing our nation's forests by doing the right work, in the right place, at the right time." He then introduced Rebecca and sat down.

"Good morning, and may I ask who the young man is with you?"

"Oh, I'm so sorry," I said with a modicum of embarrassment. "This is my son Jameson. I thought I told Dan that both of us would be here, but I guess I never gave a name."

"No problem, Dad."

The King Montezuma Trilogy

Rebecca kindly greeted Jameson and then began. "Well, I'd like to share the stories that excite me, and that's about building healthy cities. That terrible moment in 1986, when America heard 'Houston, we have a problem,' is becoming a current reality in a different way. It's called heat. The Valley has experienced record breaking heat, so we launched a web tool called 'Changing the Story of Heat in Metro Phoenix Together.' Neighborhoods that are only two miles apart can have a 13 degree difference in air temperature. Some ways it teaches to reduce heat is through lobbying for cool pavement, replacing dark roofs, and using desert scapes for your lawn. We also are proud of cooling centers, and provide help to find them." She then sat down and Sonja stood up.

"My work is in the area of climate action. The world needs to hit net-zero greenhouse gases by 2050, to avoid the worst consequences of climate change. We accelerate Arizona's path to carbon neutrality through the processes we are known for: collaboration and science-based solutions. We convene leaders across the state, because the challenge for cooperation is difficult. We strive to find a balance between the growing demand for alternative energy sources and our goal to combat biodiversity loss. We recognize that this pathway gives us a chance to demonstrate for the rest of the country how to harness the material needed for healthier energy. We also believe that protecting the natural assets of land, water, and wildlife is a crucial part of the bigger story. We are now taking on our biggest challenge. We want to be an example for the rest of America and the world, in providing clean energy and healthy air, now and in the future."

Sonja sat down to a rousing applause, and I could tell that this group was passionately committed to its cause.

The King Montezuma Trilogy

Next, I stood up and thanked them for this unique opportunity to share stories from the Aztec scriptures. "I hope you get some ideas for your storytelling messages, and before I begin, please know that I genuinely want you to feel free to interject your thoughts. That doesn't feel like normal storytelling, but my style is to go with the teachable moment. If you have a question or comment, please stop me, because the stories from the Bible do fine telling themselves. Okay?"

They seemed mildly uncomfortable, but soon nodded in agreement, so I began. "Ezra and Nehemiah were working for a better place to live, just like The Nature Conservancy."

"You got that right!" declared a jubilant Scott, who received a frown from the Director.

"The book of Chronicles was an intentional effort to deny that problems existed," I continued.

"This just must provide some fertile ground for ideas," said Diana with a genuine smile.

"Daniel," I explained, "is a dreaded story of apocalypse, which is what TNC is trying to help avoid."

"Whoa," said a surprised Sonja. "You've got my attention."

"My hope is that we can indeed find some connections in these stories, which will give new insights in how to share your stories." Everyone seemed to be on board, so I was pleased to continue. "The books of Ezra and Nehemiah were originally one book. That may not seem important, but the reason I mention it, is that editing happens, revisions take place, and sometimes history gets altered."

"Sounds like climate change opinions," said Sonja.

I nodded sympathetically, then said, "Let's first look at Ezra, realizing that your work with The Nature Conservancy may look very different in the future.

The King Montezuma Trilogy

Ezra & Nehemiah

"The story of Ezra begins with the end of the captivity of the Aztecs in Spain, and their slow return to Mexico. It is impossible for us to imagine three generations of our own family being held against our will, but this book isn't about that. It is about the joyful return home and the tasks they first chose to accomplish."

"Maybe we need to find more joy in our work," suggested Dan.

"However, the first deportees to arrive found chaos."

"There you go," grumbled Scott.

"The house of the LORD was destroyed, and there was no governance in the land. They first chose Sheshbazzar to govern them, and they set about building an altar and a new foundation for the Temple in Tenochtitlan, which is now Mexico City."

"I'm not familiar with this story, so I think tonight I'll try to find Ezra in my Bible and read it," said Rebecca.

"Great! In the second year after their arrival, Zerubbabel became the next governor. Priests were appointed to have oversight of the work on the house of the LORD, assisted by some of the Aztecs who had remained in Mexico during the exile. When the foundation was complete, they had a party, and all of a sudden adversaries started showing up. They approached Zerubbabel and said, 'Let us build with you, for we worship your God as you do, and we have been sacrificing to him ever since we came here.' But Zerubbabel said to them, 'You shall have no part with us in building a house to our God; but we alone will build to the LORD, the God of Mexico.'"

"Okay," said Dan, "I'm struggling with this one a bit. I think we shouldn't exclude anyone in our attempt to preserve land

and water."

Sonja immediately spoke up and said, "The problem is, they exclude themselves."

"If it helps any," I suggested, "Things didn't go too well for Zerubbabel. The adversaries went about causing trouble by discouraging the people from building. They then bribed officials to frustrate their building plans, and the people became afraid. The trouble makers sent a letter to the King of Persia with a list of accusations: 1) the Aztecs who have returned here to Mexico, are rebuilding the rebellious and wicked city of Tenochtitlan, 2) if the city is rebuilt and the walls finished, they will not pay tribute, and the royal revenue will be reduced, 3) this place of previous sedition was laid waste for a reason, and if rebuilt, you will have no power."

"There you go," said Scott, shaking his head back and forth. "Politics."

"Let's look at what happened next. The King replied that he had indeed discovered that the city had a history of rebellion and sedition. He wrote, 'Therefore issue an order that these people be made to cease, and this city not be rebuilt.' At that time the work on the house of God in Mexico stopped and was discontinued."

"That feels like some of the battles we had," said Scott, "with trying to get the people to understand the wildfire crisis we currently have. You'd think that with the devastating fires in California, people would feel the urgency for solutions."

I said, "Then maybe you'll like this turn of events. After a long interruption, the shamans Haggai and Zechariah show up and inspire the people to begin rebuilding. The current governor comes and asks, 'Who authorized you to rebuild this temple and restore this structure?' The current King was consulted, and

The King Montezuma Trilogy

history remembered, that King Cyrus had set the Aztec people free to return to Mexico and rebuild the temple. The King then issued a decree to, 'let them rebuild this house of God on its site.'"

Scott said, "Maybe a little hope in that for us. I guess we need to work together as a nation to elect politicians who care about the future."

The group seemed a bit on edge with this mix of religion and politics, but I thought it would be good for them to hold onto the tension for a while. I then said, "The eponymous Ezra arrives fifty-eight years after the dedication of the Temple."

"There you go." complained Scott. "Everything takes too much time."

I nodded in affirmation, then said, "He was a scribe skilled in the law of Abund, who returned from Spain with another round of deportees. The first thing Ezra had to deal with was a complaint about intermarriage among the Aztecs with non-Mexicans. By default, Ezra launches into a prayer of confession about the sins of God's chosen people, all the way to the present. He then celebrates a God who extends steadfast love, and asks, 'shall we break your commandments again and intermarry with the peoples who practice these abominations?'"

"Sorry," said Sonja, "but that's all a little too weird for me."

"I agree, but let me finish the story. The people agreed to send away their foreign wives and children, and Ezra made them swear that they would do so. The book of Ezra ends with a list of men who had married foreign women. This is a tough pill to swallow, because it feels quite threatening, kind of like trying to change the way of Americans when it comes to caring for the earth. Before we deal with Nehemiah, I would like to see if anyone made any other connections from this story, to your

The King Montezuma Trilogy

work."

I paused for a while, then Diana spoke up. "This whole idea of revisionist history you talked about, made me focus even more on the here and now. We can't affect land and water in the future, if we don't change things now. And we can't control what people might do in the future."

Sonja said, "Gotta admit, I was about ready to walk out, when I realized I could relate to the Aztecs in captivity. Hearing people still suggest that global warming is a hoax, makes me feel like my work is being held hostage." While she was talking, Dan got a phone call and had to leave.

"I was intrigued with the idea of rebuilding," said Rebecca. "Our cities are in trouble, and we have to get neighborhoods involved in doing the right things to give us a chance with heat mitigation."

Scott said, "I would never have thought it would be so difficult to get people concerned about wildfires. So let me tell you, the forest restoration effort has plenty of adversaries. I guess that I mostly related to the Aztecs, as they encountered troubles from outsiders when they tried to begin their work."

"Thanks for your excellent observations. Let's now take a look at Nehemiah. If Ezra was mostly about rebuilding the Temple, then Nehemiah was mostly about rebuilding the walls around the city. The book even begins with a concern for the safety of the inhabitants due to the broken down walls. That concern came to Nehemiah back in Spain, who was serving as a cupbearer to the King. Nehemiah immediately asked and was granted leave to help with the important project."

"I wasn't really done talking about the last book," said Sonja. I told her to go ahead, and she said, "How does your storytelling from the Bible inform us about ways to better

The King Montezuma Trilogy

communicate our message?"

"Even though I said to feel free to interject your thoughts, from my perspective the message gets through by hearing the whole story."

"What do you mean?" asked Sonja.

"The message from the story isn't about being held captive. It's about the fact that they ultimately were set free. I know you have a difficult job here at TNC, but the message I think you need to give listeners is that of hope. Focusing on a problem will rarely move a person or a group forward."

"Then what is our focus?" asked Rebecca.

"Solutions. Inspiring people to work for climate action, healthy cities, forest restoration, and land and water conservation, because all of life depends on it. It's your mission, right?" They all said yes, so I said, "If you can't keep a positive attitude about the job ahead, how can you expect others to follow?" They seemed a bit perturbed about this, but finally nodded a yes, so I continued.

"When Nehemiah arrived at the Temple in Mexico, he inspected the walls and found that they were in ruins and the gates burned. He then successfully incited them to start building, and all segments of the community supported the project and completed it. Now this made people from the surrounding areas angry, so they decided to cause trouble. Nehemiah told the Aztecs to not be afraid, and the bullies withdrew. After that, the Aztecs carried a spear at their side from the break of dawn until the stars came out."

"There you go," said Scott. "Walk softly, but carry a big spear!" A bit of tension had been building in the group, and I noticed it seemed to be after the Director left, but everyone laughed and the people were a bit more at ease.

The King Montezuma Trilogy

"That didn't solve their problems," I went on, "because the next trouble came from within."

"My money's on Scott," laughed Diana.

"The Mexicans were frustrated about the difficulty of obtaining food, the need to give up their fields to support the effort, and needing to borrow money to pay taxes. Nehemiah responded by chastising the nobles and officials who were taking interest from their own people, so they agreed to take nothing more from them. Nehemiah was then appointed governor of Mexico and treated the Aztecs properly. All in all, the wall was finished in fifty-two days.

"Soon the people gathered at the Water Gate, and told the scribe Ezra to bring the book of the law of Abund, which the LORD had given to Mexico. Ezra didn't just read to them from the holy book, he taught it in such a way that they could understand. When he was done, he broke them into small groups and had leaders read from the law of God with interpretation. After that, Ezra offered a lengthy prayer of repentance on their behalf, then closed by entering into an oath to walk in the ways of the LORD."

"Now I like that," said Rebecca. "My healthy cities task force breaks communities into small groups. Of course, I wouldn't read to them from the Bible, but I could get some legislation as handouts for them to study and discuss."

"Really like it, and here's what happened next. People began settling into the newly fortified city, along with shamans and priests, and they prepared to dedicate the wall. Companies of singers gathered, and Nehemiah took them on top of the wall. Priests had trumpets while Ezra went in front of them all. After walking around the entire wall, they went up the stairs to the city of Tenochtitlan. There they gathered and gave thanks upon

The King Montezuma Trilogy

entering the Temple, the singers sang, and a great celebration could be heard far away. The joy of Mexico was complete."

Sonja said, "Can't wait for our joy to be complete," and everyone agreed.

"Let's take a short break, see if these stories connected with you in any other ways, then move on to Chronicles." After the break, Dan returned, but of course would have nothing to say since he missed the stories of Ezra and Nehemiah. Rebecca didn't return, due to an urgent problem, so once Diana, Scott, and Sonja got back, I began. "Okay, I'm very interested in whether or not these stories were helpful."

Sonja kicked us off with, "I was particularly impressed when you talked about community support for rebuilding the walls. That seems to be my biggest challenge. Culling community support is frustratingly difficult, so I just might go back and read Nehemiah. I think you also said something about the people finding it difficult to obtain food. I'll have to think about a way to heighten the challenge for food that will come from climate inaction."

Scott spoke next. "I loved that the book started with a concern for the safety of the inhabitants. The application I see is working to decrease complacency and increase urgency. That's exactly what were doing in the midst of our wildfire crisis. Maybe the best thing I got was the need for celebration. We've had plenty of tremendous accomplishments, so I think I'm going to work on planning a celebration."

"Arizona is home to a large piece of the Apache highlands," said Diana. "It spans 30 million acres across four states, and trust me, working to protect it has caused more than its share of trouble."

"Enough with the commercials," laughed Scott.

The King Montezuma Trilogy

"Yah, but my point is that it was jarring within me when the story was about people from surrounding areas causing trouble."

"Thanks, Diana," said Dan. "Good to know you're hearing stories that may help your story, as we constantly work to improve our storytelling, so we can have the most impact."

Chronicles

"Sounds like we're ready to hear about the book of Chronicles. It was originally a single volume called *The Events of the Days*, by an unknown author, then it was divided into two books by later translators. It used to be seen as supplementary to the books of Samuel and Kings, but now is seen as selective memory." A spontaneous laugh erupted before I could continue. "There are large parts of earlier history that are simply omitted, while other parts seem to work from alternative facts."

"Wow," said Rebecca, who had just returned. "You sure know how to tell a story." I wasn't sure if I was on thin ice or what, but decided to move on.

"Chronicles was also thought to tell a unified story with Ezra and Nehemiah, but that theory is in question. Let me first give an overview of the book we now have. Chronicles is divided into four sections: 1) 1 Chronicles 1-9 is a genealogical introduction, 2) 1 Chronicles 10 to 2 Chronicles 9 is about the united monarchy, 3) 2 Chronicles 10-28 informs us about the divided monarchy, and 4) 2 Chron 29-36 runs the conclusion to the exile. Chronicles also has three themes: 1) Retain continuity with the past, 2) Have a concern for all of Mexico, and 3) Exhibit retributive justice, which is about obedience that leads to

The King Montezuma Trilogy

blessing, and disobedience that leads to justice."

"Question," requested Rebecca. "Well, maybe not so much a question as a thought. I'm very interested in this concept of retributive justice. It simply makes sense to obey the efforts at heat mitigation, so I think I'll spend some time thinking about the problems that come from disobedience."

I saw Dan flash her an approving look, then continued. "The book of Chronicles was also an intentional effort at denial: 1) Rather than ending the story on the bad note of the demise of the monarchy (like Samuel and Kings), it ended on the good note of the restoration of the Temple (2 Chronicles 36:23), 2) Rather than have the LORD angry with Mexico by inciting a dreaded, tax-oriented census (2 Samuel 24:1), it had Satan incite the census (1 Chronicles 21:1), 3) Rather than share the scandalous story of Montezuma and Bathsheba, the Chronicler simply ignored it, and 4) Rather than write about Santiago's decline in spirituality in his later years, the Chronicler only reported his good deeds."

"Wow!" exclaimed Sonja. "This really sounds like it has possible value for us."

Diana said, "I'll try to end my stories on the good note of the restoration of land and water."

Sonja frowned, and said, "But wasn't that part of the denial problem?"

"Better than ending on the bad note of demise," fired back Diana.

"Really?" snarked Sonja. "Isn't that what we're trying to avoid?"

I decided to offer a balance. "Celebrations are needed to help us feel good about progress, while urgency needs to be maintained, and complacency avoided at all costs."

The King Montezuma Trilogy

Scott said, "There you go," while the others shook their heads in pretend disgust, then he said, "I kind of like the denial intent of the book. It's where so many people are, that maybe I would do well to spend some time trying to understand where they're coming from." Several nodded appreciatively.

"I didn't like it that the scandalous story of Montezuma was ignored," commented Sonja. "We can't continue to rape and pillage the environment and think everything will be okay. I'll have to think more about that. Maybe add some stories about how we've ignored the climate and crisis and how we're paying for it already."

I gave it a moment before continuing, then said, "Thank you very much. I think we're ready to dive into the story. Since the first section is a genealogical introduction, we can begin with chapter 10. It begins with the death of Luis, reportedly for his unfaithfulness to the LORD through not keeping the commandments. The story quickly moves to the crowning of King Montezuma over all of Mexico, creating a united monarchy. Montezuma first called for the moving of the Ark of the Covenant from Guadalajara to Tenochtitlan, and after months of troubles, it was accomplished. Montezuma settled in his house, then felt bad, as he realized it was not right to have the Ark in a tent. That night the word of the LORD came to Montezuma's shaman, and it's very important, so I'll read it to you." I then opened my Bible to chapter 17 and spoke the words that came from God:

"Go and tell my servant Montezuma: Thus says the LORD: You shall not build me a house to live in. For I have not lived in a house since the day I brought out Mexico to this very day, but I have lived in a tent and

The King Montezuma Trilogy

a tabernacle. Wherever I have moved about among all Mexico, did I ever speak a word with any of the judges of Mexico, whom I commanded to shepherd my people saying, Why have you not built me a house of cedar? Now therefore thus you shall say to my servant Montezuma: Thus says the LORD of hosts: I took you from the pasture, from following the sheep, to be ruler over my people Mexico; and I have been with you wherever you went, and have cut off all your enemies before you; and I will make for you a name, like the name of the great ones of the earth. I will appoint a place for my people Mexico, and will plant them, so that they may live in their own place, and be disturbed no more; and evildoers shall wear them down no more, as they did formerly, from the time that I appointed judges over my people Mexico; and I will subdue all your enemies.

Moreover I declare to you that the LORD will build you a house. When your days are fulfilled to go to be with your ancestors, I will raise up your offspring after you, one of your own sons, and I will establish his kingdom. He shall build a house for me, and I will establish his throne forever. I will be a father to him, and he shall be a son to me. I will not take my steadfast love from him, as I took it from him who was before you, but I will confirm him in my house and in my kingdom forever, and his throne shall be established forever."

"Why is that passage so important?" asked Rebecca.

"Because it's of theological significance, in that God was guaranteeing Montezuma's throne would be established forever."

The King Montezuma Trilogy

"I kind of like that," said Diana. "Our work at The Nature Conservancy is to create enough cultural significance that we would guarantee the continuance of life on earth."

After nodding in agreement, I said, "the rest of first Chronicles is about the consolidation of the Empire, then a lengthy section about Temple personnel. That's where you get the story denying the inciting of the tax-oriented census, and the convenient ignoring of the Montezuma/Bathsheba affair. It then talks about Santiago's succession to the throne and the death of his father, King Montezuma.

"The most important thing in 2 Chronicles is the divine promise to Santiago. After Montezuma's son completed the task of building Templo Mayor and dedicated it, the LORD appeared to him in the night and spoke. Again, since this is significant, I'll read it to you." I picked up my Bible and shared the appropriate passage from the LORD:

> "I have heard your prayer, and have chosen this place for myself as a house of sacrifice. When I shut up the heavens so that there is no rain, or command the locust to devour the land, or send pestilence among my people, if my people who are called by my name humble themselves, pray, seek my face, and turn from their wicked ways, then I will hear from heaven, and will forgive their sin and heal their land. Now my eyes will be open and my ears attentive to the prayer that is made in this place. For now I have chosen and consecrated this house so that my name may be there forever; my eyes and my heart will be there for all time. As for you, if you walk before me, as your father Montezuma walked, doing according to all that I have commanded you and

The King Montezuma Trilogy

keeping my statutes and my ordinances, then I will establish your royal throne, as I made covenant with your father Montezuma saying, 'You shall never lack a successor to rule over Mexico.'

"But if you turn aside and forsake my statutes and my commandments that I have set before you, and go and serve other gods and worship them, then I will pluck you up from the land that I have given you; and this house, which I have consecrated for my name, I will cast out of my sight, and will make it a proverb and a byword among all peoples. And regarding this house, now exalted, everyone passing by will be astonished, and say, 'Why has the LORD done such a thing to this land and to this house?' Then they will say, 'Because they abandoned the LORD the God of the ancestors who brought them out of the land of Guatemala, and they adopted other gods, and worshiped them and served them; therefore he has brought all this calamity upon them.'"

"I'm sorry," said Sonja, "but where's the promise?"

"I think I get it," spoke up Dan. "It's a qualified promise, based on obedience. That certainly fits with our mission. We can promise a future on this planet, if we will simply obey those things that need to be done."

"Ooh," said Scott, "Kind of a salvation for the earth!"

"Well," I said, "it didn't take too long for things to start to fall apart. After the death of Santiago, the time was known as the Divided Empire. The southern and the northern part of Mexico each had their own kings. In the south, the king and all the people with him, abandoned the law of the LORD. They were nearly overthrown by Guatemalans, so the people repented and

The King Montezuma Trilogy

the LORD gave them a fresh start.

"Meanwhile, both parts of the Divided Empire engaged in battle. The new king of the Southern Empire stood on a hill and said, 'Listen to me, O people of the North!' This, too, is important, so please bear with me for one more reading:

"Do you know that the LORD God of Mexico gave the kingship over Mexico forever to Montezuma and his sons by a covenant? Yet your king rose up and rebelled, and certain worthless scoundrels gathered around him and defied our first king, when he was young and could not withstand them.

"And now you think you can withstand the kingdom of the LORD in the hand of the sons of Montezuma, because you are a great multitude. Have you not driven out the priests of the LORD, and made priests for yourselves like the peoples of other lands? Whoever comes to be consecrated, bows to worthless gods. But as for us, the LORD is our God, and we have not abandoned him. We have priests who offer to the LORD every morning and every evening, because we keep the charge of the LORD our God, but you have abandoned him. See, God is with us at our head, and his priests have their battle trumpets to sound the call to battle against you. O people of the North, do not fight against the LORD, the God of your ancestors, for you cannot succeed."

"So what happened?" asked Diana.

"The new king had sent an ambush around to come on them from behind. They cried out to the LORD, and the priests

The King Montezuma Trilogy

blew the trumpets, and the people of the south raised the battle shout." I then paused for effect.

"Wait a minute," complained Sonja. "You can't stop now! Still waiting to hear what happened."

After another pause, I said, "They fled." It was a wonderful bit of laughter we shared, then I asked if the story resonated with them in any way.

Scott said, "I sometimes feel like I'm standing on a hill, calling out my concerns about wildfires. Maybe I need to work on my presentation, so I can leave people in suspense."

"Yah," said Rebecca. "Knowing you, you'd be working on an ambush plan!"

The laughter this time felt like the group was coming together. Of course, they already were a group, but somehow I began to think the biblical stories just might leave an impact for their storytelling. "The rest of this third section of the book is about various kings, a bit of collusion with a northern king, and an effort at social reform."

"Now were talking!" said Diana. "What happened there?"

"Another king of the Southern Empire went out among the people."

"Hope everyone's listening!" said Dan.

"He appointed judges."

Rebecca smiled and said, "That's kind of what we do in the neighborhoods as we work to build healthy cities."

I said, "Here's the final admonition the king had for the people with respect to social reform: Deal courageously. This part continues with stories of crisis, trust, obedience, another collusion, apostasy, a coup, losing, and royal models of right and wrong."

"You know," said Scott with a big grin. "I think this Bible

The King Montezuma Trilogy

thing could almost speak for today."

"Just remember that Chronicles is a book of selective memory, or revisionist history. It serves a purpose, but one has to be careful with its use. The final section follows on the heels of the fall of the Northern Empire, leaving Montezuma's dynasty unchallenged. The point of the final section is to let the story end on the good note of the restoration of the Temple, rather than the bad note of the demise of the monarchy."

"I definitely will be working on giving hope," said Dan, "more so than fear."

"Thanks. Let's take a break and then we'll regather for one more story. The book of Daniel."

As they walked out, I heard Sonja say to Diana, "I'm not really getting this stuff. Chronicles didn't want to end on the bad note of everything falling apart, but that's where we are today. I think we need to focus on our demise, and if listeners get turned around, then I plan to work on the hope of restoration."

The King Montezuma Trilogy

SCENE TWO
Daniel

Everyone returned after the break, and I could sense an extra air of interest in this topic. "What does apocalypse mean to you?"

"End times," said Diana.

"Mad Max," offered Scott.

The others were sitting tight, so I said, "Apocalypse literally means revelation, so it's obviously not about the past. It's a prediction of current troubles giving way to peace."

"Bring it on, O teacher," said Dan.

"Daniel was written during a revolt. To encourage fellow sufferers, the author told six stories set in difficult times that ended in triumph. Those stories serve as a prologue to the apocalypse. Then four visions deliver the apocalypse proper, interpreted through their current history, with a prediction of victory. In the six stories: chapter 1 is about resistance, chapter 2 is about speaking truth to power, chapter 3 is about radical faith, chapter 4 is about true and false thrones, chapter 5 is about humiliation of the conquered, and chapter 6 is about defiance of death."

"Sure sounds useful for today," said Rebecca.

I smiled and said, "In the 4 visions: chapter 7 is about change, chapter 8 adds mystery to change, chapter 9 is about revolution, and chapters 10-12 are the final vision."

"Don't quote me," said Scott, "but I never would have thought the Bible could be useful today. Especially since some of our toughest people to change happen to be church-goers."

"This isn't about the Bible. Well, actually it is, for Jameson

The King Montezuma Trilogy

and myself, but we're here to find stories that resonate with The Nature Conservancy. If there are no other questions, let's move on to chapter 1. This first story is set after the devastating time when Cortés and the Conquistadors came to Tenochtitlan and besieged it. The king was taken into exile in Spain, along with many deportees. The king of Spain commanded young men, versed in wisdom, to be brought to his palace to be made competent to serve their new king. They were educated for three years, so they could be stationed in the king's court. Among them was Daniel, whom was renamed Belteshazzar, Hananiah who became known as Shadrach, Mishael became Meshach, and Azariah was called Abednego.

"Daniel was a sensitive sort about food, so he asked the palace master to allow him and his friends to be given vegetables to eat and water to drink for ten days. After ten days they appeared to be in even better shape, so the guard continued their request. These four young men grew in knowledge, and literature, and wisdom. What set Daniel apart was that he had insights into visions and dreams.

"At the end of the three years, the palace master brought all of the Aztec men who had undergone the training, into the presence of the king. Among all of the young men, no one was found to compare with Daniel, Hananiah, Mishael, and Azariah, so they were stationed in the king's court. These four men were found to be ten times better than all the magicians and enchanters in the whole kingdom of Spain. So, anything in that first story useful for you?"

"Obviously," said Sonja, "the power of the story comes in Daniel's resistance to the king. We're not really about the task of resistance, but the story certainly empowers me politically, so if resistance is what I have to do it, so be it."

The King Montezuma Trilogy

"Love it! Anyone else?"

"I sure didn't enjoy the deportation business," said Diana, "but not sure what I could do with that."

Sonja said, "Maybe I'll look for a connection between deportation and the idea that climate change is causing us to lose our land."

"I like it," said Scott.

Getting no other responses I continued. "The second story is about speaking truth to power. One night, the king dreamed such a dream that it troubled his spirit. The next day he commanded that someone needed to explain his dreams. He was asked what he dreamed about it, and he said, 'No, no. You tell me both what I dreamed about and its interpretation.' They responded, 'There is no one on earth who can reveal what you demand.' This made the king very angry, so he sent them far away. Well, not all of them. Daniel asked the royal official who was about to take him away, 'Why is the decree of the king so urgent?'"

"Ooh, there you go. I'm ready to hear about urgency," said Scott.

"He was then allowed to return to the king, and said, 'Give me some time, and I will tell you the interpretation.'"

"Maybe," said Sonja, "we need to take some time to make our stories very clear about the disaster that lies ahead if we don't change."

I then continued, "The king granted the request, and Daniel had a vision that night. The next morning Daniel said to the king, 'I will give you the interpretation.'"

"Perhaps," suggested Diana, "urgency needs to wait for inspiration." I was shocked to see them pondering that thought. Maybe because it came from one of their own.

The King Montezuma Trilogy

"The king nodded, so Daniel said, 'God has told you what will happen at the end of days.' Daniel then went on to tell the king what he saw in his dream, giving great detail. Daniel closed by saying, 'God has informed you what shall be,'" then I continued. "The king said, 'Truly, your God is God of gods, because you have been able to reveal this mystery!' Then the king promoted Daniel to rule over Spain, but Daniel wasn't interested. He got the king to appoint his three friends to oversee Spain, while Daniel remained at the king's court."

After a bit of silence, Diana said, "I see a lot of politics in this story, but I'm not sure how to incorporate it into my work."

Dan said, "There's a lot of politics in what we do. I'll really have to think about this whole idea of speaking truth to power. Thanks for a good story."

It felt great to realize connections were being made. "The third story is about radical faith. The king of Spain made a golden statue and prepared to have it dedicated. When all were assembled, they were told to fall down and worship the golden statue. What made it worse was that anyone who disobeyed would be thrown into a furnace of fire."

"Wait. This sounds like a story I heard as a child," said Scott.

"Probably so, if you had a religious upbringing. Remember what happened next?"

Scott looked a little embarrassed, and then guessed, "Daniel was thrown into a bear's den?"

The group laughed, so I said, "Yes, Scott you do remember, and that story does indeed happen later, but for this story, the Spaniards complained to the king. Shadrach, Meshach, and Abednego were pretty independent people, so the Spaniards reported that they were not worshiping the golden statue. That

The King Montezuma Trilogy

infuriated the king, and when he found it was true, he renewed his threat to them. They ignored his power and simply said that they would not serve his gods.

"How did that go for them?" asked Scott.

"Not too good. The king was so enraged that he ordered the furnace be heated up seven times more than was customary, and had them thrown in. To the king's utter dismay, he saw not the original three in the fire, but now four. And they were just walking about, as if it were a pleasant stroll. He approached the door of the furnace and called for them to come out. So they did, and they weren't even singed."

Sonja asked, "Now what was the theme for this story?"

"Radical faith," said Diana.

"And how can we use that in our setting?" Sonja asked with a bit of frustration.

"Maybe," said Dan, "we need to practice radical faith in our mission."

"That's how this story ended. The king said that there is no other god who is able to deliver in this way. Perhaps we can be delivered from our land, water, and air problems if we have radical faith that we can change the world for the better. Okay, any thoughts about this story?"

"I just wish," said Rebecca, "that I could have that kind of radical faith that our cities would be okay."

Dan suggested, "Maybe the job is for us to do our part, then hope for the best."

"I found myself thinking about the golden statue," said Diana. "We Americans, and probably all over the world, worship the golden idols of land and money."

"So how do we stop it?" asked Sonja.

After a very long moment, I spoke up. "Land is a precious

commodity, even in the Bible. Your efforts at conservation seem to me to lean us in the right direction. Rather than trying to prevent people from worshiping golden idols, maybe your job is to acknowledge their value. If so, you can nurture people toward the important task of conservation, preservation, education, and cooperative efforts."

"What about money?" asked Sonja.

"All I can say is that according to the Bible, we are not supposed to love money. The work of TCN needs to focus on loving and conserving nature."

Scott said, "I'm going to think about firefighters walking through a furnace, and encourage people to call them safely through their mission."

"It's just frustrating," said Diana. "When we have a government that makes things more difficult for us to do our job, it's like we are fighting ourselves. Actually, it makes me angry. Land and water are both incredibly precious, and it is beyond my ability to comprehend why it isn't any easier to get legislation to protect them now and for future generations."

"Maybe getting riled up is the purpose of an apocalypse, so let's hear the fourth story. The king made a decree to all who lived in his country, that they should have abundant prosperity."

"There's the money issue," smiled Sonja.

Diana said, "Idols are hard to topple."

I nodded in agreement, and said, "He told them that he was living at ease in his palace when he had a frightening dream. He continued to tell his subjects about his dream, and that Daniel was able to interpret it, but what is amazing is that it was a bad dream about himself. The king was then to learn that Heaven is sovereign, and that his kingdom would be reestablished. Daniel told him to stop sinning and be merciful to

The King Montezuma Trilogy

the oppressed, and his prosperity would be prolonged.

"A year later the king returned to believing that Spain's magnificence was due to his own power and majesty. That's when a voice came from heaven: 'O king, to you it is declared: The kingdom has departed from you! You shall be driven out until you have learned that the Most High has sovereignty over the kingdom of mortals and give it to whom he will. Then the king's reason returned, and he made the following declaration to his people:

> I, the king of Spain
> praise and extol and honor
> the King of heaven,
> for all his works are truth,
> and his ways are justice;
> and he is able to bring low
> those who walk in pride."

"So, that's the end of the fourth story?" asked Diana. After nodding yes, she said, "I don't get it."

"Maybe," I suggested, "it would be easier to just let this story serve its general purpose of preparing the apocalyptic visions."

"I've got to admit," said Scott, "I was confused."

"Then maybe we just need to see if any of the parts had value, as opposed to the whole."

Dan spoke up, in a seeming effort to rescue things. "I liked it that Daniel was brave enough to share bad news to his boss."

"Then I've got some bad news, boss," said Scott. There was a moment of concern, until he laughed and said, "Just kidding."

"I liked the part about being merciful to the oppressed, said Rebecca.

The King Montezuma Trilogy

Sonja said, "I got something out of the call for truth and justice."

"Great! Ready for story number 5?" Getting no answer, I continued. "After the king died, the new king had a festival, and got drunk with all of his servants. They drank the wine and praised the gods of gold and silver, bronze, iron, wood, and stone. Immediately the fingers of a human hand appeared and began writing on the wall."

"So that's where that phrase comes from!" exclaimed Scott, followed by some confused looks.

"The king was watching the hand as it wrote. Then the king's face turned pale, and his thoughts terrified him. His limbs gave way, and his knees knocked together. He called for anyone to be able to interpret the words, and they would rank third in his kingdom. The queen reminded her husband that the former king discovered that Daniel could do interpretations. So Daniel was brought in, and after refusing a reward he proceeded with an interpretation. 'You have exhalted yourself against the Lord of heaven, and praised the worthless gods. So from his presence the hand was sent and this writing was inscribed: MENE, MENE, TEKEL, PARSIN.'"

"What does that mean?" asked Sonja, with no little frustration.

"That's what the king wanted to know. Anyway, here's what Daniel said, 'MENE means that God has numbered the days of your kingdom. The fact that it is said twice means that even the surrounding kingdoms will fall. TEKEL means that you have been weighed on the scales of justice, and been found wanting. PARSIN means that your kingdom will be divided up and the spoils given to the next king.'"

"So what happened?" asked Sonja.

The King Montezuma Trilogy

"That night the king was killed, and the next king received the spoils.

"Is this story historical," asked Diana, "or poetic?"

"Good question. I'd say the prose is a mixture of history and symbolism. So what did you all get out of it.?"

"Stay away from liquor," laughed Scott.

"Be careful what we worship," said Dan. "Of all the things about nature we work to conserve, we should probably be concerned not to idolize them."

Sonja said, "I liked the scales of justice. Without referring to scripture, I'll try to bring that story alive by talking about climate action as something we are failing to do. I might even phrase it as 'Can you see the writing on the wall?'"

"I think we're ready for the final story, as the prelude comes to an end, and the apocalyptic visions begin. The new king was preparing to appoint Daniel over the whole kingdom, but that made others jealous. Finding no grounds for complaint, because Daniel was faithful, they decided to look at the laws of his God. In very short order, they found something. They went to the king and said, 'We believe you should establish an ordinance, that whoever prays to anyone other than you, should be thrown into a den of Eurasian brown bears.' So the king signed the document and set the ordinance into action.

"Now Daniel wasn't afraid of anyone, so he continued to pray, and rather defiantly, he prayed in front of his open window. Sure enough, the conspirators came and found him breaking the ordinance. They ran as fast as they could to the king and reported this heinous activity. The king was saddened by this turn of events, but he felt he had no choice. So he ordered that Daniel should be thrown into the bear's den."

"These are feeling more like stories," said Diana.

The King Montezuma Trilogy

"At the king's command, Daniel was thrown in, but at least he thoughtfully said, 'May your God, whom you faithfully serve, deliver you!' A stone was placed in front of the cave, and the king had it sealed with his signet ring. Then the king went to his palace and spent the night fasting. At daybreak, the king hurried to the lion's den and called out, 'Daniel, has your God been able to rescue you?' The king nearly fell down in shock when Daniel said 'yes,' and then he gave orders to have Daniel removed.

"So Daniel was removed and found to be unscathed. The king then ordered those who had accused Daniel were to be thrown into the bear's den, and no, it didn't go well for them. Then the king made a decree that:

> 'In all in my royal dominion people should tremble
> and fear before the God of Daniel:
> For he is the living God, enduring forever.
> His kingdom shall never be destroyed,
> and his dominion has no end.
> He delivers and rescues, he works signs and
> wonders in heaven and on earth;
> for he has saved Daniel from the bears.'

"Is that the end of the story?" asked Sonja. I said yes, so she commented that, "I really liked the civil disobedience."

"Please say more," I requested.

"You know, when Daniel was not only afraid of nobody, but he also acted with defiance."

"We have to be careful with that attitude," said Dan. "Doing the right thing has to take into consideration funding."

"Agree to disagree," said Sonja, in a properly defiant way.

"I thought the king was pathetic," said Diana. "He caved in

The King Montezuma Trilogy

to the conspirators because he felt he was trapped between a rock and a hard place. I can't begin to tell you how many times I felt that way, when trying to protect the Apache Highlands, and meeting resistance from people who thought it was their land. I've learned to forge ahead doing the right thing. Come to think of it, I guess I was acting like Daniel."

"Great! I think we're now ready to experience some apocalyptic visions. The big difference between the stories and the visions is that the stories were about the king's dreams and the visions are about Daniel's dreams. Here's how the first vison starts: 'Daniel had a dream dancing in his head.'"

"Was it sugar plums?" asked Jameson.

The group groaned, and I said with a smile, "Always a thoughtful contribution from my son. What Daniel says is that there were four winds stirring up the sea, and four beasts rising to the surface. The first looked like a lion with eagles' wings, but the wings were plucked off. It was made to stand on the ground with two feet like a human, and a human mind was given to it."

"Let me try an interpretation," said Rebecca, "because it sounds like a storm trying to control a beast. I only say that because that's how I feel sometimes when I'm trying to protect Phoenix from the ravages of heat."

"Same here," said Dan, "about our conservation efforts."

"Okay," I said. "A second beast looked like a bear with three tusks in its mouth. It was told to 'devour many bodies.'"

Sonja said, "Sounds like what our climate is doing to us."

"Next, a leopard appeared, with wings and four heads, and it was given dominion."

"Reminds me," said Scott, "of our battles for the forests, because we need to be caretakers, not dominators. In other words, fight the beast!"

The King Montezuma Trilogy

I might have frowned a little before saying, "The fourth beast was exceedingly strong…"

"You'd lose that battle, Scott," teased Diana.

"The fourth beast had ten horns with eyes like human eyes, and a mouth speaking arrogantly." Scott started to say something, but Dan stopped him, and I continued. "What Daniel saw were thrones being set in place, and an Ancient of Days took his seat on a throne. His clothing was white as snow, and his throne had fiery flames. A court served him, and a book was opened. As Daniel watched, the beast was put to death. As for the other beasts, their dominion was taken away. Then Daniel saw one like a human being coming with the clouds of heaven. And he came to the Ancient of Days and was presented before him. To him was given dominion and glory and kingship, that all should serve him."

"That would be Dan," claimed Diana.

"No," said Dan. "That would be The Nature Conservancy."

An applause rang out, then I said, "Daniel wanted to know the truth of his vision about the fourth, terrifying beast. This is what was said, 'A fourth kingdom shall be different from the others. It shall devour the earth, and speak words against the Most High, and attempt to change the law. They shall be given into his power for a time, then the court shall sit in judgment, and his dominion taken away. The kingship shall be given to the people of the Most High; their kingdom shall be an everlasting kingdom, and all dominions shall serve and obey them."

"That's just the first vision?" asked Rebecca.

"Yes, so what do you think of it?"

"Well, of course there are biblical things to get from it, but I see a vision of hope for the disenfranchised. That's what we fight for in our Building Healthy Cities program."

The King Montezuma Trilogy

Sonja said, "Peace and justice may seem like religious programs, but my Climate Action is all about fighting for the good of the world."

"If that vision was considered a doomsday apocalypse," said Scott, "then I'd see it being fulfilled in the out of control forest fires we now have. Maybe we can use this vision as a story of hope, that end times have not yet come, and it's our responsibility to see that they never do."

"Well spoken," said Dan.

"Looks like we're ready for the second vision, and it's as strange as they come. Daniel saw himself in Toledo, the capital of Spain."

"I thought," said Scott, "that Madrid was the capital of Spain."

"Toledo was, until 1561, when King Philip II moved the court to Madrid. Our story takes place during the Aztec exile in Spain, which started in 1521. Daniel specifically saw himself by Rio Manzanares, when he looked up and saw a ram. It had two horns, but one was smaller than the other, and the ram charged all around. Then a male goat appeared from the west, flying just above the ground. The goat had a horn between its eyes, and it ran at the ram with a savage force, and the ram was trampled under foot. Then the goat grew, but at its height of power, its horn was broken. In its place grew four more horns. One grew great, cast truth to the ground, and overthrew the sanctuary. Then a holy one asked, 'How long will this last?' Another holy one said, 'For a long time, but the sanctuary will finally be restored.'"

Rebecca said, "I guess that vision is one of hope."

"Then listen to this. Daniel got help from the angel Gabriel, to understand the vision. He said, 'The vision is for the time of

The King Montezuma Trilogy

the end. As for the ram with two horns, these are the kings of Media and Persia. The goat is the king of Greece, and the four horns that grew are the four kingdoms. At the end of their rule, a king of bold countenance shall arise. He shall grow strong in power, cause fearful destruction, and succeed in what he does. He shall destroy the powerful, and make deceit prosper, and in his own mind he shall be great. But he shall be broken, and not by human hands.'"

"That's creepy," said Diana.

Rebecca said, "I homed in on the idea of the goat casting truth to the ground. My mind missed the rest of what you said, but I'll definitely use this idea of truth. Our task is to lift it up, and speak against those who cast it to the ground."

"I liked the idea," said Scott, "that the sanctuary will finally be restored. I know that forest fires in and of themselves are a useful part of Mother Nature, but we complicate things with our willful disregard for the environment."

Dan said, "What I like is that this vision doesn't give in to fatalism. What we at The Nature Conservancy believe is that mistakes have consequences, and our efforts are to minimize mistakes."

"The imagery was interesting," Sonja said. "Rams and goats fight by locking their horns, and sometimes I feel like I'm locking horns with the climate hoaxers. So I guess what I'm trying to say is that I agree with Dan. It is easy to give in to fatalism, so what I'm taking away from this is a renewed appreciation of the difficulty it is to change minds."

"Wonderful, and that brings us to revolution. The third vision is about Daniel's interpretation of the prophet Jeremiah, where he believes the total devastation of Tenochtitlan will take seventy years. This caused Daniel to seek further under-

The King Montezuma Trilogy

standing through prayer. 'We have sinned and done wrong, acted wickedly and rebelled, turning aside from your commandments. We have not listened to your prophets, and the shame is our own. We have not obeyed the voice of the LORD our God by following his laws, which he set before us by his servants the prophets."

"I'll never use the word 'sin,'" said Scott, "but I might try to tell a story about the wrongdoing of not listening to our concerns."

"Good," I said, then continued Daniel's speech: "All of Mexico has sinned, so the curse has been poured on us. A terrible calamity has come, and we have not sought the favor of the LORD our God. You, O LORD, are right in all you do. We are the ones who are wrong, for we have disobeyed your voice."

"Hum," said Scott. "When fires are started by people, whether by accident or on purpose, maybe we need to capitalize on the actual wrongdoing. That way we can focus on the fact that it was wrong, and what we are trying to do is what is right."

"Good. Storytelling as a sermon is supposed to end with good news, but storytelling about nature can have any end you want. Now, where was I?" I paused for a bit, and Sonja said that it had something to do with disobedience. "Thanks. Here's how it continued: 'O Lord, in view of all the good acts you have done in the past for us, your people, I pray that you would turn your wrath away from your holy city Tenochtitlan. O Lord, let your face shine upon your desolated sanctuary. I do not make this request on the ground of our righteousness, but on the ground of your mercy."

"Interesting," said Dan, "but what's the difference between righteousness and mercy?"

The King Montezuma Trilogy

"Jameson," I said, "could you Google that for us?"

He quickly pulled out his phone and announced "righteousness is about being morally correct and justifiable, while mercy is about benevolence, forgiveness, and kindness."

Dan said, "Righteousness sounds more secular to me and mercy sounds more sacred. I think I could talk about the morality of failing to care for nature."

After a short pause, I said, "While Daniel was praying, the angel Gabriel once again showed up. He said, 'Daniel, I have now come out to give you wisdom and understanding. Seventy weeks are decreed for your people, to put an end to sin, and to atone for iniquity, to bring in everlasting righteousness. So know this: from the time that the word went out to restore and rebuild Tenochtitlan until the time of an anointed one, there shall be seventy weeks. And for sixty-two weeks it shall be built again with streets and moat, but it will be a troubled time.' Okay, your thoughts?"

"I never thought of myself as a prophet," said Sonja, "but I'm beginning to see my job as prophetic."

"What I got out of the confessional prayer," said Rebecca, "was that change takes more than confession. It needs to be followed by action. I'm so caught up in action, that maybe I need to prepare my own work with confessions of my own mistakes."

Dan said, "I think what I'll remember most about this vision is that one can hold out hope in the darkest of times. I don't want to get there, but I fear we are headed that way. My expectation of the future is to cast a positive vision, which I believe we have through The Nature Conservancy. I know it's not all good right now, but somebody once said, Sunday's coming."

"That's about Jim Caldwell," blurted out Jameson.

Some smiles made their way around the room, but I think

The King Montezuma Trilogy

it was mostly because I didn't try to make this storytelling an evangelistic moment. "That brings us to the final vision. It was revealed as a true word about a great conflict. Daniel was standing on the bank of a river when he looked up and saw a man clothed in linen. His face was like lightning, his eyes like flaming torches, his arms and legs like bronze, and his voice was like a roaring multitude. When he heard this voice he fell into a trance, but a hand touched him and brought him to his hands and knees."

"I thought maybe it would bring him to his senses," laughed Scott.

"He said, 'Daniel, pay attention to my words, and stand on your feet. Do not fear, Daniel, for from the first day that you set your mind to gain understanding and to humble yourself before your God, your words have been heard. I have now come to help you understand what is to happen to your people at the end of days. Do not fear, greatly beloved, you are safe. Be strong and courageous! Do you know why I have come to you? I am to tell you what is inscribed in the book of truth. Three more kings shall arise, but the fourth will be richer than all of them. Then a warrior king shall arise, who shall rule with great domination and take action as he pleases. And while still rising in power, his kingdom shall be broken. Then the king of the south shall grow strong, but one of his officers shall grow stronger than he and shall rule a realm greater than his own. After some years they shall make an alliance. In those times a branch shall rise up who will take action against them and prevail. Even their gods shall be carried off as spoils of war. His sons shall wage war and assemble a multitude of great forces. The king of the south shall go out and do battle against the king of the north, but he will be defeated. Then the king of the north shall rise against the king of the south.'"

Now I must admit that this vision was so long, I was reading it, so I stopped for a moment and looked around. I saw confusion, frustration, and some intrigue, so I continued in a more storytelling way. "In those times many will fight the king of the south, but he will not prevail. The king will come with strength, and he will bring terms of peace." I paused again, then said, "Next, a whole bunch of war stories happen, but I won't bother you with them. Picking the vision back up, the king did as he pleased. He exalted himself and considered himself greater than any god, and spoke horrendous things against the God of gods. He shall do well until the period of wrath is completed, for what is determined will be done. At the end, the king of the south will attack and lose. Then the king of the south will settle on the holy mountain, and he will come to his end, with no one to help him.

"Ready for the last bit of the vision?" They nodded yes, so I said, 'After great anguish, your people will be delivered. Those who are wise shall shine like the brightness of the sky, and those who lead many to righteousness, like the stars forever and ever. However, many will be running back and forth, and evil will increase.' Then he said to Daniel, 'Go your way, for the words are to remain secret and sealed until the time of the end. Many will be purified, cleansed, and refined, but the wicked will continue to act wickedly. Those who are wise will understand. Happy are those who persevere, but go your way and rest. You will rise for your reward at the end of the days.' Okay. We made it. I'm ready for comments."

There was a bit of a lull, as people were processing what they could, then Dan spoke up. "Obviously, The Nature Conservancy can't use the religious connotations, but I liked a

The King Montezuma Trilogy

lot of the vision. The ending was very useful. It is good for us to remember that the wicked won't change, so it is our job to be wise, but what did the vision say the wise would do?"

Looking back at my Bible, I said, "Understand."

"Yep," said Scott. "That's our job. If we don't understand what's going on in nature, how could we expect others to understand?"

Dan then continued, "I also liked the bit about persevering, because it is the road to happiness. And the bit about going your own way and resting, I think that's an important secret for all of us here. We need to find that natural balance of work and rest."

"Thanks," I said. "Any other thoughts about the rest of the final vision?"

"It was too much, suggested Sonja. "Maybe you could lift out what you see as important, then we can offer our thoughts about those."

"Okay. What did you think about Daniel being told: 'Do not fear. You are safe. Be strong and courageous!'"

Diana said, "I don't want people to feel safe. I want them to be afraid about not conserving our land and water."

Rebecca said, "What I get out of it is that we need to be strong and courageous."

"So," I asked, "what do you think about a book of truth?"

Dan said, "It's very interesting how the past few years have seen a lot of questioning truth. To me, a book of truth is a book of science, but it seems that facts are falling out of favor."

"I agree," said Sonja. "Trying to educate people about our work on climate action has been challenging. I think it's because people these days work more out of their feelings than their thoughts."

"The vision talks about an alliance forming, but a branch

The King Montezuma Trilogy

would rise up, take action and prevail. Thoughts about that?"

Scott said, "It does seem like evil alliances get formed against our work, so I like the idea of us being the branch that takes action and prevails."

"Okay. What about this one? Those who are wise shall shine like the brightness of the sky."

Dan said, "I'm motivated to get us to have more media coverage. Maybe that wisdom would help our cause to shine bright."

"Great. I think that is a good note to end our time on. I can't thank you enough for giving up your morning for this unique experience in storytelling. I hope your stories will be told in better and better ways, so they can be heard and understood."

A kind round of applause ended the morning, and Dan gave an extra comment of appreciation. Each of the others shook my hand and said thanks, while the general tenor of their thoughts was that of surprise that it sort of worked. Jameson and I then got in the car for our thirty minute ride home. "So what did you think of all that, Jameson?"

"The whole thing was a bit of a blur for me. I preferred the stories of Ezra, Nehemiah and Chronicles, but Daniel leaves something to the imagination," he said with a grin. "I guess my question for you, Dad, is whether or not you believe in angels, since Daniel's stories had quite a few."

"As a Caldwellian, I believe in the spirit world, and maybe even more so, I believe that I don't know everything there is to know about the spirit world."

"I hear students at school talking about angelology," said Jameson. "They understand there's no developed doctrine, but many have experienced seeing angels."

"Certainly better than experiences seeing demons," I said.

The King Montezuma Trilogy

"Another question I have," said Jameson, "from hearing Daniel, is about warfare."

"Well, this is a different kind of warfare," I explained. "It's called spiritual warfare, which is a battle against evil spirits."

"Like alcohol?"

"It certainly can be, but this kind of evil spirit is from the spiritual realm."

"Okay, one last question. I remember in my high school economics class when the teacher said, 'Never forget this. Everything boils down to money.' Do you agree, Dad?"

"It's a rather disheartening thought, but right in too many ways. What I don't like about it is that truth isn't about money."

"What is truth about?"

"Remember when Dan suggested the difference between mercy and righteousness was that one is secular and the other sacred?"

"No."

"Well, first of all, nice job of listening." I said with a grin.

"So, what's your point?" Jameson asked with intrigue.

"You asked if I believe everything boils down to money, and my answer is no. Perhaps the secular answer is yes, but the sacred answer is that truth isn't about money."

"So what is truth about?"

"Truth is something we all need to find on our own. As a Caldwellian, I find truth in the resurrection. That truth rises above, if you will, any earthly powers. It gives the kind of hope that can never be defeated, because even death doesn't defeat the believer." About that time we rolled into the driveway, and were warmly welcomed by Sol.

I told her that I wanted her to come with us on our final trip to Flagstaff. She smiled and said, "Okay," and Jameson and I

The King Montezuma Trilogy

were ecstatic. Now I had a month to think about the last five books for our Old Testament experiences. I had heard they are known as the Megillot, and now I was getting excited to hear about them from an Aztec in an Aztec synagogue. That night I drifted off to sleep with a flurry of memories from our first two trips to Mexico, and the new understandings I had gained thus far from these experiential education excursions.

The King Montezuma Trilogy

ACT IV
Liturgies in Flagstaff

The King Montezuma Trilogy

SCENE ONE
Lamentations, Ecclesiastes

    We had a 9 a.m. appointment with Atzi, a docent at the beautiful Flagstaff Aztec Synagogue, but I was losing hope that we would make it on time. My plan was to rise and shine at 6 a.m., and hit the road by 7 at the latest, to make the two hour journey. It was now 6:50, Jameson and I were ready to go, and Sol was nowhere to be found. After repeatedly calling, she emerged from the bedroom closet with two dresses in tow. "Which one do you think I should wear?" she asked innocently. Pointing to the one on the left, I said, "We're getting in the car. Please hurry."
    Sol responded, "Mi amor. You seem to forget that I work on MST (Mexican Standard Time)."
    Don't get me wrong, I love my wife. Sol is truly my soul mate, and the best thing that ever happened to me. But when it comes to timeliness, she stresses me, because I don't ever like to be late. That's just one way we grew up differently. As we got in the car, Jameson kindly suggested that I needed to chill. It was a good reminder, and Sol actually got in the car a little before 7.
    The trip up I-17 to Flagstaff is the kind where you hold your breath. In just over one hundred miles, you ascend a series of mountains, going from one thousand feet above sea level in Phoenix to over seven thousand feet in Flagstaff. That's more than a mile of climbing, and the car acts like it. My hybrid chugs up the mountain about as well as I do on foot, but the experiences are far more than that. The road is narrow and has lots of turns, and the drivers act like they're in a road race.

The King Montezuma Trilogy

The other way you inhale is with the breath-taking views. The wonderful Sonoran saguaros are an icon of the American Southwest, and they are plentifully in view as the journey northward begins. After about three thousand feet of elevation, the saguaros give way to scrub brush, but the lengthy views across the landscape are beautiful. Jagged mountains on the other side of expansive valleys are postcard picturesque. At about five thousand feet, the beginnings of pine country come into sight. Even though I hate I-17, the geographic changes along the way make the trip enjoyable.

When it was all said and done, we pulled up to the Synagogoue at 8:58 and went in. The receptionist greeted us, and after identifying myself, she said that Atzi was waiting for us. She escorted us back to Atzi's office, where a pleasant woman in her late fifties stood up and greeted us. "Good morning, my name is Atzi. I'm looking forward to chatting this morning with you about the Megillot." We then introduced ourselves, and Jameson asked about her name. She responded, "It is an Aztec word that means rain, and it's reserved for those who can't help but splash in the puddles." A surprisingly impish smile spread across her face before saying, "Enough about me. Let's move down the hallway to the first of the five scrolls we have on display. They are copies, but the originals were lost in the destruction of Tenochtitlan."

She stopped before getting to the first exhibition window, and turned around in good docent style to speak. "Megillot is the Aztec word for five scrolls, imitating the five books of the Law, as do the five books of the Psalms. What I find interesting is that several of the books had trouble getting into the final canon of the Aztec Scriptures." That same impish grin all of a sudden spread from cheek bone to cheek bone. When Sol

The King Montezuma Trilogy

asked what her smile was about, Atzi said, "I just relate to the trouble makers in the Megillot, because I wanted to become an Aztec priest, and as you know, women aren't allowed. I guess that's why I decided to become a docent. I love my faith, my religion, and my Synagogue, and hang on to hope that I might someday be fully included." Sol stepped forward and hugged her in a way that only a person who has lived with exclusion their whole life could understand.

Atzi was obviously moved by this kindness, then asked Sol about her religious upbringing. "My parents are from Mexico, and I was raised in the Aztec faith. While I was still young, my parents moved to America, and my mother was converted to the Caldwellian faith. It is really the only faith I remember, but the prejudice I have experienced as a Mexican-American woman is unforgettable."

All four of us stood there in silence for a moment, then Atzi continued her docent-trained talk. "The five writings we'll be looking at this morning gained importance after the return from exile in Spain by being read during holidays. The Song of Solomon is used at the Passover Feast. Ruth is read for Pentecost, the Aztec holiday celebrating the giving of the Law to Abund on Mount Cerro Raxon. Lamentations is solemnly read on the 9th of Av, which is the date Templo Mayor was destroyed in Tenochtitlan. Ecclesiastes is liturgically employed at the Feast of Tabernacles, a time when we remember our ancestors wandering in the wilderness for a long time, and Esther is used at the Feast of Purim, commemorating the defeat of Haman's plot to massacre the Aztecs."

Atzi then turned and we followed her to the first display window, which was surprisingly large. The glass-enclosed environment was backlit with a medium bright light, which Atzi

The King Montezuma Trilogy

explained was to protect the book.

"I have a question," stated Jameson. "I thought the five scrolls would be, you know, scrolls."

"Not a question," smiled Atzi, "but I'll answer anyway. The originals were scrolls, but since the invention of the printing press, copies started being made into books. This is the first book we'll talk about," she then turned to the side so we could all move up to the glass, "and it's called Lamentations.

Lamentations

"This book is a collection of five poetic laments written after the fall of Tenochtitlan, to express the grief and despair of the people. For me, the beauty of the book is that it gives permission to vent anger, even at God. In other words, there is nothing that we cannot bring to divine attention."

"That's amazing," said Sol. "I never believed it was okay to get mad at God."

"Where did you go wrong with that Caldwellian faith?" Atzi asked with a mild grin. It was about that time I realized I would have to pay attention, because these two were really connecting. I think Atzi was being genuinely interested in learning when she asked, "So Jim Caldwell gives you permission to get angry with the LORD?"

"Well, I'd say its permission from Pablo. When he was writing about the New Life in Jim, he said, 'Be angry but do not sin' (Ephesians 4:26). For me that suggests that God has big shoulders and can take our pain. It's certainly better to get anger out than to keep it in."

"But isn't that sin?"

The King Montezuma Trilogy

"Not at all," replied Sol. "Keeping it in can destroy a person, and I would call that a sin. Anyway, I heard a sermon once that said, 'All sin is wrongdoing, but not all wrongdoing is sin.'"

"Okay," said Jameson. "I'm lost."

Sol said, "Wrongdoing is the big picture, while sin is just a part of it."

"Still confused," I said.

Sol explained, "You can exceed the speed limit while driving here, and that is against the law. It's wrongdoing, but it's not a sin." She then looked at Atzi and said, "You are being excluded from the priesthood. I would call that a sin rather than wrongdoing."

We all just stood there stunned for a moment, then Atzi said, "So I can be angry about my exclusion, but I should be careful not to sin?"

"Yes!" said Sol. "That's what you just said is the beauty of the book of Lamentations. We can feel free to even be angry at God, because it's not a wrong thing to do. In my opinion, the sin would come in if you don't push to make things right in the Aztec faith."

"Nice segue," said Atzi. "I guess its time to get back to the book. Lamentations gives voice to the reason for the disaster known as the Exile, and offers the balance of promise. Dwelling on Cortés conquering the Aztecs, it's called a theology of doom. It is when the returned deportees expressed grief, despair, and alienation from God, prior to the rebuilding of Templo Mayor and the city of Tenochtitlan. It is about blaming God and asking questions like 'Why me?' It is mostly about feelings, so the way out is to start thinking. This balances us through a theology of hope, which entails confession, submission, and loyalty.

"Here's a quick overview. Chapter 1 is a dirge over the dead

The King Montezuma Trilogy

city Tenochtitlan. It is impossible to fathom the pain they felt upon returning from Spain and seeing the disaster that used to be the holiest place in the world. Chapter 2 is a cry to God for mercy, because the poet believes the LORD used justifiable anger in the assault of Tenochtitlan. Chapter 3 is a personal lament and prayer, expressing confidence in God's steadfast love and faithfulness. Chapter 4 is a recounting of the suffering and hardships endured by the survivors, and Chapter 5 is a community psalm of lament and a prayer for mercy during restoration."

Sol asked, "So how is this dirge meaningful to you?"

"Because," Atzi replied, "it is a search for meaning in suffering."

"And has it helped you?"

"It has caused me to think that even God lamented the fall and destruction of Tenochtitlan."

"How did you come to that conclusion?" asked Sol.

"For me, it comes in Lamentations 3:19-24, which says:

> The thought of my affliction and my
> homelessness is wormwood and gall!
> My soul continually thinks of it
> and is bowed down within me.
> But this I call to mind,
> and therefore I have hope:
> The steadfast love of the LORD never ceases,
> his mercies never come to an end;
> they are new every morning;
> great is your faithfulness.
> 'The LORD is my portion,' says my soul,
> 'therefore I will hope in him.'"

The King Montezuma Trilogy

"Amen!" proclaimed a smiling Sol.

"Love it!" offered Jameson. "But what did you say was the liturgical purpose of Lamentations?"

Atzi smiled with patience and said, "It is used at the annual Aztec commemoration of the ninth of Av, the date when the city finally fell to Cortés. So yes, it is a very sad reading, intended to be cathartic. Just listen to how it begins." She then opened a Bible she was carrying and read it aloud: "'How lonely sits the city that once was full of people! How like a widow she has become, she that was great among the nations! She that was a princess among the provinces has become a vassal.' (Lamentations 1:1). What is sad to me, is that the city's downfall is considered to be its sinfulness."

"Why is that sad?" asked Sol.

"Because, deserved or not, the author's blame of Tenochtitlan seems hardly useful for moving on. I give in to the thought only because confession of sin is necessary before healing can begin. My frustration is that I get tired of pretending I have never confessed."

"Oh, I get it," said Sol. "My church sometimes has congregational confessions that I don't feel any particular need to confess."

"Thanks," said Atzi, "That also feels real, and the poem certainly gets real. Listen to these verses from the second chapter: 'Look, O LORD, and consider! To whom have you done this? Should women eat their offspring, the children they have borne? Should priest and prophet be killed in the sanctuary of the Lord? The young and the old are lying on the ground in the streets; my young women and my young men have fallen by the sword; in the day of your anger you have killed them, slaughtering without mercy. You invited my enemies from all around as if for a day of festival; and on the day of the anger of the LORD no one escaped or survived; those whom I bore and reared my enemy has destroyed.' (Lamentations 2:20-22)."

"That's terrible!" complained Jameson.

"What I really like," continued Atzi without acknowledgment of what Jameson had just said, "is the hope part from chapter three that I already mentioned. Here's how it continues: 'The LORD is good to those who wait for him, to the soul that seeks him. It is good that one should wait quietly for the salvation of the LORD.' (3:25-26)." Atzi then looked at Sol and said, "That's me, when it comes to my relationship with this Synagogue. I wait quietly for God's salvation to make things equal and right. I wouldn't say this to most people here, but I especially relate to 3:49-51. 'My eyes will flow without ceasing, without respite, until the LORD from heaven looks down and sees. My eyes cause me grief at the fate of all the young women in my city.'"

"Wow," said Sol, as she slowly bowed her head. "I think I'll start praying for you, and all of us who suffer."

Atzi graciously acknowledged this kindness, then said, "Now imagine the dereliction of duty pronounced in chapter four. Verse 1 talks about the sacred stones lying scattered in the streets. Don't forget that this was their Promised Land. They never believed God would let them lose it, so they blamed God. You know it's much easier to blame than to be responsible. Verse 4 describes the 'tongue of the infant sticks to the roof of its mouth for thirst; the children beg for food, but no one gives them anything.'"

I mentioned that it reminded me of the children in Ukraine and Gaza, but Atzi wanted to continue. "'Those who feasted on delicacies perish in the streets; those who were brought up in

The King Montezuma Trilogy

purple cling to ash heaps' (vs. 5). 'Now their visage is blacker than soot; they are not recognized in the streets. Their skin has shriveled on their bones; it has become as dry as wood.' (vs. 8). Then the blame returns: 'The LORD gave full vent to his wrath; he poured out his hot anger, and kindled a fire that consumed the foundations of Tenochtitlan' (vs. 11)." The visceral reaction I was getting was making me want to ask Atzi to stop, when I realized that was the purpose of the reading. If it's memorable, we are less likely to forget.

Atzi droned on, at least in my mind. Obviously she was giving us a liturgical experience that required extreme solemnity, but for some reason I just wasn't in the mood. Then she said, "'The LORD himself has scattered them, he will regard them no more; no honor was shown to the priests, no favor to the elders'" (vs. 16). Jameson started to say something, but Sol and I both gave him the stare. "Here's how this chapter ends. 'The punishment of your iniquity is accomplished, he will keep you in exile no longer; but your iniquity he will punish, he will uncover your sins' (vs. 22).

"There is one final chapter, and it serves as a closing communal lament. 'Remember, O LORD, what has befallen us; look, and see our disgrace! Our inheritance has been turned over to strangers, our home to aliens' (5:1-2). Here's one that's quite poignant: 'Our ancestors sinned; they are no more, and we bear their iniquities' (5:7). And another: 'The joy of our hearts has ceased; our dancing has been turned to mourning. The crown has fallen from our head; woe to us, for we have sinned! Because of this our hearts are sick, because of these things our eyes have grown dim' (5:15-17).

"Are we done yet?" asked a weary Jameson.

"No. "Here's how it closes: 'Why have you forgotten us

completely? Why have you forsaken us these many days? Restore us to yourself, O LORD, that we may be restored; renew our days as of old—unless you have utterly rejected us, and are angry with us beyond measure' (5:20-22). Any thoughts?"

Jameson said, "Well, if I can speak now, it felt like a roller coaster of emotions."

"I'm drained," said Sol.

My thoughts wanted to take a back seat, but I went ahead and said, "The hope is easier to take than the despair. I suppose it's good to have an annual time of remembrance. The community can gather and experience what they need, because it seems to all be there. Anyway, thank you very much, Atzi. Can we take a quick restroom break before moving to the next window?"

Ecclesiastes

When we regathered, Atzi took us to the next window. "Can you get the book out for us to look at it closer?" asked Jameson.

Atzi said, "I was hoping there would be that level of interest. Few visitors ever make that request, but these are copies, so the answer is yes." She then retrieved a key from her pocket and gingerly opened the window. "Keep in mind that this is still a part of our Sacred Scriptures, so we must show reverence and appreciation." She then pulled the book from its stand and said, "Follow me."

Sol said, "Sounds intriguingly like Jim Caldwell."

We went to a small room and Atzi turned on the lights. We all sat down at a table and Atzi lovingly opened the book of

The King Montezuma Trilogy

Ecclesiastes. Jameson said, "Say more about the scroll stuff."

"This is a copy. The originals are gone, just like I said." I was getting a little frustrated, because I sensed prejudice against Jameson and myself. Finding equality wasn't the purpose of our visit, so I let it go, and Atzi went on. "Over the nearly five hundred years since the stories were told, they slowly made their way into book form." Atzi then read the first verse, "'The words of the Teacher, the son of Montezuma, king in Tenochtitlan.' This is probably a false claim, because the words used are from a much later time. The Aztec word for teacher is *Qoheleth*. The person was probably an important official in Tenochtitlan who expressed views of an elite group of people. He or she (*Qoheleth* is the feminine form of the word) counseled acceptance of the current economic and social conditions, because opposition was useless.

"Let me go back for a moment. There's just so much to say about this book, that I get a bit excited when talking about it. Here's some of the things I love about the book. I view *Qoheleth* as a practical theologian, because he or she is honest about the ways of God in the world, then instructs the listeners on how to live. In a strange way, the book helps to discern God's will. If you are a pessimist, you'll find God talking to you in this book. Likewise, if you're an optimist, you'll find God's Spirit nurturing you. In my opinion, that's the power of the book. It honestly addresses the tensions inherent in life, by embracing them, and then confessing that life is still better than death.

"Here's the structure of the book. The first two chapters decry experience, while the third chapter admits that humans cannot know the times. Chapter 4 is about human relationships and the fifth chapter suggests that wise people revere God. Chapters six and seven recommend enjoying what is good

The King Montezuma Trilogy

because it is fleeting, while chapter 8 complains that the meaning of life is hidden. The ninth chapter says that fate is random, while chapter 10 offers observations on life. The eleventh chapter says to enjoy life, or at least youthfulness, and it ends with a talk about the end of life.

"Okay, one more thing. This book is read each year during the Feast of Tabernacles, a seven-day holiday that appears in the book of Leviticus. Since the book relates to issues of doubt, it is a proper reading for that feast. It is a time when we remember the struggles our ancestors had wandering in the wilderness, and their groanings and lack of faith. Here at the Flagstaff Aztec Synagogue, the more daring of us build shelters in the parking lot and camp out."

"Do you do that, Atzi?" asked Jameson.

"Yes, I do, from about 10 a.m. to 7 p.m. We cook lunch on open fires, play games during the day, then cook and eat dinner. Most of us go to our nice comfortable homes for the evening, but the youth group usually camps out all night."

"Why do you still celebrate it?" asked Sol.

"It is obviously a very important festival because it is mentioned often in our Aztec Scriptures. It was during the Feast that Templo Mayor was dedicated, and again at the rededication of the Temple under the leadership of Joshua and Zerubbabel. Ezra read the Word of God during the Feast in the book of Nehemiah. And I dare say that it was during the Feast that your own Jim Caldwell said, 'If anyone thirsts, let him come to me and drink' (John 7:37)."

Jameson smiled and said, "That's pretty cool."

"Let's get back to the book. After the introductory verse, the author's theme is revealed: 'Vanity of vanities, says the Teacher, vanity of vanities! All is vanity' (1:2). *Qoheleth* uses

The King Montezuma Trilogy

the word vanity because the original Aztec word is vapor, which is figurative for worthless. Can't you just see this person debating in a public assembly? I sense anger from the words, where he is almost taunting people to disagree with him. Like, 'Go ahead and say anything you want, because you have no chance to win this argument.'"

"Can't that word also be translated as breath?" I asked.

"Yes," said Atzi, with a surprised look on her face. "In that sense, it's like the teacher would be saying 'I won't waste my breath.'"

Jameson said, "That's grim."

Atzi agreed. "It's a painful way to express the thought that we never know if we will be alive from one moment to the next."

Sol said, "Please tell me it doesn't mean that life isn't worth living."

"I don't think so. As negative as the book begins, it does celebrate some good things, but not right away. Verse three asks, 'What do people gain from all the toil at which they toil under the sun?'"

"Why were they so negative?" asked Jameson.

"Don't forget that the book was compiled after my people returned from exile. They had unbelievable work ahead of them, and it must have made them angry that they had been taken into exile in the first place. The feelings continue to be expressed in verse eight: 'All things are wearisome; more than one can express.'"

Jameson said, "I can just see people listening to *Qoheleth*, and thinking that there was nothing to debate about. When you're right, you're right."

"Maybe," said Atzi, "just maybe, and that might be why the Teacher hammered away with verse 14: 'I saw all the deeds that are done under the sun; and see, all is vanity and a chasing after wind.'"

"I prefer that metaphor," said Sol. "When I was growing up, we dried our clothes outside on a clothesline. When the wind would kick up and blow some of the clothes off the line, there was nothing we could do except pick them up. We could chase after the clothes, but chasing after wind is nonsense."

Atzi said, "Here's another level of understanding about the wind metaphor. It's that we can't discern God's spirit or purpose in our lives."

"I disagree," said Jameson. "I'm thinking about going into the ministry because I feel God's spirit calling me."

"There you have it!" proclaimed a rather excited Atzi.

"Huh?" asked Jameson.

"A debate!"

We smiled and laughed a bit before Atzi said, "But remember that Ecclesiastes spends its first half with negativity." She then carefully turned the page and asked Jameson to read 2:11. "But before you do, the context of the verse is a bit of bragging about the Teacher's accomplishments. Okay, let's hear the words."

Jameson readied himself for the assignment and said, "'Then I considered all that my hands had done and the toil I had spent in doing it, and again, all was vanity and a chasing after wind, and there was nothing to be gained under the sun.' Reminds me of the old saying, 'There's no need for a U-Haul at a gravesite.'"

After a mild frown, Sol asked, "May I read something?"

"Of course. Why don't you move to where the book is, rather than moving the book to where you are?" Sol exchanged places with Jameson and Atzi said, "Please read 2:24-26."

The King Montezuma Trilogy

Sol rubbed her eyes, then read, "'There is nothing better for mortals than to eat and drink, and find enjoyment in their toil. This also, I saw, is from the hand of God; for apart from him who can eat or who can have enjoyment? For to the one who pleases him God gives wisdom and knowledge and joy; but to the sinner he gives the work of gathering and heaping, only to give to one who pleases God. This also is vanity and a chasing after wind.'" She looked up and asked, "Is this a good thing or a bad thing?"

There was a moment of silence until we all four said in almost unity, "Another debate!"

Atzi then looked at me and said, "Your turn." I slid into place as she was saying, "Read 3:1-8."

I looked down and said, "Oh, I like this one."

> For everything there is a season,
> and a time for every matter under heaven:
> a time to be born, and a time to die;
> a time to plant, and a time to pluck up what is planted;
> a time to kill, and a time to heal;
> a time to break down, and a time to build up;
> a time to weep, and a time to laugh;
> a time to mourn, and a time to dance;
> a time to throw away stones, and a time to gather them;
> a time to embrace, and a time to refrain from embracing;
> a time to seek, and a time to lose;
> a time to keep, and a time to throw away;
> a time to tear, and a time to sew;
> a time to keep silence, and a time to speak;
> a time to love, and a time to hate;
> a time for war, and a time for peace.

The King Montezuma Trilogy

Sol said, "I'm guessing that's not as debatable."

We smiled in agreement and Atzi lovingly pulled the book back towards herself. "Then try this one: 'Better is a poor but wise youth than an old but foolish king, who will no longer take advice. One can indeed come out of prison to reign, even though born poor in the kingdom. I saw all the living who, moving under the sun, follow that youth who replaced the king; there was no end to all those people whom he led. Yet those who come later will not rejoice in him. Surely this also is vanity and a chasing after wind' (4:13-16)."

"Sounds political," I said, "so wouldn't it be nice if we simply used wisdom?"

Sol said, "I'm just glad the Teacher wasn't debating the existence of God. *Qoheleth* was wise enough to just talk about the things people believed about God."

"Very wise, mom. Very wise."

After a moment of appreciative silence, Atzi continued by reading. "There is a grievous ill that I have seen under the sun: riches were kept by their owners to their hurt, and those riches were lost in a bad venture; though they are parents of children, they have nothing in their hands. As they came from their mother's womb, so they shall go again, naked as they came; they shall take nothing for their toil, which they may carry away with their hand. This also is a grievous ill: just as they came, so shall they go; and what gain do they have from toiling for the wind? Besides, all their days they eat in darkness, in much vexation and sickness and resentment" (5:13-17).

Jameson rather excitedly said, "That reminds me of Jim Caldwell's Parable of the Rich Fool."

"Great connection," I said. "Both stories warn about the peril of possessions."

The King Montezuma Trilogy

Sol said, "Greed is the biggest problem in America today."

"That brings me to 6:1-2," said Atzi. "There is an evil that I have seen under the sun, and it lies heavy upon humankind: those to whom God gives wealth, possession, and honor, so that they lack nothing of all that they desire, yet God does not enable them to enjoy these things, but a stranger enjoys them. This is vanity; it is a grievous ill."

"I'd be willing to try enjoying wealth," said Jameson with a wink.

Atzi said, "I get it that you're joking, but many people want riches without toil. Here's 6:9, 'Better is the sight of the eyes than the wandering of appetite; this also is vanity and a chasing after wind.'"

My youthful memories in Indiana kicked in and I said, "I kind of liked chasing after tornadoes."

"Yes," said Atzi. "Sometimes wind is good and sometimes it is bad, so the Teacher was suggesting that we should try to know the difference. Maybe that's why *Qoheleth* then moved to proverbial speech. Listen to this one: 'A good name is better than precious ointment, and the day of death, than the day of birth' (7:1). Or even this one: 'Do not be too righteous, and do not act too wise; why should you destroy yourself?' (7:16)."

"Whoa!" said James. "This guy was pretty dark."

"Oh, and it gets darker. Listen to 7:26-28: 'I found more bitter than death the woman who is a trap, whose heart is snares, and nets, whose hands are fetters; one who pleases God escapes her, but the sinner is taken by her. See, this is what I found, says the Teacher, adding one thing to another to find the sum, which my mind has sought repeatedly, but I have not found. One man among a thousand I found, but a woman among all these I have not found.'"

The King Montezuma Trilogy

"That seems pretty rude," complained Sol.

"What I found," said Jameson, "was the identity of the Teacher."

"Say more," I requested.

"*Qoheleth* must be a man. Otherwise, why talk so despairingly about a woman?"

"Maybe," said Atzi, "and then again, maybe not. Anyway, try this: 'There is vanity that takes place on earth, that there are righteous people who are treated according to the conduct of the wicked, and there are wicked people who are treated according to the conduct of the righteous. I said that this also is vanity. So I commend enjoyment, for there is nothing better for people under the sun than to eat, and drink, and enjoy themselves, for this will go with them in their toil through the days of life that God gives them under the sun' (8:14-15)."

Jameson smiled and said, "So that's where that comes from. Every once in a while I hear fraternity boys on campus saying to eat, drink, and be merry."

"So you walk right on by, correct?" questioned Sol.

"Mom! Of course, but then again, a little bit of eating and drinking and merriment after a tough class is in order."

"Let's move it along," I implored.

"As does the Teacher. He, or she," said Atzi, with one of those impish grins, "says, 'whoever is joined with all the living has hope, for a living dog is better than a dead lion. The living know that they will die, but the dead know nothing; they have no more reward, and even the memory of them is lost. Their love and their hate and their envy have already perished; never again will they have any share in all that happens under the sun' (9:4-6)."

"It's almost as if," I said, "the author takes death so

seriously, that it somehow gives permission to take life seriously. I would never have guessed that Ecclesiastes was a morality story, but it seems to me that the groundwork is laid to act ethically."

"That may be a stretch," said Atzi, "but certainly worth consideration." I must admit that I once again felt a little put down for being a man, but decided my job here was to listen. "Which brings us to chapter 10." She once again turned the page, capturing our attention. "Here's verses 12-15: 'Words spoken by the wise bring them favor, but the lips of fools consume them. The words of their mouth begin in foolishness, and their talk ends in wicked madness; yet fools talk on and on. No one knows what is to happen, and who can tell anyone what the future holds? The toil of fools wears them out, for they do not even know the way to town.'"

Jameson said, "Sounds like a practical ethic to me, Dad."

"Okay," said Atzi. Maybe you'll like this one: 'Just as you do not know how the breath comes to the bones in the mother's womb, so you do not know the work of God, who makes everything' (11:5).

"Yes," said Sol. "We should always defer to God, who is infinitely smarter than us."

"Not to mention, our judge," said Atzi with a surprisingly solemn countenance. "The ninth verse of chapter 11 says, 'Rejoice, young man, while you are young, and let your heart cheer you in the days of your youth. Follow the inclination of your heart and the desire of your eyes, but know that for all these things God will bring you into judgment."

"In other words," said Jameson, "make judgments of your own, but be sure they build up rather than tear down."

Atzi ignored him, then said, "How about 12:5? 'When one

The King Montezuma Trilogy

is afraid of heights, and terrors are in the road; the almond tree blossoms, the grasshopper drags itself along and desire fails; because all must go to their eternal home, and the mourners will go about the streets."

"What do you think about that, Atzi?" asked Sol.

"The message I get is to not give in to fear. I like the idea of choosing to notice the blossoming of the almond tree. That doesn't mean to ignore what's going on all around, but to find peace inside. Here's how the book ends: 'Vanity of vanities, says the Teacher; all is vanity' (12:8). An epilogue finishes the book with this intriguing saying, 'Of making many books there is no end, and much study is a weariness of the flesh' (12:8)."

Jameson teasingly said, "I think I have a brand new favorite verse for school." I laughed and Sol frowned, and Atzi suggested taking a break before looking at the final three books.

"Before we take a break, if you don't mind, I have a tradition over the last three summers of occasionally checking in to see what was either learned or appreciated." Atzi nodded that she was fine with that, so I looked at Sol and Jameson and said, "So, what do you think?"

Sol immediately spoke up and said, "I really liked hearing about the holidays the books are associated with. That made them come alive in a wonderful way. I grew up surrounded by the Aztec faith, but I was too young to appreciate the details, and then became a Caldwellian. I also liked that Lamentations gives permission to be angry, even at God, if it's useful."

Jameson said, "I learned a whole new appreciation for Lamentations as a search for meaning in suffering."

I said, "There was something very special to me. Reading Lamentations 3:1-8 from an extraordinary copy of the book, right here in the Flagstaff Aztec Synagogue. I'll never forget it."

The King Montezuma Trilogy

Sol said, "I never thought of Ecclesiastes as a debate, and I particularly liked that it's not a debate about God's existence. It's a debate about how people think about God."

"What about you?" I asked as I looked at Atzi.

"I learned that my desire to become an Aztec priest may be little more than striving after wind, so I need to focus on eating, drinking, and being merry, in case it never happens. Anything else?"

"Not from me," said Jameson, "but I do want that restroom break."

The King Montezuma Trilogy

SCENE TWO
Solomon, Esther, Ruth

We were all excited to see the other three windows holding the Megillot. Atzi said, "The first two books only took an hour, so we're in great shape to be done by noon. Would you care to have a quick tour of the Synagogue?" We were very interested, so she led us down the hallway to the sanctuary. I was surprised that it wasn't very big, and Atzi noticed my expression. She said, "You know, I'm sure, that we Aztecs are God's people. We were spread all over the world after the exile and some are here, but not very many."

"Why don't you evangelize?" asked Jameson.

"We are the chosen ones, but that's not so much an honor as it is a responsibility. Our task isn't to bring others into the fold, but to follow the Law, and most non Aztecs aren't interested." She then surprised me by opening a closet and bringing out a beautiful copy of the Law. It was a surprisingly large book that she held with great reverence. Jameson and I looked at each other with smiles, as memories of our first trip to Mexico flooded back. I particularly remembered Geraldo telling the story of the giving of the Ten Commandments, then frowned inside when I realized the story was told at the beach at Playa Del Carmen rather than at Cerro Raxon mountain.

Sol asked, "Do you have any copies of the Prophets?

"No. These are very expensive, and we're a small worship community. Between the Law, the Prophets, and the Writings, Aztecs most highly honor the Law, so we were honored to have this copy donated to us. That's the same with the Megillot. Another family blessed us with that gift."

The King Montezuma Trilogy

This time my mind went to our second trip to Mexico, when we sought to experience the Prophets. I had to quickly stop myself, because I am supposed to be learning about the Writings. We then went into a small auditorium, and Atzi said, "This is where we spend most of our time. We have special events here, and we collect most of our missional items in this area to box up and send out."

"So, you do mission, but not evangelism?" asked Jameson.

"That's right."

"Hmm," said Jameson. "Sounds an awful lot like many of the Caldwellian Churches I know. The one we attend in Phoenix has a wonderful missional program, but the thought of someone taking 'my seat' in the sanctuary, seems to outweigh any desire for evangelism. It got so bad, that our bishop sent out an email suggesting that evangelism and mission were two sides of the same coin, and both need to be practiced." Atzi seemed uninterested, but Jameson added one more thought. "The bishop later chastised our Arizona congregations for complaining too much. He suggested we put on an apron to serve rather than a bib to be served."

"So," said Atzi, "it sounds like putting mission and evangelism together is a great theory, but challenging to put into practice."

Solomon

With that sad thought, we headed to the third window to hear about Solomon. Atzi explained, "This book goes by several names: the Song of Solomon, the Song of Songs, or the Canticle of Canticles. They mean 'the best of the best,' but I just

The King Montezuma Trilogy

like to call it Solomon. Nobody knows who wrote it, but a very common understanding is that it is a celebration of God's love for God's people. What do you think it's about?"

"Sex," declared Jameson.

Sol was embarrassed, I wasn't surprised, and Atzi said, "Well, maybe. I think of it more about passionate love. Our priest even did a wedding homily from Solomon for two people who truly burned inside to be together. Some say the book is an allegory, which goes back to that common understanding. Others suggest it is cultic, with pagan religious rites, and nature myths that celebrate the seasons. It is also commonly seen as a drama, with characters and a plot, or an Aztec wedding song, or simply a secular piece of love poetry."

"What do you think it's about?" asked Sol.

"Oh, I certainly see it as symbolic, but that's what makes it fun. You can read this book from many different angles and get something new out of it every time. Another thing I love about this book is that it complemented the quite different language of law and prophecy."

"Why was it included in the final canonization of the Aztec Scriptures?" I asked.

"The answer is probably in the purpose of the song, and that has never been agreed upon. Isn't that one of the fun things about the Bible? It's openness to interpretation allows it to breathe new life into each generation."

Sol smiled and said, "My early years are beginning to come alive in good ways. Thanks, Atzi."

"Now let me do one of those things I like to do, and that's to give a quick preview of the book. Chapter 1 is a dialogue of the lovers. Chapter 2 has the lover arriving in spring. Chapter 3 is a wedding procession of the bridegroom. In chapter 4, the

The King Montezuma Trilogy

bridegroom praises the bride, and in the fifth chapter, the maiden dreams of finding her lover. Chapter 6 returns to the groom's praise of the bride's beauty, while chapter 7 lists the maiden's charms and her love is offered, and the final chapter expresses the desire for marriage.

"Okay. Ready to delve into the passion that is the book of Solomon?" All three of us looked mildly like deer caught in headlights, which is what I think she wanted. "Here's how it gets started, 'Let him kiss me with the kisses of his mouth! For your love is better than wine' (1:2)

"That's how God and the Mexican people relate?" asked a rather stunned Jameson.

"Well, first of all, it's symbolic, and second that's just one of the ways to think of it. Maybe this will help. Think of it like C. S. Lewis' *Chronicles of Narnia*. You can take it at face value or find many more layers. Next, the bride seeks a tryst. 'Tell me, you whom my soul loves, where you pasture your flock, where you make it lie down at noon' (1:7).

"I'm not catching the tryst thing here," said Jameson.

"It's artful. He would be resting at noon with his flock, making it a convenient time to get together. Use your imagination," Atzi said with a slightly devilish look. The groom responds with, 'Ah, you are beautiful, my beloved, truly beautiful' (1:16) I imagine he has just removed her clothes."

"Wow," said Sol with some minor frustration. "Jim Caldwell never talked like that."

"But he loved God, right?" asked Atzi.

"Of course," I offered, trying to settle things down, "because Jim went about trying to get people to understand God better."

"Now you're sounding like Ecclesiastes," said Sol.

"Next, the bride reminisces about her groom, 'The voice of

my beloved! Look, he comes, leaping upon the mountains, bounding over the hills' (2:8).

Sol said, "That's easier to take. She truly loves her beloved."

"To be honest," Jameson said, "that's not where my mind went."

Atzi was pleased, and said, "Yes! Just allow the story to touch you where you need." Jameson looked embarrassed as she continued. Chapter 3 begins with, 'Upon my bed at night I sought him whom my soul loves; I sought him, but found him not; I called him, but he gave no answer' (vs. 1)."

"Now that," said Sol, "is much easier to see as a story between God and God's people. Loving God, seeking God, and not finding God, is something I can relate to."

"Not so for chapter 4," continued Atzi. "'Your two breasts are like two fawns, twins of a gazelle, that feed among the lilies' (vs. 5).

I suggested that it could be a pagan ritual, because "it sounds like a celebration of undefiled nature."

"Okay," said Atzi, "try this. 'My beloved thrust his hand into the opening, and my inmost being yearned for him' (5:4)."

"Help me again," said Sol. "How did this make it into the Aztec Scriptures?"

"Passion, war, blood, and prostitutes elsewhere. Why not this?"

I said, "I'm talking it as secular love poem."

Atzi continued, "When she is asked what is so special about her lover, she says, 'His speech is most sweet, and he is altogether desirable. This is my beloved and this is my friend' (5:16)."

"Now that rings true for me," said Jameson, "as a

The King Montezuma Trilogy

description of God."

"Chapter 6 is about the groom extolling the bride's beauty, like, 'Turn away your eyes from me, for they overwhelm me!' (vs. 5).

Jameson said, "Explain that one to me, please. I want it to be about Mexico and God, so what does it mean?"

"Ah!" said Atzi, "you are discovering the beauty of poetry."

Jameson looked at me and said, "I thought we did that for the book of Psalms."

"Yes," I responded, "but Atzi's point is that poetry can have more than one interpretation."

She then continued, "Chapter 7 is a dialogue between the two lovers. He says, 'How fair and pleasant you are, O loved one, delectable maiden!' (vs. 6). She responds with, 'I am my beloved's, and his desire is for me' (vs. 10)."

Jameson said, "Wouldn't it be nice if the Caldwellian Church felt God's desire like that?"

"But the church, my son, is the people," said Sol, "and Solomon can also be seen as a poem about Jim Caldwell and the Church."

"The closing chapter says, 'I adjure you, O daughters of Tenochtitlan, do not stir up or awaken love until it is ready!' (8:4), then the bride offers this stirring testimony to the power of love:

> 'Set me as a seal upon your heart,
>   as a seal upon your arm;
> for love is strong as death,
>   passion as fierce as the grave.
> Its flashes are flashes of fire,
>   a raging flame.
> Many waters cannot quench love,

The King Montezuma Trilogy

>   neither can floods drown it.
>   If one offered for love
>   all the wealth of his house,
>   it would be utterly scorned'
>   (vv. 6-7)."

"Any questions?"
Jameson said, "More than I want to admit."

Esther

We laughed for a bit, then moved to the next display window. Atzi immediately removed the book for our perusal, and Jameson asked, "Why didn't you take Solomon out for us to see?"

"Ah, the treasures of love are always somewhat hidden," Atzi said with another impish grin. "Even old movies and television shows never showed sex. It was certainly implied, but in my opinion, today we leave nothing to the imagination. Leaving the book inaccessible was my offering of poetry." We then took the book back to a room and sat down. "Esther is the only book in the Bible that never mentions God."

"I have to ask," said a surprised Sol. "How in the world did it make it into the sacred scriptures?"

"Unfortunately, we don't have those responsible for the decision. They aren't alive, so we have no one to ask. In my opinion, its value comes in accomplishing divine will, even when God is silent. Let me once again do a book preview. Chapter 1 is a banquet given by King Ahasuerus, and the subsequent fall of Queen Vashti. The second chapter is the selection of Queen

The King Montezuma Trilogy

Esther. In chapter 3, Haman bribes King Ahasuerus to destroy the dispersed Aztecs. Chapter 4 has Mordecai inciting mourning. In chapter five, the King and Haman dine with Esther, while in the next chapter, Mordecai is honored by the King. In chapter 7, Esther is granted the hanging of Haman, and in the eighth chapter, the edict for the killing of the Aztecs is revoked. Chapter 9 has the Aztecs killing those who were going to kill them, and the last chapter sees Mordecai become popular.

"As we get started, let me also say that I take this book as a novel which addresses the question of how an Aztec should live in society. The tale probably originated in Persia, because Esther is the Aztec name of the Persian goddess Ishtar, and Mordecai means worshipper of Marduk, also a Persian god. I think the story was transposed into an Aztec novel to speak to the dispersed Aztecs after the exile. It reflected nationalistic pride when antagonism toward Gentiles ran high among Aztecs. It also purported to give the historical basis for the Festival of Purim: 'These days should be remembered and kept throughout every generation, in every family, province, and city; and these days of Purim should never fall into disuse among the Aztecs, nor should the commemoration of these days cease among their descendants' (9:28)."

"I'm getting mixed up between Spain and Persia," commented Jameson.

"Yes," said Atzi, "it's a bit confusing. The Aztecs were exiled to Spain, then Cyrus of Persia conquered the Spaniards and allowed the Aztecs to return home to Mexico. What happened was that some Aztecs remained in Spain, some went to Mexico, and some went to Persia, among other places. The story of Esther takes place in the Persian Empire during the reign of Ahasuerus. It features a young Aztec orphan who becomes the

The King Montezuma Trilogy

Persian queen. Along with her cousin Mordecai, they rescue the Aztecs from a genocidal plot by Haman.

"When you read this book as a dramatic play, you begin to catch the four characteristics of narrative: comedy is written to cause the audience to laugh; tragedy is the opposite of comedy as it deals with catastrophe; romance is about the fulfilment of dreams; irony happens when the audience's expectations don't happen. Irony is the main theme in this book. The orphan Esther becomes a queen, and the antagonist Haman becomes the victim. Any questions?"

Sol asked, "What does Haman mean? I've known a few people with that last name."

"Funny you should ask. All of the characters in this play have meaning behind their name except Haman. That's because biblical scholars are uncertain what it means. So, here we go." She turned to the first page of the book, and said, "After two banquets were served up by King Ahasuerus, with plenty of heavy drinking, Queen Vashti gave a banquet for the women. On the seventh day, when the king was pretty much drunk out of his mind, the king commanded that the queen be brought to him. She refused and the king was enraged. The queen had wronged the king, and that didn't sit too well with him. After consulting many people, he discovered that disobedience was against the law and it was unalterable. It was then decided to give her position to another, so that all women would learn from this, and give honor to their husbands."

"Sounds pretty patristic," said Jameson.

Sol chimed in, "not to mention chauvinistic."

"Of course! Too bad the world hasn't learned any better by now. Shouldn't a play turn people around?" The three of us looked at each other, and agreed, then she said, "The first chapter ends with a declaration that every man should be master in his own house."

"There you go again," said Sol.

Jameson said, "That doesn't fly too well today."

Atzi said, "Trust me. It only gets worse. The way the story goes, the king's servants suggest he find a beautiful young virgin."

"What's wrong with that?" asked Jameson.

"Because the servants paraded all the beautiful young virgins before the king, after they were fancied up with cosmetic treatments."

Jameson said, "Still not seeing a problem."

"Oh, my heavens!" complained Atzi. "If the only requirement to become queen is to be young and beautiful, then the story is objectifying women."

"Oops, sorry," he said, as his mother looked disapprovingly at him.

"The problem improves because an Aztec man named Mordecai had a cousin named Esther. He adopted and raised her when her parents died, and she was collected up into the harem at the king's palace after a raid. There she gained favor and quickly advanced to the best place in the harem."

Sol asked, "Did it matter that she was an Aztec?"

"It would have. That's why Mordecai told her to keep it a secret. He also walked by the front of the court of the harem every day to see how Esther was doing. After a year of preparation, a select group of women were presented to the king. One at a time they spent the night with the king, and would only return if invited. When Esther was summoned, she asked for nothing. Now the king ended up loving Esther more than the others, so she was crowned as queen, replacing Vashti.

The King Montezuma Trilogy

"That brings us to Mordecai. One day he was sitting at the king's gate, and heard two guards conspiring to assassinate the king. As the Queen's stepfather, he had access to Esther, so he let her know the terrible news. Esther told the king, in the name of Mordecai, and the matter was investigated. When it was found to be true, the two guards were abruptly hanged on the gallows in the public square. Mordecai did this favor for the king, but asked for nothing, just like Esther had done previously. Nonetheless, Mordecai was surprised that the king showed no appreciation.

"Five years later, a man named Haman rose through the king's ranks, and the servants were commanded by the king to bow to Haman. One day, Haman became infuriated when Mordecai refused to bow to him, and the matter was investigated. When Haman discovered that Mordecai was an Aztec, he plotted to destroy all the Aztecs in the kingdom. He told the king that the Aztecs in his kingdom followed other laws, so the king granted permission to have the Aztecs destroyed. Letters were sent to all of the provinces to kill every Aztec, in one day, and to plunder their goods. When all of the people were called upon to be ready for the day, the king and Haman sat down to a celebration banquet. The problem was that the people of the kingdom found the decree to be confusing."

"As all heinous crimes should be," stated a rather angry Sol, with her arms folded.

"Agreed," said Atzi, "and the story fortunately improves. Esther's maids told her the terrible news, and showed her a copy of the decree. Esther was not allowed to approach the king without an invitation, so Mordecai got word to her that it would be wrong for her to keep silence at such a time as this. Esther told Mordecai to use this time of confusion to pray, and then she

The King Montezuma Trilogy

would approach the king. Esther said that it was strictly against the law of the country, but she was willing to die for her people if necessary.

Esther got adorned in her royal robes, and stood in view of the king. He was sitting on his royal throne and saw his queen, and decided to allow her to approach. He asked what she wanted, and Esther invited the king and Haman to a banquet she had prepared. While drinking wine, the king asked Esther again what she wanted. Esther surprised both Haman and the king by issuing yet another invitation to a banquet. The caveat was that the king was becoming further indebted to grant her request.

"Haman departed with a smile on his face, not knowing the confusion being observed in the kingdom, rather than the decree. When he saw Mordecai, Haman was again infuriated because Mordecai continued his refusal to bow. Haman went home and bragged about his accomplishments, his invitation to join the king in a private banquet put on by Esther, and another invitation for tomorrow. He then complained about the Aztec Mordecai, and his wife suggested a gallows be made to hang him.

"That night the king couldn't sleep, so he decided to do some reading in the royal archives. He discovered that Mordecai was the one who alerted the king's guards about his assassination conspiracy. He called a servant in and asked how Mordecai was rewarded, and found that nothing had been done. That morning Haman arrived to tell the king his plan to have Mordecai hanged on the gallows, but the king spoke first. 'What shall be done for the man whom the king wishes to honor?' Haman thought the man he talked about must surely be himself, so he says,

The King Montezuma Trilogy

'Let royal robes be brought, which the king has worn and a horse that the king has ridden, with a royal crown on its head. Let the robes and the horse be handed over to one of the king's most noble officials; let him robe the man whom the king wishes to honor, and let him conduct the man on horseback through the open square of the city, proclaiming before him: Thus shall it be done for the man whom the king wishes to honor' (Esther 6:8-9).

"I'm sensing potential irony here," said Jameson with a smile.

Atzi nodded and went on. "The king was delighted by Haman's thoughtful plan, and told him to go and do as he suggested for the Aztec Mordecai. Haman was beyond shocked, but he had to obey the king, so he honored Mordecai as instructed. When the parade was done, Haman went home in shame and mourned. A knock at the door was heard, and it was the king's servants coming to take him to the second banquet planned by Esther. Soon the king arrived at the banquet by Queen Esther, with a rather downcast Haman.

"On the second day, as they freely partook of wine, the king once again offered to grant any request the Queen had. She shocked the king when she requested that she and her people not be killed. The king angrily asked who was planning to kill her people, and she said, 'Haman.' The king got up and left in a fit of rage, while Haman begged for his life from the Queen. When the king returned, he saw Haman far too close to his Queen, and he yelled out that Haman was assaulting her. One of the king's servants mentioned that Haman had constructed a gallows for Mordecai, so the king ordered the execution of Haman on his own gallows.

The King Montezuma Trilogy

"Irony fulfilled," said Sol.

"Oh, there's more. In an ironic twist of fate, the king gave Esther the house of Haman, and she told the king that Mordecai was her cousin. Mordecai was told to immediately report to the king, so he went with no little bit of trepidation. Standing before the king, he was shocked to see the king remove his signet ring and hand it to him. Esther then pleaded to the king to avert the evil that Haman had devised against the Aztecs. She explained that she could not live with herself if her people were destroyed. The king told her that she could write a letter to her people in any way she wanted, sign his name to it, and seal it with the signet ring.

"The edict was written to the Aztecs, and all of the officials of his kingdom. Letters were then delivered by riders on the king's fastest steeds, and the Aztecs were told that they could take revenge on their enemies. In every city there was gladness and joy among the Aztecs, and they had a festival and a holiday. Their joy was even greater because the very day they were to be destroyed, was the day they were allowed to take revenge. To everyone's surprise, the Aztecs chose not to slaughter. The day turned from mourning into gladness, and the festival was called Purim."

Atzi said, "That's four stories down and one to go. What do you think so far of the Megillot?"

"I like," Sol offered, "the variety of their contexts. Correct me if I'm wrong, but I think Lamentations was set in Mexico after the deportees returned, as was Ecclesiastes. Solomon was a timeless song, and Esther was set in Persia during the Dispersion."

Jameson said, "I like their association with festivals. Pretty cool that Ecclesiastes can be celebrated by remembering the

The King Montezuma Trilogy

tent camping hard times of wandering in the wilderness. Esther is used at the Feast of Purim, and Lamentations is read on the date of the destruction of the Temple in Tenochtitlan, but I forget Solomon's purpose."

Atzi said, "It's used at the Passover Feast."

"Oh, that's why I was confused. I thought Jim Caldwell started Passover."

"Not uncommon," said Atzi. "Most Caldwellians, at least in my experience, think Pentecost was started by Jim." I asked which festival it was read at, and she said, "Ruth. It's read during the celebration of the giving of the Law."

"Oh, I get it," I said. "Aztecs celebrate the Law coming down on Mount Cerro, just like Caldwellians celebrate the Spirit coming down on the Hole in the Rock Gang."

Sol and Jameson still looked confused, so Atzi said, "Both religions call those experiences Pentecost, which comes from the word *pente* and means fifty. The Aztec Pentecost happens fifty days after Passover, while the Caldwellian Pentecost is celebrated fifty days after Easter."

"Nope," said Jameson, "sorry. No help."

Sol said it was starting to bring back a few memories from her childhood, so Atzi said, "Just let it sink in. This is good for Aztecs and Caldwellians to learn more about one another's faith traditions. That brings us to the final book of the Megillot."

Ruth

We walked down to the last window, where the four chapters of Ruth were displayed on four pages and in full view. Atzi didn't take the fragile pages out, so we stood back and

The King Montezuma Trilogy

listened to the story. I couldn't help but look into the glass and see our reflection. I know I was supposed to see through the glass and listen to Atzi talk about the book of Ruth, but the idea of reflecting on our own past was very tempting.

Any hope of that was shattered as she began. "First of all, who do you think is the main character?"

Jameson said, "Sounds like a trick question, but I'll still say Ruth."

"No," said Atzi, with an almost fiendish gleam in her eyes. "That was a trick question." We all laughed, then she said, "It's Naomi. The Caldwellian Scriptures place this book right after the book of Judges, to set its context at a time when there was no king in Mexico. The reason was to let it pave the way for King Montezuma, whose great-grandmother was Ruth. The Aztec Scriptures include it among the Writings part of the Bible, because the attitudes of the major characters in Ruth fit a post-exilic mindset.

"This book showed that the LORD was concerned for people of every nation. It helped counter the opinion in the Aztec religion that said marriage to foreigners was wrong, like in Ezra and Nehemiah. Another purpose seems to be about redemption. Variations of the word show up 20 times in the 85 verses of the book.

"The plot focuses on Naomi, an Aztec, and her Honduran daughter-in-law, Ruth. Here's my traditional preview of the book. Chapter 1 is about Ruth deciding to leave her homeland to return with her mother-in-law to San Miguel Ajusco, just south of modern day Mexico City. In Chapter 2, Ruth finds favor with a man named Boaz, and in the third chapter, Ruth and Boaz become engaged. In Chapter 4, Ruth marries Boaz. To add a little flavor, here's the meaning of the characters:

The King Montezuma Trilogy

Elimelech means my God is King.
Naomi means my joy.
Mahlon means weakening.
Chilion means pining.
Orpah means cloud.
Ruth means water abundantly.
Boaz means quickening.

"Okay, ready to get started?" We all nodded a yes, so Atzi began. "One day, a famine in the land became unbearable. A certain man of San Miguel Ajusco went to live in the country of Honduras, he and his wife and two sons. The name of the man was Elimelech, the name of his wife was Naomi, and the names of his two sons were Mahlon and Chilion. They went to the Honduras and remained there. Elimelech died and Naomi was left with her two sons. They took Honduran wives named Orpah and Ruth. About ten years later, both Mahlon and Chilion died.

"Naomi started to return to Mexico with her daughters-in-law from Honduras, because she heard that the famine was over. However, Naomi insisted that Orpah and Ruth stay and return to their mother's houses. Then she kissed them and they all wept aloud. They insisted on continuing with her, but Naomi begged them to turn back. Finally, Orpah agreed to stay in Honduras, but Ruth clung to her. Naomi tried one more time to talk some sense into Ruth, but Ruth said,

'Do not press me to leave you
    or to turn back from following you!
Where you go, I will go;
    where you lodge, I will lodge;
your people shall be my people,

The King Montezuma Trilogy

and your God my God.
Where you die, I will die—
there will I be buried.
May the LORD do thus and so to me,
and more as well,
if even death parts me from you!'

"When Naomi saw how determined Ruth was, she said nothing more about it. So the two of them traveled along until they reached San Miguel Ajusco. When they arrived, the whole town was stirred up. They asked, 'Are you Naomi?' She said, 'Yes, but now please call me Mara, for the Almighty has dealt bitterly with me. I went away full, but the LORD brought me back empty.'"

Jameson said, "I'll bet that didn't sit too well with Ruth!"

"Probably not, but things started to get better. Now Naomi had a relative whose name was Boaz. Ruth said to Naomi, 'Let me go to the field and glean, in hopes of being seen by someone who might favor me.' Naomi gave her blessing and Ruth went. As it happened, she came to the part of the field belonging to Boaz. When he saw her, he inquired about her, and discovered she was the Honduran who had returned with Naomi."

Sol asked, "Why is it that the story continues to refer to her as Naomi, rather than the requested name of Mara?"

"Good observation," said Atzi. "I don't know. But Ruth had been toiling all day without a moment's rest. Boaz went to Ruth and told her to work only in his field. He said, 'I have ordered the young men not to bother you. If you get thirsty, drink from what the young men have drawn. I have heard all that you have done for your mother-in-law, and that you left your native land

The King Montezuma Trilogy

and came to a people you did not know. May the LORD reward you for your deeds.' Ruth replied, 'May I continue to find favor in your sight, my lord, for you have comforted me.' At mealtime, Boaz offered her some bread and food. She ate until she was full and she had some left over."

"That reminds me of the time Jim Caldwell fed the multitudes," said Jameson, "and they had bread left over."

Atzi continued, "Boaz further instructed the young men to leave extra grain in the field for her, and to not rebuke her. That evening she came into town and Naomi saw how much she had gleaned. Naomi asked her where she had gleaned, and she told her it was in the fields of Boaz. Naomi said that he was a relative, and both women were pleased. Ruth was living with her mother-in-law, so they returned home that night.

"In the morning, Naomi suggested that Ruth should seek some sort of security for her future. She told Naomi that Boaz would be winnowing barley at the threshing floor that night, so she should put on her best clothes and go down to the threshing floor. She said, 'When he lies down, go uncover him and lie down; he will tell you what to do."

"Is this a sex scene?" asked Jameson, to the disgruntlement of his mother.

"Ah," said Atzi, "you have again found the joy of storytelling. It doesn't have to mean what it says, but it can certainly mean what it means."

"What do you mean?" asked Jameson.

Atzi said, "Fill in your own blanks. Anyway, our task is to listen to the story. When Boaz had eaten and drunk, he went to lie down at the end of the heap of grain. Ruth stealthily approached, uncovered him, and lay down. At midnight he woke up and was startled, and asked who it was lying with him.

The King Montezuma Trilogy

She told him it was Ruth, and he complimented her because the townsfolk knew she was a worthy woman. He then told her to lie down until the morning.

"The next day, Boaz gathered the people of the town and said, 'Today you are witnesses that I have acquired from the hand of Naomi all that belonged to Elimelech. I have also acquired Ruth.' Then all of the people said that they were witnesses, and offered blessings. So Boaz took Ruth and she became his wife. When they came together, the LORD made her conceive, and she bore a son. They named him Obed, and he became the father of Jesse, the father of King Montezuma."

"In the Caldwellian faith," I said, "we refer to Jim Caldwell as having come from the house and lineage of King Montezuma."

"Yes," said Atzi, "and that is one thing that separates your faith from the Aztec faith."

"In what way?" asked Sol.

Atzi said, "Our faith is looking for a messiah who will come and bring peace on earth. I look around and don't see that has happened yet."

Sol said, "I agree with you, but the important thing is that Jim Caldwell brings peace within."

Atzi smiled and said, "I have another tour group coming soon, so I need to get ready. At that point, Atzi walked us to the front door and thanked us for our interest. Sol gave her a hug, and Jameson and I thanked her for her time and we departed.

"Before going home," asked Jameson, "can we stop for lunch?" When I asked where, he said, "Fat Olives." I thought it was a great idea. Not only was it right on our way along Route 66, but we had plenty of time to catch the lunch specials. Soon enough we were pulling into the small parking lot for Fat Olives

The King Montezuma Trilogy

Wood-Fired Pizzeria and Italian Kitchen. Sol never requests Mexican food, because she's spoiled on her mother's cooking. Being a week day, we got right in and seated. They are famous for their authentic thin crust, wood-fired Neapolitan pizza, but everything is good.

We got our menus and started salivating. The server came by quickly and I decided to spring for an appetizer. I ordered a classic bruschetta board, then asked everyone to be ready to order when it arrived. Meeting the task at hand, Sol was first. She requested a smoked salmon sandwich, Jameson went for the margherita pizza, and I chose their signature lasagna.

After a great meal, we started back down I-17 toward Phoenix.

"Hey, mom."

"Hey, son."

"Why don't we finish the story after Ruth? Would you please read Matthew 1:6-16?"

Sol gladly picked up her Bible and quite solemnly read:

> Montezuma was the father of Santiago,
> Santiago was the father of Rehoboam,
> Rehoboam the father of Abijah,
> Abijah the father of Asa,
> Asa the father of Jehoshaphat,
> Jehoshaphat the father of Jehoram,
> Jehoram the father of Uzziah,
> Uzziah the father of Jotham,
> Jotham the father of Ahaz,
> Ahaz the father of Hezekiah,
> Hezekiah the father of Manasseh,
> Manasseh the father of Amon,

The King Montezuma Trilogy

Amon the father of Josiah,
and Josiah the father of Jeconiah.
After the exile to Spain:
Jeconiah was the father of Shealtiel,
Shealtiel the father of Zerubbabel,
Zerubbabel the father of Abihud,
Abihud the father of Eliakim,
Eliakim the father of Azor,
Azor the father of Zadok,
Zadok the father of Akim,
Akim the father of Elihud,
Elihud the father of Eleazar,
Eleazar the father of Matthan,
Matthan the father of Jacob,
and Jacob the father of Joseph,
the husband of Mary,
and Mary was the mother of Jim Caldwell
who is called the Messiah.

She serenely closed her Bible and Jameson and I thanked her. "Now tell us," requested Jameson, "how Jim Caldwell ended up in Phoenix."

"Oh, that's easy. You just need the last name of Joseph, the husband of Mary."

"Please remind me," said Jameson.

"Joseph's last name was Calderon, and his wife's name was Maria. During the Mexican-American War, which ended in 1848, the U.S. gained control of the Phoenix area. In 1851, Jim Calderon was born to Joseph and Maria. The Gadsden Purchase of 1854 was a treaty that gave $10 million dollars to Mexico for land south of the Phoenix area, where Joseph, Maria

The King Montezuma Trilogy

and Jim lived. This made them United States citizens, so Maria started going by Mary, and Joseph changed his last name from Calderon to Caldwell."

When we pulled into our driveway, I was beyond ecstatic to have experienced the three parts of the Aztec Bible in such a unique way. I'll never be able to read it the same again, because now I will connect the stories to the sights and sounds of the area. As we got out of the car, I hugged my wife and thanked her for joining us on this particular trip, not to mention the second trip to Mexico. Then I gave my son a hug and thanked him for allowing me to participate in his original high school graduation gift that paved the way for the remainder of our journeys.

As I got back in the house, I saw my copy of *The Four Agreements* given to me so long ago by Maria, who helped me plan the trips. She also asked me to live with my understandings, so I reflected back on the excursions. All of a sudden it started coming together. The poetry of the Psalms were wonderful examples of the first agreement: Be Impeccable with Your Word. I decided right then and there to live my life in a more poetic way, by loosening my self-imposed strictures of agenda. It takes time to find the words that truly express oneself, and then becoming a person who keeps your word.

The wisdom expressed in Proverbs and Job became an illustration for me of the second agreement: Don't Take Things Personally. That will be a monumental challenge, because my ego is fragile. The next time I feel confronted, I'll remember Job. He dealt with a divine attack and came out the better for it. Then there's Proverbs. I realized I needed to absorb more of its wisdom, so I opened my Bible and read the opening verses. This caught my attention: "Let the wise also hear and gain in

The King Montezuma Trilogy

learning, and the discerning acquire skill" (1:5). Lord, help me to gain the skills needed to not take things personally.

The storytelling was a unique experience. It helped me gain new appreciations for Ezra, Nehemiah, Chronicles, and Daniel. As I looked back again at the agreements, the third one says: Don't Make Assumptions. The hidden agenda of Chronicles taught me to research carefully, so I wouldn't get caught assuming what a biblical book is about. The same goes for Daniel. I've never been interested in an—or *the*—apocalypse, but my assumption about it was all wrong. It is full of useful lessons about life here and now.

The close encounter with the Megillot was very revealing. I never knew how the Aztecs used Lamentations, Ecclesiastes, Solomon, Esther, and Ruth. The fourth agreement: Always Do Your Best, taught me openness, so I could get a greater appreciation of Jim Caldwell's roots. I hope I can practice what Maria preached about living the agreements. It helps to bridge the gap between scripture and life. Most importantly, the Aztec Scriptures and the Caldwellian Scriptures give us some idea of what it was like to experience God. That became my prayer: that people would be open to the many ways people experience God, and to know that we are all God's people.

Shakespeare wrote: "All the world's a stage, and all the men and women merely players." My Old Testament trilogy is offered as a play, and it is now complete. May our lives be more than merely players, but movers and shakers, toward the task of leaving this world better than when we arrived.

The King Montezuma Trilogy

If you want to read about the Caldwellian Bible, check out my fictional trilogy about the New Testament, comprising the Jim Caldwell Trilogy.

The King Montezuma Trilogy

ACKNOWLEDGMENTS

The *New Revised Standard Version* (NRSV) of *The Holy Bible* is used throughout this book when texts are referenced.

Many thanks to Dave Raines, who I met in seminary in 1980. He had a Masters Degree in English Literature, and has been immenently useful in my attempts to write over the past fifteen years.

My heartfelt gratitude to my wife and life companion, Yvonne Cuenca Oropeza. Her copyediting suggestions made this book much better than it would have been without her. She graciously hand-drew all of the pictures, graphics, and maps found throughout this volume.

Finally, my thanks to God, creator of life, and inspiration for my effort to take a fresh look at the Bible.

The King Montezuma Trilogy

BOOKS BY THIS AUTHOR

Nonfiction

A Natural History of Scripture: How the Bible Evolved—Book 1.

This is the first book in my serious, in-depth, Bible Study trilogy, written for those who want to get serious about the Bible. It is a deconstruction of biblical formation as seen through the lens of evolutionary biology.

Wrestling with Scripture: How to Interpret the Bible—Book 2.

This is the second book in my trilogy, written for those who want to know what a particular word means in its own setting. It shows how to interpret the Bible's original Greek and Hebrew by using word study tools.

Practicing Scripture: How to Live the Bible—Book 3.

This is the third book in my trilogy, calling upon my Doctoral work in Practical Theology. It explains how to put the ideas from the Bible into every day practice.

The King Montezuma Trilogy

How to Lead a Celebration of Life

This is an indispensable guide, built on my 37-year career as a pastor, teaching laity and clergy how to conduct a funeral with meaning and integrity.

Don't Look a Camel in the Mouth: Pilgrimages through the Land of Jesus and Paul

This book shares five pilgrimages I led with my wife through the Holy Land, Turkey, Greece, Italy, and the Mediterranean. It brings the Bible alive through storytelling from a modern perspective.

Don't Look a Camel in the Mouth: Includes Journal

This book begins with *Don't Look a Camel in the Mouth: Pilgrimages through the Land of Jesus and Paul*, and ends with a Journal that contains spiritual questions and space to reflect on them with your own answers.

Parish the Thought: An Eye-Opening Look Behind the Pulpit

This book is a candid look at the joys and concerns of pulpit ministry. In it, my wife and I share stories of our years as ordained clergy.

The King Montezuma Trilogy

Austria, Germany, and the Oberammergau Passion Play

This book shared the experiences my wife and I had taking a group to the famous Oberammergau Passion Play, and our adventures through the surrounding region.

Your Year of Spiritual Growth: A Biblical Journey

This book is designed for people who love to journal. It creates spirituality through daily scripture readings, devotional questions, and debriefing with others.

Fiction

The Forming of the Diamond: A Jim Caldwell Story—Book 1

This is the first book in my New Testament historical biblical fiction trilogy. It is a retelling of the life of Jesus, drawn from the four gospels, looking through the lens of the American Old West. It focuses on The Sermon on the Mount, and shares some of the parables and healings from Jesus' ministry.

The King Montezuma Trilogy

The Secret of the Diamond: A Jim Caldwell Story—Book 2

This middle book of my Jim Caldwell trilogy is a creative reimagining of the last days of Jesus, set in Phoenix in 1881. It deals with the Passion Narrative, from Gethsemane to the grave, which I call the diamond of the Gospel.

The Value of the Diamond: A Jim Caldwell Story—Book 3

This final book of my biblical fiction trilogy deals with the resurrection, and tells what the early church's mission might have looked like if set in Mexico and the American West. It share the Good News from the Book of Acts and the Letters of Paul, and ends with the Book of Revelation.

The Secret of the Diamond: A Lenten Devotional

This booklet coordinates with *The Secret of the Diamond: A Jim Caldwell Story: Book 2*, and is designed for spiritual growth during Lent.

The Jim Caldwell Trilogy

This is a combination of all three books of the Jim Caldwell series.

The King Montezuma Trilogy

The Forming of the Empire: A King Montezuma Story—Book 1

This is the first book in my Old Testament biblical historical fiction trilogy. It is a reimagining of the Law section of the Hebrew Scriptures, through the book of Kings. It is set in the Formative and Classic Periods of Mesoamerica, beginning in the jungles of Guatemala and ending in what is now Mexico City.

The Secret of the Empire: A King Montezuma Story—Book 2

This middle book of my King Montezuma trilogy deals with the development of biblical prophecies. The Aztec Empire ended when Hernan Cortés and the Spanish Conquistadors overthrew Mexico. The book reimagines the Prophets section of the Hebrew Scriptures by setting them in the Postclassic Period of Mesoamerica.

The Value of the Empire: A King Montezuma Story—Book 3

This is the final book in my biblical fiction trilogy. It retells the Writings part of the Hebrew Scriptures, sharing the legends, wisdom, poetry, and stories left behind in Mexico. It also paves the way for the Jim Caldwell Trilogy.

The King Montezuma Trilogy

The King Montezuma Trilogy

This is a combination of all three books of the King Montezuma series.

If you enjoy my books, please review them on Amazon, Goodreads, Barnes & Noble, or any of your favorite places.

The King Montezuma Trilogy

www.ingramcontent.com/pod-product-compliance
Lightning Source LLC
Chambersburg PA
CBHW050847160426
43194CB00011B/2055